GATE OF HOPE

GATE OF HOPE

A novel

by

ELON SALMON

LONDON
VICTOR GOLLANCZ LTD
1987

First published in Great Britain 1987
by Victor Gollancz Ltd,
14 Henrietta Street, London WC2E 8QJ

British Library Cataloguing in Publication Data
Salmon, Elon
Gate of hope: a novel
I. Title
823'.914[F] PR6069.A48/

ISBN 0-575-03983-3

Photoset in Great Britain by
Rowland Phototypesetting Ltd, Bury St Edmunds, Suffolk
and printed by St Edmundsbury Press Ltd
Bury St Edmunds, Suffolk

To my daughter
Naomi

PART ONE

Chapter 1

"Blessed is the Lord our God, Creator of the World. With His help, the fourth day of the week. I'll not mark the month nor the year, for this is a mere passage before real time and real life begin again for me. Besides, we're at sea. The sea is neither time nor place but is, like sleep, a suspension of life, so say our sages of blessed memory."

Solomon paused. The creaking of the ship was thrusting into his thoughts. He took up his writing again, sitting uncomfortably, his back pushed against the vessel's swaying side, the wad of pages propped up against his knees.

"I'm in the belly of this creature. Not reluctantly, like Jonah, but of my own free choice, and with a glad heart. My prayers carry me to the land where God fulfilled His promise to Abraham, Isaac, and Jacob, and whence He cast our poor people out and dispersed them, for our sins. There I must take up my destiny."

The last sentence sounded too portentous; his hand was posed to strike it out.

Kedainai, his home town in Lithuania, came into his mind: he saw Mad Berl Zeff standing on the edge of the roof of Pfeffer's warehouse, his stunted body transfigured by his purpose, poised to jump. His eyes turned to heaven, arms flapping, flapping with all his might. And the people below, watching. No one really believed Berl would jump; the warehouse roof was very high. Solomon knew he would, he felt it in his heart with terrible inevitability. Berl leaped. Roared out "Hallelujah", turned a somersault in the air, and landed with a mighty crash on his head. Died instantly.

"Poor devil, that's what comes from having crazy dreams," Pfeffer had said and, to atone for the guilt he felt, undertook the expenses of a funeral. Then there was a big argument over whether Berl took his own life and should not be buried in consecrated ground, or whether he was just crazy and therefore not responsible for his act.

What were Berl's dreams? He dreamed of the Promised Land where his spine would be straightened and his mind cleared of its fog. He had prayed and prayed until his heart told him he could fly there, just like that, as though he were a bird!

Such an act of faith by an idiot had moved Solomon to the depth of his soul. He had stood among the people who looked up and shook their heads —some even laid bets. His heart was in his throat as he watched Berl flex his knees and wave his arms. The thud of Berl's head cracking on the courtyard's flagstones went through him like a blow from a hammer.

That night, as he lay awake beside his sleeping wife, Solomon's own yearnings for Jerusalem gathered into one simple, ineluctable command: "Take your wife and child, and go!" All his doubts were at once resolved. The lengthy arguments with Ada and with himself were no longer relevant: If you believed, you had to act on your belief, that was all. If the Almighty looked down caringly on his creatures, then surely poor Mad Berl, who had never harmed a living thing in his life, couldn't die in vain: his spirit soared to Jerusalem even as his body plunged to the ground. What clearer sign could there be for Solomon? How else could Berl's sacrifice be vindicated?

He began to write again: "Whatever people say, I know I've done the right thing."

"The ship smells, and Ada, dear heart, has been sick for most of the voyage. May God comfort her. Little Aaron, he sleeps like an angel, and I'm well. I suffer only in the imagination—for her, for my dear gentle wife whom I value more than anything else. But what's our suffering, hers, mine, when measured against the reward that awaits us? Nothing of value is ever gained without pain and effort. Did not the Lord make our forefathers wander forty years in the wilderness so that they might better appreciate His gift? So it is with me. I'm a simple man. My suffering is simple."

Now he heard voices from the deck, shouting. The ship steadied. He hurried to complete the account of their journey. Who could tell? One day his son would read it, maybe his grandchildren too. The thought made him overcome his natural disinclination to write. "Once I'm there," he thought, "there'll be living and working. The past will flow naturally into the future without a need to explain, as it should be. Only now . . . God forgive me if I'm being vain."

Ada stirred and looked at him from the bunk with tired eyes. "Are we there?" she asked.

"Nearly, I think. Come, let's go up on deck with the boy. You'll feel better in the fresh air."

Under the rising sun the mist began to disperse. As soon as the boatswain shouted out that the harbour was in sight, the passengers clambered out of the hold and crowded the deck. There were not many of them, but shoved together against the rail of the small run-down Russian schooner—a ragtag group of peasants, traders and Jews—they made the ship appear still smaller, and squalid.

Solomon and Ada found space at some distance from the crowd, and there they stood huddled together, with their eight-year-old, thin-faced son Aaron between them. Solomon put his arm round Ada's shoulders, to reassure her and protect her from the morning chill.

The sails were flapping against the spars. There seemed hardly any breeze yet the ship was gliding smoothly on the still sea. Slowly the domes and towers of Constantinople took shape in the distance among the hills and dark cypress trees. The City of Cities, braced by the flat, brilliant stretch of the sea, was beckoning them to come, Solomon thought, and smiled.

At the sight of Constantinople the fatigue of the journey lifted from him as if by magic. He felt elated. He never imagined such a large majestic city could exist, except in fantasy. Ada pressed closer to him, her mind in a turmoil, and stared wide-eyed at the unfolding views. Solomon lifted his son and held him above the rail. "Look, the biggest city in the world," he said.

"Jerusalem!" the boy said in awe.

"No, Constantinople. Capital of the Empire."

Aaron was silent for a moment. "We're not home yet," he said, disappointed.

"Not yet, boy. But now we really are on our way."

The child mouthed the difficult name. He could not imagine anything so grand as the city he was now seeing, so that Jerusalem all of a sudden lost its meaning to him. Solomon put the boy down and stared at the sea.

Sounds from the shore, no longer fragmented, broke through the chaotic cries of the gulls. The shouts of porters and sailors could now be heard, and the braying of donkeys against the deeper, more distant rumble of the city from beyond the walls. After the sea voyage, all this was a sudden assault, and Ada trembled. Solomon tightened his embrace and pressed his mouth against her hair. "Afraid?" he whispered.

She looked up at him and smiled, "Yes . . . maybe a little . . . I don't know."

"Don't be," he said, and immediately added in a practical tone, "Is everything packed and ready?"

"How long do you think it takes to pack the few odds and ends we have? It's been ready since last night," she said.

To distract himself from thoughts of their poverty and how they would manage, Solomon pointed to the narrow spur of water that cut into the mainland on their right, dividing the city. "This is called the Golden Horn, because . . ." And he went on to recount what he had read in a Russian travel book. Neither Ada nor the boy listened to him. Their attention was fixed on a Turkish man-of-war which was just pulling out of the harbour, ensigns flying, guns glinting in the sun.

The crew were busy on deck preparing for landing. On shore the men were swarthy, healthy-looking. They wore baggy pantaloons with broad sashes, like in illustrations Solomon had seen in books on the East. He was almost overcome by the flashes of colour and by the strange smells. Aaron too was shaking off the lethargy of the journey. Tugging at his father's sleeve, he pointed and asked questions animatedly. Then Ada, leaning her bosom against Solomon's hand, suddenly asked in a quiet voice which he couldn't ignore: "What shall we do when we get off the boat? We know nobody who speaks our language, we have no money." Her anxiety invaded him. Now they were looking at him, the boy and she, trusting yet worried.

He said, "We shall seek our brethren. There are Jews here, I know that much."

The boat tied up in the port of Galata. Constantinople proper was on the other side of the Golden Horn which was spanned by a number of wooden bridges. But it was here, on the Galata side of the water, that the Jews lived, the more prosperous among them, anyway, as Solomon found out. Where exactly, he had no idea. Nor was he in a hurry to find them. It was a brilliant mild summer morning. The gardens, the rich of colours, the foreign vigour of the people who jostled against them as they made their way through endless bazaars, all seduced his senses. Such was the magical power of the city over the young family, that they had forgotten that not a morsel of food had passed their lips since early that morning.

The stall of a silk merchant caught Ada's attention. She stopped to look. Never before had she seen such a magnificent display of materials, saffron yellow, poppy red, purples and blues. The merchant was sitting in a low chair under a canvas awning, languidly sucking on a water pipe. He smiled at her but did not get up to solicit. His practised eye told him that this outlandish couple with their child and untidy bundles were not potential customers. But his mercantile reflexes compelled him to contemplate their boots just as Solomon turned round to admire the sight of his wife against the splendid background of silk.

There was a commotion at the far end of the street: angry shouts, a terrified scream. The row drew nearer. The merchant tensed. He stood up quickly and pulled Solomon, Ada and the boy into the recess of his shop behind the stall.

A half-naked man came bounding down the alley. His face was set in terror. There was blood streaking down his chest from his shoulders. He was running and stumbling, mouth wide open. Close on his heels were three thick-set men wielding whips with many leather thongs. They shouted as they ran, and the slashing of their whips made a fearful cutting noise in the close confine of the alley. The man, driven forward, suddenly tripped and fell. Before he could rise to his feet, his pursuers were upon him. They kicked him and lashed at him until he lay a quivering, torn heap. The men stood over him, breathing hard. Then two of them dragged him by his feet out of the alley, and left him in a corner crumpled up against a wall.

Soon the bazaar returned to normal as though nothing had happened. The silk merchant gently shoved Solomon and Ada out into the alley, and smiling, seated himself on the stool and took up smoking again.

Aaron stood very still. His eyes were fixed on the dark recess from where the man's legs protruded and twitched spasmodically. Solomon took hold of him by the shoulders and turned him away. He said to Ada, "Probably a thief or some sort of criminal". And he added quickly, "Such things happen everywhere, why, even at home, didn't you ever see louts beat one another senseless, or some Jew . . .?" Ada said nothing. He noticed how her lower lip began to tremble. In his own imagination he had already come to terms with violence. But seeing her now, he wondered how he could cope with her fears, the reality of terror which he saw reflected in her eyes. The Jews. He must find out where they lived and go there, quickly. With this in mind, he turned to the silk merchant who was now regarding them with what might have been compassion, if his cold look did not contradict the smile and the gentle shaking of the head.

Haskui, situated some way beyond the bazaars of Galata, along the Golden Horn, was where the Jews lived. The first thing that struck Solomon and Ada was the appalling squalor of the place. If it hadn't been for the *mezuzas* on the door jambs, they wouldn't have believed Jews lived here. At last they found a synagogue, just when the people were coming in for evening prayers, and before the evening was out, Solomon had managed to contract a humble room in the home of a poor widow who lived not far from the synagogue.

The Rabbi, Haham Bashi of Haskui, was the leader of the Jewish community, and he honoured Solomon. Seldom did they have such guests; Haskui was not like Saloniki with a large, prosperous Jewish community, in constant touch with the larger world. Nor like Pera further north along the Golden Horn, where rich Jewish merchants lived. Besides, it was easy to like Solomon. He was young and strong, and his manners were pleasing. For a man only twenty-eight years old he spoke with diffidence and wisdom that often eluded men years older and more experienced than he. But above all, the Rabbi honoured him because he was ascending to the Holy land. To fulfil this ancient commandment, particularly in such hazardous times, was an act deserving of the deepest respect.

Solomon towered above the slight Sepharadi Jews of Haskui. His dark chestnut beard fanned out richly across his broad chest. His clear hazel eyes looked with candour on whoever spoke to him. The Jews of Haskui took to the young family whose enterprise fired their imagination and distracted from their own drab existence.

The tiny room where Solomon and Ada stayed overlooked a small walled garden where a few bitter lemon and apricot trees grew. Above the wall you could see the curve of the street which led to the synagogue. Tonight they would dine at the house of Haham bashi with some of the community's honoured elders. A wealthy merchant from Pera, a benefactor, was among the guests. It was he, the Haham bashi had told Solomon, who would secure a passage for them on a boat bound for Palestine, at his own expense, as a gesture of brotherly love.

Ada was sitting on a stool, the only piece of furniture in the room besides the mattresses on which they slept. She had Solomon's only coat on her knees and was stitching a torn lapel. They had left their native Lithuania dressed for the journey like peasants. But she had packed a change of clothes for each, to be used only on special occasions. These were now laid out on the floor for her inspection.

She bit off the end of the thread, and said smiling, "They call you a learned rabbi. Did you know that?"

"Well? What of it?" Solomon answered, pretending to be lost in thought. She laughed. "You, a learned rabbi. If they could only hear that back home!"

He turned to look at her. Her slender back and long soft dark hair which he had forbidden her to crop as married women did, sent a wave of warmth through him. He wanted to tease her, to say, "And why not? Aren't I as clever as any of those prattling rabbis back home?" Instead, he said, "What matters is what you call me."

"I call you my man, my love, my life," she answered.

He took her in his arms and held her tight. He turned to look at Aaron who lay on the mattress against the wall, curled up in his sleep, and started to say something, but there was a knock on the door and the widow's toothless face appeared. She put the jug of water on the floor and retreated. Through the window he could see that it was already getting dark. Any moment now the Haham bashi's servant would come to fetch them, and they weren't ready.

The merchant of Pera was fat and jolly. He laughed frequently, and when he did his small lively eyes would disappear in the shiny folds of his face. Dressed in fine robes and a splendid turban, he stood out among the other guests like a great ball of colour that lit up the drabness of the place. Solomon wondered what a man like that was doing here among these poor Jews of Haskui who milled about him obsequiously. Later in the evening he learnt that the merchant was born to a humble Haskui family. Fortune had smiled on him; he had fought his way to reach his present eminence, but never forgot his origin.

The Sabbath feast was laid out on a Bukharan carpet of reds and browns. Platters were heaped with steaming pilaw, sweetmeats, bread and a large cask of wine. Along both sides of the carpet there were rows of cushions for the guests. The Haham bashi had gone to great trouble and expense to make this a very special occasion. The women sat at one end, where, chuckling and gesturing, they were making a great fuss of Ada who could not understand a word of what they were saying. The merchant of Pera sat at the centre, propped up by the largest and most ornate cushions. Next to him sat the Haham bashi and, on the other side, Solomon.

After the Rabbi said a prayer, the merchant, being the guest of honour, broke the bread. Solomon caught Ada's eye. She smiled nervously, and he smiled back as if to say, "See how they love you, relax and worry about nothing." The merchant's wife hugged Ada and kissed her cheek, murmuring endearments in Turkish.

In addition to his native Turkish, and Ladino the merchant could speak French and even a little Italian. Where these failed, he had a range of gestures and winks he could rely on. But German, Russian, not to mention Hebrew, were beyond him. He wanted to know everything that Solomon had seen on his journey. Most particularly he wanted to hear news of the war, for he had heard that Napoleon had begun to march into Russia. Speaking broken school Hebrew with the Haham bashi translating, Solomon told his story from its beginning. What he had seen on the way, his adventures. Of the war he had very little to say. The merchant listened attentively, stroking his sparse beard. The Haham bashi, too, listened head cocked, now nodding, now raising his eyebrows, his lips pursed. Whenever Solomon paused, the Haham bashi drew himself up and began to translate, not only for the benefit of the merchant, but for all the guests. He made a great act of it. Solomon suspected that his host was not merely translating but reshaping the story to his own taste. The guests' eyes were riveted on their leader, they hung on every word that came from his mouth.

Was it a surfeit of food and wine that diffused his concentration? The smooth cadence of the Haham bashi's voice, rising and falling like waves, made him languorous. "I'm among brothers. Safe," he told himself, and relaxed. Open-eyed, he dreamed of water, of earth fragrant in the rain in Kedainai which he had sworn to blot out of his memory. But his memory was stubborn, like himself: again and again images and voices rose into his wine-washed consciousness.

"Have you no pity, to break an old man's heart like that? Is that your gratitude for all I've done for you? What were you? A poor orphan! And I took you into my home, to the bosom of my family. Put food in your shrunken belly and clothes on your back. You married my Ada, the apple of my eye, too good even for a saint. Did I say anything? I treat you like my own flesh and blood. And you want to take her away, with my only grandson, to the end of the world, never to be seen again!" Reb Ephreim weeps and rocks from side to side, pulling at his beard. His anguish burns Solomon like fire, even though Ephreim had ill-used him, even though he knows too well the dissembling nature of the cunning old man.

Broad-backed and strong, he towers over his father-in-law and faces him impassively: "We've been through all that. I must. I cannot change my mind."

"Books!" Bobke screams. "Instead of working for his keep, he reads books! That what comes from all that reading, you go crazy!"

And Reb Ephreim, made bold by his wife's hysteria, strikes Solomon in the face with his fist. "Are you a Jew? I wouldn't believe it! Who are you? I don't know you any more!" he shouts.

Ada smiles from across the room. The Turkish ladies tickle her and she laughs. Gentle Ada, quiet yet strong, unyielding in her sacrifice. How she stood by him right to the half-hearted reconciliation with her parents, before their departure. Without thinking, he had given the name Zeff to the Lithuanian officials who prepared their travel papers. It had been an inspiration: Berl's fatal jump – his own starting point. Ada had been too overcome at the parting even to notice.

It is the month of Iyar. The trees are ablaze with green. Seated at the back of a cart with their bundles, with Aaron squeezed in between them, Solomon and Ada turn to look at their native town receding in the distance. Even now he can feel her hand.

The Haham bashi, it was plain to see, was greatly exercised by the story. He had entered it so fully that the effort exhausted him. When sweet black coffee was served in small china tumblers, with little almond cakes, the merchant's head began to droop. The Haham bashi leaned across, behind the merchant's back and said "Rabbi, I marvel at your courage. May God protect you and your wife and child. Yet, I fear for you."

"Why so, Rabbi?" Solomon asked.

The Haham pulled a face. "I've never visited Jerusalem. God willing perhaps one day I shall. But from what I hear, it is not a good place. No, not in this world."

"This world must, nevertheless, be endured." Solomon laughed.

"Jerusalem is a dirty, unhealthy city, full of wicked lawless Arabs who have no love for our people. Besides," he paused,"they say your people, the Ashkenazi, will not be suffered there on account of an old feud with the Arabs. Of course there are ways . . . and life is constantly changing, who can tell the Almighty's designs? But we hear stories. . . . There's danger, always danger. I tell you this for the sake of your pretty young wife and child."

At that moment, after the good food and the attention people paid him, danger seemed to Solomon a very abstract thing. He said light-heartedly, "As you say, Rabbi, who can tell what the Almighty has in store for any of us? My mind is made up and nothing will dissuade me."

The Haham raised his hooded eyes and his lips moved in silent benediction.

The merchant surfaced from his torpor and burped. Putting a plump hand on Solomon's knee, he began to speak to him in French, then remembering, turned to the Haham for help. In a few days' time a ship he had once contracted to carry some of his merchandise was sailing for Palestine. He would make sure Solomon and his family would be taken on board. There was also something he wanted to give Solomon, a small token of his esteem. The merchant beckoned to his man and whispered something in his ear. The man made off and presently returned with a little wooden box. The box contained an amulet, a polished blue stone encased in stained silver filigree, and attached to a dirty leather thong. Without another word the merchant fastened the amulet round Solomon's neck. The thing emitted a mildly unpleasant and unfamiliar odour.

"This", the Haham explained, "is a potent charm against all evil and misadventure. The merchant was given it many years ago by a Persian who had travelled all over the world. So long as you wear it, no harm will come to you. Guard it well, and it will guard you."

The merchant clasped his hands together and blinked happily. He had worn the amulet, he wanted Solomon to know, on all his travels. But now, thanks be to God, his fortunes had increased, he seldom travelled and no longer needed the protection of magic. He was glad to have found someone worthy of the precious charm.

Solomon was moved. He thanked him—though the smell from the talisman irritated his nose and made his eyes water. The merchant seized his hand and pressed and patted it. Solomon promised that he would return the gift as soon as he had safely reached Jerusalem, so that it might be passed on to other travellers like himself.

The day of departure arrived. The merchant had kept his word, he sent his man from Pera to say that a Greek cutter, named *Calypso*, had just entered the harbour in Constantinople, and would be weighing anchor in two days' time, bound for Acre. Solomon should be at the port early that morning; everything had been fixed with the Master of the ship. Solomon and Ada went to the bazaar to buy provisions for the journey. Ada also bought some tough woollen cloth that would serve them in their new home: who could tell what was available in that unknown land where conditions were said to be so hard? There were a few farewells before Solomon and Ada settled in for an early night, having packed their belongings and left them by the door ready for the morning.

The night was chilly. From their window they could see the flickering lights of the city. The smell of honeysuckle wafted in from the garden, and with the gathering darkness, those distant lights seemed to merge with the stars and shine with a cold brilliance. At last Aaron, tired from imagining the journey, fell asleep. Ada leant against her husband's familiar solid body. Together they gazed out at the lilac sky. For a long while they didn't speak. He put his arm round her and stroked her hair. He knew what was going through her mind. They had travelled a long distance, but for all that they were still in Europe; even sailing into Constantinople had not taken them beyond the world they knew. Now at last, they had come to the edge of the great leap from which, as in death, there was no return. Ada had no sense of direction, no commitment like him; she clung on to his faith as a child clings to the steady hand of an adult. He knew he could not reason her fears away. Only his own calmness and tenacity of purpose could give her support.

"Look at the stars," he said, "how fixed they are in the heaven, how brightly they shine, ever more so tonight. This is the covenant of our people with the Ineffable Name, that the seed of Abraham will be as numerous as the stars in the sky. Think that we're going home so that the promise may be fulfilled even through us."

She gave a small laugh, "The stars shine on all the world, on man and beast alike."

"But no other people understand it in quite the same way."

"So who's right?"

"I'm right," he answered, and kissed her. "You'll see. The land we're going to is a pleasant, welcoming land. We'll work hard, we'll be happy and have many children."

"Talk to me about it as you used to," she said, because suddenly she had visions of home. And he began to tell her of the visions he had seen, of his dreams, quoting from the Book of Books, describing the scenery which had burnt itself on his imagination until, reassured and aroused by one another, they made love.

Somewhere a dog howled. In the elemental silence Ada and Solomon could hear one another's heartbeats. She said, "What shall I do in Jerusalem?"

"Why, the same as you always do. Just the same. Everything you want, with gladness and joy."

"Say you'll always be with me as you are now, no matter how hard things get. Even when I'm no longer pretty."

"You know I will, I swear," he said.

"Do you know, Solomon," she said after a pause, "that we'll be spending the High Holy Days on board a ship among goyim?"

"We'll celebrate all the more joyously for being alone and on our way," he said to her.

After she had fallen asleep in his arms, he remained awake long into the night. The darkness seemed to expand until he felt as though he were shot into a vast space, somewhere out he knew not where. He could hear the voice of his soul: "I'm travelling, even now. Not only outward but inward, into an equally uncharted place within myself. My God, is this the *Ein Sof*?

The Divine Infinity? Teach me what to make of it. I feel lonely in this featureless space. Ada and Aaron, if anything should happen to me, what would become of them?" Tears began to well in his eyes. "Yet she is my strength, my other half, slender and fragile though she is, with small girlish breasts. Yes, for all that, she is my strength. Now I understand what Rabbi Simeon Bar Yohai of blessed memory taught: "It behoves a man to be male and female always, so that his faith may remain stable and complete, and in order that the Presence may never leave him."

He began to pray, and as he prayed he felt comforted. Surely the Lord had heard him. He would give him strength, sharpen his judgement so that he might not stumble in the darkness of ignorance; more than that he couldn't ask. A pleasant drowsiness came over him just as the knife-edged voice of the Muezzin began to proclaim the break of day.

Chapter 2

The *Calypso* was roped to a capstan alongside a quay. Dwarfed by the other ships around her, she creaked and swayed on the littered brown water of the harbour. The paint was flaking off her wooden hull. The name "Calypso" had all but faded from the prow. She smelt of decay.

On board was a hive of activity. The Master of the ship stood leaning against the quarterdeck rail, shouting to the sailors and porters below. He was an elderly man with a bulbous nose and mean eyes. His face was covered with an untidy stubble of beard.

From the bottom of the gangplank, Solomon looked up at the ship. He didn't like her or the look of her crew. Even her name sounded frivolous and untrustworthy. The Captain caught his eye and stared back insolently. The merchant of Pera's agent suddenly materialized at Solomon's side. He shouted a few words at the Captain, then beckoned Solomon to take his wife and all his belongings, and follow him aboard.

When Ada saw the quarters they were allotted, she burst into tears. In a filthy corner in the bowels of the ship, among heaps of dusty, unrecognisable cargo, a couple of burst sacks of straw were thrown on the floorboards. Here they were to sleep. The merchant, it seemed, had secured their passage in the cheapest possible way as though they were nothing more than lumps of merchandise.

"I'll speak to the Captain. I'll pay . . . we won't put up with this," Solomon vowed, and stormed out.

Meanwhile on deck, some sense of order had been created and an expectancy of departure was settling over the ship. A few passengers had arrived, and were chatting, or trying to get a better view when the ship pulled out of the harbour.

There were six of them, all Europeans. One was a crusty lady of indeterminable age, small and steely with birdlike features made sharper by her wide-brimmed hat. Two gentlemen were standing talking to her. One was tall and had a dark pointed beard. The other, an older man, looked soft like a plump woman, with childishly innocent eyes. They were talking in French and laughing loudly. Every now and again the tall bearded man would point out things on shore with his cane.

Not far from this group, a pair of Greek ecclesiastics in black cassocks stood in silence, leaning against the rail and staring into the distance. The sixth passenger was a German. He had just come aboard. All his luggage was about him. His broad, serious face was flushed and covered in perspiration. He kept pushing back his cork helmet to wipe his brow. The lady gave him a stiff little smile which he returned with a bow, then continued agitating among his leather suitcases, muttering to himself and polishing his glasses.

Solomon approached the Master of the *Calypso* who was arguing with two uniformed men, apparently shore officials. His mind was seething: surely the Merchant had paid for their berths? This rascal, sensing easy picking, had pocketed the money and thrown them down below with the cargo.

"Remember what you are and where you're going. Be calm," Solomon said to himself.

At last the Captain was free. He didn't look at Solomon but deliberately ignored him, as though he didn't exist. Solomon cleared his throat. Not a muscle moved on the Captain's face—he might have been contemplating a fresh insult. "Sir, I wish to talk to you about the place you've put us in, which isn't fit for animals," Solomon spoke in German. "I'll pay extra for proper quarters where my wife and child can sleep like human beings." He had little money, but his honour and the dignity of his family rested on this issue. The Captain looked at him blankly; there was no mistaking his contempt. The obvious surfaced through Solomon's dammed-up rage: how foolish of him to expect that creature to understand German! He tried again, this time using gestures and the few Turkish words he had picked up. The Captain worked his mouth, gathered it to a spout, and shot a gobbet of spittle on Solomon's shoe. In Kedainai, for a lesser insult, Solomon would have sent him flying out of his filthy vessel with one blow. Now he stood rooted to the spot, unable to control the trembling brought on by the outrage.

The Captain began screaming insults. Advancing on Solomon, he pushed him in the chest, and Solomon retreated to avoid even proximity with his obnoxious tormentor. The other passengers stopped whatever they were doing, to look. So did the crew.

There was no telling what the outcome might have been were it not for the sudden arrival of a new passenger of such compelling presence that at once all attention was shifted to him. He stood at the top of the gangplank, arms akimbo, fists clenched. Short, muscular, with a flame of red hair and beard, he glared at the Master of the ship.

All at once order was restored on board: the crew resumed their work as though a power of greater authority than their Captain had taken over the ship. The Captain himself slunk away from Solomon and moved towards the newcomer, all humble and obsequious. The Europeans prepared to greet and claim their fellow-traveller.

For a moment, Solomon met the stranger's gaze. There was no hint of sympathy in the man's eyes, nor any sign of emotion. His look was one of intense curiosity which invited no communion. Solomon was the first to avert his eyes. The man turned to supervise the portage of his luggage aboard. He had more than all the passengers had together—a whole train of boxes of varying sizes, as well as an assortment of suitcases. He was an Englishman, it transpired, a man of elevated rank who held much sway in the Sultan's court.

Released at last, Solomon sought his son. He found him standing by the mast. His expression was grave, as though having witnessed his father's humiliation, he was prematurely acquainted with dangers and evils he could never before imagine or understand, and with that, had aged beyond his years.

Ada didn't have to ask. She read the failure of the mission in their faces. They sat quietly together for a while until the swaying of the ship told them that they had weighed anchor. Then Solomon sighed and said, "What can we do but trust in God?" It was Aaron, who after a moment's thought came up with a practical suggestion, "We needn't be here at all. It's warm outside. We can sleep up there after everybody's gone to their places. And we can spend the day looking at the sea."

Chapter 3

"The month of *Elul*, five thousand five hundred and seventy-two years to the creation of the universe. Blessed is the Lord," Solomon wrote in his journal. "It is now two days since we put to sea, and they say that tomorrow, God willing, we shall anchor at Smyrna. I've heard it said that this time of the year the Creator calls off the tempest and all other perils, and commands the sea to rest. And so it has been, with only fair winds to speed us on.

"I am learning the virtue of patience. The Captain, a villain though he is who will doubtless pay for his villainy before the Highest Judgement, no longer scowls at me. We sleep mostly on deck, for the nights are soft and luminous. During the day we sit quietly out of the crew's way and watch the other people. They smile at us kindly, except the two Greek monks. They are like two testy crows. I can see in their eyes how they hate us.

"Aaron, bless him, is a brave and resourceful boy. Already he knows as much about seafaring as any of the sailors who make much fuss of him. I can see that he'll grow up to be a man of action. Maybe that's good. When we touch the shores of the Promised Land, I shall call him Israel. Israel Zeff. That's a good name for a man of action. And dear Ada's good spirits are restored. Today, one of the sailors, with the approval of the Captain, I'm sure, brought us clean mattresses to sleep on so that we don't have to lie on the hard deck with only blankets. The Englishman is the strangest man I've ever come across, and everyone on board, from the passengers to the Captain, treats him as though he were a prince, which perhaps he is, though I doubt it."

At that point Solomon stopped writing. The sun was touching the horizon. Beyond the stern, the water shimmered red and silver. Earlier on, a school of dolphins had followed the ship, racing through the waves. The sailors said it was a good omen. Now the sea was empty. Shadows moved over its surface. This hour, as at dawn, when he woke and said his prayers, was for Solomon a time for thought and reflection. Inevitably his mind turned to his destination. He could see it all in perfect calm, as though security of possession had already been granted to him: Jerusalem, his heart's desire, the object of his prayers.

Aaron and he had the deck almost to themselves. Four sailors sat grouped together near the bow. They were throwing dice and laughing. One of them began to sing. At the other end of the ship the Englishman stood in silent meditation. The flat horizon cut him at the chest, his wild-looking head silhouetted against the hazy sky. The boy was not paying attention to his father. He was looking at the Englishman. Solomon whispered impatiently, "Don't stare so. If he should turn and see you . . ."

"What would he do?"

"Nothing, it's not nice to stare at people. It makes them feel uncomfortable." But Solomon didn't think anything could make the Englishman feel uncomfortable. He didn't seem to mind in the least when the boy and the sailors, or indeed anyone who chanced to be on deck early in the morning, looked at him as he sat on his peculiar box, his face set in concentration. The strange contraption, Solomon soon realized, was a portable lavatory. Early in the morning, as Solomon prayed, the Englishman would place his box at the stern, set a canvas screen about it and sit there, staring out to sea, oblivious of the ship and her company. Even now Aaron couldn't take his eyes off him. He had encountered him many times on deck, had looked him straight in the eye, and the stranger gazed through him as though the boy didn't exist. Solomon himself had had dreams in which he saw the Englishman striding across a landscape he didn't recognize, stocky, fearless, indestructible. The fact that such a man was travelling to the land that was to be their home, added to its magic and was, at the same time, reassuring.

"Father, why is this man going to the Holy Land?" Aaron asked.

"He wants to visit it, like so many people, like the other passengers. Don't keep looking at him like that," Solomon answered flatly.

"If he's going just for a visit, how come he has more things than we do?" the boy persisted.

"Some people need more things even for a visit, and others need less. We don't need many things. Our possessions are here and here." Solomon touched his bosom and tapped his head.

"Maybe he's going to live there, like us. Maybe secretly he is a Jew."

"I don't think so, son," Solomon laughed. "In Palestine there are Arabs and Turks and all sorts of other people, as well as Jews."

The *Calypso* anchored at Smyrna for a short while, then they were at sea again. At Rhodes they went ashore. The passengers disembarked and returned laden with souvenirs. Solomon and Ada took Aaron for a short walk, just to feel the firm ground under their feet. They bought no souvenirs, only some honey, apples, a few loaves of bread and some smoked fish to last them for the rest of the voyage.

They saw that the Englishman was on deck when they returned. He had not gone ashore. To their surprise he greeted them with a nod of the head, and meeting Aaron's eyes, smiled at him as if to say, "We know one another, and in our way we have talked, haven't we?"

"He's a missionary, now I know for sure," Ada whispered once they were out of earshot. Aaron's eyes followed the Englishman as he paced leisurely up and down the deck, ignoring them.

"Maybe he is, so what?" said Solomon. The way she looked at him, he might have uttered a blasphemy.

"Did you see how he smiled at the boy? And you say 'so what?'", she mimicked him. "I've heard how missionaries ensnare Jewish children."

"What nonsense you talk!" he snapped at her.

But she went on, "Nonsense is it? Why did he all of a sudden greet us? And smile like that at Aaron? Look how your son is already enchanted by him."

"It's nothing, just a nice day, and he's probably feeling good. There's no one about, so he greeted us. What of it?"

"I tell you, Solomon, that man deliberately stayed on board when everybody went ashore, just so that he could work his charm on our son. I shan't let the boy out of my sight for the rest of the journey, even if you think I'm a silly woman."

"You can be very silly at times," said Solomon. "Even if he is a missionary, what can he hope to do with one little Jewish boy with a fussy hen for a mother?"

"They always try, no matter where and against all odds. Look," she added, catching her breath, "he's coming towards us."

The Englishman was no longer strolling aimlessly. Suddenly he changed course and approached with the obvious intention of talking. Solomon stood up. The Englishman stopped a few paces away, smiled at the boy, then addressed Solomon in German. He had a deep, booming voice. "My name is Richard Pike," he said. As Solomon was slow to respond, Mr Pike took another step forward, stretched out his hand and took Solomon's in a firm grip. "Like me, you're making a pilgrimage to the Holy Land," he said, "though in quite a different way, I suppose."

"I'm going there to live, to stay for good," Solomon replied, withdrawing his hand. Suddenly the Englishman switched to Hebrew. "You are returning to Zion. May the Lord be with you, may there be many more like you, for it was prophesied that you should return, and I have prayed for it."

His Hebrew had a biblical resonance and was certainly better than Solomon's.

"See? What did I tell you!" Ada whispered.

"You speak our ancient tongue very well, sir. Incredible, you being a gentile . . ." He paused; perhaps the Englishman would contradict him and reveal himself to be a Jew! But Mr Pike smiled and said, "I've taught myself, with great difficulty, so that I may read the holiest of books." He took out a leatherbound bible from his pocket and held it high. Solomon noticed that it had the crucifix emblazoned on it. He said in German, and with some reserve: "So you are a churchman?"

"Oh, no," Pike laughed deprecatingly. "I'm what you might call a student of the past and of mystery. I'm particularly interested in archaeology."

Solomon knew nothing about archaeology. He had heard it said that it was a futile, if not a blasphemous thing, which some gentiles engaged in, often as a cover-up for missionary activities.

Mr Pike fixed his eyes on a far distant point and said in a quiet voice, "I don't know how long I shall sojourn in the Holy Land. Maybe I'll never see England again." Now his thoughts came out in snatches, spaced by silences. "I've had visions . . . I've had an idea, a theory . . . I shall prove it . . . the origin of creation, proved beyond doubt in the formation of rocks . . . out there in the desert. . . . Rock, the first things to have emerged out of the void, the *tohu vavohu*, as it is written."

Aaron was fingering a wooden shackle he had found on deck as he watched uncomprehendingly the strange Englishman talking to himself. It dropped from his hands and spun close to Mr Pike's feet. Emerging from his reverie, Mr Pike bent down, picked up the piece of wood, and held it in his large hand for a moment. "Every matter has its origin," he said, as though the object had offered him a revelation. "Do you know, *Mein Herr*, what became of the tablets on which your ten commandments were etched?"

Solomon made no reply.

"They were written by the finger of God on the pristine rock. Those were broken by Moses. Those which he brought down from the mountain the second time, do you know what became of them?"

"The man is crazy!" Solomon thought. Aloud he said: "Who can tell?"

"Somewhere they lie hidden beneath the sands. If they could be found, the Messiah would come and the world will be redeemed. Think of that!"

"Found? How? They're lost for ever. Only the commandments endure within us," said Solomon.

"Ah," Mr Pike stabbed the air with his finger, "that's where you're mistaken. I've had a vision, not once, not twice, but many times over the last years. I've maps. I've researched. . . ."

Their conversation was interrupted by the arrival of the European lady and her two companions on the quay. They hailed Mr Pike cheerfully. In a moment they had clambered on board and drew the Englishman into their company. The taller man with the beard, produced a bottle and a few tumblers. Solomon watched them as they toasted one another and laughed. "He behaves naturally with them, but with me he's like a madman. Is it him or is it I who's the cause of it?" he thought. To Ada he said, "Well, I thought we might have found a useful friend. Now I understand that we can look to nothing from him."

"Wise Solomon! I could've told you that long ago! A man who does his things on deck for everyone to see . . .!" Aaron said, "He might find the tablets, he can, I know he can."

"Hush child, don't talk such nonsense. Who's ever heard such foolishness," said Ada, and added with a laugh, "If I didn't believe in the Law and in the Almighty, I'd say that in such a land, where such people go, anything was possible."

Mr Pike didn't speak to Solomon again. He would greet him with a nod whenever they met on deck. After a while he stopped doing that too. The closer the ship drew to the shores of the Holy Land the more withdrawn the Englishman became, as though he was concentrating all his mental powers and purifying his soul for the awesome task he had set himself.

Yom Kippur, the holiest day in the Jewish calendar, fell on the second day out from Rhodes. It was expected that, all being well, they would reach Cyprus the next day, and then it was just another day before they reached their final destination, the port of Acre. Solomon fasted and prayed as he was accustomed to do, but now, for the first time in his life, he felt that his prayers had an immediate meaning, that no hindrance came between him and his maker. So he prayed fervently, with a pleading passion, for Aaron and for Ada, and that no sin he had committed might encumber him as he set foot on holy soil.

Throughout Yom Kippur, there was hardly a breath of wind. The sky was leaden. Its greyness flowed into the heavy greyness of the sea. The little ship was held fast in a dreary vastness. The passengers turned lethargic and moody. The Captain stood on the aft deck staring gloomily into the emptiness which engulfed them. Only Mr Pike went on with his usual routine as though nothing in the world mattered to him.

In the middle of the night, Aaron woke and vomited. At that moment the sea heaved, the ship shuddered and shot upwards. A sheet of lightning rent the darkness, and for an instant a ghostly illumination lit up the sea. Then the thunder came, rolling in from the distance and breaking over the ship. Water swept across the deck. With each lightning flash Solomon thought the ship would be smashed to splinters. He could see nothing, feel nothing but the vortical pull against which he was helpless. He groped in the dark for Ada and the boy, clutched at limbs, held on to them with all his might, and cried with what little breath he had: "*Shema Israel Adonai Eloheinu Adonai ehad*." "Hear O Israel, the Lord is one."

He felt he was plummeting to the deep. Water washed over him. The deck pushed him into the air, smashed him against the mast. He regained his senses enough to undo his belt and loop it round a solid projection near him. Then he slipped his leg through the loop as far as it would go. Fixed thus, he held on to Ada and Aaron like a wrestler, and prayed: "If I'm to perish for my sins, please God, let it not be at sea among thieves and gentiles. But deliver me to where you have commanded me to go that I may die with my dear ones in the land you gave to our forefathers Abraham, Isaac and Jacob."

At last there was a lull. Light filtered through the darkness. Voices were heard shouting. Hands were touching him. Still clutching his family, he half-walked and was half-carried below. The storm rose again soon after and raged for another day. Then as suddenly as it had come, it ceased, and all was still again.

Weakened and grateful, Solomon, Ada and Aaron clambered out of the stinking hold on to the deck. The scene that greeted their eyes was stupefying. There was débris everywhere. Bits of broken rigging lay strewn along the deck. A boom dangled disjointedly like a broken limb. The sea was calm and sparkling, the sky pure blue with puffs of cloud scudding across it. Against all this, the destruction stood out monstrously cruel, as if some evil spirit of vengeance had been at work. Mr Pike was sitting serenely on his box surrounded by the screen, and staring out to sea.

For two days the crew laboured on the battered ship until the damage was repaired. During that time it appeared that the captain was not at all sure how much off-course the storm had blown them. In all his life as a sailor on the Mediterranean he had never experienced such a storm, he told the Europeans. It was as though the Devil himself had plucked up the ship, spun her madly and cast her far away from any recognizable coastline or stretch of water. He had no navigation instruments except a compass; who needed a sextant or marine charts after having sailed that route so many times? He knew it by heart. The two Greek monks became more morose than ever, but the Europeans took it all in a spirit of adventure. Mr Pike calculated that the ship had drifted far to the north and any hour, the northern coast of Cyprus should come into sight.

What came into sight instead was a larger ship with red sails, and it was fast closing on them. The Captain followed its progress through his telescope, and as the strange ship came nearer, his face grew ashen, the telescope shook in his hands.

"First the storm. Now this. Who knows, perhaps a deadlier peril. Oh Lord, what further trials have you in store for us!" Solomon said under his breath as he watched the pirate ship swing to head them off. The *Calypso* was too slow to escape. As this became obvious, the cohesiveness of the crew fell apart; even the Master abandoned his authority to seek anonymity among his men. It occurred to Solomon to go and hide below, among the bales of cargo, an idea he dismissed after a quick thought: there was no telling what might happen once the pirates boarded the ship. Surely they would find them. Would they not then be singled out for a worse treatment? And if they should sink the ship . . . no end could be more terrible than going down with the rats. Better stick with the crowd, the Europeans. If there was safety in this awful situation, it must be with them, he decided.

To have come all this way—the Holy Land so close—only to be snatched by the maw of hell! It was too terrible, too painful to contemplate. "They'll have to kill me before they lay a hand on Ada and the child," he swore to himself, "I'd kill and die a thousand deaths before I see Ada abused, and my son taken away screaming." Aloud, he said, trying to sound as calm as he could, "Keep quiet and don't leave my side whatever happens."

Impassive and undaunted, the Englishman stood at the prow and looked on. The Europeans who were grouped around him likewise showed no sign of fear. "They think their governments are so powerful that no one would dare harm them," Solomon said to Ada, "Let's go and join them." At that moment, the pirate ship fired her cannon. The ball hit the foremast which splintered and crashed on to the deck. No one was hurt but the noise induced hysteria among the crew; the Greek monks shrieked and fluttered away to hide below.

Now the pirates were crowding the yards of their ship, swinging grappling hooks as they drew alongside the *Calypso*. They didn't look much different from the *Calypso*'s company, Solomon observed.

All but a few who stayed behind to man their own ship swarmed on to the *Calypso*, about twenty of them, armed with muskets, pistols, and swords. Their leader was a grizzled elderly man whose face was pitted with scars. "Albanians!" Solomon heard someone say. The *Calypso* offered no resistance, and soon the pirates were in full control. The pirate chief took a commanding stance on the deck, a pistol in each hand, and shouted orders. His mates rounded up the crew at sword point, and having corralled them around the mast, dragged the Master whining and kicking, to face their chief. There followed a brief interrogation during which the Master of the *Calypso*, his obsequious compliance notwithstanding, was severely beaten. Soon, parties of pirates set off to search the hold. One returned with a few bundles and the two Greeks whom they threw in among the crew. The pirate chief was angry: the booty was disappointing.

Among the crew of the *Calypso* there was a handsome youth with lively eyes and a mass of curly hair. One of the pirates noticed him, and dragged him before the chief, to appease his wrath. The more terrified the youth became, the louder the pirates laughed. The chief examined him slowly, passing the barrel of his pistol over the youth's neck and shoulders, then gave an order. The lad was bound up and laid with the rest of the booty. Solomon saw the Englishman's jaw tighten. Another search party arrived carrying loot from the Europeans' quarters. Among these were the Englishman's boxes which the pirates proceeded to open and empty on to the deck. The chief looked amazed to see so much worthless junk. His face grew darker with every moment. When he saw the thunder-box, his fury erupted afresh; he began kicking it and would have tossed it overboard. Mr Pike could no longer contain himself. He sprang at the pirate and seized him by the throat. But before he could throttle him, he was overcome by a rain of blows from the other pirates.

The pirate chief conceived a special end for the Englishman. He had him trussed up like a chicken, and stuffed into one of his boxes. The box was shut and secured with ropes. The pirates then knocked loose an iron capstan from the deck, and tied it to the box. As soon as the Englishman regained consciousness, he was to be thrown into the sea: the pirate chief didn't want his victim to drown without knowing it.

Meanwhile, he turned his attention to the Europeans who were now shaken and frightened no less than the hapless crew. "Aaron!" It flashed through Solomon's mind that they'd do to him what they'd done to the young sailor. He moved forward. The pirate chief cocked his pistol and aimed. Solomon continued to advance, slowly, hands raised. He heard a loud report and felt something hot and wet slap him hard on the forehead so that he staggered. Regaining his balance, he took out the amulet which hung round his neck and held it at arm's length, pointing at the pirate chief. No one moved, even as he came face to face with the man. He could see his contorted face, his bulging eyes and gaping mouth. He could smell his sweat, as he grasped his neck and with his remaining strength rammed the amulet down the pirate's mouth. He felt the pirate convulse in his grip, then go limp. He backed away; the ground was sinking beneath him; a red veil was lowering before his eyes. Then everything went silent and all movement seemed to slow down. He saw the pirate chief lying lifeless in a heap, yet somehow he knew he hadn't killed him; he saw the terrified pirates pick up their chief's body, clamber back to their own ship and cast off. Turning in search of Ada he saw her standing over him. A weight he couldn't shift seemed to be holding him down; he opened his mouth to speak but heard no sound. He saw the Europeans open the box and pull Pike out, who, unfettered, straightened himself, rubbed his arms and legs, then began to come towards him.

His first words when he came round were: "Ada! Our son. They've taken our son!"

"Be calm, they've gone," she said. "Aaron is here. Don't worry."

He was lying in the shade. His head was bandaged, and Ada was wiping his brow. "It's just a graze," she said. "An angel of the Lord came between you and the villain and made him miss. Rest now, soon you'll be well."

The Europeans were looking down at him, smiling beatifically. Mr Pike appeared and knelt at his side. "The Lord has wrought a miracle through you, Solomon Zeff," he said in Hebrew. "You've saved our lives and confirmed me in my purpose. Glory be to God in the highest." And he began to pray.

"Ada, I want to sleep. Take me somewhere where it's quiet," Solomon said.

"Father's like the great rabbis now, doing miracles. Everybody on the ship admires him," Aaron said gleefully.

"Hush child, your father's a man like other men. The good Lord saved us all, that and nothing else," Ada said, casting a wry smile at her husband. And Solomon smiled back at her.

"Tell me, where was the boy when the pirate shot me? I looked for him and couldn't see him."

"I hid him under my skirts. What else could I do?" she replied.

One morning, the coast of Palestine appeared in the distance, a dun-coloured wasteland and broken cliffs, with Acre blazing white in the sun. Solomon scribbled hurriedly in his journal: "The day before Hosana Raba, 5572 years to the creation of the world, 1812 in the calendar of the Gentiles. Blessed be the Lord God of our fathers, who has delivered us safely to the land He gave to Abraham and his seed. Blessed be the Lord for having come to my aid when we were in peril on the high seas, blessed is He, the Almighty, Creator of the world, supporter of the infirm and provider of the needy. I have arrived, at last. I trust in you, my God, to direct my steps heretoafter, that I might serve you and glorify your name in my deeds."

A wish undefined, hovered in his mind: Ask for good health? For the success of his enterprise? That his seed might multiply and fill the land? He sighed and put the paper back in the leather pouch. "I shall not ask for anything," he said to himself.

But as they disembarked and his feet touched land, he fell on his face and kissed the earth, and then it suddenly came to him. He murmured, "Lord God, I have but one thing to ask, fill me not with pride, but as was asked of you by the great king whose namesake I am, give me an understanding heart."

Chapter 4

Acre, a city surrounded by a thick crenellated wall, spread stoutly along the wide bay, whose beach gleamed with soft white sand. She was nothing like as majestic as Constantinople. In fact, apart from the pleasant sweep of the coastline and the dull grey walls, there was nothing particularly arresting about the place. But neither was there a threat about her, not at first glance, anyway. She looked solid, comfortable and dirty, like a peasant woman squatting by the waterfront, with her thick feet in the water.

The harbour was crowded with fishing boats, jostling one against another. Standing among the sun-blackened brawny Arabs who milled about before the walls, Solomon wanted to feel he had arrived home. He was tempted to shed his boots, to feel the sand and stones under his feet. Ada was unimpressed. She had expected something grander or welcoming, and Acre was neither. She was not afraid, but she had a dull, persisting feeling that from here there was no return.

Two porters dressed in rags solicited Solomon for his baggage. He waved them away. They left him to join the others who swarmed around the European passengers. The latter, now that their feet were on firm ground, seemed to have forgotten the miracle at sea; they ignored Solomon. The lady and her two companions stayed together, the Englishman was talking to a fellow countryman who had come to meet him. The solitary German succumbed to the porters who surrounded him as ants surround a helpless beetle. Two Greek priests had arrived to greet their co-religionists. They embraced and kissed without affection, then sneaked a glance at Solomon and smirked. Mr Pike suddenly remembered. He looked for Solomon, found him, walked over, and shook him warmly by the hand. "I shall always remember how you saved my life," he said, "I know in my heart that we shall meet again. God be with you."

The city gate with its rusty iron grille opened on to a spacious stone-paved esplanade that ran between the sea and the walls. Stalls laden with fruit and vegetables, sacks of oriental spices and strange foodstuffs stood along the esplanade from one end to the other. Men, women and children were walking about among the donkeys and the mules that were driven leisurely in and out of the gate, or else stood motionless as if lulled by the hot October sun. The tangy smell of the spices mingled with the smell of sea —and of fish, lying in glistening rows on the fishermen's stalls.

Solomon, Ada and Aaron stood in the midst of all the noises and smells and colours of their new homeland. The grey, scarred walls held the town like a hand, firm and assured. Above them they could see a minaret, straight and white as a bleached bone. Solomon had heard of Jizzar Pasha who had ruled the city, the Butcher, he was called, because of his legendary cruelty. His notoriety had spread throughout the Ottoman Empire. The Jews in Haskui had many tales about him, how Jizzar personally used to disembowel his enemies with a slash of his sabre, about his dark moods and moments of munificence, and his raw courage. It was only thirteen years before that he had faced and repelled the armies of the Emperor Napoleon outside the city's walls. Thank heavens he was dead.

Aaron, catching hold of his father's hand, said: "Father, if this is our home, why is it that we are strangers here?"

"When you've been away from home for a long time, you feel like a stranger when you come back. But you're not really a stranger, not really, son," said Solomon.

"But we've never been here before," the boy insisted.

"Our forefathers were here, a long time ago. Let's go now."

They went through the gate. Aaron was silent for a while. Solomon's mind was moving ahead. Jerusalem! A home, work. They would not stay here for long, only a day or two, until they could find means of travelling to the Holy City. He balanced their bundles across his shoulders and walked on, urging Ada to follow. Aaron began to lag behind, and Ada was getting cross with him. "Father, the people who came on the boat, they were all met by friends. But nobody came to meet us. Is that because this is our home?"

"Questions, questions! Enough of that," Ada said irritably, "Shall I tell you what happened to the little boy who asked too many questions?"

Inside the walls, the cooling sea breeze did not reach the narrow alleys which reeked of sewage and spices. The heat was oppressive and Solomon felt exhausted under his burden. He noticed how passers-by were staring at them, not with hostility as he might have expected, but with open curiosity. Aaron was boldly staring back, which made Solomon realize how all three of them had relaxed their habitual guard. He was pleased. There were Jews here, of that he was sure, and some might have passed by them and stared at them. But how could he tell them from the Arabs?"

Two armed men were loitering in front of a shop which had a sagging canvas awning stretched over its dusty patio. They had an official look about them. The shopkeeper brought out chairs and a stool upon which he placed a brass platter. The two men sat down. The shopkeeper brought water pipes and small tumblers with black coffee. Unbuckling their swords, the men settled down to smoke. They were jovial; they looked friendly. Solomon hesitated in front of them, then approached. The older of the two looked up, stroking his huge black moustache. Solomon tried several variations on the word "Jews", gesturing questioningly as he pronounced the words. The soldiers exchanged looks and laughed. Then the younger one pulled a chair and invited Solomon to sit down.

"Yehudim?" Solomon said.

At last they understood. *"Yahood, Yahood."*

Solomon nodded. "Yahood," he repeated. He took out two coins from his belt and offered them: "Yahood."

The soldiers led them through the narrow streets. So many times they seemed to change direction, turning now here, now there, that Solomon began to doubt whether his guides understood what he wanted. They kept ahead of him, talking among themselves, paying no attention to their charges who began to straggle behind. At last they arrived at a wider street, where the low white houses were well spaced between pomegranate trees heavy with fruit. Here the soldiers stopped. The older one made a sweeping gesture with his hand over the entire length of the street. "Yahood," he said.

The soldiers were gone. The sun flattened the landscape. Beyond the walls, on the far horizon, Solomon could see a ridge of purple hills. There was not a soul in the street. A mangy dog lay panting in the scanty shade of a broken wall and looked at them with tired eyes. The windows of the houses were all shuttered up. There was not a sound from within.

Ada broke the silence. "What sort of place is this?" she said. "Those men have been making fools of us. They've taken our money and brought us here where there's nobody. Who could imagine Jews living here? There's no sign of life."

"Let me be, Ada, for God's sake. It's hot. What do you expect? Haven't you seen enough life already? People are probably inside, resting. We're in a strange country!"

His sharpness cut her, and she turned on him: "Strange it certainly is! But you say, 'our home, the land God promised to our fathers'" she mimicked him. "We nearly died coming here. And for what? Open your eyes and look around you for a change!"

He was exhausted, and her rebuke stung him. He threw down the load of their possessions he was carrying, and gave the nearest bundle a kick for good measure, "Can't you hold your tongue for just a little longer? You're not the only one who's tired and wants a rest! And what do you know about people that you're always so suspicious of them? Can you divine who's good and who's bad? Can you read minds?"

Ada shouted back: "You're a fine one to talk of knowing people! A stupid madman kills himself and you see it as a sign from heaven! A filthy Turk cheats you, we get put in a hole like animals, and you let it pass. And now, having brought us here, you let two bored louts make a joke of us! What am I supposed to say, 'wonderful'? When will you ever learn,

Solomon? Never! Not even if one of us dies! I wish I'd stayed behind . . ." and she broke into bitter tears.

So absorbed were they in their quarrel that they didn't notice Aaron running off up the street covering his ears with his hands. When at last they wore each other down to silence he was nowhere to be seen. Solomon ran up and down the street, shouting "Aaron, Arele, where are you?" A man came out through a narrow door in the yard of one of the houses, and stood before him. He was short, stocky and barefoot and wore a white galabiya and a coarse woollen skull cap. "Salaam aleicum," he said, showing strong white teeth. Solomon, too distraught to return the greeting, made a gesture to indicate a small child and said in Hebrew, "The boy, a little boy."

The man pointed behind him, where a dusty path cut through an arid patch of a garden to the house. The door was open and at it stood Aaron, together with two other boys and a gentle-faced woman who had her hand on his shoulder.

The man said in slow throaty Hebrew, "You see? All is well. I am Rahamim Ben Ezra, this is my humble home. Honour me and be my guest, you and your family."

Ben Ezra's home was small and functional. Amina, Ben Ezra's wife, kept the place spotlessly clean, which made it look more spacious than in fact it was. Outside in the courtyard, two goats and a dozen black and brown hens roamed about. There was a donkey too, a fine grey animal, tethered to a post underneath a rickety shelter made of wood and coarse black cloth. Ben Ezra and his wife had four children: Miryam, the eldest, a girl of fourteen and already betrothed, Jacob, a fine, sturdy youth of fifteen, who helped his father in his shop, for Rahamim Ben Ezra was a saddler, and twin boys, David and Elazar, who were about Aaron's age. Ben Ezra was not wealthy by any means, but neither was he poor: he seemed to possess all he needed for a comfortable, secure life.

Amina fetched a large earthenware jar full of cool water from the well in the yard. After they had washed, she served them bread, cheese and yoghurt. That evening, Rahamim Ben Ezra bought at the market a freshly slaughtered lamb. This was a great luxury for the family, Solomon realized. But they were glad for the occasion to celebrate. Amina and Miryam baked fresh flat bread, and cooked rice spiced with saffron. As hosts and guests sat down to eat, Rahamim broke the bread and blessed, thanking the Almighty for having given him the honour of hospitality. Solomon too prayed, blessing the house of his kindly host, and giving thanks for his own good fortune. His coming upon this house he now believed with all his heart, was not fortuitous but divinely directed through the agency of his son. The thought so moved him that tears came to his eyes. He hugged the boy and said, "This has been your day, son. You've put me to shame but I'm proud of you, and I bless you. From now on your name will be Israel. I decided on this name when we set out today."

Ben Ezra, turned to his wife and whispered, "It's a good thing we have been granted to do, wife. God alone knows what misery and hardship these poor brethren of ours have endured on their journey here."

Solomon was eager to learn about the land, and about the Jews in Acre, in Jerusalem, anywhere in the country. But Rahamim stayed him with his hand. "My brother," he said, "what's the hurry? You'll soon learn that this country dislikes impatience. Eat, rest, enjoy the humble comforts of our home. There'll be plenty of time to learn all you seek to know. After all, you've come to live here."

That night they could hear the wind rustling the pomegranate trees, and the muffled thudding of the sea. Occasionally a jackal howled in the plain far out beyond the walls, and the dogs began to bark. All this was like music to Solomon's ears. "I shall learn to recognize these sounds, like my own thoughts," he said to himself. "Then I shall really feel at home at last. Home is when nothing seems strange to you."

Through the thin wall which separated their room from that of their hosts', he could hear Rahamim's steady snoring. They had all gone to bed early, as soon as darkness fell. Solomon observed how rapidly night thickened here, so unlike the lingering dusk in the Baltic countries. Ada lay at his side silent, pretending to be asleep; he knew she was awake. He put his arm round her and she stiffened. He persisted; she pushed him off, until he drew away from her. For a while they listened to each other's breathing, and waited for the other to say something. At length he said, in a hurt voice: "So it has come to that, and so soon. Now, when we need each other more than ever. . . ."

"Come to what?" she asked after a pause.

"You, shunning me."

"I'm tired," she said.

"Do you blame me for what happened?" she went on.

"No. What's the point of blaming you or me or anything? I'm saddened. I . . ." The wind rose. In the courtyard, the animals stirred and once again the jackal's wail was heard, contesting the wind.

"You've changed, Solomon," Ada said. "The journey's changed you. I don't know what it is . . . sometimes I feel I hardly know you."

"What are you saying? How have I changed? Towards you? The boy? Tell me . . . How can you say such a thing?"

She made no reply. So he turned his back on her and drew the blanket round him. "You wish you hadn't married me, you wish you'd stayed at home," he said unhappily.

She touched his shoulder. "I didn't mean what I said when we quarrelled,

I spoke in anger. No, no, of course I don't regret things. Only . . ." she hesitated, "I was afraid. I still am."

He turned to her and took her in his arms. "Afraid? Why? Things will turn out, can't you see?"

"Aren't you ever afraid?"

"Only when I'm not sure of what I'm doing. Now I am, I have been all along, about coming here, what it involved, that is." In the darkness he could imagine her drawing her mouth sceptically. "You seem to wish that I were afraid," he chided her, to which she replied by hitting his chest with her fist.

"I do," she cried in exasperation. "If only you were, just a little. You see no danger in anything. That stubborn confidence. Where did you get it from?"

"Faith, Faith!" he replied. "If you don't have faith, you have nothing, you fear everything. What better proof do you want than the miracle with the pirates?"

"Proof! Is that what makes you feel no harm can come to you? That stroke of luck which, thank God, saved us, you call proof?"

"It was an act of God, Ada," he said.

Ada laughed at his solemnity. "Listen to the noises of the night. I've never heard such terrible sounds. Danger. That's what's out there. And you think God will protect you because you've harmed no one, because you pray and observe the Law. Well, I think God has other things more important to mind. God hasn't stopped brutes in Lithuania from slaughtering Jews and He won't stop evildoers here from doing the same to us, if you go on the way you do!"

"Hasn't everything gone well for us so far? Why fret?" he tried to reason with her.

"Too well, and it worries me because it seems to have dulled your senses. Trust less in God, Solomon, and more in your own caution and judgement. That's all I ask."

"Ada, Ada, dearest, stop tormenting us both, take heart from our good fortunes," he pleaded.

"Oh, how simple you are! I'm tired," she said, and turned her back on him.

"But you must stay with us, at least to celebrate the Rejoicing of the Law," Rahamim implored, then added with an exaggerated tone of hurt, "Is my hospitality not to your liking? Have I not given you all the honour a guest could have?" His Hebrew, with the guttural Arab accent, was difficult for Solomon to follow, far more difficult than the expressions on his host's mobile face, on which he had come to rely more than on words.

"No, no," he protested. "Never have I enjoyed more generous hospitality. I don't know how I could ever repay you."

"By staying with us," said Rahamim.

"I've come a long way, friend, and now Jerusalem is near. How can I languish here?"

Rahamim lowered his eyes. "Jerusalem is further than you imagine, for people like you," he said. "If you don't believe me, speak to our Prince Farhi. Do you want to risk your life and the lives of your family? You must stay here for the Rejoicing of the Law. There's no other way you could meet Lord Farhi." And Rahamim spread his arms out in a gesture which closed the argument.

It so happened that the eve of the Rejoicing of the Law fell on the fifth day of the week. Rahamim and his family prepared for the big evening at the Synagogue. Early in the afternoon a tub was filled with steaming hot water and the children, including Aaron (now renamed Israel), were washed and anointed with olive oil. Then came the turn of the adults. At last they were ready to go.

Rahamim had put on his finest robe which he wore only on festive occasions. It had wide sleeves and embroidered hems. Underneath he wore a striped white tunic held up by a silken girdle. But it was the tall black turban that turned him into a princely figure, emphasizing the dark vitality of his eyes and his grey-streaked beard. Solomon envied him; how drab he himself looked by contrast, in his own best clothes which were foreign and time-worn. And Amina, her hair gleaming, the gold and silver coins on her headdress twinkling like little stars, how she glowed, like Sabbath itself.

"It is their holiday, not yet ours," Solomon reflected. "Why else does the radiance of the occasion pass us over? Poor Ada, a little sparrow beside Amina. But Israel—" Solomon had to smile—"how well he wears his new clothes and name! Israel Zeff! If his grandfather could see him now!" The boy was given clothes of one of the twins, and like his two new friends, he held a small flag attached to a stick, upon which Rahamim's eldest son had skilfully painted a rampant lion and the Tablets of the Law. An apple crowned the end of the stick, and on top of it there was a tiny wick to be lit when they arrived at the Synagogue. His complexion had been darkened by the eastern sun. He could have easily passed for one of Ezra's boys. Now he was laughing with them as they adjusted his turban and pulled at the girdle which braced his tunic.

Rahamim said, "See? Your boy is already one of us. Fine boy. May he bring you much honour and happiness in your old age."

"And may he have many brothers and sisters," said Amina with a sceptical glance at Ada's slender hips.

"If only you weren't so big I'd have gladly lent you my finest clothes," said Rahamim, looking at Solomon admiringly. And Solomon laughed, wishing for once that he were smaller and less conspicuous.

All along the street the Jews were coming out in their festive clothes and making their way to the Synagogue which stood not half a mile away, in the heart of town. They greeted and showered benedictions upon one another. In between encounters, Rahamim told Solomon about Farhi, a lord in Acre, light of the Jews and prince among men. It was due to him and him alone that Jews in Acre, and indeed throughout the land, were treated with respect. He was his people's shield and judge. So long as he prospered no Jew would feel the oppressor's hand. That was why each day a prayer was said for his health.

"It was in the days of Jizzar Pasha that Farhi had reached eminence," Rahamim explained. "Nothing was done without consulting him. Jizzar held him in higher regard than any other of his men. But Jizzar was a cruel man. Savage, like a wild beast. Even a leopard when he loves is still a leopard. One day in a fit of anger, Jizzar gouged out Farhi's right eye and cut off his nose. Then he threw him into a dungeon. This saintly man would have surely died if the good Lord had not made Jizzar repent. So Farhi was saved and taken back into Jizzar's favour. Our present Pasha, Selim, may he live forever, is a mild God-fearing man. He appreciates a good and loyal subject. And he has given Farhi more honour and power than Farhi had in his best days with Jizzar."

They had come into the heart of Acre. Here the Jews mingled in the larger crowd of Arabs. Ada walked beside Amina and her daughter, a few steps behind Rahamim and Solomon, the children were running back and forth, shouting and laughing. The sun had settled on the horizon with a flush of red that fanned across the water and illuminated the city walls and domes.

"Lord Farhi knows me. When he wants a saddle mended or a new bridle, who do you think he comes to? Me, Rahamim Ben Ezra," he said proudly. "He is a modest man, humble in spite of his position. You shall see him at the synagogue. He mingles with the people. But he is a sad man. What Jizzar had done to him has made him shy and quick to take offence, so don't look at him boldly but lower your eyes if he should look at you."

"But how can I approach him to beg his help so that we can go to Jerusalem?"

Rahamim looked horrified. "Approach him? Put such a thought out of your mind. No one approaches Lord Farhi without an intermediary, not even on a Holy Day. But pray hard. If God answers your prayers, Farhi will call for you. He knows you're here. He knows everything that goes on in Acre."

The synagogue had a large white dome and a heavy ornate portals, it stood between two rundown houses which looked uninhabited. A crowd of worshippers were singing outside in the street. The Torah scroll was brought out by a stalwart man whose head was covered with a prayer shawl. Chanting and singing, the worshippers followed the man in a procession, round and round the synagogue, as was the custom. Hands reached out to touch the Holy Scroll, and then kissed in devotion. Parents lit the wicks on top of their children's painted flags. The children's piping voices rose above the singing of the adults.

"This day", Solomon said to himself, "Jews all over the world celebrate the end of the Torah reading, and begin afresh from Genesis. And so it is with me. The beginning, at last. From this moment may the Lord open a new account for me in His books, and may I always do the right things." He looked for Ada and saw her with the women. She was smiling happily at him as his eye caught hers. "Please God," he prayed, "let me not quarrel with her over foolish things. Give me strength to make her happy and secure. And let us have many children."

There was a stir in the crowd. A knot of people agitated excitedly not far from the synagogue's gate. Then, riding a white thoroughbred Lord Haim Farhi came into sight. His crimson robe cascaded over his horse's flanks. His face was half-covered by a veil which came down from his black turban, in the fashion of desert warriors. A group of foot-soldiers surrounded him and gently kept the people back, for the crowd sought to touch their prince, his horse, the hem of his robe.

At the entrance to the synagogue, Farhi dismounted. He unbuckled his girdle and handed his sword of office to the sergeant-at-arms who stood near him. Then humbling himself with a swift gesture, he went up the few steps and into the synagogue.

The service was noisy. Solomon could barely recognize any of the prayers, let alone follow the reading of the cantor. But even if he could have, Farhi's presence was too compelling. It totally absorbed his interest, and he could not keep his eyes off him. Rahamim's warning was forgotten but luckily Solomon was standing some way from the great man. In the synagogue, Farhi unveiled his face. Here, among his own people in the house of God, he was ready to be seen in his deformity. From where he stood Solomon could see only the good side of Farhi's face. It was a lean, sad and severe face. Dark complexion, a pointed beard streaked with grey. Not a muscle moved in his face, only now and again he would blink, like a brooding hawk.

The Haham bashi, who conducted the prayers, moved in front of the ark, now reading from the scroll, now making room for the cantor. Solomon wondered fancifully whether he too, as a stranger from afar, might be called to read a passage from the Torah. Lord Farhi, in his awesome stillness, seemed to set the tone of the proceedings by invisible pulses; people moved, sat down, or rose to their feet as if at his command. Moments of fervour alternated with longer casual periods during which the worshippers chatted with one another. Once during such an interlude, Farhi gestured to the Haham bashi, who immediately came over and leaned his ear towards Farhi's lips. A little later, Farhi suddenly turned. His glance swept the hall and Solomon saw him full-faced for the first time. Where the right eye had been, there was a hollow over which the skin had stretched. The good eye glittered with dark brilliance; it dominated the broken face and gave it majesty. The nose was cut from the bridge, and the piece of bone stuck out in a downward curve. So forbidding was Farhi's expression that Solomon wondered if he was at all capable of smiling. Suddenly Farhi was looking straight at him, and Solomon, held by his gaze, was unable to lower his eyes.

"Listen to me, my brother. What you want to do is madness. Forget Jerusalem. There are more dangers to life between here and where you want to go than you've seen in all your nightmares," Rahamim pleaded.

"Forget Jerusalem! After all the journey, when it's so close? No, Rahamim, that I cannot. I might as well not have left my native town if this is how it should end. I must speak to the Prince Farhi, since he's the only one who could help me."

"Even he won't do that. He's not God. He won't listen to you," Ben Ezra repeated.

"I must see him."

Ben Ezra heaved a sigh. "Once a month, the Prince holds court, as is our custom. On that day every free man can come and the Prince will hear his petition. In three weeks you may see him."

"I cannot wait three weeks, Rahamim. I must see him tomorrow, the day after, within a week at the most. I must have his undivided attention, if only for a moment. Advise me, I beg of you."

"You can't force your presence on a man like Farhi. If you offend him, it will be the dungeon, not Jerusalem, that you'll end up in. We have customs, and ways."

"If God has seen me through all the dangers and allowed me to reach the Holy Land in safety, surely He will open the Lord Farhi's heart to my pleas," insisted Solomon.

"I know your kind of man, brother," said Ben Ezra resignedly. "Either you'll come to a sorry end, may God protect you, or you'll prevail against everyone and everything. Let me think and ask around for a few days. Who knows, maybe a solution will be found."

Solomon didn't leave it at that. He himself followed the Prince's daily routine, observing where he passed, where he stayed. But Farhi was always unapproachable, always surrounded by his guards who kept people away from him.

"Often at dawn, the Lord Farhi takes his favourite colt for a gallop on the beach," Ben Ezra said one evening.

"Then I shall be there and speak to him," Solomon said, delighted that at last an opportunity was found.

Ben Ezra laughed wryly. "Do you imagine he'd be alone? His guards will take you for an assassin and cut you down before Farhi even sees you."

There was a large sprawling rock on the beach just on the line of the waves, and not far from the city's gate. It marked the end of Farhi's gallop, Solomon deduced after reconnoitring the place. Early in the morning, as soon as the gate was opened, Solomon came out and positioned himself behind the rock. Soon he saw two armed riders issue out. They rode at a trot up and down the stretch of the beach, then waited. A few minutes later, two more horsemen appeared. One of them was Lord Farhi on his unmistakable grey colt. The company cantered some distance, turned, lined up, then broke into a full thundering gallop. As they came bearing down towards the rock, they slowed down. Solomon stepped out, and raised his hand, hailing the Prince. The three guards veered towards him while Farhi galloped past, reined in, and turned to watch his men surround Solomon, ride into him, and buffet him. But when one of the guards drew his sword, Farhi shouted an order, and came trotting up.

He looked irritated and puzzled, but not dangerous. "What is it you want?" he said in Hebrew. The words Solomon had prepared evaporated from his mind.

"My name . . ."

"I know who you are," the Prince cut him short, underscoring the grossness of Solomon's impropriety. It was too late to back down.

"I must go with my family to Jerusalem. I've made a vow. You have the power, Prince. In God's name, help me . . ."

Farhi fixed Solomon with a piercing gaze for a moment then without a word wheeled his colt and cantered away to the gate.

In the afternoon of the next day, the Haham bashi of Acre paid an unexpected visit to Ben Ezra's home. It was about Solomon the Ashkenazi he had come, on the orders of Prince Farhi. He was polite and sympathetic, but firm. The Prince, said the Haham, appreciated courage and was tolerant of strangers' alien manners. He had heard of how Solomon faced the pirates aboard the *Calypso*, for which there was a reward on behalf of Pasha Selim himself—enough money for Solomon and his family to rent their home and live frugally for a whole year. In the Galilean town of Safed, which was under Acre's jurisdiction and therefore of the Lord Farhi's, there lived a friendly, law-abiding community of Ashkenazi Jews. On the morrow after the next, Solomon and his family must leave Acre and go there. The Prince would provide an escort with riding animals for Solomon to keep. That was Lord Farhi's judgement against which there was no appeal, said the Haham, and handed Solomon a pouch containing the reward money.

Seeing how down-hearted Solomon looked, the Haham tried to console him: "It's for your own good, believe me. Judea is a lawless country. In Jerusalem there are Jews but not like you. If you set a foot there, the Arabs will kill you, and that would be bad for the Sepharadi Jews who live there. Prince Farhi will not allow that to happen."

"But why will the Arabs kill me? I've done nothing," said Solomon, bewildered.

"Some fifty years ago, there were Jews like you there. They borrowed money from the Arabs to build their synagogues. They quarrelled with the Arabs and defaulted on their debts. They were chased out, and their houses burnt. Ever since, no Ashkenazi Jew has been seen in El Kudz, and so it will be for as long as you and I live. Now do you understand?" And with that the Haham rose to his feet. "Go and buy what you need, and be ready at dawn when Lord Farhi's man will come for you."

Chapter 5

Ada could not conceal her joy and relief that they were not making the dreaded journey to Jerusalem, but were instead going to Safed where there were European Jews who spoke Yiddish. She immediately started packing and preparing for the journey, muttering prayers of thanks as she worked.

At first cock-crow, they rose from their mat and dressed for the journey. The boy was still asleep. Ada shook him gently, dressed him, and gathered his belongings. Rahamim, his wife Amina and their children were already up. Oil lamps were lit. The smell of freshly-baked bread filled the house. Before sitting down to breakfast, Solomon and Rahamim and his son put on phylacteries and prayer shawls and prayed together. Amina, meanwhile, was discreetly weeping. Soon they heard the sound of hooves approaching. There was a knock on the door. Farhi's man had come. Without a word he pointed to the end of the yard. There, tethered to the gate, stood three saddled donkeys, their heads hung low. Behind them, half-hidden by the wall, there was a horseman. His face was partly covered. He held a long spear in his hand. This was their escort whom Lord Farhi had sent to see them safely to Safed. The Prince's servant bowed, touched his lips and forehead and departed.

Rahamim Ben Ezra recognized the horseman immediately. His name was Farid el Sallah, a Druze from the mountains of Lebanon, a former bandit of such notoriety that mothers in Acre and the surrounding villages used to frighten their children with stories about him. Rahamim swore that el Sallah recognized no power in the world save Allah's and Lord Farhi's, nor was he given to speak more than a dozen words in the course of a day. Solomon was therefore assured of silent company and complete safety.

Rahamim and his sons helped Solomon load the donkeys. At last they were ready to move. Ada and the boy sat on the sturdiest animal, the second was loaded with all their belongings, Solomon took the third. The Druze set off at a slow walk. "God speed your journey and deliver you safe and sound," Rahamim said and clasped Solomon's hand between his own.

"God bless you for all you've done for us," Solomon returned.

"How strange it is," Solomon thought. "We arrive at a port full of noise and people. We leave as if by stealth on a dark, empty morning. It should be the other way round. Come quietly, depart in triumph. Is this a bad sign? Who knows. I think this fellow won't look back to see if we're still behind him, and yet I know he watches over us."

He turned round to chat with Ada. Sitting sideways on the donkey and holding Israel in front of her, she looked biblical. He told her so. She laughed. "At this rate," she said, "when do you think we'll reach Safed? Not before the Messiah, I tell you."

"Once we get into our stride, you'll see how time and distance shrink," he answered.

She pointed to the Druze, "if the Ishmaelite should only increase his pace he would lose us in no time at all."

He looked at her questioningly. "Why did you call him that?"

"How else should I call him?" she retorted cheerfully.

It occurred to him for the first time that she was more aware of racial difference than he was. "But he's the best of guides, a faithful servant of Farhi's, how can you even imagine that he should leave us?"

"Did I say that? Listen to him! All I said was that the Ishmaelite could, unless he paid attention, leave us behind and lose us, seeing that we're so slow and his animal's so fast. And he doesn't even look back or say anything."

Acre fell behind. Ahead stretched the plain, blasted by the heat. Clumps of trees stood here and there, and in between them withered shrubs and dust. In the distance the hills interlocked, grey and purple against a brassy sky. A few buzzards wheeled slowly above. The sun, dim and red, seemed fixed on the lance tip of the Druze.

In his native country Solomon knew the points of the compass by the bends in the rivers, by the way moss gathered on the trunks of trees, or from the position of the sun. Here he had no sense of direction. He knew nothing about the land. The trees were unfamiliar, nothing connected with anything he knew. His dependence on his silent guide was complete and it made the land appear all the more alien and inhospitable. It did not correspond at all to what he had imagined.

To help him feel a little at home and pass the time, he tried to remember passages from the Bible which described places. The first passage that came to his mind, however, was from Genesis: "And Jacob went on his journey, and came into the land of the people of the east." Now, Solomon began to deliberate: in the Hebrew text it clearly states that Jacob, the Patriarch, walked. No donkey. Shouldn't he, Solomon, therefore emulate that humble setting forth? The idea appealed to him. He pulled at his donkey's mangy mane. The animal went plodding on. "Stop," he ordered. The donkey walked on. Solomon leaned forward and put his hands over the animal's eyes. The donkey stopped dead in its tracks, and Solomon fell to the ground.

"Father, what are you doing?" Israel shouted.

"Can't you see? I got off. I've decided to walk," Solomon shouted back; how could he expect a child and a woman to understand!

"You'll only get tired, and what for? Besides, it'll slow us down even more," said Ada.

"I can walk much faster than this creature," said Solomon, and tying a piece of rope round the donkey's neck, walked ahead, pulling the donkey behind him.

Meanwhile, the Druze rode on, neither stopping nor looking back. The distance between them grew steadily, and Ada was beginning to worry.

"He has a sword and a lance, and a horse. He doesn't think much of us," said Israel. "When I grow up I'll also ride a horse. Then everybody will want to talk to me."

The Druze had reached the foot of a rise and Solomon suddenly anticipated a river. He was getting tired, he longed to see running water.

The Druze reached the high ground and stopped. Here he waited impassively for his charges to catch up with him.

There was no river in sight, nor any sign of one. The ground rolled down from the edge of the escarpment into a wide plain which had more trees in it and looked lusher. It was past noon and clouds began gathering in the sky. "Will it rain?" Solomon thought. "Who could tell here? Except the Druze, he knows everything intuitively, like the fowls of the air and the beasts of the field."

El Sallah was resting on his lance, looking out to the distance. Solomon followed his gaze. At first he could see nothing. But soon he was able to make out a party of horsemen moving like dots towards them. "Robbers!" he thought. El Sallah was calm, and Solomon, mindful of the Druze's reputation, relaxed too.

"Why have we stopped?" Ada asked.

Israel said, "To give the animals rest, of course. That's what you do."

"If you keep the Ishmaelite busy for a moment, I'll go and relieve myself behind that bush over there," said Ada.

"There're horsemen coming," Solomon said.

She went all the same. Solomon started talking to the Druze, making signs and using whatever few words of Arabic he had picked up in Acre. He wanted to know who the horsemen might be. To his surprise El Sallah responded. Even though his back was turned he had noticed how Ada had slipped away and he sought to reassure Solomon that there was nothing to fear.

The party now approached within a few hundred yards, trotting at an easy pace. There were ten of them all well-mounted on fine Arab horses, and armed with lances and rifles. To Solomon they looked, from their bearing and the way they were dressed, like a group of distinguished Bedouin warriors out hunting. Then he saw that three were Europeans who, although dressed as Arabs, carried more compact rifles of a kind he had not seen on Arab horsemen.

El Sallah nodded in the direction of the receding party. "Englese," he said, and added "Libnane", pointing with his lance to indicate that the English, whoever they were, were riding north to Lebanon. El Sallah, it seemed, held the English in great reverence.

By late afternoon they had passed through the foothills and began to ascend into the higher reaches of Galilee. Solomon's legs and back ached from the effort of the climb but he would not mount his donkey. He stopped every now and then to rest, and to admire the rugged beauty of the hills. At dusk clouds began piling up on the horizon. It also became noticeably cooler. El Sallah chose an olive grove on the hillside for their overnight camp. They set about erecting tents, using blankets and other pieces of material they had with them. When that was done Solomon built a fire which Israel lit, using a flint and a chunk of steel as Ben Ezra had taught him. Ada prepared their supper of flat bread, goat's cheese and olives.

El Sallah didn't join them but withdrew and sat apart beside his mare which he had tied to an olive tree away from the other animals. There he built his own fire. Ada and the boy were unconcerned, they were too preoccupied with the fire and the food. But Solomon was troubled.

"Perhaps I offended him in some way," he said to Ada.

"Why do you bother with him? He has his world and we have ours, and this is as it should be. Tomorrow, God willing, we shall reach Safed and be among our people. What does it matter whether this man, to whom I am grateful for what he's done for us, wants to sit with us or not?"

Darkness fell quickly. The jackals began to howl. The wind picked up the sounds and mixed them. El Sallah sat with his robe wrapped round him, absorbed in thought, listening to the sounds of the night. When Solomon looked at him, he smiled. "If only we had a common language, how much I'd want to listen to you," thought Solomon; "I envy your understanding, everything that happens, each and every sound, whatever passes by, you know and recognize."

A shower of sparks flew off the fire. Stars glittered through gaps in the pall of cloud. Israel, tired from the day, pulled the blanket around him and fell asleep against his mother's thigh.

Before they retired El Sallah piled more wood on to the fires. In their improvized tent—a lean-to with a flap that came down and was secured to the ground with rocks—Ada pressed herself against Solomon. He pushed his hand between her legs. Her warmth aroused him. She raised her hips gently against his touch.

With dawn it began to rain. The raindrops rattled like pebbles against the drooping flank of the tent. Gradually the rain became stronger, turning into a torrent. Peering out, they could see nothing but whirling water. The water came through, gushed under them, soaked them to their bones. They huddled together to keep warm. When the rain stopped, large areas of blue sky appeared among the broken cloud. The air had a sweet crispness and the earth was dark and thick among the puddles. The olive trees glistened as though they had been anointed.

The first thing that struck Solomon and Ada as they stepped out of their collapsed shelter, was the silence.

There was no sign of the Druze or his mare.

"He's abandoned us, just as I knew he would," Ada moaned and burst into tears. Solomon climbed to a nearby hill and called out, "El Sallah, El Sallah!" His voice echoed in the hills. From his vantage point he could see their disorderly little camp, his wife and his child standing among their cast-about belongings, afraid and confused. "It can't be," he said to himself, "he's Lord Farhi's trusted man. He couldn't have left us and gone just like that!" Again he scanned the landscape. Nothing but hills and hills, climbing seemingly to nowhere. Not a sign of human habitation. He sat down on a rock. "Now Solomon, your hour of trial has come," he said aloud. "There must be a reason to all this. I shan't lose heart. But which direction is it to Safed? Can't be too far away. A distance of two days' ride, they told me. So we must be half-way there. To the right? Left? No. It must be only up, straight up. There, from the heights, we're bound to see the city, a village at least . . . and, no doubt we should meet someone on the way." A thought flashed through his mind: "Who travels in these wild parts? No pilgrims, only robbers . . . I'm unarmed. Anyone can see I'm not a man of violence. And what have we got that a robber would want?" He touched the girdle under his robe, where the money Farhi had given him lay hidden. "They'd take the donkeys and our few possessions. As for the money, Ada will wear the girdle under her clothes. Abraham, on his way to Egypt, bade Sarah his wife to pose as his sister, to protect himself. It's not me I want to protect but my family and their future." He stood up.

Ada dried her tears. Obediently she took the money belt and secured it round her waist next to her skin. Solomon turned to face where he believed Jerusalem was, and sang his morning prayers. Ada too, prayed, fearful for her life and the life of her son. When they had finished saddling and loading the donkeys, both realized that Israel, who had been silent all the while, was feverish. Solomon remembered the path they had been on the evening before, not far from their camp, and made for it. The path led towards the hills for a short stretch then finished in a deep ravine. Pulling his donkey by the rope, Solomon strode on with Ada riding behind holding Israel against her breast. They had not gone far when the boy began to moan loudly. Solomon stopped. Israel's face was deathly white and covered in perspiration. His eyes were shut, he was trembling uncontrollably all over.

Ada rocked him back and forth, speaking to him, promising him the world if he would only open his eyes and say something. When she saw Solomon look at her, she calmed down all at once and said quietly: "I only hope that we shall not have to bury him in this wilderness, all on his own."

The sun scattered the clouds. The air was so clear that from every rise they could see the Galilee heave and dip all around them, great provinces of grey, brown and purple, streaked with green, all glistening from the rain. After an hour of steady climbing, the ground levelled on to a straight plateau which ran for some half a mile, and then seemed to end in clouds. There was a bare hillock crowned with jagged heaps of black basalt rocks, and on it they saw El Sallah astride his mare. A direct sign from God could not have pleased Solomon more than seeing the Druze again. He let go the donkey and jumped up and down waving his arms in the air, "El Sallah, O hero, El Sallah," he yelled. "See? I knew he wouldn't abandon us," he said jubilantly. "He must have had some good reason for going off, probably kept an eye on us all along. Hey, El Sallah!"

The Druze waved his lance and trotted down the hillock towards them. He had brought food, freshly-baked bread, and some cheese. When he saw the state the boy was in, he clicked his tongue and immediately set about lighting a fire. He gathered some herbs that grew on the hillside among the prickly bushes, boiled them, and soaking Ada's kerchief in the solution, applied it to the boy's chest. Having done that, he motioned Solomon to mount his donkey, and himself taking the rope of the loaded donkey, attached it to his saddle and rode away at such a pace that the humble beast was nearly pulled off its feet.

Early in the afternoon Safed suddenly came into view. The sight made Solomon forget for a moment his son's condition and gasp for breath with wonder. The ancient Galilean redoubt, one of the four cities in the land holy to the Jews, was perched on top of a high hill separated from the other hills by deep ravines on all sides. So insubstantial yet perfectly formed she looked, that one might have imagined her resting lightly, like a crown, on the summit. The houses, pale blue and white, stood clustered together. The sky filled the spaces among the gentle curves of walls and domes. A wall surrounded the city and from it several chalky paths snaked down through the wooded and shrubbed slopes of the hill. Here the Druze bade them farewell and rode away.

There were few people in the first streets they came to, and no Jews. The Arabs in their way regarded the newcomers with indifference. Solomon led the donkeys through the narrow cobbled streets where thin torpid dogs slunk about, to where he imagined the heart of the city was. He hadn't gone far when he heard a murmur, growing louder. It sounded like a congregation at prayer. He prodded the donkeys to quicken the pace. Soon they arrived at a wide, stone-paved square which stood in the shadow of a square fortress-like building. Here a strange sight greeted his eyes.

Gathered in the square were some hundred Jews, men, women and children, all dressed in their best clothes, the men in long striped kaftans and fur-trimmed hats, like the men wore in Kedainai, and the women wrapped in shawls. The children looked scrubbed clean, their long side-locks brushed and curled. A few Arabs stood by the entrance of the fortress and looked on with languid curiosity. It was they who spotted Solomon and Ada and cried out to the Jews, who immediately turned to look.

When they saw Solomon, they all fell silent and stared. One of the men, a tall thin fellow, whose hat was as big as a target, stepped forward. He looked at Solomon ecstatically for a long moment. Then he lifted his eyes to heaven, and clasping his hands before his chest, cried out aloud in Yiddish, "It has come to pass, just as Zipple dreamed!" Immediately the entire congregation chimed in with a loud "Amen". Solomon was completely bemused. Before he could say anything, the thin man rushed towards him, embraced him as though he were a long-lost brother, and kissed him on both cheeks, choking with tears as he did so. "Oh miracle, Oh deliverance. Welcome, welcome, you bringer of life. Now Reb Mendle shall live," he murmured excitedly. "Our prayers have been answered, Glory be to God." The men began to chant and dance in circles round Solomon and Ada. But Solomon grabbed the thin man by the sleeve. "Brother, what's all this about? My child is dying and my good wife is half mad with worry. Help us first, for pity's sake," he said.

The wife of the thin man took the feverish Israel to her home, washed him in warm water, and wrapped him in a prayer shawl which, legend had it, belonged to a holy man many years ago, and had healing properties. The thin man, whose name was Reb Isser from Shklov, said, "Rest at peace, you and your good wife. Your son's in the best of hands. Now come to my house and wash, and I'll tell you what good fortune you've brought us." But before they reached Reb Isser's house, a lad came running towards them crying: "He lives! He opened his eyes and smiled. He lives!"

"Come," said Reb Isser, linking his arm through Solomon's, "let's go and give thanks and rejoice for the miracle that has been wrought."

The house of Reb Mendle of Shklov, who was Isser's kinsman, was thronged with people. In the largest room, the saintly old rabbi was lying in his bed which had been moved from the bedroom so that the congregation outside could look through the windows and the open door and see how their revered, beloved judge and teacher had been restored to life. The room was alight with candles and fragrant with incense. Reb Mendle was covered with a patchwork blanket the colours of the rainbow. His white beard fanned out over the blanket and was held down by his fragile, almost transparent hands. His head was propped up by pillows, and covered with a *kippa* embroidered with gold and silver from which his splendid side curls reached down to his thin shoulders. To Solomon he looked aged beyond count of years, far older than his supposed seventy.

"Come closer and kiss his hand," whispered Reb Isser. And Solomon drew near, too bewildered not to obey. As he bent over the old man's hand, Rabbi Mendle opened his eyes. They were brilliant and blue. He smiled. His lips moved silently. Then he closed his eyes again.

"He knows you, he has blessed you," Reb Isser said tremulously.

"How does he know me? How does any of you know me?" Solomon whispered, because involuntarily he was beginning to enter into the hallowed atmosphere of the place.

Reb Isser nodded in the direction of the corner where, seated against the wall, apparently unconscious, was a sallow-looking young man.

"Zipple, dreamer of dreams. It was he who foresaw it all. But visions always drain his life away for a while. That's why he's as you see him."

"You speak in riddles, Reb Isser. Tell me, make me understand or like Zipple I too will pass out."

Reb Isser took him by the arm away from Reb Mendle's bed. "It was like this," he began. "A month ago, during the Awesome Days, just after the New Year, we all rode to Meron, as is the custom, to pray at the tomb of our blessed sage Rabbi Shimeon Bar Yochai. That day Reb Mendle excelled himself in wisdom and piety. His words were pearls. What a memorable day it was! But on the way back, the Devil, always jealous of saintliness, made Reb Mendle's mule stumble. Reb Mendle was thrown on his head. He lay on the ground as though he were dead, and the light went out of our lives. We bore him back home and put him in his bed. There he lay, his saintly soul hovering between life and death, unheedful of our weeping. No medicine, nor prayers, not even charms from the Caballa were of any help. Then the Great Ari appeared one night to Zipple in a dream, and told him that on a certain day a stranger would arrive in Safed, an Ashkenazi Jew, pure of heart and full of strength. And the Presence would be with him. His strength would flow into Mendle, and he should be healed.

"We waited and prayed and fasted. Every day we gathered in the square by the synagogue where Reb Mendle taught, and waited. You see? It all came to pass, just as Zipple had seen in his dream."

That night another miracle happened: the boy Israel opened his eyes and called for his mother. Before morning his fever had abated and he slept peacefully. Ada, exhausted, put her arms round Solomon and wept from joy and relief.

According to tradition, a boy who was close to death and recovered, was given a new, additional name. The name Solomon chose for his son was Zvi, in Hebrew, the hart, symbol of the Promised Land and her excellence, as it is written in the Book of Books: a name which had graced many an illustrious rabbi.

Chapter 6

In Safed, the Arab saying went, you stood at the pinnacle of the world; from here you could only go down. The city was as elevated as Jerusalem, and a good deal more salubrious. Misfortunes and unhappiness stopped at the foothills. In Safed, people had fresh complexions and clear eyes. Old age came on with the gentleness of an autumn breeze. The pace of life was slow, and old men were gathered to Abraham's bosom with a peaceful heart and a mind as pure as the mountain air. "When your time comes," Rabbi Mendle used to say in happy anticipation, "your soul drifts up the short distance to Heaven, like a white feather." Small wonder it was that the Jews of Safed were renowned for their piety and learning; was it not providential that here the Cabala flourished and legends were created?

Some six hundred Jews, men, women and children, lived in Safed. None was rich—no Ashkenazi Jew was in Palestine. But neither were there paupers, not real paupers anyway, for the community took care to provide for the needy from its meagre resources. There was no shortage of food, and there was always water in abundance, cool clear water from mountain springs and deep wells.

Only a few worked for their living, and only for a part of their living at that. Most of the men spent their time studying the Torah and praying. Their subsistence money came from Jews in Europe who were ready to pay so that their brethren in the Holy Land might live in piety and pray for the redemption of all the Children of Israel. Once every three years an emissary would travel to Europe to collect the money which, having been brought back, was dispensed to every household by a select group of elders. The system was known as *haluka* which in Hebrew means distribution.

There were some who earned part of their living in small trade with the Arabs, or as artisans. Relations with the Arabs were mostly friendly though never close. The Arabs seldom abused the Jews. As for the small garrison, the Ottomans, universally despised, were content to let things run as they did, so long as taxes were paid and there was no trouble.

Beyond the city's gates, which, as in any other walled city, were shut at sunset and opened at dawn, there was no security: bands of robbers roamed, preying on wayfarers. Once in so many years, Solomon learnt, disasters visited Safed, just like any part of the country. There would be an earthquake, an outbreak of plague, a drought that withered the crops, or the mountain Druze would swoop on the city in a riot of pillage. When that happened the garrison would withdraw into the fortress and not come out until the Druze's fury was spent. Reb Mendle used to say all this was God's way of keeping man aware of his mortality and testing the resilience of the Jews.

The Jews in Safed had their social order. Rabbi Mendle was the spiritual leader and ultimate authority in matters of dispute. But the saintly old man had little understanding of material things. To deal with these he appointed his two astute kinsmen Isser and Israel, who administered the affairs of the community, saw to the distribution of the money, and dealt with the Turks and the Arabs. Safed was within the Ottoman Pashalik of Sidon whose Pasha resided in Beirut. Minor officials, like the overseer of Safed, were often local Arab sheiks who were given the right to levy taxes and enjoined to keep the peace and provide the basic public services of which the most prominent and lucrative was justice. Such local rulers were receptive to bribes, and at times cruel, but they instinctively understood the advantage of flexibility in government: they imposed taxes according to how much they believed they could extort. Even the most stupid official realized that little could be squeezed out of prayers.

There was a larger and older community in Tiberias on the western shore of the Sea of Galilee which, like the Jews in Safed, subsisted on haluka money. These were Hassidim with whom the men of Safed had differences over the interpretation of the Torah. The Safed luminaries considered the Hassids obtuse if not heretical, and their ritual simple-minded and vulgar. But Jews are Jews, and all are equal before the Creator and accountable to one another. So the two communities kept council and helped each others in times of need.

Such was the world in which Solomon found himself. With the money Lord Farhi had given him, he was able to rent a small dwelling, not far from where Rabbi Mendle lived. It was a modest affair, two rooms and a courtyard surrounded by a wall, a shared well in the middle. The kitchen was a recess in the wall across the courtyard. But there was a fine stone oven in which Ada soon learnt to cook good thick Sabbath *cholent*, and bake fragrant bread and raisin cakes, just as she used to in Kedainai. In a half-dilapidated shed adjoining one of the rooms, Solomon set up his workshop. Solomon had decided that in the Holy Land, he would earn his living from the sweat of his brow, if he could, rather than depend on charity. He seized the opportunity of learning silversmithing from their host in Odessa – a relative of Ada's with whom they sojourned for a month before continuing their journey to Constantinople. It had taken a good deal of sweat before the master silversmith could pronounce Solomon proficient in the basics of the craft. The shed was cramped and cold but after he had installed his work table, a bench, arranged all his tools on shelves, and brought in an old oil burner, the place generated a cosy atmosphere of industry. He bought four hens and a rooster, and a she-goat.

The animals were kept in the yard. Looking at them as he stepped out in the morning, Solomon, for the first time in his life felt he was a man of property.

Israel Zvi attended the Rabbi's classroom, the *cheder*, where, together with other children of his age he learnt to read the Torah and nothing else. For Solomon, work was infrequent and hardly remunerative. He soon discovered that people came to his workshop more to talk than to employ his skill, because apart from everything else, people had no money to spend on such luxuries as ornaments.

Rabbi Mendle seldom visited Solomon, nor did he invite him often to his own home. Not because he didn't like Solomon. He loved him; he was grateful to him for having restored him to life as he believed. Balance and moderation were his guidelines in all he did. For fear of going to excess he tended to give of himself in small portions and at wide intervals. But on one or two occasions he was seen emerging from Solomon's retreat with a distant and radiant smile on his face, as though a glimmer of Heaven had been revealed to him.

That Solomon had taken up residence close to Reb Mendle's dwelling was enough to confer on him a special privilege in the community. Added to that was the fact that he was different: stories of his adventures on the way to the Holy Land circulated with varying degrees of exaggeration. And when Reb Mendle who never tired of listening to Solomon's stories, and whose disciples never ceased to marvel at his new glowing health and how his deliverance was brought about, was seen going in and out of Solomon's home, simple folk began to believe that Solomon was indeed an exceptional man, far beyond the understanding of ordinary mortals.

"Reb Solomon, listen to this, I had a dream. . . . What do you think it means? What would Reb Mendle say? Here, I've brought you a round of fresh goat's milk cheese." And Solomon would unleash his imagination, and give an answer. "Reb Solomon, my donkey's developed a swelling on its fetlock. What should I do? Will you look at it?" "Bring it round and let's have a look," he would say. Life's wisdoms, things he had learnt in his youth from Lithuanian peasants and Jewish pedlars, lined up in his mind like old familiar tools.

Those who couldn't gain access to Reb Mendle, came to seek advice from Solomon, and he seldom let them down. As his reputation grew so he prospered. Had he not always been an innovator, an improviser when others had learning and experience? Reb Mendle loved him: in his company, the old man felt rejuvenated; his innocence of spirit found kinship in the younger man's innocence of demeanour. "Fresh minds bring forth fresh ideas," he would say of Solomon, "I know in my heart that the Blessed Name directed this young man here not merely to save my life but to reawaken us all, for we've been like a still pool, locked in stone."

At night, when they were in bed together, Solomon would regale Ada with stories he had heard from his visitors during the day. He would mimic them, making her laugh. But she would caution him, saying, "The higher you rise in people's esteem, the harder you fall when they tire of you. Beware, husband, not to overreach yourself."

"What joy is there in never-changing routine, Ada? Look at them. Superstition and tradition. Nothing new, nothing that hasn't been tried before. Is that to be our life too? Sometimes I'll succeed. Sometimes I'll fail, that's inevitable. But I want to discover, Ada, more than anything I want to discover." He spoke with passion, because already he was beginning to chafe against the rigid constraints of his new life.

Chapter 7

Winter came with sudden ferocity. A dense chill settled over the city. The people of Safed woke up one morning to a deep silence. All about, the hills white with snow crowded the city, cutting her off from the world. Soon life came to a standstill. Not even the donkeys could negotiate with safety the steep tortuous paths which led in and out of Safed. When it stopped snowing, the cold became so intense that water froze in the cisterns. There was treacherous ice on the paths and in the streets. Children stopped playing outside and huddled together with their parents wherever there was a fire or a stove to gather round. The freezing weather continued for over two weeks, by which time food and fuel began to run low, for the Arabs from the villages who brought these to the city did not come. And if they came, they charged such prices—particularly for the charcoal—as the Jews could barely afford.

The Rebbetze Baile, Mendle's wife, fell ill. On two occasions she had stopped breathing and was given up for dead, only to stir again. Mendle's fearful prayers kept her in this world. The community mustered their resources to keep Mendle's hearth burning. Solomon had a premonition that the Rebbetze would soon ascend to Heaven in grace that had eluded her most of her life. Of course he didn't tell Mendle. Ada said mournfully, "The way things are going, I shan't be surprised if poor Baile takes all her friends and neighbours with her."

One morning Israel came in blue with cold. He brought with him a small log of wood which he had found somewhere. He shoved it into the oven, and through the grille watched it crackle and smoke until it caught fire and the aroma of burning wood filled the room. "On the hillside there's plenty of wood," he said, "why don't the men go out and bring it in for everybody?"

"From the mouths of babes comes good counsel," said Solomon, and kissed his son.

"We've never done such things before," said Isser and Israel, pulling at their beards.

"Well? There's never been a need for it, has there?" said Solomon.

"God forbid that we should fall foul of the Arabs who profit by selling firewood."

"Where are they now, when we need fuel more than ever? Think of the Rebbetze."

"Reb Solomon, you tempt Providence," said Isser.

Solomon led a party of young men armed with axes to the slopes of the hill. They took with them four donkeys and Isser's white she-ass. It was hard work. Their hands were numb from the cold. But by the end of the day enough wood was gathered to be distributed at least to the widows and the poor. And when they congregated in the synagogue for the evening prayers, Rabbi Mendle clasped his hands together and said, "Just as the Blessed Name brought manna to the children of Israel to sustain them in the wilderness, so in His infinite mercy He inspired our Reb Solomon, to bring us warmth. May he go from strength to strength."

Mendle's wife, Baile, died that night in the glow of her hearth and was buried the next day before Sabbath, just as the thaw began.

When the snow and ice melted, rivers of water ran through the city's streets, and Mendle, in his grief, observed, "Even the city weeps for my dear departed Baile."

The roofs began to leak. An epidemic of influenza broke out in which two children and an old widow died.

But the bad weather didn't last for long, and balmy days followed when the air was so sweet it reminded Ada of spring in Kedainai. Children were singing in the Rabbi's cheder. Only now and then it rained, and then it rained so hard the sky seemed to fall right into the city. Donkeys pattered up and down the glinting cobbled alleys from morning till evening. The Arabs greeted their Jewish neighbours as they passed them in the streets, or from darkened cafés where they sat drinking coffee, idling away the leisured hours of the afternoon with games of backgammon. Once more convoys of camels passed in and out of Safed.

Reb Israel, Isser's maternal cousin and his senior by three years, had never warmed to Solomon. When he heard people talk admiringly of him, or praise his candour, extol his courage, or note how Reb Mendle, whose saintly nature and judgement were beyond questioning, doted on him, Reb Israel would remind whoever cared to listen that from the day Solomon first set foot in Safed, he disliked the man.

It wasn't that Solomon had done anything to offend Reb Israel. Reb Israel disliked him simply for being what he was, for the unguarded look in his eyes, for his strong hands, for his pretty wife whose tresses of shiny hair carelessly fell out of her kerchief. Above all, he disliked him for the affection Reb Mendle showed him which was denied to himself. This was more than a personal hurt; it was, in his eyes, intolerable injustice.

He was not a great light in the Torah like his uncle Reb Mendle. Nor was he a charmer who got things done no matter how difficult they seemed, like his cousin Reb Isser. But Reb Israel was cleverer than his two kinsmen put together; he was, in fact, generally held to be the cleverest man in the community. Without Reb Israel's advice, Reb Isser's endeavours would not have had the aura of infallibility they had. Yet it was Isser who married well, had children and a nice home, and who, in spite of his youth, had been sent once as the community's haluka emissary to Europe. While Reb Israel, devoid of charm and social warmth, unprepossessing in his appearance, lived unmarried as a lodger in his cousin's home. Power, whose subtle nature Reb Israel understood better than anyone, was there for him to seize, yet forever beyond his reach. He knew that without a home and a family of his own to serve as a collateral, a guarantee, he could never hope to be sent abroad as an emissary, and without the status that followed such an honour, he could never hope to make a good match. All this didn't make Reb Israel bitter. But he was, or tended to be, impatient with fools and harsh of judgement, particularly where other people's seemingly easy success was thrust before him.

So long as Reb Mendle favoured him, Solomon needn't have feared Reb Israel. And Mendle's affection, like his faith, was constant. The cold shafts from Reb Israel's pale beady eyes dissolved before the overwhelming warmth of Mendle's generosity. No one knew that better than Reb Israel himself. But Solomon was troubled. In Reb Israel's presence, he would feel self-conscious; he always imagined Reb Israel's eyes boring into him like cold drills. The gossip he heard hurt too: that he was an ignoramus, a simple-minded upstart who took advantage of Reb Mendle's sweet nature, all flowed from Reb Israel's contemptuous persecution.

"If I've offended you in any way it was in innocence and I beg your forgiveness. For the love of Heaven let's be friends," he once said, stretching his hand to Reb Israel. Reb Israel stared at the offered hand and replied with a tight smile, "You shouldn't listen to people's idle prattle, Reb Solomon, idleness breeds idle thoughts and conceit."

After that, Solomon kept well clear of Reb Israel. And Reb Israel, having gauged his quarry's vulnerability, sharpened his darts and aimed them mercilessly, discreetly, and elusively from behind the shield of people's insensitivity. The city with her crowd of whispering homes became oppressive, and Solomon fled to the countryside to find his peace.

The earth was a deep and lusty green at this time of the year. Flowers and dark glistening shrubs speckled the hillside. He thought of them as nature's secret moles and beauty spots, for they suggested intimacy. He was filled with longing of a kind that was new to him. His peace was that of an outcast: intensely personal and raw-nerved. His wanderings became adventurous. At times he stayed out for a whole day. Once, after a particularly balmy day, he camped under the stars, by a fire he had lit. The rhythm of the countryside became his own, punctuated by the sound of sheep-bells, the cry of the eagle and the jackal's bark. His orientations were the morning star, the pale sun, the lengthening shadows of the approaching evening. No longer would he feel lost: he knew instinctively where the city was when he couldn't see her, or the Sea of Galilee which appeared from high points like a dazzling eye sunk in the dented purple mountains of Bashan.

The Jews of Safed marvelled at his outings: did ever a Jew sally forth into the open, away from walls without fear of his life? Was he a fool or a hero destined for great things? If there were many who admired him, there were also not a few who became converted to Reb Israel's jaundiced view of him. Solomon became aware that he had critics, even enemies who would pounce on and amplify every mistake he made. This depressed him. He longed to break loose from the jealous tribal embrace of Safed.

Much to Ada's disapproval, Solomon began taking Israel out on his walks. The boy was hardy and could walk without tiring almost as far as Solomon could himself. More than that, he was sharp and quick to observe and remember details. In his son he discovered a natural comrade, a kindred spirit who shared his own love of adventure. He delighted in him; in his company he felt his own youth recaptured.

One night, as they were lying in bed, Solomon said to Ada, "Soon we'll be celebrating the Passover, our first in the Land of our Fathers. We shall be saying to one another, 'next year in Jerusalem', as we have been doing for generations in the diaspora. And yet Jerusalem is so far away, as far as she ever has been. Might as well be in another country."

Ada sighed. "What is it you want, Solomon?" she said tensely, "You heard what people say about Jerusalem. Isn't it enough that we've travelled across half the world to come here, because you wanted to? Isn't it enough to live in a holy city full of good and wise people? Isn't it enough for you to be respected and admired? For God's sake, what more do you want?"

"I can't live with half-done things, Ada. Nothing more," he said morosely.

She got angry. "Half-done things? You haven't yet gone halfway through your life! If you'd done everything already what would you do when you're old?"

"You should be a rabbi, not me," he said. "I have quite a few grey hairs in my beard already, you know."

"I too have grey hair, too soon, thanks to you and this country!" she retorted.

"I get old, old from waiting Ada, old without achieving anything." He had it on the tip of his tongue to add "without love."

"You never knew what you wanted," she cut him. Then, taking his hand, she placed it on her belly. "I'm with child, Solomon. Remember that night when the Druze left us? It shall be born in the summer, in the month of Tamus."

He hugged her, trying to recapture the passion they once shared. After a while he said, "I so wanted our next one to be born in Jerusalem."

"What does it matter where it's born, so long as it is well and healthy?" She snuggled up against him.

"Yes, you're right, still. . . ."

"We used to laugh," Ada said quietly, "We used to have so much fun, thinking about the future, what's happened, Solomon? What have I done?"

"Hush, what nonsense you talk," he said.

"But things aren't the same. I know, I feel it." When he didn't answer she went on, "Is it because we're here and not there, in Jerusalem? You've always been telling me to trust in God. Now I'm telling you. If it's His will that we should live there then the sign will be given and the way will be found." In the dark she imagined him smiling. She kissed his hand, pressed it to her breast.

He didn't move. Then he said, hollowly, "Some treat me as though I knew things others didn't. Others say ugly things behind my back. I accept presents. I've learnt a trade to win our bread, and I haven't used it." Bitterness came into his voice. "You know what people like Reb Israel want. They want me to conform. They can't stand someone being different. They want to look at you and not be able to tell you from the other women."

She touched his mouth lightly. "Well, is that so terrible? A small sacrifice for peace and quiet. Let Reb Israel say what he likes. We both know what we are. That's what matters."

Next morning, which happened to be a Friday, Solomon stole away and made for the hills before Ada awoke. In the evening he returned and confronted her. She could tell from his face that he had something on his mind. He said with a solemnity that froze her: "Cut your hair like the others, and wear a kerchief," and walked out.

Ada wept and pleaded but Solomon would not be moved.

"Why? Why all of a sudden? You're tired of me, I know it."

He watched her, hair loose, tears streaming down her face. She was holding the scissors in her hand. His heart went out for her. But guilt at his own cowardice hardened him. He said, "All married women crop their hair. Do you want to be the exception? It was after all your idea!"

When Ada realized that he was not going to relent she turned her back on him, and began slowly cutting her hair. The dark tresses he had so loved fell to the floor like bits of discarded cloth. At last she turned to face him. With her head shorn she looked drawn and wide-eyed as if age had suddenly crushed her. "Let it not be said that Reb Solomon's wife does not walk in modesty as befits a mother in Israel," she said.

Winter was over; the rains ceased. The voice of the turtle dove was heard in the land. The Arabs from the nearby villages said that because of the harsh winter there would be a bumper crop of wheat and barley "Life is one day all onion, one day all honey. We've had the onion; now comes the honey. May Allah keep predators and pestilence away."

Solomon and his family celebrated the Passover at Mendle's home with Reb Mendle's large clan. Reb Israel, whether out of politics or touched by the spirit of the holy days, was kind and friendly through unrepentant. Israel Zeff, being the youngest child, read the Ten Questions while Reb Mendle nodded approvingly. When they all said, "next year in Jerusalem the blessed," Solomon looked sideways at Ada and thought "I may never set eyes on Jerusalem. But my son, whom she carries in her belly, will. He will go there, even if Israel won't."

The thought of Ada, pregnant with their unborn child, who might, God willing, succeed where his father had failed, introduced too many imponderables into his mind, and this was a night of rejoicing, a celebration of liberty from bondage. Solomon shook his head, as if to clear it from vapour. It was then that he caught sight of Dinah coming in from the kitchen carrying a platter of food. He saw the thrust of her full high bosom, the proud carriage of her beautiful head. As he followed her progress he marvelled at the gracefulness of her gait, and felt a thrill of discovery, as if he had never seen her before until that evening. "Has time flown so quickly? Could it be that she's changed so much without my noticing?" He thought.

But Dinah, Reb Mendle's orphaned grand-niece, now in her prime, twenty years old, still unbetrothed and unwooed, had always been beautiful, as anyone would have acknowledged. It was her reputation which overshadowed her beauty: people—women in particular—said of her that she was high-minded, too clever for her own good. Dinah, who while the rebbetze Baile was alive was more like a household servant than a relative, had been elevated by Reb Mendle to be his housekeeper. This was as much as he could do to compensate her for past deprivations, or for the fact that she was, so to speak, left on the shelf, with no prospects of a husband in sight. At least the women didn't talk about her as much as before. Nor did men cast lustful glances at her so openly when she passed by. Yet still the *shadchan* wouldn't take up her case: finding a match for a girl who was poor, tongue sharper than a razor, who could read and write as well as any rabbi, and who wilfully shunned the company of women her age and kept her own council, always aloof! No beauty could outweigh such vices. No successful shadchan would risk his reputation arranging a marriage for such a girl, unless he were out of his mind. Not after she had turned down Reb Israel who never forgot nor forgave the insult.

Dinah took her place at the end of the table, opposite Reb Mendle, where the rebbetze used to sit when she was alive and mistress of the house. Dinah, Solomon thought, looked queenly in her festive white dress, with the embroidered shawl on her shoulders. He contrived to watch her unnoticed. He strained to catch her words as she inclined her head to talk with the guests around her. The expressions of her face, together with her economy of gestures, set her apart from the rest of the women, and suggested to him a manner of self-possessed reticence as he had never before encountered.

He drank one glass of wine, then another. The wine was going to his head; it was just as well that they had begun to sing the Passover songs, because swaying from side to side, he could look at Dinah more boldly, take in those hyacinth eyes with the long dark lashes, and her hair which was the colour of ripened wheat and as smooth as silk. "She's not of this place," he thought. "She's a foreign creature, a bird blown off-course to be stranded where she didn't belong. Could these be her kinsmen? How like a rose among the thorns she is among them." Now he heard her voice, subdued, steady as her gaze and as non-committal. He began to sing with greater gusto, clapping his hands: " . . . and then came the water and put out the fire . . . a kid for two farthings, a kid for two farthings. . . ."

All of a sudden she was looking at him, not with the lupine detachment he had seen in her before, but with amused interest, as though she had caught and acknowledged a coded message he had sent her. He felt his face flush. He sobered up immediately. He began to fuss over Ada and Israel.

In the days that followed the Passover holiday, Solomon, on several occasions, saw Dinah as she went in or out of Reb Mendle's home. Not once did she look in his direction. "Fool," he said to himself. "What did you think? And you a married man! It was just a look. She was feeling happy. It could've gone to anyone."

He tried to put her out of his mind by working harder. He stopped himself from going out of his workshop in the hope of catching her on her way in or out of her house. "Work banishes idle thoughts," he repeated to himself as he tapped furiously at a piece of metal. Then, sensing a movement at the door, he lifted his eyes. She was standing there, still as a statue, holding something in her cupped hand. He jumped to his feet. "I've startled you," she said. "I did knock, but you were so deep in your work."

The thought of her watching him as he was bent over his tiny anvil discomfited him. Instinctively, he looked beyond her to see if Ada was there, for no woman ever came into his workshop unattended. Ada was not to be seen; was the Devil tempting him?

"Your wife told me I'd find you here," Dinah said simply.

"Yes, I'm here, mostly, this time of day." His hands fumbled on the table for something to hold.

Dinah stretched out her hand to him. In it was a gold locket on a chain. "It's broken, just there. Reb Mendle wondered if you could repair it." He took it from her, careful not to touch her as he did so. It was a delicate object; he had never worked on such a thing before.

She said, "It belonged to Baile, blessed be her memory."

"It has no value. Surely he doesn't want to sell it?" said Solomon looking up.

Dinah gave a short laugh, "Oh no, he'd never do that, he's never sold a thing in his life, I don't think. He wants me to have it."

"Not an easy task," Solomon said examining the locket again with deliberation. "What if I should spoil it during the repair?"

"It wouldn't matter, as I had no intention of wearing it anyway. No one would blame you."

Because he hesitated, lowering his eyes—his heart was pounding so hard—she said after a moment, "Still, if you're worried about it, let me have it back. I'll tell Reb Mendle it couldn't be done, just as I had told him."

"No, let me try, maybe I can do it," he said, closing his fist.

He expected her to leave at once, but she lingered. "You go for walks in the hills, don't you?" she said.

"Sometimes. How do you know?"

"Oh, people talk. I've also seen you leave early in the morning once or twice."

"Sometimes I feel a need for open spaces," he said.

She smiled. "People here think such a desire is madness." She was looking at him as if she was trying to gauge the measure of him. Then she said, "Would you let me come with you? I too feel a need for open spaces."

And all he could say in answer was, "What a very unusual thing to ask. . . ."

"Does that mean no?" She seemed neither surprised nor disappointed.

"It means I don't know what to say."

"You know what you want to say. But you're afraid, aren't you?"

Again he looked beyond her to see if Ada was nearby.

"There's your good name to think of."

"Not my good name," said Dinah with sad mischief in her eyes, "There's your wife, your family, your standing."

"That too," he agreed.

She turned to leave. "Well, it was a thought."

"Wait! Yes, you can come . . . I'll think of a way . . ." he blurted out.

She looked at him over her shoulder. "See what you can do with the locket. I'll come back for it in a day or two."

Dinah showed him a breach in the wall, shielded by a thicket, in a forgotten part of the Jewish Quarter. Solomon went out first to wait for her at an appointed place a short distance away. Soon she arrived. Wrapped in a long shawl, she was unrecognizable: she might have been any Arab woman of the town out in the early hours of the morning to collect firewood.

Out in the open, Solomon no longer felt nervous in her company. They walked briskly, hardly talking to each other. About an hour's walk from Safed, there was a secluded grove of wild almond trees in blossom, figs, and bitter oranges, in a sloping ravine. From here you could see the falling levels of the hills down to Lake Genesereth, which sparkled and darkened alternately with the passing clouds.

"My own private hideout," he said, guiding her to the tree beneath which he took a nap from time to time. Here they sat down, she hunched up, hugging her knees and gazing into the distance, he reclining on his elbows.

"I've never heard such silence," she said at last.

A heifer appeared on a far hillside. They both looked at it.

"Strange," she said after a long silence.

"What?"

"Being here. I've lived around here all my life and hardly ever stirred beyond the walls, never seen such beauty except in my dreams. And here it is, real. Perhaps I should never have seen it if it weren't for you . . ."

He wanted to say some words of endearment, to touch her, but didn't dare for he sensed her independence. Instead he said, pointing at the heifer: "Esau lost his inheritance by Jacob's trickery. Now his seed possesses the land while Jacob's is exiled in it. I suppose there's justice in that."

"Why do you say that?"

He picked up a twig and began breaking it bit by bit. "I have these thoughts when I'm here. Our people live in books, and in the past. They shut themselves in walled cities. Never see the countryside. Only roads, when they travel from one walled city to another. These hills are foreign to them, and frightening."

She leant back on her elbows, like him. He felt himself engulfed by the beautiful lucidity of her eyes. He wanted to put his hand underneath her shawl, to feel her skin.

"Did you know", he said, "that once Hebrew peasants herded their flocks on these very hills? On the Feast of Pentecost they'd bring the first fruit of the land to the Holy Temple in Jerusalem. Now we read books and wait for the Messiah. . . . Do you think he'll ever come? Do you think we'll ever be peasants in our own land again?"

"Probably not," said Dinah, and her eyes seemed to tell him: "Be the peasant, plough and sow."

Tentatively he removed her shawl. The sweet scent of almond soap from her exposed neck reached his nostrils. He tried to kiss her but she sat up.

"Don't," she said.

"Why did you come here with me?" he challenged her.

"For this," she snapped at him gesturing at the view in front of them, "for a bit of quiet beauty. What did you think?"

He made no answer. Her sudden anger made him want her even more.

"I thought you were different," she went on but without the harshness.

"I want friendship. Trust. I was hoping we'd be alike, not like the others. Why are you telling me about our people being slaves to their narrow vision, when you. . . ." She turned her head away from him.

He drew in his breath and said, "We're not like others. Or we would not be here. Only I couldn't bear it if we were . . . if we were just friends."

"Perhaps we'd better get back then," she said, getting up.

But she didn't move away when he came and stood close to her.

"Dinah, we've already done something very unusual. Let's not go back feeling angry and disappointed. I couldn't help myself. Because you are different, so beautifully different from any woman I shall ever meet. Sit down enjoy the view. I shan't touch you again."

She lay her hand on his cheek and kissed him gently. "I want you too, Solomon," she said. "I've wanted you ever since you sang for me at Reb Mendle's *seder*. It's wrong. It's dangerous. It would be terrible beyond imagining for both of us if people found out. That's why it must be right. Do you understand what I'm saying? I don't want to be seduced. I want to come to you as an equal, as I am. If we're to be lovers, let us, above all be friends, companions. Don't you see how rare, how precious that would be?" Then she was in his arms, pressing her mouth to his, and he wondered how he could have been alive before such sweet dangerous passion.

They taught each other how to perfect deceit to secure their trysts in the hills. She filled his thoughts to the exclusion of all else. So painfully he longed for her between meetings that he prayed for forgetfulness which never came. They became reckless in their love.

The danger of it all, too great to contain by stratagem, for long, as they both realized, heightened their feeling of urgency. At times Dinah was terrified. "What if someone should come here by chance and see us?" she said to him.

And he covered her body with kisses, saying, "A guardian angel stands at the gate of this Eden, with a turning sword in his hand. No one dares come near."

"If I were to die now, Solomon, I should be content. Most people don't have such happiness in a lifetime."

"Think of life, imagine us together, in another place, a home of our own, children of our own," he said.

"Oh my love, don't speak like that. We promised we'd never talk of home and children and all that goes with such things, remember?"

"Is it so wrong to hope, Dinah?"

"Yes. When it's useless. When it's a waste of precious time. You know very well there's no tomorrow for us. Only now, and we mustn't waste it."

She might have told him the sky would soon fall down, for he could not imagine life without her.

Summer arrived. *Hamsins* came fast one upon another, like the breath of hell. The hills were scorched yellow. The mountain springs dried up. Wells ran low. Animals, overcome by the heat, collapsed and died. You could tell where the carcases lay from the buzzards wheeling in the sky. Solomon hadn't seen Dinah for days. When at last they met, he was frightened by how unwell she looked. He ran to her and took her in his arms. She said not a word but when at last she lifted her face from his chest, tears were running down her cheeks. "It's finished", she said in resignation. His heart sank, for he thought she might be mortally ill.

"Tell me, what is the matter?" he said.

Even through her tears, she managed a smile. It was the saddest smile he had ever seen. She took his head in her hands and kissed him once on each eye. "What I dreaded most has happened, Solomon. I'm with a child. And I'm afraid, so afraid."

Reb Mendle stood with his back to Solomon, facing the shuttered window through which the morning light filtered in and made a broken pattern on the floor. He was trembling, with emotion, or with rage, Solomon wasn't sure which. In fact Reb Mendle was talking to himself and to his Maker, arguing, reasoning, searching for a meaning, as he tended to do when beset by a crisis. When at last he turned, his eyes looked at Solomon sadly and gravely. "Poor Dinah, poor child, my heart breaks for her," he said. "I don't want to judge you, Reb Solomon. You, like any other man, will have to give account for all you've done in life before the Supreme Judge, the King of Kings, blessed be His name, when your time comes. And this sad affair, for which you bear responsibility, will no doubt be on your list of debit and credit."

The slow deliberation of his voice was the strongest rebuke he had ever shown, and it cut deep.

"As the girl's kinsman, I forgive you. I know there's no wickedness in you. You've spoken to me from your heart. You're courageous and honest. I never doubted you and I don't now." He sighed. "Unfortunately this doesn't make much difference in the circumstances."

"Reb Mendle, I love Dinah, we love each other. . . ."

The old man's face turned severe and there was a sharpness of impatience in his voice: "That's neither here nor there, considering that you're married and cannot, would not, must not leave your wife, who is with child."

"I've come to tell you Reb Mendle, because I had to. But I also want your help, for Dinah's sake. . . ." said Solomon.

Reb Mendle's mouth tightened. "What help, what advice can I give? Only the Almighty would know what to do. Who can fathom His design?" His voice dropped to a mumble: "Has He not afflicted Job only to strengthen and enrich him? And did He not send Samson to the arms of a Philistine woman that he might redeem his people?"

Mendle's unfocused abstractions irritated Solomon. His mind was heavy with a sense of loss, for Dinah, for Ada, vulnerable in her pregnancy, whom he would have to tell everything and face her misery and accusations. Mendle went on mumbling, "Who but a saint is immune to the weakness of the flesh? The girl is beautiful. Is it God's work, or the Devil who made her so to tempt men from the path of righteousness. . . ." Suddenly he surfaced: "Have you told anyone else?" he asked.

"No. I was going to tell Ada my wife. I've never hidden anything from her."

"Deceit has already been committed. Don't add to her injury by telling her now or she might abort in her misery and sin would be added to sin. Don't say a word to anyone. Perhaps there is a way out."

"How?" Solomon was ready to seize on any solution.

"My nephew Reb Israel, has always been fond of the girl, even though she turned him down. Now, more than ever he wants a wife" Reb Mendle said heavily.

"You call that a way out! Dinah despises him!"

Mendle gave him a cold look. "I've seen hatred turn to affection and respect with time," he said.

"There's no other way. That is the price she must pay for her forbidden happiness with you, Solomon. What you'll pay, I dare not imagine."

Solomon opened his mouth to answer, but Mendle raised his hand. "I'll speak to Reb Israel. I'll tell him the truth. I believe he'd do as I ask. But from now on, you must know that I cannot shield you from his hatred. And another thing. You must promise me now that you two will never see each other again."

"Just to say. . . ."

"Never! Not for anything. Never, I say." Mendle cried.

No one in Safed in his or her right mind, would have imagined that such an alluring if questionable a prize as the girl Dinah, would fall to Reb Israel's unwarm and uninviting bed. But wasn't Safed a city of miracles and the unexpected? Besides, Reb Israel and his bride both found their match in each other, people said. Marriages were arranged in Heaven, and if ever a man and a woman thoroughly deserved one another, they were Reb Israel of Shklov and his comely, sharp-minded distant cousin, Dinah.

Reb Mendle himself officiated at the wedding. Four stalwart members of his clan held up the canopy over the bride and bridegroom. The guests remembered that the newly-weds looked too sombre for the occasion, but that night Reb Israel, like Jacob, was going to wrestle with his Angel and the outcome was not at all certain.

Solomon caught Dinah's eye as she was being led to the canopy. She looked defeated; her gaze passed through him as though he weren't there. He went away to a spot on the city's wall which overlooked a deep ravine and a sun-blasted hill on the other side, and wept and cursed his helplessness.

On the eve of the fast of the Ninth of Ab which marks the destruction of the Holy Temple in Jerusalem, the heat reached such a searing intensity it seemed the Creator was bent on wreaking another destruction of sorts, just to chastize his chosen for past and future sins. Ada sweltering in her pregnancy woke up that night gasping for air. She had nightmares, she talked feverishly of hills made of burning metal, and breath of fire. Solomon sat at her side wiping her brow. He thought of the two children, both his, that would soon come into this inhospitable world. "God," he prayed, "make them strong, healthy and happy. Punish me if you will for I'll never repent of loving Dinah."

The Jews prepared for the solemnity of the fast. It was a day of prayer and reflection. No leather shoes were worn. Instead, people wrapped their feet in rags, for the ground was too hot to walk on barefoot. But as they made their way to the synagogue at midday, they sensed a strange tension in the city. Soon afterwards wails could be heard from houses, and by evening, the news spread like wild fire: the plague had struck Safed.

In the days that followed there was hardly a house in which someone did not die of the plague. Doctors and Turkish officials from Acre arrived and placed the town under quarantine. Fires were lit in the streets to burn contaminated clothes, anything that was thought to have been in contact with the afflicted. The stench of quicklime and smoke hung over Safed. Neighbours shunned one another. Those who had means bribed the Turks and escaped into the hills, where they lived in caves or in isolated villages with friends and relatives. As the death toll mounted, old suspicions and superstitions were revived: Arabs began to stir darkly against the Jews. Was it not during the fast of the Jews that the plague broke out? They were being punished and innocent believers suffered too. A shepherd reported that he had seen a strange-looking Jew wandering alone in the hills, gesturing and shouting at the sky and the earth. Solomon had a premonition of something hateful and violent, hissing in the depth like snakes in a pit. Walking in the streets, he felt people were looking at him in a new way, with reserve, almost with hostility; Arabs with whom he had had dealings, as well as some of the Jews. He shut himself at home and went out only when he couldn't avoid it.

In the night he was awakened by Ada's moans. He thought she was having a bad dream, so he touched her head and realized that she was awake and covered in sweat. She complained of pains in her stomach. He got up and made her some tea. She drank a little then vomited. He thought, "Now she's got the plague, a sacrifice for my sins." He went out to get help. When the neighbours heard that Ada was sick, they slammed the door in his face and pleaded with him to go away.

As the hours of the night dragged on, Ada became delirious. There was nothing Solomon could do except wipe her brow and hold her hand as she heaved and writhed in bed. Israel sat on the floor in the corner of the room and looked on with a sombre expression on his face. Then something seemed to burst inside Ada, she heaved and screamed. The bed was filled with her dark blood. Terrified, Solomon rushed out and, standing in the middle of the alley bellowed at the top of his lungs, "My wife is dying in agony. Is there no more mercy among Jews? Are you no better than the beasts of the field?"

After a while he saw a lone woman coming towards him. Her head was covered with a kerchief and she was holding a jug and some towels in her hands. It was Dinah, but he didn't recognize her until she was quite close to him, for his rage and despair obliterated familiarity and made all human forms look alike. When he saw who she was he began to cry with total release, surrendering to the emptiness that was in him, grateful only that it was she who had heard him and come reaching out for him.

Dinah approached and without a word put her hand on his bowed head. When his sobbing stopped she said quietly: "Let's go and do what we can to help her. What have we got if not each other, and what have we to lose but this wretched life?"

Dinah's courage brought out two elderly women to the scene: if Reb Mendle's great-niece dared sally forth into the shadow of death on mercy's mission, what would be said of Safed's virtuous wives and mothers who held back? And who would sing their praise when the fury of the plague had abated? Such were their thoughts as they came forward to offer their help.

Whatever afflicted poor Ada, it was not the plague. This was quickly diagnosed by one of the older and more experienced women who, having assessed the situation, summoned more help. A group of women arrived and formed a fussing barrier around Ada. Solomon took the boy and found refuge in Reb Mendle's home. By late morning the word reached him that Ada had passed through the worst of her travail, and was asleep. She had had a miscarriage. Feigle, midwife and healer, said she was certain Ada would recover in a few days but barring a miracle would never have children again. Solomon rushed back home. Lying in bed, propped by pillows, Ada looked pale and wasted but her eyes were bright and calm. She hugged Israel and smiled at Solomon as he kissed her. "I thought I'd never see you again in this world," she said faintly, "but here I am, blessed be the Lord. The woman told me I'd never be able to bear a child again."

"Rest. Think of nothing but peace and getting well," he told her.

On the morning of Ada's recovery the favourite son of Sheik Ja'abar

Ali, died of the plague. He was a boy of three, the tenth child and last issue of the eighty-year-old Sheik's unending potency. Sheik Ja'abar Ali was the *Mukhtar* of Safed's Arabs. As chieftain he had been wise and tolerant as he had been a fierce warrior in his younger days. Reb Mendle had come to greet the Sheik on his latest son's birth, had laid his hands on the infant's head and blessed him that he may lead a long life, be guided by divine wisdom and goodness, and be a joy unto his aged father. Now the Arabs, in their grief, gathered in the streets to vent their anger on the Jews. The Jews barricaded themselves in their homes—some moved to other houses for more safety and not to be alone—and waited for the worst to come. Two homes had been set alight by the mob; a *shochet*'s apprentice had been dragged out of his bed and beaten within a breath of his life, before the old Sheik bestirred himself from his bereavement and tried to calm his people's frenzy. But it seemed that the mob had a particular aim in mind, above their random attacks upon the Jews. This became apparent when later in the day Sheik Ja'abar Ali himself came to see Reb Mendle.

After the Sheik had left, Reb Mendle sent for Solomon. He received him alone in his room. There was a sombre, anxious expression on his face. "The Arabs", he began, "are mustering against us. Already there has been violence, and there'll be more. Jewish blood may be spilt. Unless . . ." He paused. "We have men. And the soldiers . . ." Solomon interjected.

Reb Mendle shook his head. "They're many and trained in fighting. We're few. The soldiers will do nothing to protect us."

"What are you saying then, Reb Mendle?"

The old man looked at Solomon in resignation. "They're after you, Reb Solomon," he said with a sigh.

Solomon stared at him, open-mouthed. "Me? In the name of merciful heavens, Reb Mendle, what have I done?"

"Nothing, Reb Solomon. You're blameless of anything. I know that as does the Lord above. But the Arabs have got it into their heads that it's because of you the plague broke out and it's no use trying to reason with them. They want blood, they need a scapegoat."

"What am I to do? My wife's on her sick bed, my son is still a child. Would you abandon me to the mob, Reb Mendle?" Solomon said quietly.

"God forbid that any one of us should even think of doing such a thing," Mendle protested. "If there had been no way out we'd have all stood together and put our trust in the Lord as our people have done for generations in all parts of the world."

"And what is this way out, for which, I presume you summoned me?"

"I called you here first of all to warn you," Reb Mendle answered. "The way out has been shown me by the old Sheik Ja'abar Ali who came to see me not more than an hour ago. If you were to leave, he said, then he would be able to restrain his young men, and there would be no bloodshed."

"And where am I to go?"

"I thought of Tiberias where there are Jews—*Hassidim*, where I once was with my friends and family before we came here. But I'm told the plague has made them more unwelcoming than ever. Then an idea came to me. Why not Shefar'am? A friendly healthy village hardly a day's ride from here, in lower Galilee. A few Jews live there. Many of our people have fled there since the plague broke out. In Shefar'am you and your wife and son will be safe. And when all this is over, I shall send for you and you can return. It won't be long, a month or two maybe. . . . Don't you see? It's the only way out. I cannot do more than advise," Reb Mendle said, and stretched his hand to touch Solomon's shoulder.

"I came here against my wishes. I was greeted like a saviour. Now you say you know I'm innocent yet you tell me I must leave like a thief, like an unwanted dog?"

"Don't say that. What has been with you and Dinah hasn't lessened my affection for you. I tell you what I believe is the best course to follow, bearing in mind your wife and child, and other women and children who might be killed if you stayed. But tell me you won't go and I shall stand with you no matter what."

Solomon didn't answer right away. He stood, eyes downcast, his brow furrowed in thought. "No, I don't want to be held responsible for anything that might happen to Jews here" he said at last. "Tell the Sheik I'll go as soon as Ada can travel. You know in your heart as well as I know in mine, who it was that set the Arabs against me. May God forgive him, and may I find it possible to forgive him too."

Reb Mendle nodded his head. "Without evidence I cannot accuse him. But I did warn you at the time," he said.

"So we're outcasts," Ada said.

Having recovered better and sooner than Solomon could imagine was possible, she was stronger of spirit, steadier within herself. She didn't complain; she didn't accuse. She accepted it all in calm dignity.

"But why? What harm have you done to that man that he hates you so much?"

"I've done him no harm. Nothing at all. But you might as well hear this from me, because before all this happened, I never kept anything from you." And he told her about Dinah.

Ada didn't cry. Nor was there hatred or anger in her eyes when at last she met his gaze. She said quietly, "If my father knew, he'd have died of grief. If he's not dead already."

They were both silent.

"Would you have left me for her, Solomon?" she asked at length.

She looked so drawn, and her cropped head, like something near-destroyed, played up remorselessly the sadness of her eyes. His heart was breaking for her. Yet he knew that no doubt must remain between them, which might one day accumulate more pain, since they had reached rock-bottom, since they had nothing more but each other. He said:

"Yes, Ada. I believe I would have."

"Once, it seems so long ago, I used to dream that one day I'd love as you and she loved," Ada said thoughtfully.

"We have a bond, you and I. Our love is a wider, more enduring thing. I'd never leave you now. If you'll still have me."

She laughed bitterly. "If I'd have you? My parents have given me up for lost. I've come as close to death as one can and still return, and I shall never bear children. What else have I other than you and our son?"

"I'll never leave you. I'll never let you down again," he repeated.

"I'm glad we're going away. I hate this place now. Where is Shefar'am? I've never heard of it."

"I was thinking, Ada. We don't want to go there."

"Where to, then?"

"Jerusalem," he said.

"That's where you always wanted to go. If not now, then when?"

He put his arms round her and kissed her head.

"Go," she told him. "Make preparations for the journey. Don't worry about me. I'm well. I'm strong enough to face anything we might come up against."

From his window Reb Mendle watched Solomon coming and going as he prepared for his journey. Daily, the mark of defiance deepened on his face. He set up his standard in public places where, like a hawker, he called out to people to come and join him. Nobody came. He was a voice crying in the wilderness with no one to listen. The men of Safed chose to cling to the débris of what they knew rather than set out on a hazardous journey to a strange place, led by Solomon whose good name had been eclipsed by rumour and insinuation.

Reb Mendle sensed Solomon's loneliness. He was tormented by the vision of the couple and their child trekking alone across the country. The look of resigned despair he had seen in Ada's eyes haunted him. His very sense of justice rebelled against the cruel arbitrariness of the expulsion about which he could do nothing. "I'm old, Lord," he prayed. "What I've done, I've done and You alone are my judge. What is there left for me to do? What is there left for me to lose but the living breath of my frail body?" The answer came to him like a gathering of light in the dark even as he asked these questions. "Strengthen my spirit O Lord, give me a sign," he called out loud.

Yossel Binderman, the spice trader, had been following Solomon around the whole morning. Suddenly Solomon stopped and turned to face him. "What do you want of me?" he asked.

Binderman grabbed him by the arm. "I want to go with you. Safed is finished. There's no future here for men like us, Reb Solomon. Yes, me too. I don't want to sell them spices any more. I can tell a brave man when I see one. Take me with you, Reb Solomon."

Binderman, a Galilean from birth, had travelled even as far as Jerusalem in his day. He knew the routes to the coast and through the hills. When Binderman declared himself, other people began to take note. But no one came forward, until Reb Mendle embraced Solomon outside the synagogue after the Closing Prayer of the evening, and said to him, "You came to me when I was in the grip of the Angel of Death, and I was restored to life. I'm an old man yet I've done nothing I can truly call remarkable. If I should see Jerusalem with my own eyes, I would be fulfilled. If I die on the way, so be it. Take me with you."

Twelve families, numbering forty men, women and children, rallied round Solomon, resolved to go with him to Jerusalem. The number twelve inspired him and filled him with confidence. Did not the twelve tribes of Israel set out from bondage to freedom? These were not the twelve tribes, for sure. Nor was he Moses by any means. But the omen was good. He counted them: there was Lefkowitz, a sturdy man with a ruddy complexion and his square-faced, thick-armed wife; Buxbaum and his wife and three children; Sontag, Altman, Fuchs, Weiner, all with their wives and children; Pfeifer whose donkey kept running away; Druckman and his spinster sister; Lame Barash with his deaf wife; Binderman, and Kor the giant who was bigger and stronger than Solomon, but gentle as a lamb. Lastly there was Reb Mendle, their mentor and spiritual light. All upright God-fearing people, true children of Israel. A soft and wide saddle was procured for Reb Mendle for his comfort on the long journey.

Solomon prepared for the expedition like a general. He gathered information from every available source. He dispatched the invaluable Binderman to question Arabs who knew the by ways of the coastal plain and Judea, who could provide information about Jerusalem. Again and again he pondered over possible routes, weighed one option against the other, dropping this, taking up that, changing his mind as he counted advantages and hazards. He listened to advice, consulted his friends, then, in loneliness, pondered over details. There were many: what baggage to take, what clothes to wear, how many pack animals they needed and could afford. And should they carry weapons? None of them was trained in self-defence. And how should they cope with illness on the way? What provisions should they take and what purchase on the way? The responsibility weighed heavily on him.

When they were at last ready to move, Solomon gathered the men and laid down the rules of the convoy, outlining the role of every man. He told them all to bring their Ashkenazi gabardines and pile them on the ground. They would not need those any more, he said. From now on, everyone was to wear local oriental garb, robes, girdles and turbans, lest they should be recognized and banned from entering the Holy City. They lit a fire and threw in their old gabardines, the wide brimmed hats, and the striped kaftans. Some of the men stared sad-eyed into the fire that was consuming their past. Others shook their heads and muttered under their breath. Solomon was the first to throw his own clothes into the flames. He did it with a glad heart and a sense of release.

After morning prayers the next day, the company assembled in an open field just outside the walls. Dressed as oriental Jews, they looked at one another and made jokes. Kor's robe came down only as far as his knees, and his sleeves were ridiculously short. He could not find clothes large enough to fit his enormous body, but he wore a huge turban which made him look even more of a giant than he was.

The two camels, Methusala and Terach, would not suffer themselves to be loaded. They snarled and spat but refused to kneel. Kor lay his mighty hands on Methusala's halter and pulled down with all his strength, until the poor beast groaned and began to wobble on his ancient feet. "Reb Kor, Reb Kor, go easy on the animal or you'll make it kneel untimely before its Maker," Lefkowitz cried. Neither force nor entreaties prevailed upon the two stubborn creatures. Leftkowitz ran back to town and returned after a while with the Arab who had sold them the camels. Uttering a gentle throaty sound, the Arab immediately brought the two creatures down to their knees. and then showed the Jews how the camels were saddled and loaded so that the weight of the burden would rest securely and comfortably on them. Since Lefkowitz showed some aptitude for dealing with the creatures, they were placed in his care.

The preoccupation with the camels distracted everybody's mind from the absence of Weiner and his family. It was Kor in his innocence who suddenly cried out, "Heavens, Weiner's not here!" Solomon's questioning was greeted with silence. All at once the mood had changed. The people hung their heads. There was unease in the company, as though the full realization of what they were about to embark on hit them suddenly at that moment. Solomon sensed that if there were any more delays the less resolute among them would turn back. He grabbed hold of one of the mules by the halter and pulled it forward. "Let us not tarry any longer," he called out. "As it is written, House of Jacob, come let us go."

Slowly and silently the people began to move after him. Just then Weiner could be seen running towards them waving his arms. He came up to Solomon and grabbed him by the shoulders. He was so agitated, he could barely speak. Solomon held back and stared stonily: "What is it with you, man? Has the plague hit your family?" he said.

Weiner's face flowed from one grimace of distress to another. At last he stammered, "It's my wife . . . she's been crying all night . . . I say to her, 'Feigle, my dove, what is there for us and our children here? Haven't we been saying all our lives 'next year in Jerusalem'? And she just cries and cries and says, 'A city that has no river is not a city. Better go on saying next year in Jerusalem as we always have done.' I tell her this is madness, the *Dybbuk*'s got into her. What would I say to all our friends? But she keeps crying and mumbling about a river. She won't budge, Reb Solomon. Not for all the riches in the world. What can I do? Leave her behind with my three little ones? You tell me. Thank God for not having made me a woman. A river! What a crazy notion!"

Solomon looked round and saw the people laughing. He gave Weiner's arm a squeeze, and patted him on the back. "Reb Weiner. Stay with your family and look after your wife. I cannot help you. I can't create a river. If the Blessed Name had meant there to be a river in Jerusalem there would have been one. Farewell. We cannot wait any longer."

Chapter 8

From the Dung Gate, Jerusalem, the holiest of cities fanned out and up the slope into what was commonly known as Dar el Yahud, the Jewish Quarter—a cluster of dilapidated, grey and dun-coloured houses, separated by narrow twisting alleys in which scraps of food and excreta were washed over by rivulets of filthy water. But above the Gate to the right, the perimeter wall of the Sacred Compound, Harem El Sharif, rose in grim grandeur, and above it, like a dark sun, the dome of the Mosque of El Aksa.

After days spent in the open countryside the stench of the city hit Solomon like a blow in the face. He had never seen such an ugly, utterly repelling view as greeted his eyes from the portals of the Dung Gate. What made it even worse was an air of immutable starkness that brooded at least over that part of the city. Had it not been for the fact that ten frightened and confused men looked to him for leadership, he might have cried with disappointment and despair.

A solitary dove cut across the nacreous sky. City of his dreams; oh that he should never have woken up to such a reality. If poor Berl Zeff had seen this when he stood on the warehouse roof, he wouldn't have dispatched his spirit from his tormented body so trustingly. What of all the songs of praise to Jerusalem's beauty and excellence, which had sustained them all for generations? And who would believe him if he were to shout so that they could all hear back where he came from: "Wake up, it's all lies, dreams, illusions!"

Ada hung on to his arm and said nothing. She felt dead inside. Then, as he looked about the others, he caught sight of Reb Mendle. The old man's face was radiant with a gentle beatific light, even as his eyes looked on the ugly, crudely grouped houses in front of him. "To be here, to be here, at last. To breathe the air and pray at the Western wall of our holy Temple, to die here . . ." he spoke softly.

"It's all in the mind, all the substance of the world, all the beauty, all the beastliness. And my mind is dark, while his is full of light," Solomon said to himself.

Israel, tugging at the hem of his robe, said drily: "Things can only get better from here and now, because nothing could be worse than this."

The Sepharadi community of Jerusalem received their Ashkenazi brethren with courtesy, but also with some caution. They had heard of their misfortune in Safed, all the people who died of the plague, the plunder and persecution which followed. How could they not open their hearts and take in a broken branch of their people? And yet, how different were the branches of that same ancient trunk; what a strange improbable tree it was, which had risen from Abraham's seed!

The Haham bashi of the Sepharadim went out of his way to ensure that the newly-arrived fugitives were found quarters quickly and unobtrusively in the very place which at first sight offended Solomon's sensibilities. Solomon, Ada and the boy were settled in one room with a recess for cooking, in an old house which, like some frail dying creature could only stand up because it was supported on both sides by other houses in a similar state of dilapidation. Below, at the ground level, lived Buxbaum with his wife and children. The house was built round a communal courtyard in the middle of which was an empty cistern. To reach their room, Solomon and his family had to climb an external flight of stairs with a rusty iron balustrade. Behind the house there was a huge mound of rubble, full of discarded things. Here weeds grew in untidy profusion, and stray dogs fought and fouled. The heap gave off an evil smell which hung over the neighbourhood day and night, without relief.

Solomon soon discovered that the dirt and decay of the Jewish Quarter prevailed in other parts of the city as well: Jerusalem was dirty as she was holy. In the dark maze of alleys all sense of geography was lost. Only from the more salubrious parts where the wealthier Arabs lived, was it possible to see the majestic sweep of walls, minarets and cupolas, and the tessellations of stone and tile which made up the patchwork pattern of Jerusalem's roofs. As in Safed, hills surrounded the City on all sides. Only here they did not shut her off from the world. There was constant traffic of people and animals, from Bethlehem, from Hebron, from Nablus, from far and near, filling the narrow streets and bazaars. Beggars were everywhere, displaying their deformities. The smells of the city clung to clothes; and at night the stench from the nearby abattoir plagued Solomon and his fellow Galileans who were used to cleaner, fresher air.

Sometimes, the dirt in the alleys of the souks piled up so high that the Ottoman authorities left the city gates open for the night, and hyenas would come and devour the refuse left over from the day. In Jerusalem beauty married squalor and each fed on the other.

Even in Constantinople Solomon had not seen so many people of different origin and cultures crowded together. There were proud aristocratic Arabs, Bedouin from the desert in their black robes, peasants from the hills. There were black Ethiopians and Sudanese, Christians of all denominations. Behind the walls of their well-kept gardens Armenian priests moved sedately like chess pieces. And there were Europeans who always wore an expression of abstinence. Travellers from across the sea came and left like the migrating storks, and looked on the city with wonder or distaste.

The different communities led a self-contained existence, yet together they were like the various parts of a large complex organism that moved, breathed, made noises, emitted smells without ever really engaging directly with one another. Overseeing all this, were the Ottomans, rapacious and corrupt, hated or feared universally, but the only authority to which a man could relate when order or protection were needed.

According to the legend of the blessed saints, God created ten measures of beauty. Jerusalem took nine and the rest of the world, one; and ten measures of wisdom, Jerusalem took nine, and the rest of the world one. Solomon read this to Ada and Israel. They looked at him sceptically. Israel said, "If that's so father, where has it all gone?"

"It's not all gone, son," Solomon tried to explain, for with the memory of Mendle's face as he glimpsed at the city, he was beginning to understand, so he felt. "Look, it's like this. There is one point, like the peak of a high mountain, where the Creator comes closest to His creatures. This is Jerusalem. Here, on the threshold of the Divine Presence, all the beauty, the ugliness, the wisdom, the foolishness, all aspects of our existence come together in one concentration. And it is the mark of the man what he sees. Jerusalem is simply more of everything—a distillation of life."

"You really believe that?" Ada said later.

"With all my heart," he replied, for he needed to believe if he were to survive.

"Teach me to believe like you," said Ada forlornly, for she needed faith even more than he.

He began to learn Arabic, and work. He directed his energy to the routine of everyday life. Their meagre means and possessions made this very fundamental: eat, sleep, pray, get whatever bits of work he could, teach his son and learn with him, be good to Ada. Hope. But without expectation; hope alloyed with patience and forbearance. Occasionally the memory of Dinah would come back to him like a spasm of pain.

After the epic journey to Jerusalem, and the portage of Reb Mendle on the shoulders of Kor the Giant, when Mendle's mule died, Kor swore that he would devote his life to looking after the old man; never let him out of his sight. Wherever Reb Mendle went, Kor followed, and where he cast his giant shadow, there was safety.

One day Kor fell ill, and on that particular morning Reb Mendle decided to go to pray at the Western Wall which was called the Wailing Wall by the Arabs, but a short distance from the Jewish Quarter. Reb Mendle got there, just as he had done on many other occasions, and began to pray. He never wept in remembrance of the Temple's glory like many of the others. He pressed his face against the massive stones and let his thoughts flow. Standing thus, he felt engulfed by the Divine immanence, it went into him, like a flood of benevolence. He thanked the Lord for all life had given him, for his understanding of others, for the gift of joy he had. He prayed for the well-being of his people—those who had come to Jerusalem and those who stayed behind in Safed. He prayed for Solomon to find peace of mind and happiness. Then he scribbled a wish and a prayer for Dinah on a piece of paper, kissed it, and stuffed it deep into an interstice in the wall.

He felt pure, clear of vision and light of spirit. So full of joy he was that he wandered absent-mindedly and instead of arrriving at the Jewish Quarter, found himself in an unfamiliar part of the city not far from a formidable-looking church which turned out to be the Church of the Holy Sepulchre.

The two young Greek monks who were sitting outside taking the morning sun, were stupefied to see the old Jew dreamily walking by where Jews never ventured. They might have let him pass with nothing more than a perfunctory insult if two youths and a boy hadn't suddenly come thumping on to the scene shouting in Greek, and seeing Reb Mendle, began to jeer and chide the monks.

Reb Mendle didn't understand what the agitation was about, but sensed danger. He averted his eyes and quickened his step. He didn't get far, for the monks and the youths, aroused by one another, set upon him, knocked him to the ground, and began kicking him. Mendle called out aloud "Hear O Israel, the Lord is one. . . ." He thought he was done for. And he may well have been if one of the monks didn't suddenly have an idea. He had a sack of flour in a nearby shack, which would have been taken to the baker but for the want of a beast of burden. Now they dragged out the sack and tied it to Mendle's back. It was much too heavy for the old man. He strained and gasped; the monks laughed and kicked.

How Reb Mendle survived the ordeal was in itself a miracle. When at last he returned home, soiled and crumpled and clutching at his chest, all he could do was to shake his head and repeat again and again "Why? Why?" When he recovered he said to the people around him, "Let it pass, make no complaints. I'm alive and that's what matters. Blessed be the Lord." Kor the giant wept and beat his breast. It had taken all the powers of persuasion Reb Mendle could command to stop Kor from going in among the Greeks, as Samson had gone to the Philistines to avenge the wrong done to Reb Mendle.

At the New Year, the Reverend Haham Bashi Isaac Ayish, Head Rabbi of the Sepharadi Jews, invited the newcomers to join in the prayers and celebrations. In the ornate, colourful synagogue of the Sepharadim, where the Haham Bashi Ayish presided, the small Ashkenazi group witnessed for the first time the humbling of their own Rabbi Mendle; he was not called to sit beside Rabbi Ayish nor to read from the Torah.

The chants and prayers of the New Year's service which they all knew from childhood, were barely recognizable here, concealed as they were by the trilling embellishments. The ark where the Holy scrolls lay was too gaudy for their taste and the ram's horn, blown with great panache by a sturdy Sepharadi, was a large spiralling thing like some pagan instrument. It emitted a bellow of deep resonance that vibrated in the crowded synagogue, so unlike the ethereal note of the Ashkenazi *shofar*.

Solomon had seen all this before, in Constantinople, in Acre. He liked the colour and vitality of the Sepharadi services.

Mendle was happily praying, as always, in total concentration, unheedful of the slight he had received from Rabbi Ayish. He never did place any value on personal honour. Looking at him, Solomon noticed how he had aged, even since that ordeal at the Holy Sepulchre church. Or was it the collective vigour of the Sepharadim which so magnified Mendle's fragility?

How much there was to learn in this city of strange, undirected currents. Solomon juggled, arranged, modified, took in, or discarded the flow of daily information which came his way. He asked questions; he listened. The Sepharadi Jews—particularly those close to the Haham Bashi Rabbi Ayish—knew everything, so they claimed:

"Never wear green, carry weapons, or ride a horse. These are forbidden to Jews," he was told. Well, he was happy enough to see green in the fields, not on his person. Jews never carried weapons. As for riding a horse, who among his people needed one, or knew what to do with it?

"Green and yellow for Moslems. Black for Greeks. Crimson for Armenians. We Jews wear no colour, unless it's blue. Never spit near a mosque, that's a deadly insult. . . ."

"Wait!" He would interrupt, "Why not tell me first what we can do without offending anyone."

"The Ottoman Empire? Imagine a giant with a weak head, whose parts rebel, legs, arms, guts, all go their own way and do what they want. That, in brief, is the Empire. And no part of it is as backward or as unruly as Palestine. Here, there's no law but the law of the bribe and the sword. The powerful grasp; the weak submit and are robbed. The peasant fears the landlord. The landlord despises the government and the Turk. And all live in terror of the bandit who fears neither man nor God."

Of the more specific information, Solomon took notes: Palestine: divided into two *vilayets* or *pashaliks*, each an autonomous province. Jerusalem belongs to the eastern vilayet whose capital, where the Pasha governs, is Damascus. Its territory stretched east and west of the River Jordan. The other province, to the west, embraces Acre, the whole of Galilee, and the coastal plain down to Gaza; its capital is Sidon. The Pasha, governor of a vilayet, is personally appointed by the Sultan himself, for which honour he pays a considerable sum of money. The vilayet is subdivided into *sanjuks*, whose governorship the Pasha sells, thereby recouping his own outlay, and making a handsome profit. In addition, he levies taxes throughout his vilayet. The Chief *Wizir* in Constantinople is the most powerful man in the Empire, next to the Sultan. He executes his master's orders by means of *firmans*—Royal statutes.

Firmans and taxes were of great concern to the Jews, who were classed as *Ra'ya*, that is, non-Moslem subjects, and paid a poll tax called *Jiziye*, negotiated annually between the Governor of Jerusalem and the Haham bashi.

At the top of the social pyramid were the *Askari*, who were the military caste, the government and court officials, and the landowners. Then came the *Ulama*—Islamic judiciary and clergy. The Ra'ya were at the bottom of the heap. He might have guessed: Jews and slaves mostly of Sudanese and Circassian origin. But there was another class, not strictly speaking integrated into the larger scheme of things. These were the *Hamiya*—resident citizens of European countries who, by virtue of the Capitulation Agreement between the Ottoman Sultans and the European powers (an agreement dating from the sixteenth century and periodically reaffirmed), were exempt from Ottoman taxation and jurisdiction, and could be judged solely by their own consuls. It occurred to Solomon that a great advantage for the Ashkenazi Jews could be won if they contrived to join that class. And with that in mind, he began to ponder the possibilities of establishing their own money-collecting haluka, independent of the Sepharadi community.

During the Holy Days between the Rosh Hashana and Yom Kippur, the Sepharadis lavished hospitality on their Ashkenazi brethren. But once those days were over, this friendly attitude diminished rapidly. The source of the changed mood was the Haham bashi Rabbi Ayish and his côterie, who distanced themselves from Solomon and his friends.

Buxbaum's wife returned from the butcher's one day in tears; on the order of the Haham, she was refused meat. Other wives rushed to the butcher's shop and confirmed that this was so. There was an outcry—but not such a loud one as when shortly afterwards it transpired that the Haham's officials had reduced the amount of haluka money due to the Ashkenazis. In some cases—such as Rabbi Mendle's, it was withheld altogether.

Solomon together with the men marched to Rabbi Ayish's residence and demanded an immediate audience. The Rabbi had been expecting them. After making them wait outside for over an hour, they were finally admitted to his study. There, among carpets and divans, sat the Haham bashi Rabbi Isaac Ayish on a high-backed chair, flanked by his aides. There was a pleasant redolence of Arab tobacco in the room. Rabbi Ayish greeted his visitors with a gracious nod of the head, and waited for them to speak.

"We've noted with sorrow how you've changed towards us Rabbi," Solomon began. "Tell us what we've done to offend you and we shall ask your forgiveness if we are to blame. If you find us wanting, teach us and we'll try to learn. But don't deny us the haluka money on which we depend, and which is ours by right no less than it is yours."

"Rights you talk about?" said Ayish urbanely. "Have you forgotten that your very existence here is unlawful?"

"He thinks he has us in the palm of his hand," Solomon thought, but aloud, he said: "There are the laws of the gentiles and the righteous ways of our people. It's the latter to which I was referring, Rabbi."

Rabbi Ayish began to drum the fingertips of one hand against the other. "Of course, we're all Jews, accountable to one another. But this responsibility, Rabbi Solomon, runs both ways. . . ."

"What responsibility can we have towards you, when we're in your power?"

The Haham bashi wagged a finger at him: "Not power, Rabbi Solomon. Hospitality, generous care. For which people show appreciation, if not gratitude.

"This world, Jerusalem, is delicately balanced. Its ways are intricate, hard to learn in a short time. Its pitfalls are legion.

"How I hate his devious formality . . ." Solomon thought.

"What one Jew does here inevitably affects the rest. Therefore, one must tread with caution. And have we not guided you securely? Given you homes, a place where to pray?"

"Next to a stinking heap of rubbish!" cried Buxbaum, unable to contain himself.

"Ah," said Ayish, raising his voice to a point of emphasis, "the heap! Do you know what's beneath it? Your past! On that very spot once stood the grand synagogue of your predecessors, which was burnt to the ground and defiled by the Arabs of Jerusalem, who banished your people from here for ever. Is there not a lesson for you in this? They too walked in arrogance, unheedful of other customs. They paid the price!"

"We are not arrogant, Rabbi Ayish. Not ungrateful, for all the help you've given us. All we want is to live in peace and to go about our business. I don't understand your anger. I don't understand what you have against us."

The Haham bashi smiled coldly. "Reb Solomon, do you understand the meaning of Jiziye? The hardship it can inflict? The skill and painstaking trust it takes to negotiate an acceptable rate? It seems that you *do* understand who is Ra'ya and who is Hamiya. Yes, after all the questions you've been asking! Don't look surprised. There's little if anything that is said among Jews that doesn't reach me. No secrets are hidden from me. Not even your scheme to send your own emissary to raise money from your brethren in Europe."

"There is no scheme, Rabbi. If or when we decide on such an action it would be done with your agreement and co-operation or not at all. Of that I assure you," Reb Mendle interjected.

"Revered and learned Rabbi Mendle, how can I rest peacefully on your assurances when you know not what you do? When you wander alone by the Church of the Sepulchre where no Jew in his right mind would walk? You might have got yourself killed! Dreadful consequences, for all of us! But of course, you do not understand."

He paused to measure the effect of his words. "You want to live in peace with us?" he went on in a flat harsh voice, "Obey our rules. Take advice. Never agitate. Above all, dispel all idle thoughts from your heads. The haluka stays where it always has been. In the hands of the Chief Rabbi of the Sepharadi community, the Haham bashi. Oppose him, and you'll rue the day."

When at last they were outside Reb Mendle began to shake so violently they feared for his life. They took him by the arm and led him home. There, seated, the old man gradually recovered his composure. He looked at the anxious faces around him and his limpid eyes shone. "Well, children," he said, nodding his head, "now we know what to expect. Or rather, what not to expect. Our trials are far from over, I fear."

Pfeifer began to argue: "If we submit, we may just as well go back to Safed. I say let us defy him. For him nothing's good that isn't Sepharadi. Let us send our own man to Europe. And I say let this man be none other than Reb Solomon Zeff!"

Solomon rose to his feet. "Friends," he said, "it's been a taxing day. Ideas are like fruit, they mustn't be picked before they are ripe. Let us not rush into anything before the time is right. Let us go about our business as though nothing had happened. And when the moment comes, we'll act."

Solomon set up a little workshop at the back of one of his rooms. Ada took in some sewing from the wealthier Sepharadi ladies. She had patched together a curtain from odd remnants and strung it across so that Solomon's workshop was partitioned from the rest of the room. The earnings from his work were pitifully small and sporadic. Nevertheless, he derived satisfaction from going about the bazaars, buying bits of metal, mostly copper and brass but occasionally a strip of silver, then returning home to tap away at his bench. He seldom ventured beyond the city walls as he had in Safed: Jerusalem was unpredictable; untold dangers lurked beyond her walls. And yet for all the severity and decay, the city, like a deity, could reward devotion by glimpses of her beauty among the dirt, exquisite as they were unexpected.

It was not through a pilgrim's soul that Solomon made Jerusalem his own, but through his feet, his senses, and, not least, through the innate instincts of a fugitive that every Jew had. In the Moslem Quarter, which was the largest, stretching along the western flank of the enclosed Temple Mount to the north and then east, he learnt to walk with caution, stepping out of the way whenever a group of Arab youths came sauntering towards him down a narrow alley. He learnt to blend in with the crowd whenever armed Ottoman gendarmes came into view, walking idly with bored expressions on their faces. He learnt that boredom often made those hated officers wantonly cruel.

The Governor's house stood at the heart of the Moslem Quarter, dominating from its elevated vantage point the forbidden enclosure of the Temple Mount. On that same spot, the Christians claimed, once stood the Palace of Pontius Pilate, on the site of which the city's centre of authority remained ever since. Close by the Governor's house were the courts of law, where flogging was done and public executions held. Here was the caprice of the Turks at its most promiscuous, it was a place to be avoided. Solomon had heard stories of how innocent passers-by had been seized and thrown into the Kishle's dungeons where, forgotten, they languished in a dingy twilight for the rest of their lives.

The Christian quarter stretched north from the Jaffa Gate along the western part of the city. From the outside, it gave an impression of enclosed cleanliness. No Jew ever set foot in there for fear of being beaten up or even murdered. Many stories were told of how Latin and Greek monks snatched Jewish children and kept them in locked rooms where crucifixes hung on the walls, until they renounced their creed and became Christians.

Of all Jerusalem's quarters, none was so beautiful as the Armenian; these peaceful reflective people may well have prepared their environment painstakingly in anticipation of the hereafter, so that their passage to eternal life would flow from their worldly existence with the same easy pace to which they were accustomed.

The wide street curved languidly from the Citadel by the Jaffa Gate and ran south along the crenellated city wall. Palm trees and pines whispered from behind tall stone enclosures, and shaded passage-ways opened on to gardens full of trees and flowers. On one side of the street, not far from where it rose to meet Mount Zion, stood the Church of Mar Jacob, the most beautiful church in the city, so pilgrims said. But all you could see from the street was the strong majestic gate in the wall, and the cupola rising above it. The sound of donkeys' hooves echoed in the vaulted arches above the street. Bead curtains tinkled in the high windows in the walls. The darkly robed and cowled monks lived with their folk in their enchanted cloisters secure as trees. Not even pestilence could have dominion here.

How miserable by contrast was the Jewish Quarter which bordered on it. It seemed to plunge into the darker recesses of the City where all the dirt and sorrow concentrated. Whenever there was an outbreak of epidemic its source was invariably traced to the Jewish Quarter and hence the blame fell on its unfortunate denizens. The Quarter ended at the Street of Chains, fast by the outer wall of Temple Mount. Here, and all along the western wall of Temple Mount, lived the Moors, a fearsome dark-skinned race who guarded the consecrated ground of the El Aksa Mosque and the Dome of the Rock. Woe betide any unbeliever who, by misadventure or folly, wandered into the sacred grounds. The Moors would flail the life out of him with their heavy clubs. Often it was on their Jewish neighbours that the Moors perfected their deadly art.

It was said that the Jewish Quarter was situated where it was because no shrine belonging to any other faith existed there, therefore the place was of no interest to anyone. The municipal abattoir was there, and its heavy stench added to the misery of the Quarter's residents.

Not far from the Jewish Quarter stood that ancient wall, sole remnant of the glory that had once been the Holy Temple. It rose in massive gloom from among the dingy houses in the narrow alley. Weeds sprouted from the cracks in the huge masonry. Here the Jews would find relief in tearful prayer, hence the gentiles called it the "Wailing Wall".

But although the wall was the only shrine the Jews had, even here they were not free to worship in peace. They were frequently set upon by the Moors and chased away. Bribes had to be paid and presents given to buy the fickle protection of the authorities.

Day by day and street by street Jerusalem was filling out in Solomon's imagination. What a chaos of beauty and ugliness she was. Even the Messiah—if he ever came—couldn't untangle the mess of a thousand generations and impose His order on her. Maybe Ayish was right, maybe it was better simply to submit and let things take their own course. How can you oppose anything in such a city which has an indomitable will of her own? These thoughts passed through Solomon's mind as he stood on the Mount of Olives, on the slope of which a host of Jewish saints lay buried, and looked down on the walled city below.

The wide, stone-paved expanse of Harem el Sherif, once the sanctuary of the Temple, conjured up images of prophets and kings in his mind. The two mosques, Al Aksa and Omar, did not disturb him; on the contrary their magnificence emphasized the austere purity of the place. The bricked-up portal of the Gate of Mercy stared at him like two blank eyes. The Arabs had walled it up a long time ago because some Moslem seer had pronounced that if ever anyone came through it Moslem rule over Jerusalem would crumble. How simple-minded of them to imagine that mere brick and mortar could stop the Messiah, and yet how perverse, for who would want to come through these gates but the Redeemer of the World, the Messiah, son of David who would bring comfort to all men? Jerusalem once David's City, now a jumbled altar of a universal religion. The names all about were Hebrew names. Why, there was even the "Pool of Israel" not far from the Governor's house. Yet what Jew could claim it? What could a Jew claim in this city except memories? Even here he was no more than he was among the gentiles in the diaspora; a creature of contempt. So where and how should redemption begin?

His mind reeled back to the long journey, and to Berl Zeff. If a miracle had happened—for miracles were known to occur when least expected—and Berl had actually flown instead of plunging to his death, what would he have made of all this? He remembered what Rabbi Ayish had said about the midden heap behind his house: "your past". Even now he was haunted by that revelation. He tried to think of a psalm to comfort his spirit. But instead, the first sentence of Genesis came to his mind: "In the beginning God created the heaven and the earth."

"May I perish right now if there's a blasphemous thought in my head," Solomon muttered to himself, "but is there not a moral in this? And is it just chance that the verse came to my mind this moment? In the beginning there was void—*to hu va vohu*. Out of which the Ineffable Name began to create. A heap of filthy rubbish is something like a void, something from which to begin. Reb Mendle says reality is in the imagination. True, for out of the mind's reality comes the reality of matter."

Ideas rushed at him, a host of them. He pressed his hands to his face and his son's imaginary voice spoke to him: "You think only of stones and ruins and buildings. I think of earth, of trees, of birds and of water," the boy was saying, holding two fistfuls of grass. "You rebuke me for playing truant and wandering about. But see, I've already learnt some Arabic, I'm learning about the land, what I'm learning you can't find in the Rabbi's books."

"I'll build," Solomon said aloud. "Out of that stinking nothingness I'll build the synagogue. What's the use of a past if it's not a base for the future?" And in his mind's eye he was seeing the proud edifice of the synagogue rising like the sun out of the rubbish.

Chapter 9

In the twilight hour of dusk, the city noises subsided into a reposeful stillness. The bul bul's liquid warbling, riding on the lilac-scented air, reached even the squalid recesses of the Jewish Quarter, bringing reprieve from the day's oppression.

There was a knock on Solomon's door. Standing there, alone, was Reb Isser. In his arms was a baby wrapped in a white embroidered shawl which Solomon immediately recognized as Dinah's.

"I arrived only a few hours ago," Reb Isser said. Solomon had already heard.

"You know who this is. . . ." Isser's manner was at once solemn and sympathetic.

"Is Dinah all right?" But the answer to his question was already rolling over him like a breaker.

"She is at peace, eternally. She died in childbirth," Isser replied. "This, her baby son, was duly received in the covenant of Abraham, Isaac, and Jacob. His name is Ariel Baruch Mendle, as she would've called him. I deliver him to you, as she would've wished."

Solomon sank to his knees, covered his face with his hands, and wept in silence, for the misery and his failure; for the beauty he had been allowed to embrace briefly but not to keep, which he knew he would never again experience. Isser stood over him, murmuring condolences, unknowingly pushing wide open the floodgates of Solomon's sorrow.

At last he stood up. The baby was asleep in Isser's arms. He said: "I won't come in, Solomon. I'll only say this, the poor orphan has been with us like one of our own, since his mother died. He's a lovely baby, an angel. He's your child. But if you say no, I'll take him back and not another word will be spoken about it."

But Solomon took the baby from him, and kissed it lovingly. "Thank you, Reb Isser, for bringing my son home to me," he said.

Ariel had clear blue eyes like his mother, flaxen hair, and a fair complexion. When Solomon told Ada what had happened, she looked silently at the baby for a long while. Then she took him in her arms and began to rock him gently. "This poor baby will see enough misery when he grows up. At least for now we can shield him and give him love and warmth. You have done the right thing, Solomon."

To his son Israel, Solomon said, "Here is an orphan boy. Now you have a baby brother to love and to look after, blood of your blood and flesh of your flesh. He is the only sibling you shall ever have for your mother can bear children no more. Love your brother Ariel and cherish him."

What Solomon didn't show his wife or anybody, was a sealed note—from Reb Israel which Isser delivered with the baby. It read: "Your whore died in misery and shame. Take your bastard son, the fruit of your lust, for I have no use for him. May God spare him the pain and suffering which are rightly yours."

One day in late summer, a mounted courier, one of those who brought the post from Jaffa and were commonly known as "Tartars", came galloping in bearing the news of Napoleon's defeat at Waterloo. No one in Jerusalem could appreciate the immediate significance of the event, least of all the Governor, a medium-ranked officer of one Horse Tail, who had only recently moved into the Governor's Palace. Nevertheless, to mark that remote defeat or victory, he ordered the public execution of three convicted thieves, chosen at random from among the prisoners in the Kishle. The three condemned men were brought out chained together. They wore white *galabiyas* and no shoes. Docilely they stepped on to the gallows without a word. They seemed grateful to be together even at this their last moment on earth. Two gendarmes struck up a discordant roll on their drums, while a third went round kicking the stools one by one from beneath the condemned men. It was over too soon; the Governor looked disappointed.

As they walked away, Mendle covered his face with his hands and wept. "Why all this wanton evil? Did He create us in His image so that we may behave like beasts," he said, choking on his tears. Solomon put his arm round the old man to hold him up. "He's grown old and weak, he can't take these things any more", said Binderman in a low voice.

If there was a new order in Europe, it did not affect life in Palestine. Indolence and corruption continued. Summer followed winter and each punished Jerusalem and her people, first with the ordeal of frost and then the ordeal of fire. Food and other essential commodities became scarce. Even when these were available their prices were often beyond the reach of the Jews. At the height of summer, street vendors who sold water out of goatskins hardly ever came. When they did, they charged more than twice the normal price, and the water was brackish. Spurred by need, the clan of Abu Gosh increased its depredations on the roads to Jerusalem. Any unfortunate traveller, however poor, who could not pay the toll, was stripped of his possessions and sent back whence he came: at such hard times bandits too could not afford generosity.

For all that the Ashkenazi community was growing. Every month new people were arriving; the word had spread that once more Ashkenazis were allowed into Jerusalem, which was, of course, untrue. The Sepharadis, patient and forbearing by temperament and tradition, noticed the change and a rumble of discontent passed among them. The seemingly indifferent authorities too, noted the influx of Ashkenazi Jews, and raised the tax for the infidels, the "Jiziye". If Jews were coming, the Governor argued, there must be more money around, in spite of the Haham bashi's protests. Rabbi Ayish fought on doggedly, with tenacity, with dignity. Every Friday morning he could be seen dressed in his best black robe with embroidered hems and a splendid turban, making his way to the Governor's palace, followed by an aide carrying a present. But now the Governor would not see him. Rabbi Ayish was made to cool his heels in the courtyard among other supplicants, and then sent away humiliated and disappointed. The Jews—Sepharadis as well as Ashkenazis—began to say that the Haham bashi had lost his influence. It was poor Rabbi Ayish, not the Governor, who was blamed for the hardship the new taxes brought upon the community.

Among the young men who came to Jerusalem with Reb Isser was one called Shimon Tanzman. His father, a leather tanner, had died in the plague in Safed, and young Tanzman lived with his aunt. Tanzman was short and powerfully built. He had a shock of red hair and a great beard like an unruly flame. Behind his back the men called him Esau, because he was red and hairy. No one dared call him that to his face for Tanzman was short-tempered and quick with his fists. Even Kor the giant, who feared neither man nor beast, was wary of him. Like many men of brawn, Tanzman had excessive esteem for learning which was beyond his reach. He prayed and disputed heatedly, and never ceased to plague cleverer men with tiresome questions.

None of the Ashkenazi men particularly liked having to dress like Sepharadis. But Tanzman resented it with a passion. Not because he disliked the Sepharadis, nor because he liked the black kaftan and wide-brimmed hat better than the oriental robe and turban. It was because he thought it demeaning to have to live in perpetual deceit, as he saw it. He hated even more the contemptuous looks he thought he saw in the eyes of the Arabs each time he went to pray at the western Wall.

Tanzman drew trouble as a lamp draws moths. Since it was neither possible nor right to stop him from going to pray at the Wall, a special guard was put on him by order of Solomon, Reb Isser, and with the blessing of Rabbi Mendle. Whenever Tanzman went to the wall, a band of level-headed men surrounded him on all sides so that he was barely visible.

But Tanzman had his own followers, for he was courageous and generous. Not least among his younger admirers was Israel Zeff, whose respect Tanzman had won one day when he took hold of a horseshoe and, with his bare hands, twisted it out of shape.

The sight of the tight nervous group of men buzzing like bees about Tanzman intrigued the Arab *shabab* who often hung around the Wall to mock the Jews. Soon more Arab youths came to watch the strange spectacle, and thus the heroes of both Arab and Jews were brought within challenging distance of one another.

One Friday, before the setting of the Sabbath, as Tanzman and his band of restrainers arrived at the Wall, they found a larger than usual congregation of Arabs waiting for them. Among them was one Moor, a guardian in the Harem el Sharif and notorious for his violence. The Jews began to pray, rocking and gyrating as was their custom. The Arabs looked on, Tanzman and his companions ignored them, or pretended to, even as the latter began to taunt them. The taunts were not unusual or more threatening than at other times. It would have been just another Friday, nothing better or worse, if a group of Sepharadi men, who were praying closer to where the Arabs stood, and therefore more discreetly, did not suddenly break off and move quickly down the narrow alley along the Wall. In doing so, a man at the rear inadvertently brushed against the Moor. Altercations started and instantly the Moor began raining blows on the hapless Jew. The Sepharadis raised a loud cry. Tanzman and his friends stopped praying. The ring round him opened and all at once Tanzman was facing the Arabs in the full raging glory of his flaming countenance. The Moor let go his quarry. For an instant he and Tanzman stared at one another while all the others backed off to see what would happen. "Hear O Israel, the Lord is one," Tanzman roared, and charged. The Moor too shouted his war cry and cannoned forward to meet his adversary.

Around the eye of the storm, lesser battles were fought, and the clamour rose from the narrow confine of the Wall and alley, and split into the surrounding streets. When at last the fury was spent, there were bruises, cuts and some broken limbs. Tanzman was dragged away panting with a deep knife wound in his side.

That night the Moors from the Mahgreb quarter and bands of Arab youths rampaged through the Jewish Quarter, setting fire to houses, dragging Jews out and beating them senseless in the gutters. Solomon came out at the head of a group of young men to repel the attack and had his left hand crushed with a blow from a club. The Governor, alarmed by a frantic appeal from the Haham Bashi, despatched a detachment of gendarmes to the scene. They fired a few shots, arrested a few innocent spectators and withdrew without restoring order.

In the morning the news got round that an Arab youth, one of the Kahdi's clerks, had been severely wounded, and the enraged Arabs were out to seek Tanzman's head in vengeance. Rabbi Ayish's clerk, a men called Hadad brought the news. He came straight to Solomon's house, catching him just as he was leaving for the morning prayers at the synagogue.

"It was very bad, what happened yesterday," said Hadad, "Rabbi Ayish is worried, very worried indeed."

"None of us is pleased with the affair, I can assure you. Look at my hand. It could have been my head," Solomon said.

"Never before have we had such a thing," Hadad went on. "Before you came we had none of these things. Your young men acted rashly. You mustn't allow hot-heads to act irresponsibly. It puts us all in danger."

"Should we offer our throats to be cut?" Solomon asked heatedly. "You talk as though you were one of them—a Turk, an Arab!"

Hadad blinked irritably and made an impatient gesture with his hand. "What I came to tell you is that the Arab boy's father demands that this fire brand of yours, Tanzer or whatever his name is, be arrested and punished. What he really wants is compensation. A large sum of money. And should the lad die, there'll be blood. You'd better get that Tanzer out of Jerusalem or hide him until this thing blows over."

But Tanzman was in no condition to travel. Besides, he had nowhere to go to. The men gathered to take counsel. After a lengthy consultation it was decided that Tanzman should disguise himself as a woman and hide in someone's home until after the month of Ramadan. If the youth died, Tanzman would have to leave for Safed or Tiberias. Was it permissible in the Law, was it possible to shave off a man's beard—and such a splendid one as young Tanzman's at that—and humble him in a woman's guise? Was not such a thing nearly as impious as eating unclean food? Reb Mendle consulted Rabbi Ayish. Both delved into books. A precedent was found from the days of the Maccabeen rebellion against the Greeks. And so, with a heavy heart but also with some relief, both Mendle and Ayish pronounced that even a cardinal law must be waived to save life.

This was the first, albeit unhappy, occasion when unanimity and total co-operation was reached between the two rabbis. Tanzman submitted with tears of outrage: "I'm being sacrificed like a lamb," he thundered, as one tussock after another of his beard was cut and fell to the ground. When the transformation was completed, Tanzman was unrecognizable. "There, Reb Shimon, your own aunt would not know you now. You'll be safe so long as you keep your mouth shut," Solomon said.

But Tanzman, still weak from his wound, threw himself about and protested. "Should we hide like cowards? Did not the Maccabees defy their oppressors? Are we to shame their memory? Oh, how long must we be down-trodden?"

"Tanzman, Tanzman, be realistic, this is not the time to be a hero. Do you want us all killed?" the men pleaded with him.

"Better be killed and sanctify the Name than live like dogs," he kept repeating. Only after his ailing aunt raised a great lament and said she would die forthwith, he relented. He was taken away to Tusia the tailor's ramshackle house, there to pose as his relative and housekeeper.

Thanks to the skills of an Armenian healer, the Arab youth lived. No sooner had the crisis passed when the Haham Bashi summoned the leaders of the Ashkenazim to his home. "Brothers," he began portentously, "Now that you've brought us all to the brink of disaster, will you listen to reason? Or must I use my authority to curb you? Remember whence you came and where, if you persist in your hard-necked ways, you might be forced to return."

"You call us brothers but you threaten us," Solomon protested. "Is this the way a brother treats a brother?"

The Haham Bashi leapt to his feet, "You . . . you —"he shouted, pointing a trembling finger at Solomon, but all of a sudden he turned pale and sank back to his seat. His men raised a cry and began fussing about him. Slowly Rabbi Ayish recovered. "Hadad, Hadad . . ." he made an urgent motion with his hand. Hadad rushed in with a bottle of medicine, the Haham Bashi pushed the medicine away from him. It was a letter he wanted, a sealed letter with an official look about it. Rabbi Ayish did not break the seal but brandishing the letter like a weapon, said, "You know what this is? I'll tell you. It's a command from the Prince Farhi, yes, a command no less to all the Ashkenazim of Safed and Tiberias. And what does the Prince command? That no more Ashkenazis should come to Jerusalem. And more . . . that those of you who are here should submit to my authority in all things. The Prince had heard of the trouble you've caused, and as a Jew he is concerned. He has written to me, here. Do you understand? Do you understand?" His agitation rose to a pitch. Presently he began to tremble again and emit small choked grunts.

"The Haham has a seizure, the medicine, the medicine, call for the doctor," Hadad cried. While Ayish's aides fussed and fretted around him, the Ashkenazis sat in frozen silence. For a while they were forgotten. At last the poor Haham was carried, trembling and grunting away from the room. Hadad soon returned. He was visibly shaken and openly hostile. "See what you've done?" he reproached them all. "Is that how you show gratitude for all the saintly man has done for you? God forbid that anything should happen to him or it will be on all your heads."

Mendle put his hand on Solomon's arm and whispered, "Say nothing, what's the point? God sees and judges everything. We might as well go now."

No news came of the Haham's condition for a whole week. But meanwhile, all the Ashkenazi heads of families gathered in the small hall which served as their synagogue, to devize a stratagem. Rabbi Mendle was tired of strife. He advized submission. But his kinsmen supported Solomon who objected to such an attitude. "I can't believe that Farhi made those demands, and anyway, what power has he here? Why even less than the chief of the Abu Gosh tribe," he said.

"If we give in now, who knows what the Haham Bashi will want next? We shall never be able to raise our heads again," Isser said, and added, "besides, the old rogue may soon depart to a better world."

"Better the devil you know . . ." Lefkowitz chimed in.

"That kind of thinking you should have left behind in exile, Reb Lefkowitz," Isser rebuked him. "I say no. Let us make a stand now, no matter what. So that an example is set and Ayish's successor, whoever he may be, will not have us at his mercy."

Reb Isser's words caught the mood of the assembly, and as the full implication of what he had said slowly sank in, they all fell silent and one by one turned to look at Solomon.

He did not speak right away but sat quietly, stroking his beard. "I've always thought", he said at last, "that we should have our own synagogue. Now we are like a body without a centre, without a heart. That is the cause of our dependence on the Haham. If we haven't a place of our own, what are we? Who will recognize us? How can we tell our brethren abroad 'give us money' when we have no synagogue, no schools, nothing?"

"Now, Reb Solomon, you've touched the heart of our problem," Isser said. "We must send an emissary. Who better than you?"

"Yes, but not yet, Reb Isser. There's another thing we must do first."

All eyes turned on him in surprise.

"We must find a way to free ourselves from the debts of the other Ashkenazim—those who were here before us—that we may live here in our own right, in peace. It is wrong. We cannot be held liable for things that others did. And the only one who could declare these debts null and void is the Sultan himself. We must somehow reach him. The man to do this is not me but someone who has contacts in the Empire's capital, or one who can get such contacts. Until we've achieved this, we must do as Reb Mendle says, submit to Ayish."

"Pretend to submit," Isser corrected.

"As you like, so long as he believes it. And patience, always patience and discretion, so that not even Hawaji Zrubavel Hadad would suspect anything."

Chapter 10

There was a man in Jerusalem called Jacob Pach who arrived from Byelo–Russia in the thick of winter. In his native land Pach had been a furrier and something of an entrepreneur. A man of the world, he had travelled a great deal. There were stories that he had even been to America, lived with trappers and had eaten forbidden food. Pach was a repository of worldly knowledge and information; what he didn't know, he plausibly made up with his flamboyant imagination. There was nothing you could ask him that he couldn't answer.

No one really understood, or knew, why a man of Jacob Pach's calibre should have left the excitement of his past existence, all the luxuries he had enjoyed, and come to Jerusalem where there was nothing but prayer and deprivation. He seemed in good health, so it wasn't to die that he came. But there he was, with his wife and three small daughters, and nothing else to call his own except the wide horizons of his mind.

Although he was only a couple of years older than Solomon, Pach looked a good deal older. By the ordinary standards of manly good looks, Pach was ugly beyond compare. His face was fat and covered with warts, his sparse, ash-coloured beard barely concealed the folds of flesh around his jowls, and his bulk seemed to slide down from his shoulders and concentrate about his thick short thighs. But Pach had irrepressible charm. His small eyes were alive with humour, he had a quick wit and a laughter which could dispel the gloom even from a mourner. He could tell a riveting story at a drop of a hat. And in his flowing oriental garb he looked inordinately exotic, almost regal.

Since the Ashkenazi Jews of Jerusalem now faced the awesome task of dealing with the mightiest temporal power in the world, the Divine Port, Pach's presence in their midst seemed to them ordained by the Blessed Name. For what other purpose could a man like Pach have come to Jerusalem if not to obtain for his brethren the Imperial firman, that redeeming dispensation from the Sultan? "The Lord opened the mouth of Balaam's she-ass and made her speak. Was that not as extraordinary as choosing such an unlikely saviour as Reb Pach?" Mendle philosophized glibly.

At first Pach hesitated. True, he had connections in Vienna, in London, in Paris. There was a Jew in Livorno who had dealt with the Ottomans at the highest level. A lot of discreet meetings would have to be held, and bribes no less discreet, the higher they went. It was no easy matter; they could not look forward to a quick or easy deliverance, he warned. And when Reb Isser reflected on the dangers of travel, Jacob Pach laughed and said, "When you know what's before you, you see no danger, only difficulties. I was never afraid of danger. But I have a family from which I don't want to part, not even for a few months."

In the end he agreed. How could he not, entrusted as he was with such a task that nobody else could undertake? Money was collected. Rabbi Mendle took up his pen and wrote letters of introduction and appeals to all the rabbis he knew or heard of, whom Pach might chance to meet. And so, soon after the High Holy Days, with all the congregation praying for his safe journey and successful mission, Jacob Pach set forth on his travels.

Winter was unusually mild, or was it hope that kept them warm? Fewer people fell ill, more families arrived, and because the Haham Bashi Ayish claimed he had seen the Angel of Death beckon to him, he was less concerned with the doings of this world and was said to be preparing himself to meet his maker. Throughout the winter no message arrived from Jacob Pach. No one knew where he was or what he was doing. Every day Solomon waited in vain for the Tartar to bring a letter. It was as though the earth had swallowed Pach without trace.

Spring came. Young Arabs, sons of the city notables, began to go out on hunting parties. For a while Nature's generosity distracted people's minds from the hardship and misery they were constantly inflicting on one another. Israel, now a sturdy boy, fleet-footed and quick of eye, followed the hunting parties from a distance. He watched with envy as the Arabs galloped on the hills in pursuit of the Judean gazelle. Like the gazelle, he too learned to avoid them. Only two or three of his friends would follow him on his outings. Stories of his ventures had reached Solomon's ears. He said nothing to the boy except once, just before the Passover feast, when Israel came home all hot from a day in the hills. Solomon looked hard and long at his son, until the boy was compelled to say, "Father, have I done anything wrong that you look at me with such disapproval?" He would soon be thirteen. He spoke without defiance but his calm confidence annoyed Solomon.

He checked himself and replied, "No, son. I'm not your judge. Only your father and, if you want, your guide in life. Unless you do wicked things. . . ."

"I don't do wicked things."

"No, I don't think you do."

In the silence that followed Solomon realized how awkward he felt. Were they nearly equal now? he asked himself, does he think I have nothing more to teach him? He said: "I look at you and I see how you've grown. You're like a creature of the wild, quick, decisive, confident, alert. I don't think I was ever quite like that although I did roam about a good deal when I was your age. I'm proud of you, and a little afraid at the same time."

Israel shrugged his shoulders. "What are you afraid of, Father?"

"What are people afraid of but things they don't fully understand?"

"I haven't changed that much."

"You do things Jewish boys don't do, son. That's what it is, I suppose."

Israel averted his gaze and stared out of the open window into the alley where the shadow of the courtyard wall was darkening the puddles. He spoke slowly. "What Jewish boys do here cannot be the same as what Jewish boys do back where we came from. Out there, there are people different from us, with different language and different ways. What do we know about them? What does Rabbi Mendle or any of the others know about the Arabs?" He turned to look at his father. "Nothing. The Arabs might as well be like the Cossacks you used to tell me about. Mendle, all of you live as Jews do in Europe. Why come here then? And the Arabs are like Cossacks to them." He broke off but before Solomon could say anything, he added, "Why can't we too be like Cossacks?"

At that moment Ada came in with Ariel and a whole basket of food for the Passover meal, and they talked no more. But what Israel said lingered in Solomon's mind and troubled him. Where did the boy get such ideas? Cossacks means savagery. How could Jews ever be like them? How could Jews threaten anybody for that matter? Then he remembered the Book of Joshua and God's Covenant with Abraham. The promise and its bloody fulfilment. "Am I not here because of all that?" He sighed. "My son is turning his back on my ways. Soon there won't be much I can tell him. Oh God, whatever Jews must do here, let it be good. And if it is your will that they should become like Cossacks, let them at least be good, compassionate Cossacks." He washed himself and made ready to go to the Synagogue. Israel was waiting for him at the door.

On the first day of Passover, Rabbi Eliezer Rimkin from Riga arrived in Jerusalem with his family, his wife, two daughters and a son. Rimkin walked with an aura of temperance and good rabbinical breeding about him. The wisdom of a steely intellect shone from his pale honey-coloured eyes. His voice was eloquent; in a word he could impart a sense of authority. Almost at once Rimkin became the focus of the Ashkenazi Jews in Jerusalem, because apart from his compelling presence, he brought with him the long-awaited letter from Jacob Pach. He had not met Pach in Constantinople where he took possession of the letter. Pach had sent a message saying that he was hurrying away to Alexandria on a special mission which he had not specified. Since Reb Eliezer Rimkin already saw himself as a member of the Holy Community of Jerusalem, he had no inhibitions about opening the letter and reading it on grounds that its contents concerned him no less than anybody else in Jerusalem. Pach wrote that through intermediaries he had petitioned the Sultan, may he live forever, who granted a firman, declaring the old Ashkenazi debts cancelled and the Ashkenazis themselves henceforth legal citizens of Jerusalem on equal terms with their Sepharadi brethren. There was no mention of a trip to Alexandria nor was it clear why Pach had not rushed back himself bearing the precious document.

That night, with Rimkin and his family, who were very charming, sharing the Passover feast with Solomon and his family and Rabbi Mendle and his kinsmen, there was a great celebration and dancing. Reb Isser wanted to go straight after the Passover to the Governor and receive his confirmation. Surely by then the Grand Wizir in Constantinople would have instructed the Pasha of Damascus on the matter who, in turn, would have passed on the instruction to his subordinate, the Governor of Jerusalem. Others were more cautious and caution prevailed in the end. The community would wait, it was decided, until they heard from the Governor, or until Pach himself appeared bearing the firman.

Weeks passed and not a word was heard from the Governor's palace or from Pach in Alexandria, or wherever he was.

The first hamsins began to blow and the grass on the hills blanched and withered. One night Haham Bashi Rabbi Ayish died without as much as opening his eyes to say "Hear O Israel". He was quickly succeeded by the mild-mannered Rabbi Keruel who was full of years and as deaf as a post. His secretary and chief aide was a younger cousin, a septuagenarian called Zadok who replaced Hadad. The two had a special sign language between them that no one else could understand. Keruel spoke voicelessly, only his lips moved. Zadok watched him and gave voice to the words.

Keruel let it be known that whatever had been in the days of his predecessor, his own heart desired nothing better than complete reconciliation with his Ashkenazi brethren. And it was in this spirit that he invited all the Ashkenazi leaders to his house to drink strong Hebronite coffee and smoke *toombak*.

When Solomon informed the new Haham Bashi of the Sultan's firman, Rabbi Keruel nodded his head and turning to his cousin launched into a long and animated speech in their sign language. After he had finished, Zadok turned to Solomon and with an impassive expression on his face said, "The Haham Bashi says it's good".

"Was that all he said?"

"Yes, he's very pleased, for it will now remove a burden from his shoulders which must have weighed heavily on Rabbi Ayish of blessed memory."

"And he will not mind if we go to the Governor?"

There was a quick consultation. Keruel shook his head vigorously.

"The Haham Bashi does not mind in the least. Go to the Governor," said Zadok.

"It's a trap," Isser said. "Did you see his eyes? I wouldn't trust him for the world."

"To think that the Sepharadi would give up his authority over us. It's unimaginable. Something must be wrong," Buxbaum agreed.

Rimkin looked at Solomon and Solomon looked back at Rimkin.

Rimkin said, "Before we do anything we should have more definite information about the firman, don't you think?"

"I was thinking the same," Solomon replied.

"There should have been news from that man Pach by now."

"Yes, this too has been much on my mind. What do you think could have happened to him?"

Rimkin knotted his brow. His large bony nose began to twitch. "Alexandria. Anything could happen to a man in Alexandria," he said.

"Not to Jacob Pach, you don't know him."

"Ah, but neither do you know Alexandria," Rimkin countered suavely.

"So?"

"So let's see what we can find out. I know a trusty Jew in Alexandria."

Summer came and went and still there was no news of Jacob Pach. People began to say that he must have died somewhere among the gentiles and no one would ever hear of him again. Collections were made for his poor wife and children so that they should not want. But stout-hearted Mrs Pach, although her clothes began to look more and more like mourning weeds, refused to give up hope. "When he dies you'll know all about it," she would say to anyone who raised the subject. "He's been trouble all his life, and he'd be even more trouble in his death, bless him."

After ten months the terrible news finally arrived. The ship which Pach had been sailing in to Alexandria, had been blown off-course and seized by pirates. Pach himself was taken to Khartoum and sold for bondage. Rimkin's contact in Alexandria wrote saying that since Pach was an Austrian subject the Austrian Consul in Alexandria could negotiate his release if the ransom money was raised, and he gave an estimate of the sum required, 100 piastres, the price of a healthy mule. The Jews started another collection with alacrity. The Sepharadim too contributed, for it was a terrible thing for a Jew to be enslaved, even an Ashkenazi, and all for the price of a mule!

They were still collecting the money, when Jacob Pach suddenly appeared in Jerusalem. He had lost a good deal of weight but apart from that he looked none the worse for his experience, and he had certainly lost none of his resilience and good humour. After he had rested the night in the bosom of his family, he went in the morning to the Synagogue and there, before an eager audience, told his story. "The fortunate if sad truth of the matter is, that they could not sell me on account of my ugliness," he concluded cheerfully. A prayer of "He which sustained and saved us" that is said when someone is restored, was recited.

Then Solomon dared ask, "And the Sultan's firman, have you still got it?"

"Safer than my health and body," Pach said, and pulling from the inside of his robe a soiled muslin pouch, he handed it to Solomon. "Here it is. Today we are all delivered from bondage."

The Governor took his time reading the firman. He held it up, turned it round, yet he showed no reverence, was visibly unimpressed. When he had finished he whistled through pouted lips, and casually handed the document to one of his aides who, like his superior, perused it impassionately. Solomon, Rimkin and Isser, and Zadok who had come as the Haham's representative and interpreter, waited anxiously.

"You must have paid a lot of money for this," he said at last, tossing the unfurled document at the feet of the men who stood before him.

Reb Isser fell to his knees reaching for the precious firman. The Governor said, "Don't bother, this bit of scroll is worthless, a forgery. I've seen dozens like it. I might punish you for bringing a false document to me but already you've been punished. It's no news to me that European Jews have been coming to Jerusalem. Did you really think you could fool me wearing those robes?" The Governor began to laugh, he was in a good mood that day. "I'll say nothing more about this. You'll pay your taxes and obey the law and no one shall harm you. Go on wearing your oriental robes, for if the Arabs see you've come here to claim that for which your brethren owed money and were chased out of Jerusalem, they'll be sharpening knives for you."

All day Reb Mendle had been talking of their redemption, close at hand at last, thanks to the Royal firman. "I'm too old to live to see the Synagogue of Rabbi Yehuda The Pious of blessed memory, rise again, out of that heap of dirt . . ."

"Nonsense, Reb Mendle, to a hundred and twenty, long may you live!" cried the guests, elders of the community, who had come to his house to wait for the good news.

Reb Mendle lifted his hands high, "But if I should live to see the cornerstone laid, I'd say to the Blessed Name, 'Enough, your servant is fulfilled!'"

When Solomon recounted what had happened, Reb Mendle's face went deathly pale. He rent his clothes, went to the kitchen, and returned with ash on his head. "Now your servant has seen enough," he mumbled. Then he turned his face to the wall and uttered not another word.

No one wanted to talk to Jacob Pach after that. He pleaded his innocence, swore on the lives of his children that he had acted in good faith. How was he to know that the high-ranking official he had been introduced to in Constantinople was a fraud? "I'll make good your loss if it's the last thing I do, only give me a chance," he begged.

"We should have let you rot in bondage, you're not worth the price of a mule," Buxbaum spat at him.

Traduced though he was, Pach lost none of his dignity. "And to think that I risked my life to go to Alexandria in order to raise money and start trading so that all of you should benefit," he said indignantly.

On the first day of Hanuka, which the Sepharadi and Ashkenazi Jews celebrated together in a spirit of more vigorous concord than ever before, Reb Mendle suffered a stroke. Paralysed, he was laid in bed; his clan, his friends and pupils—all the Jews of Jerusalem—prepared to face his death, for no one believed he would ever rise or speak again.

Rabbi Hazan, a wise and genial Hebronite who in turn had succeeded Keruel as Haham Bashi, called Solomon and Eliezer Rimkin for a meeting. The time demanded more active co-operation between the two congregations, he conceded. Better for an Ashkenazi to go to Europe as emissary for both communities. Therefore, let Solomon go, with the hopes and blessing of all the Jews of Jerusalem, Ashkenazi and Sepharadi alike. Reluctantly, Solomon accepted. Outside, Rimkin embraced his friend. "I know what you're thinking and how you feel. But you must go, Solomon. No one else but you would do. While you're away I'll look after your family as though they were my own. In a way they are already, so I feel. Gird up your loins then, brother, and put all worries out of your mind."

At around midnight Reb Isser awakened Solomon. He had come running and was out of breath. "Come quickly," he said, "Mendle is dying. He has whispered your name. He wants you at his side."

Reb Mendle looked as if life had already left his body. The glass into which he had been bled with leeches still stood on the stool by the bed. His eyes were wide open, staring at the ceiling. He didn't move a muscle. Solomon took the old man's hand in his. "I'm here Reb Mendle, dear old friend. I'm here," he said. He felt his hand being squeezed, light as a feather. Then Mendle's lips moved. "I'm here" he repeated. "Solomon. I shall go to Europe just like you wanted. There'll be money. We shall build the synagogue. Do you hear me? Do you understand? I'm with you now. I shan't leave you."

Mendle's mouth moved. Again Solomon felt his hand being squeezed, and saw the washed-out eyes focus on him. Mendle was making broken sounds. Solomon brought his ear close to the old man's mouth, and then as he listened to the uneven reedy breathing, the words came out disjointedly: "Ariel . . . be blessed in him . . . never betray your heart . . . never give up Ariel. . . ."

It was over in an instant; he might have imagined it all, he might have mistaken Mendle's death rattle for what was in his own heart. The old man's eyes once again turned glassy, the hand went limp.

Solomon found himself standing behind his house, at the foot of the great heap. He shed his shoes and slowly walked up towards the top. The heap billowed out in the pitch darkness. His feet were bruised as he clambered up. He reached the top. Now he could see phosphorous eyes watching him, prowling round the heap, disappearing, reappearing from behind folds of blackness. Jackals? Stray dogs? Maybe the wild hyenas that sometimes came into the city. Round and round they went, making no sound. Solomon flung his arms apart and began stamping his feet. It hurt him but he didn't care. "I shall do it, I shall do it. . . ." he kept repeating. The eyes whirled round him, mocking him. Then he was falling, rolling down the sharp slope. He let go. He imagined the beasts closing in on him, he could smell their foul breath. They'd fight over his body the moment he stopped rolling.

When he opened his eyes he saw his son holding him across his knees in the dark.

"Are you all right, Father?"

"Yes. I'm not alone?"

"You're not alone. I'm with you, don't be afraid."

"I fell, I tripped."

"Yes. I saw you."

"Israel!"

"Father?"

"If only you knew, if only I could make you understand. . . ."

"I understand. I shall help you. Come, let's go in now."

On the day Solomon departed for his mission to Europe, Israel rode with him to Jaffa. They stood on the quay and watched the ship that was to take him to Constantinople swaying on the dirty water of the harbour.

"Remember how we came?" Solomon said.

"Yes. Acre. What a day that was."

"And you've grown so much. You're almost a man now." Israel smiled.

"It's the end of a period, closed between two sea voyages. Now I leave half of me behind, half my strength, half of all that I understand. Look after your mother and your brother, son. God knows I shall miss you enough."

"It won't be so long. You'll be back sooner than you realize. You'll write?"

"Of course, whenever I can. But you know how long letters take to arrive."

"Yes. I'll miss you. Look after yourself."

Solomon looked away. "Go now before I weaken and change my mind."

PART TWO

Chapter 11

Eliezer Rimkin had a gift not only for doing the right thing at the right time—his sense for an occasion was unerring—but also for making sure, while outwardly seeming diffident, that what he did was noticed by as many people as possible. He kept his word to Solomon; in his friend's absence Ada, Israel and young Ariel wanted nothing, nor did they suffer a moment of loneliness. Rimkin's untidy and effusive household stretched out and took them to its bosom, suffused them with warmth and engulfed them with smells of food. Ada yielded with relief. Israel held back for a while until his balanced sensibilites told him that only within Rimkin's embrace could he find a latitude of freedom.

The names of Rimkin and Solomon became linked in a symbol of friendship, the noblest, most committed that could be found—like David and Jonathan. And so, when in gatherings or in the Synagogue the holy commandment of "Love thy neighbour as thyself" was mentioned, eyes would turn in Eliezer Rimkin's direction; his virtue had to be seized and shared like bits of bread, as an affirmation of goodness amidst petty rivalries. And Rimkin would gaze contemplatively at some spot on the ceiling until he felt public attention had shifted away from him.

Rimkin did not attempt to usurp Solomon's position in the community. He loved his friend, and whatever he did he did with Solomon's interest at heart. He read Solomon's letters in public meetings, and always extolled his worth and modesty. Through him Solomon, absent in body, was made present in spirit, with all his virtues magnified. It was the people who thrust Rimkin into the space temporarily vacated by Solomon. And he filled it with alacrity and faith, as a custodian, a true and loyal agent. Rimkin had a manner which inspired confidence. He spoke with authority yet was never patronizing. He managed to be economical with his time without ever seeming inaccessible. If he had moods they never showed; you could approach him any time of the day in happiness as in sorrow and he would always be attentive and considerate. Moreover, he suffered fools with patience that would have surpassed even the departed saintly Rabbi Mendle. "Thank the Lord for having sent us a man like Reb Eliezer," the men said. "At times like this we need leaders like him. He is to Solomon as Aaron was to Moses." Or was it the other way round? People could no longer say with certainty.

Hannah Rimkin took Ada under her wing. She taught her how to embroider, for which Ada had little use, and how to cook cholent, the sabbath broth, to just the right consistency so that it could last well over the sabbath and lose none of its substance when you added water to feed more guests.

"But what's the point?" Ada protested with a weak laugh. "When my man is away, my son spends more time with you than at home, and Ariel will eat hardly anything?"

"Ah, my dear," said Hannah, poking a wooden spoon into the bubbling broth, "here lies the secret. What keeps the family together? Good food. Jews must eat. Our culture is centred on food. And you dear Ada, with all respects, could do with a little more flesh on your ribs and colour in your cheeks." Hannah, like many stout glowing women, regarded slender women with compassionate disapproval.

It hadn't been Reb Eliezer Rimkin's design to make a match between his daughter Sheine and Solomon's son, Israel. The Buxbaums planted the idea in his mind inadvertently, and not out of generosity at that. Buxbaum and his wife occupied the rooms immediately below Solomon and Ada's; they were a quarrelsome couple. But the more Solomon had distanced himself from them, the more the Buxbaums had taken to spying on him and his family. No one could come and go from Solomon's home without the Buxbaums knowing about it and talking about it to anyone who cared to listen. One evening someone threw a rock through Buxbaum's window. It bounced off the table and hit Mrs Buxbaum on the head. Nothing could persuade the bitter couple that it wasn't Israel who was the culprit. They never forgave the boy for what they believed he did, nor Solomon and Ada for being indirectly responsible. No sooner had Solomon departed and Rimkin taken up his role as protector and surrogate father to his friend's family, than the Buxbaums concluded that behind it all lay Rimkin's desire to secure a bridegroom for his unprepossessing daughter, and proceeded to propagate the idea with all the malice they could work into it. Rimkin, for his part, saw the possibilities and began to ponder over them.

A year had passed since Solomon had left on his journey and he kept his commissioners informed of his progress as far as the caprice of the post system permitted. News was reaching Jerusalem of his success, the good impression he was making everywhere and the eloquent plea he was making on behalf of Jerusalem's Jewish community. Hopes were rising for more contributions and therefore a better life resulting from his trip. The Sepharadis in particular hung on to such hopes. Under their new Haham Bashi Rabbi Hazan, they saw their power ebb. It wasn't that Hazan was in any way less capable a leader than his predecessors; on the contrary, he had wit and immense erudition as well as considerable social grace. Above all, he was flexible and diplomatic. But the Sepharadis, by nature and tradition, were passive and compliant. They accepted rather than demanded. To them calamities were arbitrary and inevitable, just as triumphs were a divine reward. The Ashkenazis, on the other hand, agitated constantly: expected innovations then descried them when they came about; complained about hardship but were dissatisfied when hardship was relieved; called for unity and fought among themselves when there was no one else left to oppose. But for all that, having shaken and reshaped the reality they found themselves in, they had resilience and a kind of creative toughness that carried them forward and in their wake their bemused Sepharadi brethren.

Solomon's letters came in batches at intervals of two to three months, depending on the maritime traffic and the inclination of the couriers between Europe and Palestine. He wrote to his son and to Rimkin. He had visited Germany, Austria, Italy and France. Everywhere he had been received with kindness and honour. The Jews of the diaspora cared deeply for their brethren in the Holy Land who were always in their hearts and prayers, he wrote.

Often his assessments were modest; he didn't want to arouse false hopes for things he could not achieve. Rimkin, however, added colour to the colourless, and moisture to the dry. He was a natural interpreter, not only of Solomon but of the minds and hearts of the diaspora Jews whom he knew and understood better perhaps than anybody else. When Solomon wrote that he had been well-received, Rimkin could say with certainty born of experience that a large donation was to be expected.

"My dearest son Israel, light of my eyes, blessed of the Lord," Solomon wrote. Israel stuffed the letter into the breast pocket of his coat, and ran off to some quiet spot where he could read it undisturbed.

" . . . Frankfurt is a truly magnificent city and there is a large prosperous Jewish community here and several very learned Rabbis. At this time of the year the trees—there are so many of them—are all golden and copper, and the river Main is languid and shimmering grey. I remember how on the day we set forth for Jerusalem, one of the men who was to go with us came running to me and told me with tears in his eyes that his wife would not budge because there was no river in Jerusalem. At the time I thought she was crazy. Now I understand. In Jerusalem we have the great current of our consciousness, the tides of our miseries, and the spring of our faith. But no river. Rivers make a lot of difference; they force you to look away from yourself and into a great flow of life outside your thoughts.

"The other day, it being Sabbath, I was invited to read the lesson from the Torah, as I have on many previous occasions. It fell to me to read from the Book of Samuel. I read 'Return to thy place and abide with the king: for thou art a stranger and also an exile'. And I thought to myself how very suitable it was. I am an exile here. Even the trees and the birds, which I could many years ago recognize, now look foreign to me. I look at the good people around me and I know in my heart that they too are exiles, even if they don't realize it or won't face up to it.

"Yet they seem so contented while my spirit is restless. I ask myself why they treat me with such reverence and kindness. Am I more learned or a better man? No, I never had pretences and I know what I am. Is it because they love the Holy Land? Again, no. If they loved the Holy Land would they not go there as I and many others have?

"I'm weary, son. My heart asks questions to which it finds no answers. I pray and I find no comfort in my prayers. . . ."

Israel put the letter down and looked up at the sky. A kestrel hung over the valley of Hinnom. Regiments of cloud moved slowly before the westward breeze. Suddenly he had a vision of his father and of mortality. A chill ran through him even though it was a warm day. "Is strength an illusion?" he thought. "And if so what is real?" For a moment it occurred to him to pray for his father's return. He couldn't. He had ceased to believe in prayer, if he ever did, even though he pretended to pray to please his mother and allay the suspicions of those who watched him.

"Soon, my dear son, my mission will be over and I shall return to Jerusalem. I am the generation of the desert so to speak, the generation which the Lord wasted on the wilderness of Sinai so that the bad habits of idolatry and enslavement would be finished. But you are a fresh root, rooted in our homeland. I shall watch you grow, tend to you, like a good gardener. Heavens above, you've had your Bar Mitzva and I wasn't there to watch you go up and recite your passage in front of all the congregation. What can give a father more pride than that? And what can mar a boy's Bar Mitzva more than the absence of his father? I should ask your forgiveness, except that my life is not my own now, and therefore I'm not accountable for such remissions."

That night Israel was invited to dine at Rimkin's home. In his mind's eye he could see the table, laden with food, Reb Eliezer and his family scrubbed raw with rough soap, and in their best clothes. Reb Eliezer's eyebrows would rise steeply, and his mouth pucker, ready to bless the food. And Sheine would be there, looking at him from across the table, from under those thick dark eyelashes of hers.

That night Hannah had surpassed herself, made the tastiest plumpest dumplings Israel had ever eaten. And for dessert there were glazed apples and almonds. She watched Israel eat and was not beyond hinting that this was nothing less than he might expect one day as his normal fare if . . . At which Sheine blushed and lowered her eyes and Rimkin's mouth widened in a smile.

At the end of the evening, Rimkin insisted that both he and his son Samuel who was Israel's age, accompanied their guest back to his home. It wasn't a long way to go but it was a night of the new moon and very dark. The air was still; the smells of the day hung heavily in the alleys.

Here and there a dog slunk behind the shelter of a wall. An owl hooted from somewhere on the walls. A broad pale ring encircled the yellow rind of the moon. Samuel, who prided himself on knowing the constellation of the stars and the patterns of the sky, remarked with adult dryness that it was going to be a hot day, perhaps the first hamsin of the season. They each carried a lamp, for it was forbidden to walk the streets of the city at night without light. Anyone caught without one in the dark faced a fine if not imprisonment, and woe betide the offender if he happened to be a Jew.

At the door of his home, Rimkin hugged and kissed Israel on both cheeks. "Look after your blessed mother and little brother" he said. "The Lord looks down favourably on you. Soon your father will be back and all will be well. So do what lads of your age should do: study the Torah and be a source of pride and comfort to your friends and family." Samuel, meanwhile, was contemplating the heaven with an air of superiority. Then, as an afterthought, Rimkin added, "This day I did a good act. At least I think so, an act of mercy which I hope will not bring us trouble." He turned away, waving his lamp in valediction. Israel watched them as they receded into the night. Their voices became distant, soon all he could see was the two lamps swinging to and fro like fire flies in the dark.

Ada was up waiting for him. She had cleared the table after the small meal she had prepared for herself, and had put Ariel to bed. Now she was sitting in the only comfortable chair they had, knitting. When Israel came in, she shot a quick glance at the clock which stood against the wall. Solomon had come by the clock in lieu of payment for some work he had done. It no longer kept time well, but it had a pleasant chime which reminded Ada of her father's home.

"Well, did you have a nice evening?" she said.

"Pleasant enough but too long," he replied and kissed her hands.

"They are good people, the Rimkins," said Ada. "Their home is full of light and warmth."

"Why didn't you come too, Mother?"

She shook her head. "I'm not a widow, Israel, God forbid. Nor am I poor. I have this home and this table. For you, it's different. You go, be with them. It's good for you. I was napping and I dreamt your father had returned in the month of Sivan, at the height of summer, when everything's so beautiful in Europe and here it's like a furnace." Suddenly her face clouded over. "There's a surprise waiting for you in father's workshop, and I hope it's not as bad as I think it might be."

"A surprise?"

Ada pulled a face. "Remember that crazy Tanzman? He's here, looking all drawn and wild-eyed. It seems Reb Eliezer Rimkin has smoothed things over with the Arabs. So he comes straight here. I tell him come sit, eat something. But he wouldn't. He's too used to being alone, he says, and he goes and sits in the dark in the workshop and waits for you. Poor devil. I hope he doesn't cause more trouble." She looked at Israel with concern. "But why should he come here, of all places?"

Israel shrugged. "Why not? We were friends."

Tanzman was sitting at the work table. He didn't move when Israel came in, his figure was massed up against the wall in the dark. Israel lit the lamp to see Tanzman staring at him steadily and unblinking. In the shadowy light Tanzman looked hollow, his face all caved in. The stubble of his beard marked out the valleys of his face. His eyes shone with disquieting intensity. It occurred to Israel that his friend might be suffering from some illness. Were it not for that, he might have laughed, for there was something at once comical and moving about Tanzman's posture and attitude.

"Put the light out, Israel," said Tanzman.

"Why, Shimon, what's this? Have you become a creature of the dark?" Nevertheless, he extinguished the lamp.

"Close your eyes," Tanzman commanded. After a pause during which Tanzman appeared to be counting slowly, he said, "Now open them. Do you see me?"

He did, outlined against the grey light from the window.

"Now listen, listen carefully. What do you hear?"

"Nothing. Your breathing."

"There's no such thing as nothing. Even nothing's something."

"Shimon, what's the matter with you, are you ill?"

Tanzman laughed softly. It made him sound awesomely mature, and a little sinister.

"You mean am I mad?"

"I didn't . . ."

"Don't think I'm mad Israel. I've learnt a good many things during these past months. One of them is about darkness, and night. It's a world in itself, full of sounds, full of visions. When you know it you're no longer afraid. When you're no longer afraid of it, you have power over other people who are afraid of it. This is what I want to teach you. Come, closer. Don't be afraid."

Israel dragged out a chair and sat opposite Tanzman, across the table. Tanzman kept his hands hidden in his lap. His shoulders squared up above the table's edge, block-like, with his head looking small because of his cropped hair and shorn beard.

"What does it say in our Bible? 'Watchman, what of the night?' Yet what does a good Jew do at night? He sleeps or lies awake afraid of it. I have mastered the dark. There's something I want you to keep for me, that's why I came." From his lap he produced a little bundle wrapped tightly in a piece of cloth and tied together with a leather thong.

"What is it, Shimon?"

"Better for you not to know,"

"I must. I insist, if I'm to keep it for you."

Tanzman hesitated. "Very well then, open it. Do it in the dark," he said.

Couched in its swaddling clothes the metal object lay heavily in his hands. Israel touched the smooth steel surface. It had a terrifying coldness. Even as he held it he felt perspiration breaking over his face. He was experiencing a feeling such as he had never experienced before: excitement heightened by fear. All the while Tanzman was watching him. He could feel his eyes boring in on him.

"You know what it is?"

"Yes . . ."

"Say it!" Tanzman commanded, but couldn't wait for the answer.

"It's a revolver. A Turkish army revolver," he said. At that Israel lifted his hands from the weapon as if it had scorched them.

"Where did you get it?" he asked.

"What does it matter?"

Israel pulled the cloth over the gun. "Are you completely mad?" he whispered harshly. "Do you know what will happen to you if this thing is found in your possession? Do you realize what you might bring upon all of us?"

"Should we always be fearful?" Tanzman said implacably.

"For God's sake, Shimon . . ." Israel got up.

"Wait," said Tanzman. "I'll tell you. . . . Four days ago, just before dark, I went out, still dressed as a woman. Just a little way along the wall, to breathe some fresh air. There was this lout. He started following me. He made lewd remarks. I walked on, ignoring him. In the shadow of one of the wall's casemates, he pounced on me, thinking to despoil a defenceless woman, a daughter of Israel." Tanzman reached for the gun and held it. "This is the only thing about him that remained in one piece when I was finished with him. Now what do you want me to do, present myself at the Ottoman's palace and say, 'I killed one of your creatures, a beast who'd have done sodomy on me. But here's his pistol. I'm a good law-abiding Jew, I mean no harm'? He got what he deserved." Tanzman said.

"What difference does it make?"

"Everything, Israel. I'm no murderer like them. I fight in self-defence, to save my life, my honour as a Jew."

"No Shimon, you're no murderer," Israel said, and thought, "even so death and violence gather around you. Which is almost as bad."

"Well?" Tanzman said.

"Put the gun away. I'm going to light the lamp now."

He wanted to see his friend's face when he asked him questions.

"Did anyone see you?"

"No one. The street was empty and it was dark. The Amalekite was alone. After I took the gun I threw him over the wall through a broken part in the casemate. I walked away as if nothing had happened, and returned home. No one but you knows about it. Nor ever shall. No one except you, Israel."

"Very well then. It will remain between us. Go now. I'll hide the gun. Not even you will know where." And when Tanzman protested, Israel said, "If you trust me then trust me all the way. You shall have your gun when you want it and pray God you never will."

After Tanzman had left, Israel wrapped up the weapon and tied it firmly with the leather thong. Outside, by the well, there was a loose flagstone. He waited until it was past midnight then rose from his bed. He prised the flagstone up, dug a deep hole in the soil beneath, and deposited the gun there. He replaced the flagstone and swept away the traces of earth. Looking at his work, he was satisfied that no one could think anything was buried there. He was calm now, as calm as Tanzman had been. In a sense he was an accomplice: Shimon had killed, he, Israel had buried the evidence.

Chapter 12

Reb Eliezer Rimkin liked to philosophize whenever he felt the world getting on top of him. The greater the pressure he was under, the more abstract and convoluted would become his inner discourse. One theme that haunted him was time in space, a realm he considered insufficiently explored. Thus he would say to himself that just as the contours of the land can deceive the eye and distort distances, so time can take on capricious rhythm which falsely quickens or slows down the pace of a man's life. Indeed time itself has contours: it draws you laboriously uphill, or entices you to lush plains full of pleasant sights and scents which distract your mind and dull your purpose, or it sends you hurtling down a slope fearful for your life. A man gets the illusion that his life expands and contracts alternately. If it were not for time's wanton trickery what tests would man have to prove himself before his Maker? And what could put man's mind off the terrible and inevitable moment of mortality when he must give account of himself before the ultimate seat of judgement? The concept, so he thought, had a neat symmetry, which was a tribute to reason, which afforded comfort in the face of trouble, and made resignation easier to accept. And since it worked so well for him, he felt obliged to try it on others who came to him oppressed by the tribulations of life. Kor the giant summed up the common admiration for Rimkin: "Reb Rimkin, you're wisest man as ever lived," he said, and in gratitude heaved into place the huge iron stove Rimkin had recently acquired.

Rimkin was filled with warmth in which his already considerable generosity blossomed like a lily on a balmy summer night. He imagined himself to be a steady bridge underneath which the broad stream of life gently flowed. He loved people, he never tired of listening to whoever wanted to unburden himself. And he would help anyone whenever he could, without ever counting the cost.

Only Israel resisted Rimkin's embrace. Friendly but independent, he kept his distance. "He and his father are one of a kind. Self-reliant and introspective. You can't help such people," Rimkin thought ruefully. "He marks the passage of every day. He doesn't have the comfort of forgetfulness. And one day, please God, he'll be my son-in-law."

Summer came and blasted the hillsides bone-white. Providentially there was no shortage of water and no epidemics broke out. At the Jewish New Year, in the month of Tishre, the Ashkenazis and Sepharadis, still on friendly terms, prayed together for peace and gave thanks that the passing year had brought them no disasters and no exceptional hardship. It had been a good year for both communities, but particularly for the Ashkenazim for ten more families had arrived from Safed, from Tiberias and from Byelorussia to swell their numbers.

Shimon Tanzman, now free to walk around without fear, did so, though without his former assertiveness. He had grown a new beard, larger and darker than the one he had so ignominiously lost. And as if to compensate for his temporary emasculation, he now looked more sinewy and awesomely fierce than ever in his brooding silence. Young men eager to test themselves gathered round him. And Rimkin, who already half-regretted having arranged for his rehabilitation rather than having shipped him out of Jerusalem, would look at him, nod his head and say with a sigh: "The heavens are clear and all is well. But Tanzman stalks about like the harbinger of storm."

Tanzman no longer sought Israel's company; the secret they shared from that night when the gun was buried seemed to have laid a strip of no man's land between them. He was not unfriendly towards his former young companion. But he sensed that Israel was not suited to the aims and challenges that now dominated his life. As for Israel, his instincts told him that nothing good would come of Tanzman and his doings—there were whispers that he had formed a militant group for self-defence which called itself Sons of Bar Kochba. He watched Tanzman but kept his distance from him.

When the fresh westerly breeze began to blow, and the sweet fragrance of blossoming pomegranate and the almond wafted out from the walled gardens of Jerusalem, a short letter arrived from Solomon saying that he was embarking on a ship for home and would reach Palestine, all being well, in time for the Passover.

The Messiah himself, had he arrived, could not have been greeted with more joy than was Solomon as he entered Jerusalem through the Jaffa Gate on a dazzling April morning. Both the Ashkenazis and Sepharadis declared a day of holiday. Dressed in their best clothes, the men danced around Solomon and stretched their hands to touch him. Rimkin was there together with all the elders of the community who stood apart from the women and the children. The Haham Bashi also came. Dressed in his robe of office and his splendid black turban and surrounded by his small retinue, he added some pomp and ceremony to the occasion. He waited for Solomon to approach and pay his respects while his retinue looked on anxiously to see in what order of precedence Solomon would greet those who came to welcome him.

Rimkin held on to Ada who held Ariel's hand. Together they pushed through the crowd to reach Solomon. Behind them followed Israel and all Rimkin's family. Hannah was at hand to take Ariel from Ada when she came face to face with Solomon and fell into his arms. He held her for a long moment, his eyes shut tight. When at last they drew apart, their eyes were brimming with tears. She wiped her tears away and smiled at him, "I've grown old and silly in your absence. How long it's been."

"You haven't changed at all, beautiful as ever. . . ."

And Israel, looking on, noticed how the grey had shot through his father's beard.

"Israel, my son. How you've grown! I hardly recognized you." Solomon hugged him, then held him at arm's length and looked at him admiringly. Ariel began to scream, and Solomon reached down and picked him up to plant a paternal kiss on his golden head.

He had brought presents for his family and for Rimkin and his wife and children: small things, a token, just to show that he hadn't forgotten them. At meetings in the synagogue, Solomon gave a full account of what he had done and where he had been. The money he had brought with him was substantial, but more would come, he said. There were other commitments. He had carried on his body as much as he could, dangerous though it was. At this point, a fellow traveller, a newly arrived Jew from Vienna, related with fervour how during the trip three thugs attempted to rob Solomon and how he prevailed on them and made them turn away empty-handed.

"You've brought everybody something and look at you, nothing for yourself. You're wearing the same coat as you did on the day you left," Rimkin chided him after they had finished dinner at Solomon's home. Solomon shrugged his shoulders, "The coat is as good as ever, why should I get a new one?"

"Typical of you, Reb Solomon. Do you know, they are already talking of you undertaking another trip in a year or two. You've been such a success." Ada paled and Hannah dug her fat elbow into Rimkin's side.

But Solomon said calmly, "I shall never go abroad again on any mission."

"Not even if we beg you on our bended knees? Not even to save us all?"

"Not even that," Solomon replied and smiled.

"Ah, after a few years have passed. . . ." Rimkin persisted.

"I tell you never," said Solomon with finality.

The guests had left, Ada cleared the table and put Ariel to bed. The child was tired and over-excited, he was screaming petulantly. She washed herself and put on the embroidered nightgown which for two nights, since Solomon arrived, she had been wearing and which he hadn't noticed. She got into bed. "I'm old and no longer attractive to him," she thought unhappily. Then she found some solace in the thought that perhaps he was weary from the long journey. Who could tell what hardships he had had to endure? He never talked much about such things. He didn't look at all well, she could see that. How foolish and selfish it was of her to expect his attentions. She could hear him talking to Israel in the next room.

Solomon was admiring his son. "How you've filled out. Strong as a young tree," he said and laughed. "Soon there'll be talk of marriage. I know what Eliezer has in mind."

Israel gave a short uncomfortable laugh, "Not too soon, Father, I'm not nearly ready for that yet," he said.

Solomon raised his eyebrows and stroked his beard. "It's good to start early rather than late. Sheine is a fine girl. She'll make a good wife and a good mother. And both Eliezer and Hannah love you as if you were their own son. They are well off too . . . ."

Israel's expression hardened and Solomon quickly changed the subject.

Father and son sat together and talked for hours. Solomon told Israel things he had seen and done from the day he left home. When he had finished he said, "I've written a journal, just as I used to do years ago, when we travelled here. In it you'll find everything. When I'm gone it will be yours, to show your children and their children, may the Lord make them many."

"But you've a long life ahead of you and much to do yet, Father!"

"Who except the Blessed Name knows, my son, who knows. But it's important that you keep my journals, for the future. You know why? Because people should have a past to hold on to. Not just the bible or legends about sages. No, real stories about ordinary people that give you a beginning and continuity in a place. What do I know about my forebears? What does anyone here know about where their fathers came from, and what they did generations ago? And how can you say 'this is where I belong' if you don't have the answers to these questions? Do you understand what I'm saying, Israel? Does it make sense to you?"

"Yes. I'll treasure your journals," he said.

Solomon got up and began pacing up and down the room, his hands behind his back. Twice he stopped as if about to speak, then changed his mind. At last he stood facing the window over which Ada had put up the patched curtain to hide the view of the mound. He stood looking at it for a long moment. Then he turned round.

"Once you said to me that Jews here should not be as Jews are in the diaspora. Do you remember?"

"I must have said many things, some of them foolish" Israel said, pulling a face.

"Solomon, Solomon, will you be up talking all night?" Ada cried from the bedroom.

"Peace, my love, I'll come soon," he answered, and returning to Israel, went on "I remember, I thought about it a great deal on my travels. Do you know how I saw our brethren in Europe? I saw pale plants in pots. Shallow roots. Foreign wherever they were, bunched together against one another for support. And I wanted to get back home, for even to be a common weed here is better. And I thought of what you said to me even if you hadn't quite understood what you were saying. You look at the hills and the fields and you know in your heart they are your home. You needn't explain it to yourself. Oh yes, I remember how I used to chide you for running around like a wild gazelle. I could never be quite like that. Soon I'll be old. When our forefathers lived on this land do you know what they did to mark their geography before God and man? They put up a column of stones, that's what they did."

"So? You want to put up a pillar of stones? Like Absalom?"

Solomon laughed. "Not like Absalom. He was a wicked man, a bane to his father, and he did evil in the eyes of God. But a pillar in a sense, yes."

Half-turning he thrust his finger in the direction of the window. "Out there shall my pillar be, on that filthy heap. Not a pillar, a synagogue. Not for myself but for posterity. For your children and their children for ever. This is the only thing I want to do from now on and to the day I die. And if I succeed I shall die a happy man. That's what I've decided to do, the only thing I have time and strength to work for."

Israel entered his father's enthusiasm. Suddenly what had until that moment seemed like a dream become an attainable object. Trying to sound adult he said in a practical tone of voice, "There's the question of money. Lots of it. Where will you get it? Then there's the question of the permit to build the synagogue. . . ."

"Good, good," Solomon nodded, enjoying and welcoming his son's involvement. "But do you think your father's a soft-headed old fool not to have thought of that? Have you no faith in me?"

"Oh father, faith I have in abundance but faith will not make one stone rise," Israel laughed and got up.

"Ah, that depends on how faith is applied," Solomon rejoined. "There'll be money, as much as is needed. Have no fear. That's the other thing I've taken care of on my visits in Europe."

Israel wanted to know more but Solomon suddenly pulled a large silver watch from his coat pocket, and gazed at it. "It's late now," he said. "We'll talk more another time." He clicked shut the watch's cover, stared at it for a moment, then disconnecting the chain from his belt, held the watch out to Israel. "Here, take this. I never had a watch nor ever needed one. I keep time in my heart."

Ada pretended to be asleep when Solomon came to bed. He could tell and he smiled to himself as he touched her shoulder and squeezed it gently. Ada moaned as if in her sleep. Then she turned to him. "There, there, " he said, "we should be saying 'He that hath kept us alive.'"

"He that hath kept us alive and sustained us to this day," she murmured and snuggled up to him.

Chapter 13

Israel liked to sit high on the wall by the Jaffa Gate, and watch travellers come in and go out of the city. He learned to recognize from their clothes and the animals they rode whether or not they were strangers, and where they most likely came from. Sitting thus, he would dream of the day when he too would set out to discover new places.

One morning, as he took position on the wall, in time to see a small group of horsemen come out of the gate, he thought he saw a familiar figure. He looked hard and couldn't believe his eyes: astride a large bony mount sat none other than Jacob Pach! He was dressed as an Arab but there was no mistaking, it was Pach, as real as the wall Israel was sitting on. And riding a horse!

At the earliest opportunity Israel went to see him at his home. Pach, in spite of his lingering eclipse in the Jewish community, looked more cheerful and rotund than ever.

"Soon, God willing, my fortune will change. Then, my young friend, everyone will see what kind of a man is Jacob Pach," he announced. "And when I go up to read from the Torah in the synagogue, they'll say, 'we've wronged Pach. We were blind and foolish.'"

"What are you doing? What are you up to? Tell me, Pach."

"I'll tell you what I'm not doing. Sitting at home wringing my hands. Not me. Walls depress me. I'm by nature a vagabond," Pach said with a laugh.

"I go out. Make friends among the *goyim*. I buy, I sell."

"Buy, sell, what?"

"Anything I can get that will make profit. There's hardly a thing you can buy that you can't sell at a profit with a bit of patience."

"Dressed like an Arab? Why?"

"Why not? With the Arabs a man is a man and his word is his bond."

"Until they slit your throat."

"Don't believe that nonsense. Listen to me, young Israel. . . ." And he told him of the places he had visited, people he had met, deals he had struck. And how he had learnt to sit on a horse he rents from a horsedealer in town.

"Be honest and open, and you win trusting friends. Tell a good story, and you win a favour," Pach concluded and winked.

"Could you take me with you? Just once?" Israel pleaded.

Pach rolled his eyes. "What your father and the rest would do to me I daren't imagine!"

"I'm not a boy any more."

Pach's eyes twinkled affectionately. "Did I say you were? Let me think about it. Maybe. But first you must prove yourself."

"Tell me how. I'll do anything."

"Secrecy," said Pach with a finger across his lips. "A man must know when to keep his mouth shut."

"I shan't breathe a word about you or anything you told me, I swear," Israel said.

"Reb Israel, shake my hand on this," Pach said.

When Solomon observed how restless and withdrawn Israel had become, he said to Ada, "I think it's time we made arrangements for our son's future."

Catching Rimkin one evening in a relaxed mood, Solomon said, "Reb Eliezer, supposing there are two streams which run alongside one another' drawing closer at times and apart at other times, but forever invigorating one another and their surroundings, is it right that their common course should be diverted to make them part? Would not such a thing be against nature and a wanton waste?"

"And if there are two stout trees, Reb Solomon," replied Rimkin with a smile of anticipation on his face, "which grow side by side, and their roots share the same goodness of the soil, and they give forth good fruit, is it right that their branches should be cut to prevent them touching one another?"

The two men fell into each other's arms in an embrace.

"Is it not right, Reb Solomon," Rimkin went on, "that our seed should become one shoot? That whatever we contribute to our blessed community should be a joint thing?"

Solomon hesitated.

"I have a daughter, you have a son. . . ."

Solomon took in a deep breath. "Your Sheine is a fine girl. Everything a man may wish for in a woman. I know my son Israel should be proud and happy if such a woman would marry him," he said.

"And such a woman would be happy to share her life with an upright young man such as your son, Reb Solomon. A proud and obedient wife she would be. My Sheine cannot conceal what's in her heart. Not from her father."

Solomon was silent.

"Let us pledge our children to one another, my friend," Rimkin said and extended his hand, which Solomon took.

"Let nothing ever come between us, Solomon. We are now . . ."

"Kinsmen, as we always have been in spirit, Eliezer," Solomon said. "But . . . this matter, let it remain between us for a while. The boy has a proud spirit and an unbending mind, he still has a lot to learn, a lot to do and this news may turn his mind away from what he has yet to accomplish. I'd like him to come to the idea of marriage of his own will."

A cloud of apprehension stiffened Rimkin's smile. "If that is your wish, Reb Solomon."

"Eliezer, I've pledged my son to your daughter. Marriages, as we both know, are made by fathers not in heaven. All I ask is discretion, so that nothing could mar the contract. There is time; the children are young and we are both well, thanks be to God."

"Solomon, my friend, there's no better bond for me than your word, and your counsel is wise, as always. Let's say no more about it," said Rimkin, rising above his disappointment.

"She's a good girl, from the best family. Israel will be grateful, I know for I've today opened a way to comfort and success for him. Please, God, help me make him see it this way, for the sake of us all as well as for him. Ada, to whom, God forgive me, I've not brought the happiness she deserves, will be recompensed in that union," Solomon thought as he walked away.

The road from Jerusalem to Jaffa passed through Abu Gosh, then wound down a steep twisting wadi to Bab el Whad—"Gate of the Wadi". Here, where the land levelled and fanned out on to the rolling Judean foothills, stood a caravanserai, kept by a Sudanese, former slave of Sheik Abu Gosh, who had won his freedom by his valour in the service of his master. Wayfarers stopped at the caravanserai to rest their animals and refresh themselves. Among these were merchants, landowners and peasants as well as bandits, and spies. In Babel Whad, deals were made, alliances forged, and treasons hatched. Every event of importance was first whispered about in the smoky alcoves of Bab el Whad caravanserai before it actually took place.

"Tonight, young friend, you'll see the ears and tongue of the country. You'll be a man among men in a place where the faint-hearted dare not tread," Pach said expansively.

"I've already been there. Twice in fact," Israel replied.

"That was different. Times have changed. Don't hold me so tight," Pach said curtly.

"I'm not even touching you," Israel said and stretched his arms forward for Pach to see.

They rode on, Israel sitting behind Pach on the large ambling horse he had hired, until Jaffa Gate fell behind out of sight. The other travellers soon outpaced them.

"When we get there, you must watch, and listen. You say nothing. Understood?"

"Yes."

Pach began to hum a Yiddish song.

"I still don't know who you're meeting, Pach," Israel ventured to say after a while.

"Meeting? My son, this trip is just for you. A present from Pach, which you'll remember all your life and tell your children about. You don't know anything about women, do you? Of course not. How could you, being so young? Well, listen. There's that Gazan dancer. Delilah never looked so enticing. The Arabs say she has the largest breasts from here to perdition. . . ."

Israel's mind conjured up the image of Sheine, with cow eyes, and hands stirring slowly in her wide lap.

"No harm for you to look at the Devil's work from a safe distance," Pach was saying.

At the first turning in the wadi, Pach dismounted to relieve himself. "There's no denying. You make a very good impression. I'll say you're my son. No, nephew would be better," Pach said shaking himself.

"To whom? So you're meeting someone!"

"Oh, just one little meeting. Important all the same. An Arab trader called Fawzi, from Beit Jamal. I've made approaches to him with a view of acting as his agent in Jerusalem." A hint of pomposity was creeping into his voice, which he quickly acknowledged with a smile and a wink. "Dried fruit and spices. Fawzi produces, I sell and collect a commission. And with just a little luck, there's a regular steady income and no more worries for Yakov Pach and his family. A nice little present for you too, I shan't forget that."

He led the horse to a nearby rock, climbed up on to it, and then laboriously on to the animal's back.

There were not many people at the caravanserai. Those who were there didn't seem like ordinary travellers: there was a certain nervousness about them. Most were armed. Pach and Israel took a place at the corner of the vaulted room, from where they had a good view of all who were there. There was no sign of Fawzi.

"There's something strange going on," Pach kept repeating, "No girls, no musicians, something's going on."

Fawzi arrived late. He walked straight to a group of men who were talking conspiratorially round a table, and sat down with them.

"Wait here," Pach said.

As he got up, Fawzi saw him, and waved him on. He rose, greeted Pach, then introduced him to the men round the table. Israel could see Pach's face turning grave as he listened. At last he returned. "We're riding back to Jerusalem with these men," he said.

"Why? What happened?"

"Bad news. War. There's a Jew in Acre called Farhi. . . ."

"Prince Farhi. I saw him once," Israel broke in.

"Well, he's just been murdered by Abdullah, son of the late Pasha Selim. This Abdullah is now going around killing everybody in sight, Jews in particular. He wants to purge the entire region of Farhi's friends and supporters. People are running away. An army from Damascus is marching on Acre. Everybody's fighting everybody."

Memories of Acre were so distant in Israel's mind, he couldn't relate to them with any sense of urgency. He said blandly, "It's so far away, why worry so soon?"

"When Jews are killed, no matter how far, you can't start worrying too soon. Also, according to Fawzi, a band of outlaws from around Hebron have teamed up with Bedouin. They want to take advantage of the situation, attack Jerusalem and kick out the Governor. It could happen any time. Look, the men are coming, let's go."

Thanks to Fawzi's friends, one of whom took Israel on his own faster horse, the pace was brisk: they arrived before Jerusalem with day-break, just as the Muezzin's voice was heard from within the walls, and the Bashi bazooks on guard swung open the Jaffa Gate.

"Tell your father what's going on. Tell him to prepare our people for whatever may come," Pach said, and hurried off to his own home.

Solomon had been on the point of organizing a search party to look for Israel. When he saw him his anxiety gave way to relief, which was in turn blasted away by a rage of anger. "Have you no sense at all?" he bellowed at his son. "Leaving like that without a word! And us beside ourselves wondering what had happened to you." Then, for the first time ever, he struck Israel a hard blow on the face with the flat of his hand, which nearly sent him to the floor. "I forbid you to see or talk to that man Pach, do you hear?" He shouted. "Never mention his name in this house, never!"

The news from Galilee had reached Jerusalem the night before, and made the garrison edgy. But neither Solomon, Rimkin, or the Haham Bashi, who met to discuss what Israel had told them, believed an attack on Jerusalem was either imminent or real. "If we warn about it and it turns out to be true, which I cannot believe, there will be some who will say 'the Jews knew about it'. If it's nothing but a false rumour, we'll be accused of spreading fear. Better not say a word. Let the news come from other sources," the Haham summed up. And so it was agreed to take note but no action, and wait to see how things would turn out.

Tanzman studied the news and registered the tension in the souks. He gathered hard men about him, and waited.

One evening he saw Israel pass by and motioned his friends to withdraw some distance. Israel pretended not to see and was on the point of turning into a side alley when Tanzman hailed him.

"Young Israel, wait a moment. . . ." he said with steely formality. Israel stopped and turned. Tanzman advanced with a new kind of menacing gait he had acquired.

"Do you see leper's scabs on my face that you avoid me?"

"No. You seemed occupied with your friends."

Tanzman looked at him hard. "Your father, the others, they didn't believe what you told them did they? But I do. I have eyes and ears. I can put two and two together."

"So? What do you want of me?"

"My pistol. Remember?"

"How could I forget!"

"Good. I want it back."

"Shimon!"

Tanzman raised his hand. "Don't argue. The gun is mine. Just give it back. Tonight. You see I too have my intelligence. I know what will happen and when. We'll not be slaughtered like sheep, Israel. We'll fight!"

"'We'? Who are you talking about? You're crazy!"

"We are who we are. Tonight then. One more thing, Israel. Rest in peace. That pistol will never be fired until Jewish blood is spilt. I'm not crazy."

On a morning commemorating the day Reb Mendle passed away, Solomon, Rimkin, Israel and a group of other men went to the Wailing Wall for an early prayer. Rimkin also wanted to remember in his prayers a deceased aunt he had been very fond of, and who had left him a tidy little sum before he departed for the Holy Land. It was a pleasant morning. A strip of light along the top of the wall illuminated the crevices and chased away the gloomy shadows, so that in those intense moments of prayer the shrine invited joy rather than tears. After the prayers the group split: some returned home, while Kor the giant together with a wispy cousin of his who had arrived in Jerusalem in the spring, joined Solomon, Israel and Rimkin for a stroll through the bazaars. The souks were crowded, it being the day before the Moslem Sabbath. On Thursday mornings fresh brown eggs, with bits of feather still clinging to them, were brought from Silwan, from Abu Tor or from Mount Scopus, and laid out on the stalls. There were hens for sale, black, brown, or speckled white, trussed up on the ground by the stalls. The smell of rosemary and thyme stirred the appetite. The bazaars of Jerusalem were divided into specialized souks: any housewife knew where to buy eggs, or spices, nuts and almonds, or vegetables and fruit. A good housewife could tell at a glance from which village came this cheese or these gherkins and egg plants. Passing from one souk to the other was like moving from one province to the next, each with its own colours, smells, tastes, and sounds, by which a blind man born and bred in the Holy City could tell exactly where he was.

Solomon was enjoying the stroll. His eye fell on a stall laden with fruit—plums, and grapes from Hebron which were renowned for their honey-colour and sweetness. He thought how happy Ada would be if he bought a small bunch for her, even though she would rebuke him for spending money on things that were not really necessary.

There was a calming rhythm about the noise of the souk. A man who lived in the city could tell at once from the pitch of the noise, if there was trouble anywhere. Today, however, all was quiet, the sounds were ordinary and reassuring, and the Jews were greeted with courtesy and with smiles. It was that mood which prompted Israel to suggest they went to the Damascus Gate, outside which a livestock fair was held every Thursday morning. Solomon's eyes lit up. "Why not? It's not often we go there," he said. Kor pushed his hat back and scratched his head. "Reb Pfeifer bought a jackass at the fair only two weeks ago, and he's been cheated, so he thinks."

Rimkin laughed. "That'll be the day, when Pfeifer is cheated over a donkey."

"The animal is as fine looking as any you could see, but stubborn and ill-mannered as a Russian mujik," Kor said. "How in heaven's name is one to know, until the beast is home and put to work?" He himself was dreaming of buying a mule and starting a small haulage business.

"Yes, let's go to the Damascus Gate then," Rimkin decided with enthusiasm, and seeing that Solomon was still casting hesitant glances at the Hebron grapes on the stall, he went over and bought a good size bunch. "Why not," he laughed, "let the stomach be gladdened as well as the eye." He picked off a grape and popped it in to his mouth, winked in appreciation and offered the bunch around.

A large crowd filled the wide space outside the Gate. The weekly fair here was a popular event: peasants came from near and far villages, driving before them sheep, goats, any animal they wished to sell. Beduin tribesmen from the Judean wilderness also came, bringing their camels and even rarer beasts of burden which they had plundered either from other tribes or from wayfarers. In the little huts erected for the day, or in the darkened alcoves inside the walls, men sat together drinking coffee and smoking, exchanging news and making deals.

The fair was already in full swing. Hundreds of animals of all colours and description filled the fairground. The rumble of their bleating and braying rolled into the city through the crowded gate. Beduin had set up small camps on the periphery of the fair; their horses, unsaddled, stood flicking their tails by the tents. At the Gate itself, beggars, blind or crippled milled around, rattling their begging bowls, and making pitiful cries.

"Let's go and look at some of the horses for sale," Israel said.

"Mules are more practical," Kor chimed in lugubriously.

"I've always wondered whether it's not cheaper to buy a sheep and have the butcher slaughter it for you rather than buy meat from him," said Rimkin and popped the last grape into his mouth.

The stylized cry of a *tamarindi* vendor as he wielded his long-necked brass jar bedecked with green and red beads and tassles, made Solomon feel thirsty. The vendor was singing that on a hot day there was nothing more refreshing than chilled juice of desert dates. He sang and swung his jar from side to side, and clicked the china tumblers he was holding in his free hand.

"Don't drink that. Who knows what awful stuff the Ishmaelites put in it," Rimkin cautioned.

Solomon laughed. "Just look at them, they don't look unhealthy to me, your Ishmaelites", he said.

"Look at the cripples and the blind. . . ."

"They don't buy tamarindi, they can't afford it. If they did, who knows, they mightn't have been cripples."

"We're not made like them," Rimkin said and looked away.

"Let's see if we're not" Solomon replied, and hailed the vendor who looked surprised that a Jew wanted to buy his tamarindi.

"Solomon, Solomon, always experimenting, never satisfied to accept the collective wisdom of our people," Rimkin laughed as he watched the dark brown liquid spout in a long arc from the jar into the tumbler with not a drop spilt.

"Look," said Kor, pointing over their heads towards the gate. "Look what's going on there."

"Khalili," said the tamarindi vendor without looking, meaning Hebronites.

The agitation swelled, spilt out of the great Damascus Gate, retracted into it, and spilt out again. It was like a swarm of insects buzzing around, growing bigger with every moment. There were shouts and wails, but as yet no violence, and the few Ottoman gendarmes who were present looked on with interest but without alarm. In a while crowds from the livestock fair began to surge towards the gate. The gendarmes showed some nervousness; they made ready to shut the gate if necessary.

"Shouldn't we get out of here?" Rimkin said.

"Let's find out what's happening first," Israel suggested. Thoughts of Abdullah, of what Pach had told him in Bab el Whad, rushed through his mind. "What if they shut the Gate and we are caught outside . . ." Rimkin said anxiously.

"If we move in with the crowd who knows we don't end up in the kishle and from there there's no escape," said Solomon.

While they were deliberating what to do Israel slunk away and soon returned with snatches of information he had gathered from passers-by. He was excited. The trouble had started at the Jaffa Gate, where the agitation was even greater, he told his friends. "I'm not sure what is really going on, except that it has to do with Hebron. Anyway Reb Eliezer's right. We'd better go back quickly and make straight for home."

Towards noon the Haham Bashi's man brought the news to the rest of the Jews. There was trouble in Hebron.

Nothing to do with the Jews, and that was a relief. It seemed a local chieftain and his large clan had rebelled against the authority of the Ottomans, beat up a great number of officials, imprisoned some, and evicted the small garrison from town. Now the grieved Hebronites had come with a delegation to the Governor of Jerusalem, asking him to come immediately to Hebron with troops, and restore order. Since many people in Jerusalem had close ties with Hebron, the news caused a great amount of agitation. The Governor, meanwhile, was weighing up what to do. He had a natural disinclination for action. But, the Haham Bashi's man explained, Hebron was no small village, and apart from it being an important source of revenue, here was a challenge to his authority the Governor couldn't ignore. "So what's he waiting for?" Israel asked. His question annoyed the Haham Bashi's man who didn't think it was proper for a youth to speak before his elders. He declined to reply. Solomon repeated his son's question.

"He's an Ottoman," the man replied contemptuously. "So he thinks very slowly. Also, he wants to be begged." There was a long silence during which Solomon wondered how all this would affect them. Then the Haham's man spoke again, with noticeable concern, "God knows what will become of our brethren in Hebron." He rolled his eyes. "Abu Ammar of Hebron is a hard-hearted man. Often he torments our people just for the fun of it. Rabbi Hazan, who knows him well is worried, very worried."

After the Governor had received what he considered a sufficient number of petitions, and not a small number of bribes and promises of more remunerations, he had the troops under his command mustered, and prepared to ride to Hebron to restore his authority there. He had every reason to be pleased. The Arab notables of Hebron, who were affected by the insurrection, together with their kinsmen in Jerusalem, had written a pledge that they would cover the cost of the expedition and reward the Governor personally as well. He was on the point of retiring anyway. What did he care about the endless squabbles of his subjects, unless they provided an extra source of revenue for him?

The garrison numbered some three companies of cavalry, one regular, and two made up of bashi bazooks. There was also a rag-tag collection of foot soldiers armed with muskets. Leaving only a small squadron in the city, the Governor passed before his troops on the esplanade in front of the Jaffa Gate. They looked more like a collection of convicts than soldiers. Each one was dressed and armed differently from his friend. A crowd gathered to cheer. The drummers drummed a roll. The Governor, astride a fat dappled horse, waved his hand and gave the sign to move. Judging from his expression, he didn't expect his departure from the city to last more than a day, he looked confident and slightly bored.

The notables of Jerusalem and Hebron smiled to one another and waved him goodbye. As the Governor and his bashi bazooks moved out, Israel let his gaze wander to a thick knot of people close by. He saw three men push their way in as if to get a better view. They came to a halt beside two men Israel recognized as officials of the Kadi. The three stood there looking on. Then casually, two of them put their hands over the officials' mouths. There was movement: Israel caught sight of knives. The strangers slit the officials' throats and held them upright for a moment before letting go. No one seemed to notice. One of the assailants looked about him and met Israel's eyes. He grinned and passed his hand across his neck. In a moment they were lost in the crowd. Israel thought of Tanzman up there on the roof of a house in the Jewish Quarter, with his friends, keeping watch, the pistol hidden in the folds of his coat. He wanted to run. His legs felt heavy and unsteady. He wished he could understand who was fighting whom. Where was it safe to be when slow murder can pass unnoticed in daylight, in a familiar place where he walked daily? The only thing he could think of was to be among people he knew, his people. Even Tanzman.

The sign for the uprising was given by the voice of the muezzin calling the faithful to prayer from the minaret by the El Aksa Mosque. At that moment, armed Arabs with veiled faces attacked the soldiers who were about to close the city's gates, and cut their throats. The gates were thrown open, a torch was lit and hung on the lintels. Within minutes hordes of mounted Beduin and men from the hill villages came galloping into the city. Shots were fired, there was much shouting. The Jews sat still in the darkness of their houses and prayed fearfully. Soon the citadel was taken. The soldiers surrendered to save their lives. But they were either shot or lanced to death to a man. When the rebels completed the occupation of Jerusalem they locked the gates, manned all the vital positions on the walls and in the citadel, and waited for the Governor to return.

In the early hours of the morning the Governor appeared before the Jaffa Gate, crestfallen and dishevelled. His troops took up firing positions. The men on the walls laughed and jeered. From a safe distance, the Governor began to scream threats, his thin barks of rage were greeted with louder laughter and obscene gestures. At last the Arabs in the citadel managed to manipulate a cannon to a firing position and fired one shell which landed on the crenellation of the wall, well short of target, and caused a fearful havoc among the rebels. But this was as much as the Governor could take. Scrambling on to his horse, he signalled the retreat and withdrew in a great hurry. Jerusalem was finally in the hands of the rebels who celebrated their victory by firing rifle volleys into the air. For the next two days, while Jerusalem waited to see how its new rulers would behave, hardly a person stirred in the streets. There was looting but not nearly as much as had been feared. Then, with a resilience born of generation upon generation of violence and upheaval, the city of cities began to return to normal life.

Chapter 14

Jerusalem turned her back on her new rulers and somehow continued to function on her own. No one knew who they were, who the real power was behind the new faces which were now seen in the office rooms of the deposed Governor, in the citadel. The Kishle was emptied of its old prisoners except the hard criminals, but soon filled with new ones. No one knew—least of all the Jews—what the new rulers wanted and what they intended doing. It was said in the alleys of the souks that the burghers of the city had made common cause with the peasants of the nearby villages to rebel against the heavy-handed taxation of the Governor. But who were those burghers? And since when were they able to unite among themselves in a common cause, let alone with the peasant—Fallahin—whom they held in contempt?

Solomon, like some of the others, asked these questions as he watched the comings and goings of those who now held the city's destiny in their hands. Groups of Jerusalem merchants and landowners seldom seen together before were meeting daily in the courts of justice. There were strangers in command of the citadel—some said warriors from the Abu Gosh tribe who habitually preyed on travellers passing by their hilly redoubt. Most conspicuous of all, were the Beduin, led by a grey-bearded lean and tall sheik with a fierce, aristocratic face.

These disparate groups, drawn together by an inscrutable common interest, contrived or conspired to keep the city going and give the citizens a feeling of order and security.

"It can't last," Solomon told the men. "All they wanted was some concessions. Now they're landed with the entire city on their hands. Soon they'll fall out with one another, and the worst will come about."

"What's that Reb Solomon Zeff?"

"Chaos. Nothing's worse than chaos. Any order however oppressive is better than that."

"What must we do?"

Solomon shrugged his shoulders. "We can do nothing. Except keep quiet and hope for the best."

"Jerusalem", said Rimkin wistfully, "is like a desirable woman who cannot remain without a man for long, she craves to be possessed. Those who have her now are usurpers, they don't know what to do with her, and she will not respond to them. But a husband will come and redeem her before long, you'll see."

Ada laughed. "How filth, neglect, disease, and poverty can make anything desirable, let alone a woman, is beyond my understanding, Reb Eliezer. But then men have such strange tastes."

"Everything, my dear Ada, is in the eye of the beholder, as it is said."

"Oh," said Ada and smiled tight-mouthed, "I must be blind then."

Israel too could not think of Jerusalem as a woman, desirable or otherwise. But Reb Eliezer's parable stirred uncomfortable memories of passages in the Bible he and the boys in his class used to pour over surreptitiously, passages like the rape of Tamar, or Lot's seduction by his daughters. That had been a year or more ago, almost before the vision of a woman's naked body began to haunt him. It never reminded him of Jerusalem's dank crevices and dark alleys or anything but sweet tantalizing softness, full of strange power which moved in rhythmic persistence; an image of a woman he wanted to touch yet was afraid of. He remembered the verse from Proverbs: "There be three things which are too wonderful for me, yea, four which I know not: The way of an eagle in the air, the way of a serpent upon a rock; the way of a ship in the midst of the sea; and the way of a man with a maid." Yes, most particularly the last. The others he had seen and wondered at. But this the most wonderful and mysterious experience of all, still awaited him.

Tanzman had killed a man and that had added years to his life. But had he ever had his way with a maid? Would he ever? He thought of Sheine without excitement. Placid Sheine who smelt of starch and almonds, who might be his wife as his father had arranged. "In the dark, it's all the same, beauty counts for nothing," he remembered Pach saying to him. "The rhythm, the welcoming, that's what makes a good union." Israel sighed; his desire, if desire it was, could not connect with Sheine but hovered about restlessly searching for a womanly form he could only dream of.

The Beduin who came to Jerusalem brought with them horses such as Israel had never seen before. Noble animals they were who walked with a light step as though floating above the ground. Their necks were sleek and powerful, their flanks quivered under the touch of light. The wind seemed to pass through their red flared nostrils. They were, Israel thought, nature's most perfect creation—living vessels of lightning. Often outside the Jaffa Gate, he would see them corralled together or tethered in a line to a long horizontal beam outside the citadel. The Beduin handled them caressingly; they would pass their hands over the animals' necks, withers, and flanks. Israel watched them and envied. He would've given his soul to get near, to touch such horses.

Of all these heavenly horses none was so noble, so beautiful as the mare which belonged to the Beduin Chieftain with the grey beard. She was black and shiny. Her head was small and held high. When she turned to look at something her ears would prick and her nostrils flare out ruby-red. The Beduin Sheik loved her more than he loved anything or anybody, so the Arabs were saying. When he rode her through the streets of Jerusalem everybody would stop to look: it was as though a mythic hero had come to life in their midst.

Israel liked to hang about just to catch a glimpse of the mare whenever he could. The Beduin got used to seeing him. They would laugh and beckon him to approach, or shout at him Wald el mut, Ibn is Sabbit—Child of Death, Son of Sabbath, which were names for a Jew. Sometimes they threw stones at him depending on what mood they were in. Samuel Rimkin often accompanied him, for he too, admired the horses and as with so many other subjects, young Rimkin would expound on the merit of the different horses, their breeding and their qualities, as though he were an expert.

"They call her Baraka Luck, in Arabic," he said in a matter-of-fact voice. Israel pretended he knew. "She's faster than all the other horses, no horse from here to Damascus, or anywhere can beat her" he said. Samuel gave him a side glance. "I've heard", he said, "that this mare is descended from the horse Al Bourak, on which their Prophet Mohammed rode to heaven. Of course, this is nonsense, simple-minded stuff. They're like children with their tales and they make them up so that their horses would be more valuable in the market place." He gave a snort of a laugh.

"The Sheik would never even dream of selling such a mare. You know nothing about Arabs or about horses, nothing at all," Israel said dismissively.

Samuel hated being told that he knew nothing about anything, particularly when this was said in anger which he considered an inferior emotion. His mouth curled into a disdainful smile, he said, in the quietest voice he could manages, "Tsz tsz tsz . . . you make such a thing of them and their horses. I'm beginning to wonder if you're not a bit simple-minded yourself. Our forefathers. . . ." Samuel prepared to quote.

"Oh shut up," Israel said and gave him a push. Samuel's pale eyes looked coldly at Israel. "I tell you, there's nothing an Ishmaelite won't sell if the price is right. And I'll tell you another thing. A horse is a creature of beauty and power. But give me a donkey, like Pfeifer's any day. Now there's a fine animal to ride. . . ."

"Go ride a broomstick, that's the only thing you could ride!" Israel sneered.

"Is that so! Well, we shall see . . ."

Pfiefer's donkey was indeed a splendid beast, young, bigger than most donkeys, and well proportioned. Heavy burdens and the drab routine of work had not yet dulled its gaze. Its back was straight and dove grey divided by a shiny strip of black which ran from its neck all the way to the base of its tail. Pfeifer had paid a small fortune for it, and although the animal was stubborn and difficult to handle Pfeifer loved it dearly. Absalom was the name he gave the donkey, it had a voice that could have brought down the walls of Jericho; no one could mistake it for the braying of any other donkey in Jerusalem.

Pfeifer kept Absalom tied to a withered tree in his courtyard. There it stood, his huge penis erect and drumming on its belly. The children used to stare and giggle. On several occasions, delegations of pious women came to Solomon and Rimkin to protest that such a lewd sight was an abomination, an embarrassment to women and a source of corruption to the young. Solomon laughed, but Rimkin took it upon himself to talk to Pfeifer. He urged him, in the interest of the community either to sell Absalom or have him gelded. But Pfeifer would not hear of either. "Reb Eliezer," he pleaded, "have you ever seen such a beautiful donkey? Why, imagine, if we had our Temple—may it be rebuilt in our days—would I not bring Absalom to the High Priest on the Feast of Pentecost? And you want me to maim this perfect animal!"

"Reb Pfeifer, what nonsense you talk."

"Reb Eliezer, you have your wisdom and I have my Absalom. Leave me be," Pfeifer said, and that was the end of it.

On the second Friday of the Feast of Ramadan, news reached Jerusalem that the Sultan Selim had moved to put an end to the usurpation of the Holy City. He had commanded, according to the news, Pasha Abdullah of Acre to take Jerusalem and return her to Ottoman rule.

The thought of Abdullah in possession of Jerusalem struck terror in the hearts of all, particularly the Jews. "It shows the European powers don't care what happens to Jerusalem," Rimkin moaned. He had just agreed to postpone the official engagement of his daughter Sheine to Israel until the situation cleared up, for better or for worse.

The Arabs prepared for the defence of the city. All day long they were working on parts of the walls where time and neglect had taken their toll. Rimkin observed this and remarked, "Abdullah will never take Jerusalem. The defences are strong and the people are resolute." He heaved a sigh: "Of the two evils, better the one we already know," which prompted Solomon that evening to broach to his son the subject they had both been avoiding: the inevitable union of the two families.

On the Friday all the Moslems held a day of prayer and fasting at the El Aksa Mosque. The Jews, mindful of growing tensions and of the unloving allies' holy day, subdued their activities and generally kept out of sight.

Solomon, who had been idle for weeks, took the opportunity to work on a gilded crown for the Torah scroll which he had undertaken to complete before the High Holy days. Soon after breakfast he emerged from his workshop and called for Israel. "Here's some money. Go to the Armenian smith by the Church and buy me some beaten brass and a roll of copper foil," he told him.

"And on the way back call on Hannah Rimkin, ask her if she could spare some flour for the dumplings I want to cook for the Sabbath meal. And don't be too long about it," Ada said.

The shortest route to the Armenian Quarter would have taken him no more than a few minutes' walk at a brisk pace. The silence was all pervasive. Only on a few occasions before had he seen the city in such a charged repose. He decided to walk to the gate opening on to Mount Zion from the top of which he could see the sweep of Kidron and the forbidden area of the Temple, then cut across the now empty souks and arrive at the Armenian Quarter on the way back, passing Jaffa Gate and the Citadel. He hoped the horses would be there, by the citadel, or grazing outside the gate on the hillside. If he were lucky, he would see the black mare there too.

His mind was relaxed, ready for impressions but not for serious thought. He reached the gate at Mount Zion, climbed the steps to the wall and stood there, letting the sweep of dun and blue merge into a haze before his half-shut eyes. The hot breeze fanned his face. From the Muristan came the pulsating hum of prayers. He could see the Moslem worshippers move across the paved space of the compound.

"Israel!"

Tanzman was looking at him from the alley below, shading his eyes with his hand. "Come on up," he called. Holding the hem of his coat, Tanzman bounded up the steps. He smelt of sweat. "I shall never tire of this view," Israel said. "No wonder they say God favours this city above all others."

"If only a fire could come from heaven and burn those Ishmaelites," hissed Tanzman through gritted teeth.

"You won't let up, will you? What's the point of all this hatred, Shimon? Look at them, they're praying, just as we do. Are there no good and just men among them? Doesn't God listen to them just as He listens to us?"

"That's blasphemy," Tanzman blurted.

Israel felt that if he provoked Tanzman enough, his friend was quite capable of hurling him down from the walls in his fury.

"Tell me, Shimon," he said, "just so that I understand you, what have they ever done to you that you hate them so much?"

"You ask?" said Tanzman, taking a small step back. "Do you have to ask?" And when Israel didn't answer but held his gaze, Tanzman exhaled noisily and began shaking his head. "I'll tell you. It's not that they are Arabs and Moslems. That makes not the slightest difference. What counts is that we are Jews. And because we're Jews and they are *goyim* they are our enemy."

"But Shimon. . . ."

"Wait. I didn't say enemy for ever. May be that too, maybe not. But enemy until we've shown them we too can hurt and kill. Until they understand that there can be no transgression against us without retribution. No coming together except as equals. No, not even then. Enemies they'll be to us. Always. If you don't hate your enemy he destroys you."

"There's no hope for people like you! We're taught that Jerusalem is a city of love. . . ." He searched his memory for a quotation.

"Love and hate are not very far apart," Tanzman said darkly.

"I gave you back your pistol. You said you needed the sword to defend us. What happened? Nothing. No one harmed us."

"There was an uprising wasn't there?"

"Yes, but . . ."

"It's best to be prepared, always. Best to have a weapon. Luckily nothing happened, *this time*." He spat out the emphasis, "But a true watchman never slumbers on his watch. Thanks be to God that nothing happened this time. But the sword is ready, and I shall unsheath it when the time comes. It'll be a great occasion, you'll see."

"May I never live to see the day," said Israel. All of a sudden he was angry. He felt ready to confront Tanzman even with violence, no matter what the outcome. "You're mad," he shouted at him. "All I want is a peaceful walk and you plague me with your hatred and your madness. Go away. Be like those you hate. Kill somebody. Only keep away from me, now and always."

Tanzman looked hurt. "Why do you talk to me like that, you of all people?" he said. "Why does everybody treat me as though I were a murderer or a bandit? Must it always be that those who see the truth are persecuted? Do you think it's for myself that I worry?"

"Go away Tanzman, and leave me in peace. I don't care if you're right or wrong. I just want to enjoy today without you breathing doom and hatred all over me."

Tanzman lowered his head. He scuffed the dust with his toe, searching for something to say. Then he shrugged his heavy shoulders and sighed. "Very well, enjoy your day." He turned and walked briskly down the steps.

Israel waited until Tanzman had disappeared, then came down from the wall himself. But as he began his walk down the hill, there was Tanzman waiting for him round the next corner.

"Look," Tanzman said, "let's not quarrel. We've always understood one another in the past. Must it all end now?"

"I don't want to quarrel with you, Shimon, only . . ."

"Don't say another word, let's forget it."

Tanzman held out his hand. What could Israel do but accept it?

"Let me walk with you. We'll go and watch the horses."

"I have an errand to do."

"I'll come with you. I wanted to go for a walk anyway."

"All right, we can watch the horses for a moment or two, there's time for that."

The space in front of the Citadel where the horses were often kept was empty. Two armed Arabs were sitting by the open gate, playing backgammon. Except for a quick look they paid no attention to the two Jews who passed through the gate and stood facing the open field that rolled down towards a shallow ravine above which the dusty road to Jaffa twisted. The horses were in the field, grazing, about a dozen of them. Some had their forelegs hobbled by a stretch of rope tied to the fetlocks. Others roamed freely. The black mare was there too. She was the first to notice the two men standing at the gate. She raised her magnificent head and watched them for a moment, ears pricked. Then she turned, sniffed the air and curled her upper lip, baring her teeth. She parted her hind legs and pissed. After that she resumed grazing.

"I wish we could make them gallop, I love to see them move, the mare in particular," Israel said.

"On a day like this, they deserve a rest too," Tanzman said, "Do you think you could ride a horse like that?" Israel gave him a wistful look. "Maybe. After a lot of practice I suppose. I'd like to try. Wouldn't you?"

Tanzman pulled a face, "No. I like to feel the ground under my feet. Only then I'm confident. I reckon I can move as fast as I want to on my own two legs."

"You mean if God had meant you to run as fast as a horse he'd have given you four legs, I know."

"Something like that," Tanzman said, and laughed. "Israel."

"Yes?"

"Do you realize how lucky you are?"

"Why do you say that?"

Tanzman was looking in the direction of the road above the rim of the hill. Now he turned his gaze on his friend. There was an innocence about him which surprised and moved Israel.

"You have your life before you. Wife, family, honour, everything a man could want."

"All of which could be your lot as well, Shimon."

Tanzman swallowed. "What do I have? I have no one who could speak for me. Do you think someone like Reb Rimkin would for a moment think of me as a son-in-law? Never. What prospects do I have except . . ."

"There's no one braver or stronger than you Shimon."

"Strength, courage. What are these compared to . . ." he stopped. Then suddenly he said in a flat, dead voice, "I carry the mark of Cain. A fugitive and a vagabond I shall be. . . ."

"Shimon, listen to me. I was angry with you, and I spoke harshly. But the man you killed, it was in self-defence. That doesn't turn you into Cain."

Tanzman shut his eyes. "It's not just that. It's the way I am. I look at Rimkin and I can see in his eyes how he sees me. It's the tough loners I attract. Only they trust me. We're like a pack of wolves." His voice trailed off. "Even Cain didn't die in loneliness, he had a wife and children," he said under his breath.

It was rare for Tanzman to show signs of vulnerability, but he quickly recovered his composure. "Look," he said cheerfully, "why don't you go and ride that mare. I know you want to."

"What, just like that, with those two Arabs at the gate?"

"Oh, don't worry about them. They're playing backgammon. I'll keep watch."

"But I can't ride her, not without a saddle and bridle! God knows what she'd do if I as much as got near her."

"There's only one way to find out. Unless of course, you're afraid. . . ."

"I am that too," Israel had to confess.

"Go on, go up to her, stroke her, see what happens," Tanzman urged.

"If I should . . ." Israel said as if to himself, as he began to tremble all over.

"Go on!" said Tanzman and gave him a gentle push.

He started walking down the field. The horses raised their heads and moved away. The black mare stood facing him, her ears pricked. "Baraka, Baraka," Israel whispered and stretched out his hand. The mare laid back her ears and trotted away, neck arched, tail flexed. When she stopped, Israel again advanced. "Slower, slower," Tanzman shouted. The third time Israel approached, the mare stood still. He reached her, stretched out his hand. She was all taut but extended her neck to sniff at his outstretched hand. He could feel her warm breath on his fingers. Then the awful roar of a donkey's bray suddenly tore the silence; it was the loudest most brutish sound Israel had ever heard any animal make. The mare shot up in the air. Her front hooves flashed close to his face. He fell sideways, grazing his head on a rock. The blow stunned him momentarily. Then, still lying on the ground, he saw the mare gallop up the field. Close by the wall, not far from where Tanzman stood was Samuel Rimkin astride Pfeifer's donkey. The donkey was braying so hard his stomach moved like a bellow and all the while his erect black penis was lashing about. All at once he started bucking. In an instant he had thrown Samuel off and was careering down towards the mare.

Israel let out a loud cry. Through his tears he saw the scuffle of the two animals, heard the screams of the mare. The donkey mounted her and bit into her back as he thrust into her with all his might.

Israel got to his feet and raced up the hill. By the time he reached the path which ran close to the wall, Samuel had picked himself up and come running towards Tanzman. He was bruised and shaken. Tanzman paid not the slightest attention to him; his eyes were fixed on the animals. When Samuel saw Israel come at him, his eyes opened wide and his jaw dropped. "For God's sake . . ." he mumbled. With all the force of his rage Israel hit him straight in the mouth. Samuel staggered. "You idiot!" Israel screamed, "You mindless stupid fool." And he pitched into him. Tanzman grabbed hold of the combatants, one with each hand, and pulled them apart as easily as if they were two pups. "Shame, shame, that two Jews should fight when the Amalekite is upon us. And you two, more than anybody, should be friends," he rebuked them stentoriously. When Israel at last became aware of Samuel's puffed-up frightened face, his fury abated; he was faced with the futility of his assault, for now he saw that the Arabs, the "Amalekite" had issued forth out of the gate, weapons in hand. They made no move, just stood there looking.

"I'll overlook this outburst," Samuel said smoothing his clothes and touching his face where Israel had hit him.

"Shake hands and forgive," Tanzman commanded. He pulled them together by the scruff of their necks so vigorously that they shook like fronds of palm. At that moment Pfeifer's donkey attempted to mount the Sheik's prize mare a second time. The two Arabs at the gate stood motionless, staring with horror.

"It was so easy, until the beast saw his fellow beasts, those wretched horses . . . I wanted to show you. . . ." Samuel began. "Leave off now," Israel said in a half-whisper. He was mesmerized by the frozen stance of the Arabs. He had a sudden premonition of violence. He could see it in his mind's eye, terrible and inexorable, and he could say nothing to warn Tanzman and Samuel.

Then the shot rang out. They could hear the smack the bullet made as it hit the donkey in the side. Tanzman jumped as though he himself had been hit.

"Oh my God, Pfeifer's donkey's dead, look at him, oh God, what shall I do now. . . ." Samuel began to wail.

Israel caught the eye of the two Arabs. Stupefaction had given way to hatred. They didn't level their guns but drew daggers. They let out a loud cry and a string of curses and brandishing the curved blades advanced at a run on the petrified Jews. Tanzman spun round to face the attackers. "Run, run to the Zion Gate and go hide at home. I'll take care of these," he shouted. But Israel couldn't move, his legs would not obey him. Samuel was tearing at his sleeve. "Come, quickly. You heard what he said." When Israel still wouldn't move, Samuel hit him with the flat of his hand on his cheek and left at a run as fast as his legs could carry him.

"Go! You're no use to me here," Tanzman barked as he braced himself to meet the Arabs' charge.

He wanted to run but couldn't move. Hiding terrifed, behind a buttress of the wall, he saw the Arabs bear down on Tanzman. Like rams, the three men were locked in a deadly fight. One moment they were massed together, the next they were parted only to clash again. It seemed to Israel as if they were not fighting for their lives but performing a kind of mortal and primitive ritual dance, the motion of which beckoned him to join. But he could no more move forward into the fray than he could turn and run.

Then they were on the ground, writhing and grunting in the dust. At last, it was the two Arabs who rose: Tanzman remained down, on knees and elbows, listing over to one side as though a part of him had collapsed. Israel saw bloodied daggers in the Arabs' hands. They stood over Tanzman exhausted, a solemn expression on their faces—they might have been paying him tribute. Then one put his arm round the other supporting him as they walked back to the gate.

Israel ran to Tanzman who was still in the same position, motionless. "Shimon, Shimon, get up. They're gone," he sobbed helplessly. Tanzman let out a groan. There was blood in his mouth, on his hands, and in the dust in front of him. His face was drained of life. Taking him by the shoulders Israel hauled him up into a sitting position. Now he saw the blood bubbling in the torn cloth of his coat. "Dear God, oh dear God," he whimpered.

"Take me home. . . ." he heard Tanzman rasp. Somehow he got him to his feet, put his arm round his waist to hold him steady, for Tanzman was tottering. Then taking his friend's weight on his shoulder moved along with him.

A band of armed Beduin gathered at the entrance to the Jewish Quarter, cutting it off. They were angry, as though violence were simmering. They were waiting for something . . . or someone.

Israel had come home, covered in Tanzman's blood, and told them what had happened. Now they were on the roof: he, Solomon, Rimkin, a few other men, watching the Beduin below.

"If I'd stayed with him . . . maybe this wouldn't have happened. . . . I could have explained to those Arabs. . . ." Helplessness, shame, and remorse overwhelmed him. He was crying again. "Now Shimon will die. All because —"

Still watching the street below Solomon said, "Israel, you're a man now. It's no use saying I should've done this or that. Tanzman's not dead. But what we have on our hands now could be far worse than his injuries. So don't waste time crying about what you might have done. Keep a clear head. Or go down to your mother."

His father's dispassionate tone was like cold water thrown at his face. He sat in silence, smarting under the rebuke. After a while his self-possession returned to him: sharper than ever, and cool. He walked over to another part of the roof in search of his own observation post, away from his father. From here, he was the first to see the old Arab who lived close by and was friendly to the Jews, come running to report what he had seen and heard.

Sheik Abu Ra'aba had slain the mare Baraka with his own hands. Despoiled by a donkey belonging to a Jew, she was no longer a priceless possession but a mark of shame. He wouldn't see her foal a mule, and be the laughing stock of all the desert Beduin: "Father of the Mule", they'd call him. His tribesmen wanted revenge. But Abu Ra'aba was no hot head. In his younger days he had fought many battles and buried many of his kinsmen killed in his service. Besides, it was Ramadan, when violence was forbidden. At that very moment he was washing his hands and feet in the fountain outside El Aksa, and praying for divine guidance.

The Jews began to barricade their homes.

Gunshots rang out. The Beduin increased their commotion. Crouched in his position, Israel saw Sheik Abu Ra'aba arrive, and be immediately surrounded by his men. He could tell from the Sheik's expression what decision he had reached. Abu Ra'aba drew his sword. "Now he'll shout 'Aliehum!' and they'll come at us," Israel thought. But the Sheik hesitated. The respected Mufti Husseini, whom Israel at once recognized from his red-topped turban and flowing white beard, appeared at his side and started talking to him. The Mufti, although contemptuous of all unbelievers, including Jews, was known as a scholar of renown and a mild-natured man who abhorred violence. The Sheik listened, impatience stamped on his face. Yet something the Mufti said appeared to make him consider. He turned back to speak to one of his men. The latter presently stepped forward and called out to the Jews to come and talk.

"I'll go," Solomon said. He motioned to Binderman and Kor to come with him.

"Father! Let me come too." It came spontaneously, before he could think. Binderman began to protest.

"Let him come," Solomon said.

The Sheik would not look at them but spoke through one of his men. It was Ramadan, he said. He would be lenient. He didn't want innocent people hurt. Only one thing he desired; that the man responsible for the outrage answer for his deed. They knew who he was; the Sheik had been told how in the past he had been a source of trouble. That man—wounded though he was—must be handed over to the custody of the Mufti to be tried and judged like a common criminal. Only on that condition would the Sheik relent and call off his men.

Israel looked at his father. Solomon's face betrayed no emotion. In a calm voice he told the Sheik that his condition would be considered and he would shortly have their answer. The Sheik's man accompanied them halfway. He stood leaning against the wall of a house to await their reply.

"Go inside, Israel. Tell the others to get off the roof and bolt the doors and windows," Solomon said.

A group of men now joined him in front of the house. Some of them were Tanzman's friends. Rimkin was there too. Solomon said: "The Sheik wants Tanzman, or he will attack. I say on no account do we surrender one of our people to their mercy. Tanzman is no murderer nor a criminal. We know when to yield. This is not the time for that."

The men nodded their approval. Rimkin put his hand on Israel's shoulder. "Be proud of your father today, as I am. I shall never forget, if I live to see another day. Hurry now. Go inside."

For once, Israel disobeyed his father. Instead of going inside, he joined the ranks of the men who now squared up to the Arabs, armed with sticks and rocks. Then, with a mighty cry, the Arabs charged. Above the din he heard his father's voice, shouting to his men not to break rank. Sword in hand, Sheik Ra'aba led the attack. He went straight for Solomon. But before he reached him Solomon was hit by a large rock which felled him. Israel ran to his father and threw himself over his body just as Abu Ra'aba leapt over them to attack another target. Kor was there, in the thick of the fighting, hitting out in all directions, scattering his attackers like chaff.

Then, all at once, Sheik Ra'aba called a halt to the fighting. He was looking beyond the fray, towards the narrow road next to the house from which Tanzman's old aunt was emerging. Behind her, four of Tanzman's friends bore on their shoulders a door upon which Tanzman's body lay. The grim procession advanced slowly through the combatants until it reached the Sheik. Then the men lowered the door to the ground. The corpse had been washed clean and dressed in a white nightshirt. But Tanzman's eyes were wide open, staring up at the Sheik's face. Abu Ra'aba looked down at the body. After a moment, he leant over and closed Tanzman's eyes. With that he walked away, followed by his men.

"As for man, his days are as grass; as the flower of the field, so he flourisheth. For the wind passeth over it, and it is gone; and the place thereof shall know it no more. But the loving kindness of the Lord is from everlasting to everlasting upon them that fear him, and his righteousness unto children's children. In the way of righteousness is life; and in the pathway thereof there is no death. And the dust returneth to the earth as it was, but the spirit returneth unto God, who gave it. . . ."

Lefkowitz sang the verse. His voice was pure and strong. He did not weep nor did his voice quaver as he sang, yet all the sadness and the misery that they had experienced seemed sublimated in the simple tune whose words leapt up to the hollow afternoon sky.

They had dug a grave at the edge of the plot on the slope of Mount of Olives, in the Jewish cemetery. Here, grouped together, lay buried generations of Jewish Rabbis. The tombstones were simple and polished by the wind and the sun.

"Reflect upon three things and thou wilt not come within the power of sin: know whence thou comest, wither thou art going, and before whom thou wilt in future have to give account and reckoning. Whence thou camest, from a fetid drop, wither thou art going, to a place of dust, worms and maggots, and before whom thou wilt in future have to give account and reckoning, before the supreme king of kings, the Holy One, blessed be He."

They lowered the shrouded body into the scarred earth. Then, one by one, Tanzman's friends, who seemed to grow in number with his death, threw handfuls of dust into the grave until the white of the shrouds all but disappeared, spattered as if by dried blood. Since Tanzman had no male next of kin, Eliezer Rimkin recited the Kaddish: "Magnified and sanctified be his great name in the world which he hath created according to his will. May he establish his kingdom during your life and during your days, and during the life of the house of Israel, even speedily and at a near time, and ye say ye Amen. . . . Blessed, praised and glorified, exalted, extolled and honoured, lauded be the name of the Holy One, blessed be he; though he be high above all blessings and hymns, praises and consolations, which are uttered in the world; and say ye Amen. . . . He who maketh peace in his high places, may he make peace for us and for all Israel; and say ye Amen."

The shovels ground into the earth.

"As a young tree is cut down before it had borne fruit, so has Reb Shimon, son of Isaac Tanzman of blessed memory, been cut down and taken from us in the springtime of his manhood," Rimkin eulogized. "May his soul be bound up in the bond of life. Whenever a Jew dies the whole house of Israel mourns, for it is bereft. But Reb Shimon was no ordinary man. . . ." Rimkin paused before his voice gathered force. "His soul was like pure fire, a clear, smokeless flame. His heart knew what his mind often failed to understand. Even in his wrath, even in the heat of his battles, even in his transgressions he kept his innocence. He was as a child, and yet a man. Reb Shimon knew no fear. Not because his heart was hardened but because he trusted in God and was ever ready to sacrifice his life to save our people. . . . In our glorious past we've had many heroes. There was, for example Rabbi Elazaar, brother of Juda the Macabee, who rushed forward against the elephant which carried Antiochus, the Seleucid oppressor of our people who defiled our holy temple, killed the beast and was crushed to death under it. Such pure courage, such dedication and the readiness for sacrifice we have been fortunate to witness in our dear departed Reb Shimon Tanzman. Friends, we have buried today a hero of Israel. . . ."

Incredulous, Israel looked up. Rimkin, carried away by his own rhetoric, seemed oblivious to everything about him. He might have been eulogizing somebody else, someone he had just invented, who was nothing like Tanzman as everybody had known him. Samuel was standing next to his father, his face in rapture. There were tears in his eyes. There were tears in everybody's eyes, except Solomon's. The people hung on every word that came out of Rimkin's mouth; they sighed and sobbed as his voice rose and fell, and held their breath in the tense pauses that broke the cadence of his speech. The shallow mound of dust that was poor Tanzman's grave seemed forgotten. "They don't care at all about Shimon. Least of all Rimkin, who despised him while he was alive. It's an idea they are celebrating, they want a hero, they don't want reality to spoil their dreams," Israel thought. An emptiness invaded him and in its void he heard Rimkin's lugubrious voice intone "The Lord gave, and the Lord hath taken away; blessed be the name of the Lord. And He, being merciful, forgiveth iniquity and destroyeth not; yea, many a time he turneth his anger away, and doth not stir up all his wrath."

For days after Tanzman's funeral Israel was deeply depressed. He went to the house of Tanzman's aunt where she was sitting *shiva*, seven days of mourning, as was the custom, to pay his respect. Twice he went on his own and twice more with Solomon. On each occasion he found Rimkin and Samuel there. It occurred to him that they were there if not all the time then most of the time. It also seemed to him that Rimkin was acting more as a host who accepted messages of condolence than as a visitor. On the second time he went there with his father, he mentioned this after they had left. Solomon gave him a sharp look but said nothing.

"Well, Father, isn't it so?"

Solomon slowed down. "Eliezer Rimkin's a good man. He likes to comfort people, and the poor woman has no one to comfort her, as Tanzman had no kinsman but her." When he saw that his son's face remained set in a hard expression, he added irritably, "Israel, never look askance at any man in envy, nor find faults in him until you are certain of being blameless yourself, which is never. I understand Tanzman had it in his heart to ask for Sheine's hand in marriage, and Rimkin would not have been averse to that except —" Israel stopped dead in his tracks, and Solomon, after walking on a few steps stopped too, and turned to face Israel. "Father, can it be you don't see? Are you blind to what Rimkin's up to? The airs he puts on! He didn't care a groat for Tanzman when he was alive. He thought he was primitive, and a dangerous troublemaker. As for Sheine, if Tanzman had been the only man left in the world, Reb Eliezer would never have agreed to him marrying her. But now, now! Just listen to him! If it hadn't been for that idiot Samuel, Tanzman would've been alive today. . . ."

"Are we all free of guilt for Tanzman's death that you blame Samuel alone? Did he deliberately contrive Tanzman's death?"

His father's defence of Rimkin was worse than stupid; it was a betrayal. Israel was furious. Solomon went on in a quiet, measured voice: "There's no such thing as perfection, not in this world, maybe not in the next world either. You think I'm blind, Israel. Have you yourself grown so wise that you understand everything? I see what I see. I see Rimkin, and I see you. There's good in you and there's good in him, just as there's bad in you both, in different measures and in different ways. It's the good I'm interested in. Rimkin's a good man. He's a friend. His motives are good and flow from generosity. Don't judge him too harshly, Israel or you too will be judged harshly for your weaknesses."

Israel wanted to shout: why so virtuous and understanding about them? What about Tanzman? What about me and what his death means to me? He said nothing. He was tired of conflict, tired of the violence he had seen, and of the burden of shame he was carrying.

"Come, Israel, it's getting late and your mother'll be wondering where we are," Solomon said, and stretched out his hand.

Chapter 15

A sudden turbulence in the east sent spasms of panic through Jerusalem. Peasants from villages on Mount Scopus, the Mount of Olives, and Silwan, were streaming to the city, clamouring at the Dung Gate which was quickly bolted shut by the soldiers of the garrison.

The people of Jerusalem rushed to the walls to see what was happening, for rumours were spreading in the souks that an assault no lesser than another crusade was underway: Jerusalem took her images of disaster from her past; her alleys were, as always, powerful amplifiers.

By noon, an army had appeared. It ringed the city with jagged horizons: Abdullah, marching from Acre on the orders of the Sultan himself, had arrived to claim Jerusalem's surrender. His message to the rulers inside was plain: "Yield and depart. Or die." For the rest of the day he waited in vain for an answer. Meanwhile, every man in the city who could carry arms was summoned to the battlements, ready to resist an attack. Abdullah could be seen riding with his command at a distance from the walls, examining the city's defences.

Sheik Abu Ra'aba for one was undaunted. Picking what appeared to him the easiest target, he directed volleys of musket fire at a contingent of the invaders until it withdrew, leaving behind riderless horses, the wounded, and the dead. The gun from the citadel was hauled on to the wall by the Lions' Gate. From here, it fired salvo after salvo, until no more shells were left. No great damage to the enemy was caused, except to make Abdullah's undisciplined troops scatter and regroup some distance away. The defenders were jubilant. But not for long.

The first sight to greet their eyes with sunrise the next morning, was a glinting battery of cannons among the trees on the Mount of Olives. The barrage began at once. Shells landed in various parts of the city. In the Jewish Quarter, a Sepharadi widow was killed together with her imbecile daughter. A water cistern not far from the Governor's Palace was hit, sending a dirty flood into the nearby meat market. The bombardment shook the city but not the resolve of her defenders, because no sooner had it stopped than intelligence showed Abdullah's artillery to be hardly more than sham since his gunners were ill-trained and ammunition in short supply. This was soon confirmed: after the first barrage, the cannons fell silent. As it happened so many times in the past, so now Jerusalem settled down for a siege. And as the days passed, secret negotiations between besiegers and besieged began to take place.

The Beduin, more at home in fast, open skirmishes, were the first to lose heart. With each night more of them sneaked out of the city and disappeared, until after two weeks or so, of all the Beduin only Sheik Abu Ra'aba with a handful of men, remained.

One crisp autumn morning the barrage from the Mount of Olives was renewed with unexpected intensity. At the same time, squadrons of cavalry mustered north of the city for an all-out attack. But before it could begin, a group of Arabs hoisted white flags on the walls, overpowered the guards by the Lion's Gate, and flung it open.

Pasha Abdullah rode into Jerusalem, and accepted her surrender. He was greeted by the Mufti at the entrance to the sacred Haram ash Sharif.

The Jews, remembering what Abdullah had done to their brethren in Galilee, waited in fear, for there was no escape. But Abdullah had no interest in the Jews, nor in Jerusalem. Having accomplished the mission for which he had come, he was impatient to return to his beloved Acre. His stay in Jerusalem lasted one week, during which every day a number of prisoners were publicly hanged. When he left, a lieutenant of his in command of two cavalry companies stayed behind. He too departed within a month, and in October 1825, fifteen months after the rebellion, Jerusalem was restored to the Pasha of Damascus, who appointed a new governor, an officer of higher rank than the previous Ottoman ruler, eager to stamp his authority on the city.

At Rimkin's insistence, the two families, his and Solomon's met to decide on the date for the wedding of Israel and Sheine.

Because Eliezer Rimkin was the wealthier of the two, his share of the cost of the wedding was to be, by mutual agreement, the larger. He, more than Solomon, wanted a lavish wedding, to which all would be invited, and musicians brought from Safed and Tiberius if necessary, to regale the guests. Then there was the question of the newly-wed's home. It was common practice for the bride to come and live at her husband's parents' home until they had children, or came by enough money to get their own nest.

"Ada would have been happy for them to stay with us," Solomon said with a lack of conviction which Rimkin couldn't fail to notice.

"Ada's a good woman, a good mother," Rimkin said, and in his mind's eye he was going over rooms he had heard were available for rent closer to his own home than to Solomon's.

"We should spare nothing to make them happy," he said, "Better for the young pair to have a home of their own, if it's not beyond our means, Reb Solomon."

The mention of material things reminded Solomon of the situation in the country. He drew in his breath. "I wish they'd have married at a better time. Beyond these hills Abdullah reigns like a tyrant, and there's no glimmer of hope anywhere. The Sultan's armies are fighting the Greeks. Who knows where it will all end. How can our brethren send us money if there's war in Europe?"

"Consider, Reb Solomon, if the times are bad, our children have better things to look forward to," Rimkin said, and Solomon had to smile for he saw the gentle rebuke in his friend's irony.

"As it is written in the Psalms, 'They that sow in tears shall reap in joy'".

"Amen to that, Eliezer, Amen."

"What we have failed to accomplish, the things we both dreamed about, Israel and his seed shall realize," Rimkin mused. "Just think of that. Slowly step by step we are moving towards our preordained destiny, which is that the Kingdom of Israel will be reinstated and the Messiah shall come. . . ."

"There are many things for us to do before that happens," Solomon said, and began to talk about his synagogue and the hopes he held for it even though he had made no headway with his plans.

The day of the marriage was set for the first day after the thirty-third of the Omer, that is the festival of Lag be'omer which falls in the spring, halfway between Passover and Pentecost, when it was the custom for young couples to marry. Eliezer Rimkin undertook to arrange the wedding feast while Solomon would deal with the ceremony and all the communal activities that flowed from it.

The announcement of the engagement was made after the morning prayers at the synagogue on the Sabbath. For days thereafter messages of felicitation streamed into the two homes. It was a great union between two mighty pillars of the community: Solomon Zeff, who had led a handful of Ashkenazi families across unknown and dangerous territory to the Holy City, and Eliezer Rimkin, who, with his drive, ability and imagination, gave the community a sense of cohesion and direction. Wherever men met, the talk would turn to the forthcoming marriage and the virtues of the young couple would be extolled. Stories would be recounted of the epic trip of Solomon and the first pioneers of the Ashkenazi community to Jerusalem. And in retelling these stories, the growing Ashkenazi community was rebuilding its self-confidence which the Abdullah's regime had so battered, and spinning webs of new heroic myths.

The forthcoming wedding did not preoccupy the Ashkenazi community alone, it became the centrepiece of conversation for the Sepharadis as well. The Haham Bashi, Rabbi Moses Sussin, made special mention of it on several occasions and sent to Rimkin and Solomon letters of congratulation full of flowery bendictions and learned quotations. Rimkin, in particular, enjoyed a much respected position among the Sepharadis, on account of his untiring efforts to bring the two communities together. The Sepharadis had another more oblique reason for rejoicing at the engagement: if their Ashkenazi brethren could evince such faith in the future in the present bleak climate, then surely there was hope, not unreasonable, for better things to come. Their felicitations showed like a rainbow in a grey sky, a sign of affirmation. The Sepharadis, although still by far the larger of the two communities, recognized and accepted the Ashkenazis' tough vitality, and looked to them as harbingers of ill or good in a world which was growing increasingly complicated.

Hannah Rimkin's frustrated love reached out to embrace the new additions to her family. She was determined that all her family, which now included Solomon's, should be happy, well-fed, and well-organized, according to her own understanding of these things. Solomon and Israel were elusive, and Hannah was an impatient fisher of souls. In Ada she found a defenceless target for her affection. There was no escape for poor Ada. She didn't have a moment to herself. Hannah Rimkin possessed her life, compelled her to learn new ways, and presumed to act on her behalf in every matter. When Ada realized that Solomon would not come to her aid, she submitted outwardly to Hannah's ministration, and inwardly grew bitter.

Israel had always regarded Sheine more as a cousin than a prospective wife. After the engagement became official, he stopped seeing her. She became a forbidden thing to him. They were no longer allowed to talk as they had done in the past. All of a sudden she became a new person for him. He would imagine what it was like to be with her in bed. He imagined her breath on his neck, her body against his hot and troubled loins.

She was his and there was nothing he could do to change it. Did he really want to? He began to believe that he had in fact chosen her. In her absence her attractions were magnified. He recalled things she had said, which at the time bored him but now revealed meanings he had never suspected were there. When other people talked about her he listened eagerly, even to Hannah. Ada said not a word about her daughter-in-law to be. Whenever anything to do with the Rimkins came up, she would shut up like a clam and busy herself with something however trivial.

Chapter 16

"Blessed are you Lord our God, King of the world, who has preserved our unity with his covenance, and sustained us to this day with his law, and has commanded us to light the light of Hanucah for all the wonders and miracles wrought by Him through the Maccabeans . . ."

Eliezer Rimkin's voice rang out, bright and warm as the flame which he held out to the ornate brass Hanucah candelabrum which Solomon had made. It swelled out to fill the crowded synagogue with its resonance, and the congregation sighed and swayed and said Amen. Slowly, ceremoniously, he touched the flame to the wick and lit the light of the holy day's first candle. All the dancing points of light in the room may have gathered in Reb Eliezer's eyes, for they seemed suffused with majestic radiance. As the little flame sputtered and steadied on the menorah's wick, the congregation broke into the joyous hymn: "As a rock fortress is my salvation." Reb Rimkin thought of the Maccabeans. His chest tightened with emotion. Like many gentle men who naturally shrank from violence, nothing stirred Rimkin so deeply as physical heroism, hence no holy day moved him so deeply as did Hanucah which commemorated the heroic uprising of a band of religious Jews, led by the Maccabi family, against the Greek tyrant Antiochus. The miracles and wonders wrought by the Ineffable Name, the King of Kings, in support of His people, were real, alive; the room was immanent with them. They animated the sallow and defeated faces of the people at prayer until Rimkin was, for a moment, able to believe that even from the loins of these tired men a new breed of Maccabeans could spring.

Ariel's voice could be heard above the other voices. Pure as silver, it hung on a high note, steady, a miracle of sound, like the legendary cruse of oil which kept replenishing itself for the Maccabeans to light the resanctified Temple. A rare and beautiful voice, out of no less rare and beautiful boy, for no one had ever seen the like of Ariel in Jerusalem, except when dreaming of the boy King David of the comely eyes and red-tinted locks.

Rimkin sighed. The love he felt for his people at that moment was overwhelming. "If, God please, I should have a grandson, let him be named Judah, the best and most Jewish of Jewish names," he thought. As he was growing older, Reb Rimkin was learning to value above all else the simple virtue of fundamentals.

As he thought of a grandson, his gaze fell on Solomon and Israel standing not ten paces away from him, and a shadow eclipsed the brightness he was bathing in. Three years had passed since Sheine's betrothal to Israel, three years seven months and ten days in fact—Rimkin had counted the passing days incredulously, resentfully. Each time the date of the wedding had been postponed: there had been Israel's illness and they all feared for his life, then a bereavement in Hannah Rimkin's family, followed by locusts which threatened famine in the land, and war. . . . Eliezer was tired of remembering, except that it seemed to him that Providence was conspiring with Solomon's inexplicable reluctance against the union of their children.

He could see his daughter Sheine growing old before his eyes, or so he imagined. She no longer talked of her marriage. She had closed in on herself and avoided the company of young women of her age, most of whom were married by now. She kept to her room and watched the world through the half-drawn curtain of her window. And why all this unnecessary suffering of an innocent girl? "I know she's plain," Rimkin thought as he watched Solomon's flinty face singing the Hanucah songs. "But she's a good, honest, hard-working girl. Would make a good wife, a devoted mother, more than Israel deserved. Look at him! Is he a paragon of manhood? Is he light unto his people? Who ever saw him excelling in the Torah? He's no scholar, not even a leader like his father. And he does have some odd ideas, is stubborn too. . . ." Rimkin was growing so vexed he was unable to sing. "Tonight I'll speak to him for the last time," he said to himself. ""Reb Solomon," I'll say, "this spring, not a month later even if the second flood comes, or I'll find another man for my daughter"". And Rimkin turned his eyes away and tried to recapture the mood he had lost.

Solomon didn't see the look on his friend's face; his thoughts were in another place. He could hear the trillings and vocal arabesque of the Sepharadis at prayer next door, surfacing like a rich damask through the sparser fabric of the Ashkenazi singing, and he was saddened. Oh he liked the Sepharadi ritual for its full-blooded richness. Unlike Rimkin, he found simplicity at times too bleak: what was the point of imagination if not to add colour to life and glorify it? And if this were wrong, the good Lord would not have endowed man with that unique and godly faculty. Besides, the Sepharadi style of prayer was not merely full of verve and colour, Solomon also considered it consonant with the spirit of the country. Being there, in the shadow of the Sepharadi Central Synagogue, and through their generosity, while the synagogue Solomon had so wanted to resurrect was still a stinking mound of rubble behind his home, reminded him of his failure and impotence.

As synagogues in Jerusalem went, the Ashkenazis had nothing to be ashamed of with theirs. Here they were at home, free to worship according to their tradition. Situated next to the grand Sepharadi complex of four synagogues named after the sage Rabbi Yochanan Ben Zachai where the

Haham Bashi officiated, the smaller Ashkenazi place of worship, let to them at a modest rent, was itself modest and pleasing. The Ashkenazi named it "Light of Life"; and the Sepharadis referred to it patronizingly as the tabernacle because it was not fully finished. The Ashkenazis painted the inside, repaired the chipped walls, and decorated the ark—Solomon himself had made the crowns of the Torah scroll to look like that of the synagogue in Keidanei, as he remembered it. But at the end of each service the ark and holy scrolls had to be removed and taken away, for it was illegal for the Ashkenazis to have a synagogue of their own.

Reb Eliezer Rimkin, who only half-heartedly supported Solomon's obsession with the ruined synagogue, liked their modest, provisional place of worship. "You don't need gilt arches, brocades and carved wood," he would say. "Such things distract the soul from true worship, not elevate it. God is here, in every man," and he would thump his chest.

As Solomon followed the golden thread of his son's voice through the coarse harmony of the singing, he too was thinking of the Maccabeans. Their example challenged him: if they, a small group of men issuing from the tiny Galilean village of Modi'in, could prevail against the mighty power of the Greeks and purify and sanctify the Temple of the Lord, didn't that show how courage and determination could vanquish a superior force? Of course, a miracle was needed, the Lord had to help. But would the Lord help those whose faith and will didn't override all else? It was on this last question that Solomon had to face his weakness at its starkest. Hanucahs came and went with nothing achieved. The number of those who believed the old synagogue would ever be rebuilt had dropped with the years. Even Reb Rimkin, once his staunchest supporter, no longer talked about it. "He humours me over the synagogue, as though it were a mere child's dream," Solomon thought bitterly, and at that moment his eyes met Rimkin's, and both men knew instantly that an issue had to be resolved between them without further delay, and in a way which would either cement their friendship or break it for good.

It was Rimkin who took the initiative when the prayers were over and the people began to disperse to their homes. "A moment, Reb Solomon," he called out, raising his hand. "You walk on and I'll see you at home later," Solomon said to Israel, then turned to face his friend.

Rimkin noted the brief exchange between father and son, and understood that Solomon knew what they were going to talk about. He said, "May there be as much light in your home and in your heart as we have witnessed here tonight, Reb Solomon." "And the same to you, Eliezer," Solomon replied. Rimkin put his arm through his friend's and steered him away from the crowd to a corner. When they were alone out of earshot of anyone, Rimkin placed his hands on Solomon's broader and higher shoulders. For a long moment they stood looking at one another in silence.

"We've come a long way, you and I, Solomon," Rimkin said, dropping the formal "Reb". His voice was soft and earnest.

Solomon nodded. "I know what's on your mind Eliezer, and it's been on my mind too, for a long time."

"My daughter Sheine's a good girl, Solomon. No great beauty, I know, nothing like the Prophetess Deborah who inspired men either. But a good girl, honest and trusting as a child, and brave she is. Steadfast as her mother, bless her. Why am I saying all this, Solomon? After all, you know her as well as anybody. I'm saying this because Sheine will do anything I ask her to do. But I can't ask her to go on being unhappy. That I cannot and will not do, Solomon."

"No, that you mustn't do," Solomon agreed. "You and I, Eliezer have been bound by bonds of friendship for years and we can accommodate our lives to the wants and needs of each other, even when it comes to making a sacrifice. But I cannot commit my son to such a bond, he is a man with his own will and own ways of seeing life."

Rimkin dropped his hands from Solomon's shoulders. "You mean to tell me Israel will not marry Sheine?"

"No, Eliezer, I didn't say that. What I mean is that he doesn't feel ready for marriage yet, and I cannot force him."

"You're a noble soul, Solomon. I've always admired you for that. And in a perfect world, who could dispute you?" His voice rose slightly. "But we don't live in a perfect world. We live in a dangerous, unpredictable world, my friend. To survive we must be accountable to one another. We must often force obedience to rules, we must do what is for the common good even when it conflicts with the whim of the individual. You understand what I'm talking about, you know I'm right," he concluded emphatically.

"If we could wait only a little longer. . . ."

Rimkin shook his head vigorously. "No more waiting. I must know for certain. This spring or never. Not a day beyond Lag B'omer, Solomon."

The next day, after talking it over with Israel all night, Solomon walked over to Rimkin's home and told him that Israel would marry Sheine at the date specified by Rimkin.

This time, despite, or perhaps because, of all the disappointments of the past, Rimkin threw all caution aside and applied himself to the preparations for the wedding with extravagance. He spared no expense in building up Sheine's trousseau into a treasure befitting the daughter of a man far wealthier than he was. He contracted musicians and invited guests not only from Safed but from Europe as well, even though he knew they wouldn't come. "Let them see that there's joy in Zion, not only prayers and bleakness, let them see we can put on a wedding worthy of the best rabbinical families in the diaspora. It is not only for my daughter Sheine and her bridegroom Reb

Israel, that I'm doing this, but for the sake of all the Jewish community in Jerusalem and the Holy Land," he announced solemnly. For days he sat in his room, penning letters of invitation to famous rabbis in Germany, Russia, France and the Baltic countries, as well as to remnants of his own family and anyone Solomon suggested. Solomon and Ada were hard put to come up with some names from their side. But since Solomon didn't really believe anyone from Europe would come, he added to Rimkin's list names of rabbis he had heard or met during his travels.

Sheine, fearful of the evil eye, forbore to show any rejoicing or even relief. "Please, God, let nothing go wrong this time," she prayed in her heart. Her brother Samuel whose own wife was now pregnant, delved into books to select meaningful things to say at the wedding. Although a young man, he had acquired the ponderous demeanour of a middle-aged pedant with the kind of magisterial style that could never fail to irritate Israel. Under Hannah's tutelage Ada took to sewing and embroidering bits of cloth that would serve as bedding and hangings in the home of the young couple. She worked with little alacrity and hardly more aptitude, and was always relieved to be left alone with Ariel whom she loved dearly, after she had completed her quota of work for the day. Solomon worked desultorily at his workshop and dreamed once again with renewed hope, which nonetheless had no more real foundation than before, about the ruins that lay beneath the mound of midden behind his home. Israel became more restless than before and was visited by apocalyptic visions. Or else, anticipating life with Sheine, he would lapse into precocious lassitude.

One day at the synagogue, Lefkowitz said he had an important announcement to make. For years a melody had been haunting his mind. Now, at last it had taken a form, was alive and impatient to burst out of him. What better gift could he bestow on the young couple, the children of the two men he most admired, than to grace their wedding with his hymn? Lefkowitz had by that time established himself as a cantor of exceptional versatility and range. The men nodded appreciatively and winked at one another, knowing that the music, if nothing else, was assured to be of the highest quality. Lefkowitz had departed from all received forms. The cantata he was in the process of creating would not be for a single voice and a choir of men, but an intertwined dialogue for two voices. The other voice he had in mind was Ariel's, which would rise to the highest registers and hang there like a silver rainbow. No sooner did he announce his plan than he began to coach Ariel for his part in the musical offering.

"He's been listening to Reb Eliezer going on about the Maccabeans. Don't tell me that hymn he's preparing for the wedding is about the Maccabeans too! I couldn't stand that," Israel said in a good-humoured truculent tone he had adopted with his younger brother whenever he came back from his lessons with Lefkowitz.

Ariel threw down his little satchel on the mat at the corner of the room and positioned himself in the window recess where he sat swinging his legs. "You shouldn't be unkind to Lefkowitz. After all he's doing it for you," he said. Israel raised his eyebrows. Ariel went on, "Don't worry, it's not about the Maccabeans. You think Lefkowitz has no ideas of his own? I tell you he does."

"Really? What is it about then?"

"I'm not supposed to tell," said Ariel, and added, "Anyway, I don't much care for the Maccabeans."

Israel shrugged his shoulders. He wasn't really interested in Lefkowitz's offering. He took his little brother up on his last utterance. "All boys your age like the Maccabeans because they were such heroes," he said.

Ariel stared at his feet. "Real heroes don't have to fight. They help people, they can bear a lot without complaining or saying anything because they're strong. They don't do things for people to make stories about," he said, spacing out his sentences.

"Is that so? Well, when you grow up you'll understand that there are many types of real heroes just as there are many types of good men and bad men," Israel said.

"I know. I was only talking about the kind I like. I hate fighting," Ariel said.

"What a perfect little angel you are, there's sure to be a place in heaven for you" Israel said.

At the age of ten Ariel was everybody's idea of how an angel should behave and look. Not only was he beautiful, and had a sweet nature to go with his looks, also he had a certain sharpness and single-mindedness which usually prevented people from gushing over him. As Israel prepared to leave the room, Ariel said, "Anyway, I shan't be going to Lefkowitz any more".

Israel turned, and looked severe, "What's that?"

Ariel repeated what he said, "You don't really want to get married do you?"

"Whether I want to or not is none of your business," Israel said, flushing.

"Why should Lefkowitz pour his heart out doing something for you, which you don't want?" the boy persisted.

"Lefkowitz does what he has to do, I do what I have to do, and you do what you have to do which is what you're told to do," Israel snapped and walked out.

Eliezer Rimkin put on his best coat which Hannah had brushed and smoothed. She brought him his hat which he had not worn for years. Satisfied that it still looked presentable, he put it on. Rimkin had never really liked the oriental garb he was forced to wear in Jerusalem. It reminded him of the Spanish Muranos, who had to hide their Jewishness and pretend to be something they were not. He was going to the Austrian postal office and he wanted to be recognized as a European Jew, even if the coat and hat from his country of birth looked somewhat ceremonial superimposed on the robe he wore. He didn't care if he looked a little strange. Nor did he care that for the Armenian who ran the Austrian postal agency, it wouldn't make the least bit of difference if Rimkin came dressed like the Austrian Emperor himself.

The bundle of letters lay on the table, carefully tied together by Hannah who now stood back to admire her husband. It would be a considerable expense at ten piasters a letter. Rimkin didn't mind: his letters were not merely invitations to a wedding, carefully penned and sparkling with erudition, they were his personal credentials, and testimonies to the excellence of the entire Ashkenazi community in Jerusalem. He held the bundle under his arm, kissed Hannah, and stepped out into the street.

It was a cold morning. There had been frost during the night and patches of cracked ice lay in the holes and crevices of the alley. Looking at the sky which was dense with a tangle of cloud, Rimkin knew there would be snow. He considered it a good omen, as though a breath of his native climate was reaching out to him on this significant day. Thin though he was, Rimkin never really suffered from the cold, he found it invigorating, particularly when he had work to do. He quickened his step, anxious lest the outrider would leave before he got to the postal office.

The agent for the Imperial Austrian Post kept a grubby one-room office above his souvenir shop for pilgrims by the Jaffa Gate. He was reputed to have such a mercantile flare that it was said no person could get out of his shop without having bought something, and even to get to the office and out, you had to pass through the shop. The outriders, two retained Bashi bazooks, known "Tartars", took turns to ride once a week—or twice a week during busy periods— to Jaffa to deliver the post to the Austrian Consul, and bring back whatever post was bound for Jerusalem. When they were in town you could see their horses tethered to a post outside the shop, and the two of them—or one—drinking coffee on the steps of the shop. Of all the postal services in the city, half a dozen or so in all, the Austrian was the best and most expensive. It was the one the Ashkenazi Jews preferred to use.

The Armenian was peering out into the street from the curtained window of his shop. When he saw Rimkin approach, he rubbed the window pane with his sleeve, then came to the door. Rimkin sensed right away that something was amiss: the very emptiness of the shop created an atmosphere, and the Armenian seemed edgy.

"Good morning Monsieur", the Armenian said. Over the years he had done some modest and unsatisfactory trade in French goods. His addressing

Rimkin with a French title was to indicate that he could distinguish between the indiginous Jews of Jerusalem and the like of Rimkin, and that so far as he was concerned Rimkin and his brethren were not only outside his immediate world but not to be associated with merit. That discriminatory subtlety was not lost on Rimkin who replied icily, "And a fair day to you, Hawaja Zakar. I believe the Tartar is riding to Jaffa today, and I've brought some letters. I trust I've not come too late."

Zakar stared at him, palms spread out. "No Tartar today, nor tomorrow. Who knows when we'll have post again.

Rimkin glared at him. "No Tartar? Why, what's happened?" That anything untoward should happen on this day of all days was more than Rimkin could bear. He suspected the Armenian of some devious ploy or at least inadvertency.

"Monsieur," said Zakar, "haven't you heard? There's war. Armies are marching on Jaffa. What's the point of sending the post there when the harbour could be closed at any moment?"

"War? What war?" If Solomon had told him that he'd have accused him of breaking the deal and coming up with another excuse for postponing the wedding.

"This morning a messenger came with the news that Mehemet Ali Pasha of Egypt has invaded the country. This very moment, as we are talking, a column of his army is moving up the coast towards Jaffa."

Rimkin didn't know what to say. Clutching his bundle of letters to his chest, he half-turned, ready to leave.

"Monsieur. This is a day to remember. It so happens, I have a memento your grandchildren and their children, may God make them many, will always be grateful to you for. This portrait of the great Pasha in a frame inlaid with mother of pearl. For you, Monsieur. . . ."

Even as they were talking the Egyptian fleet had appeared before Jaffa and begun bombarding the town.

Ibrahim Pasha, son of Mehemet Ali ruler of Egypt, crossed the Sinai peninsula to the north at the head of some 8,000 troops, so it was told. He overran El Arish and advanced up the coast of Palestine. Gaza surrendered without a shot fired. Jaffa, too, fell. While Ibrahim Pasha's main force moved up against Acre along the coast, a smaller force branched off and advanced on Jerusalem. There was a day or two of panic when the news reached the city. Some people fled to the hills. The Jews, Sepharadis and Ashkenazis alike, reacted as they always did instinctively to any threatened violence: they bolted their doors, laid mats to sleep on in the synagogue, and stored as much food as they could lay their hands on. But the peasants, the best indicator of approaching danger, stayed calm. They still brought their produce to the city's markets as though nothing was happening. Soldiers and officers of the garrison which numbered some 600, mostly irregular Bashi bazooks, boasted that they would defend the city to their last drop of blood. Men in the coffee houses of the souks joked and laughed about this, saying that at the first shot there wouldn't be an Ottoman soldier left in Jerusalem.

One frosty morning, as if from nowhere, the Egyptian invaders appeared before the city walls. It was a small force, hardly bigger than a battalion but it looked well-equipped, disciplined, and confident. The sight cowed the people and soldiers who came to look from the battlements. When the commander demanded that the city surrender to him in the name of Ibrahim Pasha and Mehemet Ali, there was a hurried consultation and presently a delegation of Jerusalem notables sallied forth from the Damascus Gate to greet the conquerors with bread and salt. The garrison surrendered its weapons which were piled outside King David's tower for all to see. Those who chose to leave the city were allowed to ride out unmolested.

The Egyptian troops were courteous. Their commander, a young general with piercing eyes, proclaimed to the citizens of Jerusalem that they had nothing to fear, no one would be harmed, order would be maintained and soon people would be able to go about their business as before. And so it was. New regulations were issued. The alleys were cleaned and for the first time in living memory, lamps were lit in the main streets after dark. The commander, who installed himself in the governor's palace, liked to improve what he found, not merely to hold it. The people of Jerusalem soon relaxed.

In the north of the country the war had not yet been decided. Ibrahim Pasha had laid siege to Acre and was bombarding it. Elsewhere, the Egyptians were in control, permanently it seemed. In Galilee it was said that food was short as the opposing armies confiscated all the grain and livestock. But in Jerusalem, in spite of the shortage of water which lasted for almost a month, there were signs of a better future. Hope warmed the hearts of the people towards the new regime and chased away their anxiety. In Jerusalem, the people waited with baited breath to see what would happen in Acre, and what end would be devised for the wicked Abdullah.

Samuel Rimkin, like his father, longed to know more of the world beyond the Jewish community of Palestine. Secretly—for he dared not speak of it openly except to Israel—he hankered after forbidden non-Jewish books that told of love, and for the worst of abominations—pictures such as he had seen on few occasions in foreign books. He had an archivist's memory, sharply-focused and retentive of facts and details.

When Samuel declared without a quaver of hesitation that Mehemet Ali was a forward-looking monarch who welcomed new ideas and was well-disposed to the European powers and to Jews, Israel believed they were entering a new age of enterprise and endless possibilities. "Once the war has ended, and it won't be long, Mehemet Ali will be master of all the southern part of the Ottoman Empire," Samuel said knowingly. "Jews will dominate trade in this country, Jerusalem will become a great centre of activity and learning. You'll see. Who'd care about all those rabbis in Europe? Nobody. They'll want to come here if only to keep abreast of developments." And Samuel allowed himself a tight lopsided smile.

Israel thought of Jacob Pach, "If you just sit on your backside and wait for things to come your way you might as well be dead," Pach had said to him. All of a sudden the thought of settling down to a shared life with Sheine Rimkin became unbearable to him.

The storks arrived early that spring, flying in from the north, they circled in the sky in slow wide spirals.

Solomon said to Israel, "Perhaps the time has come. God please, it's right what people say about the open-mindedness of Pasha Mehemet Ali, for I'm thinking of travelling to Egypt to seek an audience with him. I'll ask him to recognize our rights as an Ashkenazi community and allow us to rebuild the synagogue, and may the Lord open his heart to my request."

"Amen," Israel said.

"Soon after the wedding I'll go," Solomon said.

Israel bit his lower lip. "You may as well go as soon as you like, any time in fact," he said tersely.

Solomon might have known, but hearing it hit him like a fist in the stomach. He stared at Israel.

"I can't. I'd sooner die than marry her. There'll be no wedding, Father," Israel said.

"Do you realize what this means?" Solomon said after a long silence.

Israel didn't reply.

"Do you realize what it means? Everybody told, guests invited, letters sent," his voice was rising to a shout, "And Sheine, what do you think this will do to her?"

Because Israel was still silent, for a moment Solomon allowed himself to believe that his son was hesitating. He began to plead: "Marry her, the best marriages are thus arranged. She's quiet and placid, she'll never vex you or bother you only do your bidding. . . ."

Then he could tell from the hardening expression on Israel's face that his pleading was in vain.

"Will you contradict me at this late stage, regardless of all the embarrassment and unhappiness you'd cause?" he demanded.

"My mind is made up. I will not marry her," Israel said, and before the sound of his last word died in his ears stars exploded in his eyes. Solomon hit him a heavy blow on the side of the head with the flat of his hand. Israel staggered then fell to the ground. Still dizzy, he looked up to see his father standing over him, white and trembling. Solomon bent over him and stretched out his hand but Israel shunned it and scrambled to his feet unaided.

"You'll be the death of me, Israel," Solomon said and walked away.

That evening, he didn't sit down with his wife and two sons to dinner. But after Ada had cleared the table he motioned to Ariel to leave, and said to Israel, "I'll have to go and tell Reb Eliezer about this, and I can't think of anything I'd want to do less."

"I'll go and tell him myself, if you'll allow me," Israel said.

Solomon shook his head. "It was I who committed you to this and I will set you free, since that is what you want. Let not Rimkin say I have been devious with him."

Eliezer Rimkin was sitting by the stove reading a book when Solomon knocked on the door and came in. Seeing his old friend, Reb Eliezer's face lit up. "Solomon, I was just thinking of you." It was just as well that standing in the shadow Solomon's grim expression was unseen by Rimkin, who offered him some sweet almonds Hannah had prepared. "I've been reading an account of a learned Jew from Frankfurt who eighty years ago travelled to the Holy land and visited Jerusalem. He saw the Great Synagogue of Reb Yehuda The Hassid in its full glory, and went to great length describing it from every side, inside and outside. When we rebuild it, God willing, think how valuable his descriptions will be, eh, Solomon, eh?" and Rimkin gave the book a smack.

"Eliezer, I have to talk to you," Solomon began.

"Come, sit down by the fire, let Hannah bring some hot tea. Let's not talk of problems, these can wait. We've made all the arrangements, and if some small thing goes wrong, well, it cannot be helped, we're only poor humans who make mistakes. Our children will soon be united nevertheless. Think of that."

"They'll not be united, Eliezer, that's what I've come to tell you. . . ." And Solomon told him in a few words what had passed between him and Israel earlier. Rimkin sat there in deathly silence, he didn't move or say anything, and he didn't rise when Solomon bade him goodnight and made for the door.

Back home Solomon found Israel waiting for him, alone. He could hear Ada crying in the next room. He said, "I'm no longer responsible for what you do. Everything that ensues from this sorry day will be on your own head." He paused. "It is written that when King David's infant son was dying as the prophet predicted, the King wept and fasted and prayed. When the child was taken unto his Maker, David asked for food and wine: he had done all he could to no avail. There was no point in fasting and praying any more." Again he paused, longer this time. "What I mean to say is that I've tried as hard as I could to dissuade you from what you've done. But now that it's done, you are my son and I'll stand by you no matter what."

Presently there were knocks at the door. Rimkin came in coatless and looking piteously distraught. He didn't shut the door but stood there staring at Solomon and clutching his thin chest.

"Tell me you didn't mean what you said and I'll believe you. And we shan't mention the thing again, ever. Tell me your son is nervous and you lost your judgment for a spell, and I'll understand and forgive, I'm a forgiving and understanding man as God is my witness."

Solomon came towards him with outstretched hands but Rimkin thrust his hand out to stop him. "Tell me, tell me it's not true what I heard earlier," he insisted, his voice rising. Hearing him, Ada and Ariel came and stood at the door of the other room.

"Eliezer, I can't tell you anything but the truth painful though it is. There's nothing I can do. . . ."

"All this pain, the humiliation, the shame and you stand there and tell me there's nothing you can do!" Rimkin now turned his eyes to Israel and fixed him with a hard glare. "Shameless and heartless boy! You're not fit to kiss my daughter Sheine's feet," he shouted. Then he spat on the floor and stormed out of the house.

When they were alone, Solomon said to Israel, "I wonder if you realize how lonely we shall be now. He was my best friend."

Buxbaum and his wife, who stood with their ears to the wall, heard what took place between Solomon and Rimkin. They wasted no time telling it to everybody they met. The Ashkenazi community was too stunned to do anything, if there was anything to be done. Rimkin stayed behind locked doors at his home and would neither see nor speak to anybody. Samuel walked about with a solemn expression on his face and refused to deny or confirm reports that Reb Eliezer was seriously thinking of packing up and returning to his native country. Nor did Samuel respond to later reports according to which his father was seriously ill in his heart. Solomon and Israel too avoided public contact as much as they could.

After a week Eliezer Rimkin emerged from his home to dispel all rumours about his intention to emigrate and about his health. He looked somewhat leaner and more severe but otherwise none the worse for his travail. He soon resumed most of his normal activities and behaved as though his daughter had never been engaged to marry Israel Zeff.

What he couldn't or wouldn't conceal was his coldness to the Zeff family. He never said a word to Solomon about the affair, and never confronted him over any issue. But everybody knew of the rift between the two former friends, and soon the community began to divide across that invisible rift. The first bone of contention which set Solomon's camp against Rimkin's was the controversy of the ruined synagogue.

In the month of Iyar, the last month of spring, when Israel and Sheine were to marry, Acre at last fell to Ibrahim Pasha. Abdullah was hanged, or some said, banished, and the war came to an end. In the following year the great powers undersigned a peace treaty between Mehemet Ali and the Sultan Abdel Magid, in which Palestine was recognized as the legal fief of the Egyptian Pasha. Solomon made plans to journey to Cairo to plead his case before Mehemet Ali. His supporters rejoiced. Rimkin himself said not a word against the plan. It was his friends who vociferously pointed out that Solomon was off on a vainglorious venture which would end in nothing but disillusionment and trouble with the Arabs, and that apart from everything else, there was no money for such a fanciful idea to be realized.

Chapter 17

A man arrived in Jerusalem from London. His name was Rafael Mendoza, a widower of Sepharadi Portuguese origin, a man of considerable wealth. With him were his daughter Clara, and two younger sons, Jacob and Aaron. Mendoza bought a house with a walled garden, which stood between the Armenian and Jewish Quarters. Into it he brought his beautiful London furniture, his books, the ornaments he had acquired on his travels. To make his new home exotic, he had builders extend the rooms so that each flowed into the other and into the garden. Colourful Hebron glass bead curtains hung in place of doors—there was no house like it in Jerusalem. Mendoza and his family settled down to emulate—as closely as local conditions would allow—the gracious lifestyle they had enjoyed in London.

Important foreign visitors dined at his table. With time, as Mendoza got to know them, so did the Arab dignitaries of Jerusalem and the high-ranking government officials. In the serene, cultured atmosphere of Mendoza's home, to the music-making of his children who were accomplished flautists and lute players, it was easy to make friends. Mendoza himself was a large, expansive man with laughing eyes and pleasing manners. Most of all he directed his energies to learning about the Sepharadi Jews, with whom he identified, who claimed him as one of their own, and whose ancient customs and folklore he was keen to assimilate. But his place in the Jewish community as a force to reckon with came in the following way:

There lived in Jerusalem in the humblest of rooms fast by the synagogue of the Sepharadis, a half-demented man called David Hommle. On the Fast of the Ninth of Ab when Jews mourn the destruction of the Second Temple by the Romans, Hommle went into an agitated trance; it had been a very hot day. Hommle managed to sneak into the Harem ash Sharif compound. Two days later an Arab janitor, going down into the catacombs below the Mosque of Al Aksa, which some said had been the stables of King Solomon, saw Hommle's crazy eyes staring at him out of the darkness.

The Arab came running out shouting that he had seen the Devil underneath the holy Mosque. The Mufti was summoned, with two black guardians of the complex. Hommle was dragged up into the daylight. It was just as well for him that the Mufti was there for otherwise surely he would have been flailed to death by the guards. The outrage was compounded by Hommle's statement that he was summoned there by a voice from above which told him that the day of judgement was at hand and the Moslem abomination was to be consumed by purifying fire from heaven. Hommle was promptly thrown in prison and sentenced to be killed by the guardians of the Harem ash Sharif. That was how the Jews learnt about the incident, for no one had taken any notice of David Hommle's absence.

Petitions fell on deaf ears: but the more the Jews pleaded, the harder the Arabs became, saying there was complicity to desecrate their shrine. It was then that Rafael Mendoza put his social contacts to the test and liberated Hommle.

During the comings and goings over the Hommle affair, Mendoza and Solomon met. The two men liked each other. They became friends. Mendoza's interest was aroused by the story of the Ashkenazi Jews, their buried synagogue in particular. Here was a cause he could espouse, since his involvement with the Sepharadi Jews had by no means exhausted his enthusiasm or resources. It was Mendoza who urged Solomon to repair for Egypt without delay. He also lent him money for the journey and used his contacts abroad to prepare the ground for Solomon's meeting with Mehemet Ali.

Israel's first meeting with Clara caught him unprepared and left him aching with love for her. He had come looking for his father at Mendoza's home one evening. The two men were outside, talking. Solomon appeared on the point of leaving. As Israel joined them Clara came walking down the road from the direction of the Armenian Quarter. Even before he realized who she was, she aroused his interest. She had picked up a spray of bougainvillaea on the way, which she held in the crook of her arm. She moved with a curious forward glide—a barely perceptible limp which gave her gait a singularly graceful fluidity. Something came fluttering down and landed at her feet. She stooped to look, bent down to her knees, and took off the broad-rimmed straw hat she was wearing. As she did so, her hair uncoiled and fell in a lustrous loop over her shoulder. With a quick motion, she closed her hand over the object and put it in the crown of her hat. Her father interrupted his talk to call, "What is it dear?" Clara rose to her feet, covering the hat with her hand. She shook her head to clear her hair from her face. Israel had seen such an expression of alert concern on the face of a child confronted by something intensely interesting. On the face of an adult woman, a comely, intelligent-looking one at that, he found it peculiarly arresting.

"A little fledgeling," Clara said, coming towards them, "Look."

The tiny bird squeaked piteously as it tried to escape through her fingers. "A bul bul, I think," she said.

"Let it go, dear. Leave it to nature," Mendoza said.

"It'll surely die if I do. Sometimes nature needs a helping hand. I'll look after it," Clara replied.

"That's my daughter for you. Never content to leave things as they are if she thinks she can make them better," Mendoza laughed, and put his arm affectionately round her shoulder, "Lucky little bird to fall into such gentle hands."

Clara greeted Solomon. Mendoza introduced her to Israel. She asked him a few questions in halting Hebrew. Her gaze confused him; he took refuge in looking at her hand which held down the bird soothingly and firmly. As Clara joined in the conversation, he couldn't take his eyes off her. He marvelled at her articulacy; he was captivated by her candour and directness. Was it because she had not espoused the social conventions of women in the Jewish community, that there was no trace of coyness in her manner as their eyes met, as she talked to Solomon? He decided that her self-possession—so excitingly alien—was a part of her nature, and wouldn't change no matter where she was. He observed a similar directness with her father, as though they were partners, sharing knowledge, deciding jointly as of a long-standing habit.

"I must put this poor little creature in a suitable box and give it some water," Clara said, and excusing herself, went in.

As they walked back home together, Israel's thoughts lingered on Clara, on her quiet voice, the faint redolence of lavender which clung to her, and her smooth, comforting hands. It came to him with a stubborn, impatient certainty that all he had dreamed about the woman he would love, all the aspects of nobility imaginable, were contained in those proud intelligent grey and tawny eyes of hers.

He couldn't put her out of his thoughts. Day after day he hung about her house, hoping to catch sight of her as she came out. When she saw him, he greeted her nervously, pretending he was by chance passing by. The more he saw her the more inaccessible she seemed, and therefore more desirable.

"She's not for you, my son. She's a creature of another world, not our own." Solomon said. His heart was aching for Israel, whom he was powerless to help, who reminded him now of painful things he did not wish to remember.

"If she's not for me, no woman is. I'll never want another woman," Israel said disconsolately.

"Never say never. She would be the first one to tell you that, Israel. Listen to me. She's a strong girl who makes up her own mind on everything. . . ."

"I want a strong, clever woman. Do you think I could live with a fool?"

"She's older than you. . . ."

"I don't care."

"But you can't have her. She won't have you! Mendoza wouldn't agree!"

"Then I'll go away, leave Jerusalem, for good."

Solomon covered his face with his hands. For a while he was deep in thought. At last he looked up, a smile of resignation on his face. "What kind of a father and friend I am if I'm of no help to you when you most need help? Be patient and don't lose heart. When I return from Egypt, together we'll address ourselves to this business. Don't worry, she won't disappear or marry anyone during my absence."

Mehemet Ali's regime was outgoing and tolerant. Foreign visitors, who knew the Ottoman Empire, were the first to comment on this. If to the large part of the population the relaxed, innovative tone of government was bewildering, to the Jews—whose number was steadily growing—it was as sunshine and dew is to a growing flower. Rimkin's prophecy about better times could not have been more emphatically fulfilled. Sheine blossomed. Out of the blue came her redeemer, an upright young man of learning and good family—second cousin of Rabbi Mordecai Binish, a firebrand who arrived in Jerusalem with a large clan and an imperious wife. Reb Binish made two things clear from the outset: he was out to gain power and lift the Ashkenazi community to heights they had never dared imagine. And in the process of attaining that goal, he would suffer no fools.

Sheine didn't meet her husband until they stood together under the *chupa*. As the bridegroom crushed a glass tumbler under his foot, all the guests shouted *Mozel Tov!* Luck and happiness to the newly-weds, and Rimkin prayed in his heart that his troubles were over.

In the summer of 1836, the 5596th year to the creation of the world, according to the Jewish calendar, Solomon returned from Egypt triumphant. He had seen Mehemet Ali in person. The ruler of Egypt and Palestine admired the Jews for their drive. He welcomed them in his domain, Ashkenazi Jews in particular, whose debts to the Arabs of Jerusalem he had heard of, and now personally declared null and void. There, in Solomon's hand, was the firman, signed by Mehemet Ali and witnessed by the British Consul in Alexandria. They were free at last, to do as they liked, in their own way. No one had believed this would be possible; no one was more richly rewarded with a hero's welcome than Solomon.

He went to Mendoza's home, and sitting alone with Rafael in his study, said to him, "My son Israel longs for your daughter Clara. In the world you once inhabited, perhaps his qualities would not have accounted for much. But here, there's no one better than him. If you think highly of me, know that Israel excels me in many ways. If you think this marriage is impossible, tell me now and we'll say no more about it. But I would say, talk to your daughter, ask her if she would see my son, and let her judge for herself."

Ada had made Israel wear his best coat and hat. He was nervous. In addition, he felt awkward in the informal elegance of Mendoza's home. The door of the room where Mendoza entertained, where now Israel waited, was open on to the garden. The breeze came in jangling the glass beads of the curtain. He fixed his gaze on a splash of bougainvillaea on the garden wall as he tried to concentrate on what he was going to say to Clara. Presently he heard footsteps, and turned more abruptly than he wanted to. It was Rafael Mendoza, who smiled and said, "She won't be long. Why don't you wait for her outside, in the garden?" He heard the two brothers' voices in the corridor, and went out to the bench beneath the sprawling vine, to wait for Clara. The thought that Mendoza and his two sons, who were about his own age, would be in the room, seeing them, gave him a strange sense of security. They could well have been his advocates. They would also not be unsympathetic if the interview did not go well.

Clara came out. She had put up her chestnut hair in a stately-loop which made her appear taller and formidably poised. She was wearing a long dark dress of light material. He noticed how slender she was. When she saw him, she shut the door with a flick of her hand, and approached, smiling. He rose to greet her, feeling clumsy.

But Clara had the subtlest way of putting him at ease. Soon he was telling her about himself, how they came to Jerusalem from Safed, and what he knew about the country. He ended his story, waited a moment, then said, "You know why I wanted to see you." He struggled against a rising tension to preserve in his mind the little speech he had prepared. She took her time answering. At length she said, "Do you wonder why I haven't married?"

He realized at once that everything he had rehearsed would be hopelessly out of place, and fell silent. Clara waited, her hands casually clasped in her lap. She looked desultorily at the garden as if undecided whether or not to pursue the subject any further.

"My father," he heard her say at last, "is the kindest, most generous man I know. And I'm devoted to him. Not least for his vulnerability. We've always been a close family. We understood and trusted each other. When my mother died, years ago, I thought my father would die of grief." She gave Israel a lingering glance. "He has an extraordinary capacity for loneliness, you know. Don't be misled by his outgoing manner. I couldn't bear the thought of him being alone."

With each of these sentences which she spaced with pauses, Israel had a growing sense that she was rejecting him, in the gentlest, friendliest way imaginable, which at the same time imposed no finality. That gave him hope to stay, to ask, to seek answers.

"So you've made up your mind never to marry?" he said.

"I've made up my mind never to do anything which would bring my father unhappiness," she answered with a smile. And before he could speak again she went on: "Two years ago I fell ill. I nearly died, so the doctors said. I think what gave me the strength to fight on was seeing my father's face as he sat at my bedside. When I got better, he told me that he had made a vow in the synagogue that if I recovered, if I were strong enough for it, we would go to live in Jerusalem. I agreed, because I knew this was really what he always wanted to do. There was nothing in England that gripped him so strongly as the desire to live here. It was like a strange, homing instinct. My brothers will shortly return. But Father and I will stay, probably for the rest of our lives."

"You sacrifice your life for your father? I don't think I could've done that. And I love my father very much."

She tilted her head and gave a short laugh. "Oh, it's not a sacrifice at all. I wanted to come. It was a joint decision," she said.

"I've imagined you in London, in beautiful rooms full of beautiful things, meeting interesting people, doing interesting things. . . . I see there's no hope, is there?" he said with a touch of despair.

"But don't I do all those things here? What hope do you want?"

He came out with it straight: "That you could love me. That you'd marry me. Because I love you more than I can say. . . ."

She lowered her eyes, and was silent. He moved uneasily; he was seeing the empty end of his quest. "Your father's much too large in your life. I could never hope to fill his place. . . ." he muttered. To which she replied, "You wouldn't. You needn't." And when he turned to look at her, she said quietly, "I will marry you, since you want it so much. As for my father, he'd be happy. Rest assured on that." He couldn't believe he had heard right and he almost asked her to repeat what she had said, even though the confirmation was there, in her eyes which now looked at him in warmth and amusement.

"Will you love me?" he ventured to ask.

"When I say I'll marry you, Israel, I mean I'd do my best to meet your expectations. I'd never let you down," said Clara, and put her hand on his sleeve.

Liberated by Mehemet Ali's firman, the Ashkenazis were at first dazed. They blinked at the light of freedom, in disbelief and did nothing. Then, on the eve of one Sabbath, as the men made their way to the Western Wall to pray, there all of a sudden, were Reb Eliezer Rimkin, his son Samuel, and Reb Mordecai Binish, striding boldly resplendent in striped silk coats, white stockings, and *shtreimles*, the traditional fur-trimmed broad hats Jews in Europe wore on festive occasions. The sight was so arresting that passers by stopped to stare. Led by Reb Binish the three marched on, eyes straight, heads held high.

Others soon followed suit. Old forgotten clothes were taken out from hidden boxes and cupboards. The alleys of the Jewish Quarter were filled with men in trousers and gabardine coats, wearing black broad hats. Hyam the tailor struck up a lively trade making new traditional coats from old material, repairing old breeches, reviving skills he had thought he had forgotten. And Reb Saul who had in his former life been a furrier, began making shtreimles to order. His detractors said any stray cat could end up on someone's head now Reb Saul the furrier was in business.

The Sepharadi Jews noted all this with growing apprehension. Over the years they had grown used to their Ashkenazi brethren, learnt to accept their ways, had fallen out and become reconciled time and time again, and all the while watched helplessly how they grew in numbers. The clothes they now wore stridently declared their presence and all at once the Sepharadis were aware of how alien the Ashkenazis were, how they moved with graceless and assertive energy.

Solomon at first resisted the change. He had grown used to his oriental clothes: they were less restrictive of movement than trousers and coat, they concealed what he felt needed to be concealed, and gave the body a kind of dignified bulk. But Ada fought him fiercely: "How do you expect people to take you seriously when you go around dressed like an Ishmaelite?" she challenged.

"Just as they have in the past. These are the clothes of the land. The Sepharadis wear them," he answered.

"They are different from us," she countered.

"Difference should be narrowed not emphasized, dear wife," said Solomon with an edge to his voice. To which Ada replied no less trenchantly, "Times have changed, dear husband. Only you seem not to notice this."

But he did. As more Ashkenazi Jews kept arriving in Jerusalem people weighed one another up, as though the Ashkenazi clothes showed in sharper relief one's affluence or the lack of it. He became self-conscious. At last he gave in. Standing before Ada in his mended coat, a new pair of calf-length trousers, and a secondhand hat he had bought, he saw the pleasure in her eyes and understood that he was to be thrust into public activity from which he sought to withdraw in his declining years. He wondered if he would still have the energy or the stomach for it now that men like Mordecai Binish stalked about calling people to his banner.

At a glance you could tell the Reb Solomon faction from the Binish one: they sat apart at the synagogue. Solomon's followers were more subdued in their dress and more reticent. Reb Binish's disciples took their cue from their leader: outspoken and assertive they were. They gyrated extravagantly as they prayed. Their coats always looked louder, their hats bigger. With the issue of the synagogue being at the centre of the divide, the two factions moved around like wrestlers sizing each other up before the fight.

*

Clara and Israel were married after the feast of Succoth. Three months later she told Ada and then her joyous father that she was with child: a gift to sweeten Ada's life, and for Rafael Mendoza his last, most cherished dream come true.

Rafael Mendoza zestfully embraced Solomon's ideal of rebuilding the synagogue. Together, they made plans and considered means. Israel languished at home, uxorious and dreamy. His dreams seemed to vault over all boundaries, breeding ideas which thrilled him. Clara taught him discipline of thought, trained his mind to harness the outbursts of his imagination, and pointed to ways of achieving. He adored her; he wanted her to be proud of him. And she was, more than ever, when he told her a new fantasy he had conceived, which persisted in his mind: buying land, farming it to feed the Jews of Jerusalem.

"No fantasy," she said, "You'll see." And he believed her.

"Make way, make way", someone shouted, and the crowd parted to let through a small group of men who were holding up a tall old man with a cavernous face and flowing white beard and hair. Ezra Hacohen, said to be over a hundred years old, Jerusalem born, four times widower and father of countless children, had come to dig one shovel-full of dirt from the site he said he remembered in its days of glory, and at its fall.

"Don't let the old sinner defile our sacred work! Send him away, send him away," Reb Binish's followers shouted for it was said about Ezra, a Sepharadi and a near-recluse, that he had become a Nazarite. Old Ezra with his eagle stare paid no attention and no one tried to stop him as his helpers let go of him at the edge of the heap, and put a shovel in his knotted hands.

Two English clergymen stood a few paces away and looked on in concentration. In their long coats and black broad-rimmed hats, they could mix unobtrusively in the crowd. But there was no need to, the Jews were too preoccupied with their work to take any notice of the strangers. With the Englishmen was a Jew called Joseph Wolff, a Bavarian by birth, who had turned to Christianity and now worked under the missionary John Nicolayson in the infirmary which the London mission had opened by the Jaffa Gate only the year before.

The Reverends McLean and Bryde belonged to the Society for the Promotion of Christianity Among the Jews. They had come on an investigative mission to the Holy Land to look into the state and condition of the Jews. The liberal rule of Mehemet Ali was seen in some missionary quarters as a sign from God that at long last the Jews of the Holy Land were ready to be converted to the true faith as the first step towards the total redemption of Man. It was to assess the possibilities for work among the Jews that Reverends McLean and Bryde had come, and went among the Jews like the two biblical spies in Jericho.

What they saw at once depressed and filled them with hope. They saw poverty, oppression, timidity and, they surmised, ignorance. All of which in itself was nevertheless conducive to successful missionary work. They had travelled through Galilee, visited Safed, Tiberias, then southwards along the coast to Haifa and through Samaria and Judea, to Jerusalem. Here in the cosy Christian hospitality of Nicolayson's home, they began sorting out their notes and preparing their report.

"Of all the people that I've seen in my days and on my travels," wrote the Reverend McLean, "none are so dirty, so unhealthy-looking as the wretched Ashkenazi Jews of Jerusalem. My heart ached to see the children with their pitifully sallow faces and large frightened eyes, as if the sunlight never touched them. It is said that an Ashkenazi Jew washes but one time in his life, before his wedding. Whenever a disease breaks out in this city, its source is invariably traced back to the insalubrious Jewish Quarter and the blame falls on the hapless Jews. The Sepharadi Jews are somewhat healthier and comelier than their Ashkenazi brethren. They dress like the Arabs so that they are hardly distinguishable from them. . . . It seems to me the Jews, being so down-trodden, would be receptive to help and to persuasion."

The Reverend Bryde wrote down in his neat uncompromising hand the statistical findings he had collected: 13,000 Jews lived in the land, the largest population being in Jerusalem where nearly 7,000 were believed to live. The other towns of Jewish habitation were Safed, and Tiberias,with small communities in Haifa, Acre, Jaffa, Nablus, and Hebron. The Sepharadi Jews formed the great majority, except in Safed where they were in the minority. "Although a few Jews—mostly of the Sepharadi community—earn their living working as small traders and by other menial tasks such as tanners, butchers, and dyers, the large majority of them live from charity of their brethren whose donation is collected by travelling emissaries, and distributed among members of the community according to size of the families. The system is known as the haluka.

"The Jews of Palestine are so wretched that they are incapable of work, either physical or intellectual, or indeed of any form of self-help. They have no doctors and we have heard stories of so-called healers whose remedies are so barbariously awful that only the lucky among their patients survive the treatment. It is our view that more medical facilities should be provided for the Jews by extending the infirmary and employing there Christian Jews who can speak to their brothers in their own language," the Reverend Bryde noted in his diary.

Joseph Wolff, "The Accursed One", was known to the Jews of Jerusalem who shunned his company and often abused him, though not even the fiercest of Reb Binish's followers ever did more than spit in his direction. Before Wolff turned his back on his faith and became a Christian he had been considered one of the more promising young scholars in Jerusalem. But it was said when he was still talked about, conceit and arrogance had made him an easy prey for Satan. His wife had taken their children, left him and changed her name. The only people who kept Wolff's company were a handful of converts like himself, and a few outcasts. It was he who had brought the Englishmen to the site of the old synagogue, for he was still proud of his people, even though they spurned him.

The enthusiasm of the Jews astonished and uplifted the two clergymen. Was it a sudden inspiration, or had their assessment of the Jews been ungenerous, they wondered? So moved they were that when McLean remarked under his breath that in such a way the New Temple would be rebuilt even in their days, Bryde, the dourer of the two, was compelled to nod in agreement and was heard to mutter "Amen".

The Jews now set up a rhythm of work. The level of dirt and rubble markedly reduced and presently broken bits of masonry began emerging from the midden. When this was noticed, the diggers gave a great cry of joy and Samuel Rimkin blew the shofar. McLean and Bryde clasped their hands to their breasts and prayed silently. Then other cries were heard, a strident chanting rising in pitch. A group of Arabs had arrived. They cursed in unison and shook their fists and staves at the Jews. An exchange developed between the Jews and the intruders.

"What's going on?" McLean whispered to "The Accursed one". "The Arabs are saying they will burn down whatever the Jews build on this site, since the Jews have no right to build anything in Jerusalem. The Jews are saying the property belongs to them and they have a firman from the ruler of the land to prove it," explained Wolff.

A shot cracked above the din. The Jews made ready to flee. Solomon clambered to the top of the heap and shouted at the top of his voice "Let no man leave this site until our work is done!" And switching to Arabic, he berated the Arabs and waved in his fist Mehemet Ali's firman which he carried with him. The Arabs began to retreat; they were not afraid, but neither were they ready for violence. They laughed contemptuously and threw a few stones at the Jews. The work continued.

When all the dirt had been removed on the backs of donkeys, and deposited outside the Dung Gate, it became apparent that two walls forming a corner of the old synagogue were almost intact, as was a large stretch of the floor. The area of the entire compound was also a good deal larger than had been possible to appreciate before. Then the truce between Solomon's faction and Reb Binish's broke. "The place is not the patrimony of Reb Solomon Zeff to do as he pleases," Reb Binish's words were unyielding as flint. "What shall be built will be decided by the entire congregation, not by the conceit of one man. And it should be considered whether we want a grand house of prayer with a tall dome, higher than any minaret in the area, a tower of Babel, or a couple of functional buildings to serve several useful purposes."

"I shall rebuild the synagogue as it was," Solomon stubbornly insisted. Until Rafael Mendoza pointed out that even with his full commitment to the idea there was not enough money available for the grand scheme Solomon had in mind. "Let us do what we can on a part of the plot where the walls stand, and let Binish and his friends do what they can or would on the rest," he suggested. And so two rival synagogues were begun on the ancient site.

In the month of Shebat, at the end of the winter of the following year, the frame of Solomon's synagogue was completed, windows were hurriedly put in, the dome—a more modest construction than that which he had conceived—plastered over and painted white, and the door set in below a heavy lintel. Inside, the west and north walls were still bare masonry but the synagogue was ready for consecration and for use.

When at last the time came to consecrate the synagogue and give it a name, a few of the men gathered to discuss the issue. Solomon was there, and Mendoza, and Israel. Reb Binish had declined to come but softened enough to delegate Reb Eliezer Rimkin to the meeting. By common consent the synagogue was named "Menachem Zion", Consoler of Zion.

Just after the naming of the temple, news reached Jerusalem of a terrible earthquake that had shaken the northern part of the country and all but levelled Safed. Depredation by the Druze and the hill Beduin followed the earthquake like a tidal wave.

Among the unfortunates who arrived in Jerusalem in the wake of the Safed disaster was Reb Israel, Reb Isser's cousin. Solomon had hoped not to meet him again but there he was, hollow-cheeked and pale, except for the fire in his eyes. The two men encountered each other in a crowd on the way to evening prayers. As Solomon's eyes fell on his old adversary and recognition dawned, he realized that Reb Israel must have been staring at him a good moment before he, Solomon, spotted him and instinctively he felt at a disadvantage. He hesitated. His heart was pounding. Then in a conciliatory gesture he stretched his hand towards Reb Israel. Reb Israel stared at the hand just as he had done on another occasion in Safed, then turned his back on Solomon and walked away. Soon he became one of Reb Mordecai Binish's closest advisers. Solomon always suspected that it was thanks to Reb Israel's counsel that Reb Binish sought and won the hearts and minds of the rich rabbis of Amsterdam with whose backing he became the leading force among the Ashkenazis of Jerusalem, and built a spacious yard with rooms and another synagogue on the vacant space beside Menachem Zion synagogue.

Clara gave birth soon after Solomon's synagogue was consecrated. The stress of the time—for she had been working hard helping the refugees from Safed, together with her father—made her go into labour a month before she was due. It was a difficult birth. For a while her life hung in the balance. Israel kept watch in the room next to hers, and read psalms. It was the closest he had ever felt to God. Mendoza kept repeating to him, "Clara will not die. A host of angels are fighting death for her." Before dawn, on the twentieth of the month of Nissan, which is April, in the year 1838, an assertive baby's scream was heard from Clara's bedroom, and the midwife came out to announce that a baby boy had been brought into the world. It was Clara's wish that he should be called Yoel. It had, she said, a gentle consoling sound suited to the time, and was also the name of Mendoza's father. As a middle name, Moshe was unanimously chosen, for it had a ring of promise to it. Mendoza dispensed large sums of money to the poor in thanksgiving for his daughter's life and the birth of a healthy grandson.

After the birth, he took Israel aside and said, "I came here determined never again to leave Jerusalem. But the building of the synagogue and the disaster in Safed have cost a lot. My money is nearly gone. I don't want you and my dearest Clara to live in poverty. I want you to be happy and comfortable, and bring me many grandchildren." His eyes shone. So, my dear son, I must for a while leave you. Soon I shall return to London where with my two sons I will, God willing, recoup my losses, and make a little fortune. I've done it before and I think I can do it again.

"Here, for the time being, I can do no more." A note of disappointment crept into his voice. "I see your father, Solomon, may he live to a ripe old age, and his followers, competing senselessly with Binish's people, each building more to keep up with the other, more rooms, another synagogue, sinking deeper and deeper into debt, drawing further and further away from one another. And I ask myself, why, what for? In the end all their work will end in ruin. A heap of rubbish will remain as a monument to all these quarrels. Have we not enough difficulties without all this?"

He didn't let Israel reply but gently squeezed his arm. "Look after my daughter and sweet Yoel. You shall hear from me soon and regularly. I've already booked my passage on a steamer that leaves for Genoa next Friday. I hate partings so don't come to see me off."

Chapter 18

The region of Adullam lay a day's ride from Jerusalem. Now, as in biblical times, it was a fertile country, where fields of golden corn or of richly dark ploughed soil, stretched endlessly, punctuated by groves behind low stone walls and barriers of cactus.

To reach Adullam you rode southwest from Bab el Whad. If you took the hill route, at a brisk pace you could reach Adullam well before sunset. Travellers who preferred the variety of company along a busy highway, avoided the hills even though Egyptian rule had scattered the bandits to the wilderness of Jordan, and made the byways of Palestine safe for a girl to travel on unmolested, so it was said. But Israel Zeff was impatient to arrive at Adullam, and the shifting scenes of the hills in solitude seemed to quicken his journey.

He had been making these trips regularly since his contract with Ayub Mansour, a wealthy landowner, but particularly during the past three weeks of the harvest. There, in the fields, he would watch the *falahin* at work, talk to them, observe their ways. Often he would spend the night under the sky by the threshing floor where, daily, sheaves of corn were gathered. Like the stars, his dreams and hopes were legion. He would think of Mansour, turned placid with surfeit of comfort—a Boaz of his time—and wonder if one day he too could be like him.

The falahin were friendly. They would greet him with a smile; they called him Effendi. "Why come here to sweat in the heat and sleep in the fields like one of us," they would say to him, "when for the money you paid Effendi Mansour you could've had the harvest from two *fedans* instead of only half?"

What could he tell them that they would understand? And was he indeed paying exorbitantly for his tuition? Could the ageless wisdom of the land be cheaply bought, having been lost to the Jews for countless generations? Such thoughts would console him, and fortify his spirit against the bemused questioning of the falahin.

Only Reb Binish's admonition would occasionally invade his peace, hang there threateningly, not letting go: "We're not here to work or trade Reb Israel, but to sanctify and beatify the Name by study of the Torah, until the Messiah comes." He had uttered these words incisively, in front of all the congregation, for Reb Binish was like a master archer with his warnings: his shafts were perfectly timed, never missed their target.

Above the swaying cornfields, Mansour's house came into view: a handsome house built of stone. All around it were the sheep pens where Mansour kept his flocks. A plane of sunlight set out the house against its surroundings. On the verandah, beneath a trellised awning overhanging with vines, sat Mansour, enjoying the cool of the evening in the sweet fragrance of his laden fig trees.

Ayub Mansour saw his guest arrive. He rose to his feet and waited for Israel to ride up to the house and dismount.

"Ahalan wa sahalan," he said, smiling. His eyes, however, had a weary unwelcoming look. A servant at hand led Israel's mule away, to be fed and watered.

"D'fadahl." Mansour invited Israel to sit with him on the verandah, where soon, cool water was brought, with dark grapes and figs, followed by minted tea. Mansour partook of the refreshment only as a gesture towards his visitor. His galabiya, made of the best Egyptian cotton, was spotlessly white. His eyes moved langorously, he might have been measuring the horizons of his possessions with the same preoccupational habit as his deft fingers played with the amber worry beads he held. His movement, as his speech, seemed guided by an innate economy of effort.

"To what do I owe the honour of your visit this time?" He asked at last, as if he didn't know.

"The harvest is all but finished, and I almost regret it," Israel said, breathing in the air.

"But you should be glad," Mansour said with only a hint of laughter.

"Glad to miss these days and nights? How could I be?"

Mansour clicked his tongue. "For us"—how he emphasized the distinction! "Harvest is either good or bad. Reward for hard work, or disappointment. As Allah sees fit."

"And what will it be this year, Mansour?"

A small, uncharitable smile played on Mansour's lips as he looked away, to the distant fields, "Why do you ask, when you've come here yourself so many times to check?"

"To learn, Mansour, not to check."

"Ah, didn't my falahin teach you then? Didn't they give you good advice?"

The patronizing irony stung Israel. He said tersely: "We're partners. Yet you tell me nothing. You talked to me about profits after the harvest. Is it not right that I should know what I'm getting in return for my investment?"

Mansour allowed a moment to pass. His face betrayed a touch of irritation in its immobility, as though he resented the intrusion of business on his serene and beautiful evening. He sighed, or laughed, "Look around you, any direction. As far as your eye can see. Mansour's fields, his animals, the falahin who work for him. A complete world which will go on after we're both dead and buried. You give me the price of two pairs of oxen, and you tell me 'Mansour, we're partners'?"

Israel's heart sank. How could he move this aloof Arab to understand what the venture meant to him, the hope he pinned on those 3,000 piasters, raised with so much effort? The magic the word *fedan* conjured for him, which to Mansour was nothing more than a mundane unit of land?

He said flatly, "We made an agreement. I ask for nothing more than what we agreed on."

Mansour smiled. "The terms depend on Allah's bounty."

"And on you, Mansour."

"We talked of percentage. Partners must trust each other. But you show no trust. I'd have told you anything you wanted to know, as Allah is my witness. Why do you go out questioning my men?" For the first time he looked hurt. Then all at once his manner changed, "My friend, why this idle talk on such an evening? You've ridden a long way, enjoy the peace of my home. Next week, when the work in the fields is done, we'll settle accounts. What's due to you you'll get."

There was no mistaking his finality.

Mansour protested, though not vigorously, when Israel thankfully declined his invitation to spend the night under his roof, and rode away to bivouac in the open as he had done so many times before. Lying awake looking at the stars, he understood that he would be lucky if he retrieved from Mansour only that which he had invested. He felt no regret, not even for the hurtful rebuke he knew would be his lot in Jerusalem if his losses were large. He would not have foregone the experience for anything, the lesson, the possibilities he had seen. Only Clara would see it all as he did. Even here, in the mellow field, listening to the noises of the night, he could feel her comforting presence steadfastly urging him to try again and again. Buy land, lease it to falahin for a fifth of the yield and a fifth to the Pasha. Remember what he had learnt. Above all, be patient and not give up.

Sir Moses Montefiore set up camp on the slope of the Mount of Olives. Daily the city was beckoning to him—bone-pale at dawn as he faced her in his morning devotions, darkly amber at dusk as he sat for his supper with the tent flaps drawn wide open. Yet this was as close as he could get to Jerusalem, the city which was to be the high point of his second visit to the Holy Land.

By order of the Governor, a cordon had been thrown round the campsite. Sentries stood guard to enforce the quarantine. Couriers were at hand to take messages to and from the city. Sir Moses and his entourage were to want for nothing. Within the city walls, a typhus epidemic was killing as many as ten people a day. The Governor would have gone to any length so that Sir Moses could enjoy the city in a style befitting his eminence. In spite of the disease, which of course he couldn't stamp out, he contrived to give his guests glimpses of selected sights, cleared of people in advance of the tour. The least he could do in the circumstances was to protect the visitors.

Sir Moses had not anticipated the possibility of languishing outside the city. He had come with an aim, the frustration of which tested his patient, forbearing nature.

In the autumn of the previous year he had set out from London, not on a mere journey this time but on a mission he and his wife Lady Judith had conceived of, to do something for the Jews of Palestine. In Alexandria he was received and fêted by the Khedive Mehemet Ali, who duly instructed the officials in Palestine to afford Sir Moses any help he needed. While travelling through the land Sir Moses's resolve took form; plans were shaping in his mind, which he discussed at great length with his dear friend and adviser Dr Loewe. The poverty of the Jews in Tiberias and Safed stirred him deeply. He was received there as though he were the Messiah himself: he became aware of a strange responsibility being thrust upon him. His moods changed with the alternating scenes of loveliness and desolation through which he passed on his way south. And in that changing frame of mind, his hopes rose and fell and rose again, never so high as when a group of Jewish horsemen greeted him in Galilee and escorted him part of the way to Jerusalem.

And after all that, the plague, halting the momentum of his discovery!

Outside the boundaries of his camp, delegations of Jews congregated daily, bearing petitions. After three days, during which he had been visited by the Governor and by Her Britannic Majesty's Consul in Jerusalem, who arrived accompanied by a number of prominent Jerusalem Jews, Sir Moses could stand the isolation no longer. He asked that the sentries be removed so that his fellow Jews could come into his camp, to tell him of their condition and to receive alms—the most he could give as an immediate relief.

Watching the Jews string along the downward path towards the city, Lady Judith was moved to observe, "We hear so many different stories in each place we visit. But the truth, my dear, is that we don't even know how many Jews there are in Palestine, let alone of their condition." That night, before retiring to bed, Sir Moses talked to Dr Loewe about the Jews. If anything meaningful was to be done for them, it should first be ascertained how many there were, where they were concentrated, their division into various communities or sects, and the general condition of every community. Only with that information could a sensible allocation of resources be made. And once that was done, Sir Moses would present the Khedive with a comprehensive plan for the improvement of the Jews in Palestine. As a first step, he wanted a population census carried out. Dr Loewe agreed. He made a note to consult the Consul in this matter.

*

A bashi bazook stood in front of the British Consulate. It was hot, and he was drunk. He slung his musket over his shoulder, pulled down his pantaloons, and pissed in full view of Vice–Consul William Young's window. Then, without bothering to hitch up his pants, he unslung his gun and discharged volley after volley at the Union Jack on top of the house until it hung in shreds from the pole. When he had run out of ammunition, he dropped the weapon to the ground, sat down, and waited. Two *kawasses* came out cautiously. Seeing that the soldier was harmless, they hoisted him to his feet and dragged him inside.

That afternoon William Young had the distasteful duty of witnessing the offender publicly flogged senseless outside the Citadel. No offence had been meant to her Britannic Majesty's Mission in Jerusalem, Young was assured. The garrison's Commandant offered full apologies on the Governor's behalf and, comically, on behalf of the Divine Port in Constantinople itself. Young noted the frivolity with its barely concealed disrespect. It fitted in with a new attitude locals had developed towards Europeans: they were no longer in awe of them.

It had not been like that in the beginning, the year before, when Young, dispatched from Alexandria, opened the first European consulate in Jerusalem. Now there were the French, the Austrian, the Prussian—the Russians too were coming, he had heard. You could see their flags proudly crackling in the breeze above their consulates. Indeed, flags had become something of a fashion in Jerusalem. No drunken or discontent bashi bazook had taken pot shots at other nations' banners so far. True, the British flag was more colourful, could be a more inviting target, as flags went. The respect—never an abundant commodity in Palestine whoever ruled it—which he once commanded virtually alone, now had to be shared among the other consuls. Young had resigned himself to that reality, as he did to their petty rivalry which was, after all, the normal reflexes of diplomatic life. He could envisage his European colleagues writing dispatches home about an "incident" involving the British Consulate, after humorously chatting to him about it. He'd have done the same.

For all it was worth, and it was worth some consolation, in one area Young had the field more or less to himself: no other foreign representative enjoyed the trust and sympathy of the Jews as did the British Vice–Consul. That, in spite of the fact that the other European powers had a stronger claim to the allegiance of the Ashkenazi Jews than did the British. Young justly attributed the Jews' preference of him to his own endeavours. One of the first instructions he received on taking office came directly from Prime Minister Palmerston himself: The British Consul was to afford protection to Jews in general, and to represent their interests whenever possible. It was an instruction that Young had welcomed, despite his own ambivalent feelings about the Jews. He worked hard to win their trust, even when his superior in Alexandria, Major Campbell kept reminding him pointedly that he had other duties in Jerusalem beside spending time on the "Hebrews". The returns on his efforts were multiplied with the arrival in Jerusalem of Rafael Mendoza, in whom Young found a congenial as well as useful friend. The Austrian Consul had formally recognized Rabbi Mordecai Binish as *Wakil*—head—of the Ashkenazi Jews in Jerusalem. But it was Solomon Zeff who still wielded more influence among the Jews, with Mendoza right behind him, and thus Young had secured his assets.

The garrison Commandant was not abreast of the latest realignment of social precedence in Jerusalem, Young observed humorously to his wife, for while he was doling out punishment to the errant bashi bazook and being impertinent about it, his superior the Governor of Jerusalem, was falling about ingratiating himself with Sir Moses Montefiore who only the day before had honoured the British Consul in the presence of the Governor.

Among the papers on William Young's desk was a letter from Sir Moses, outlining his plan for a population count of the Jews, and asking for the Consul's assistance. Young read it again carefully, making notes on a separate sheet of paper. Then he gathered a few documents he had put aside, called for his horse to be saddled, and prepared to pay a visit to Sir Moses.

Israel sat down to pen a letter to Sir Moses Montefiore—the Benefactor, as the Jews now called him. Mendoza had told him that Sir Moses was searching for ways to improve the condition of the Jews. What he had in mind was something far-reaching and imaginative. No longer was he satisfied with mere alms-giving. Israel, encouraged by Clara, decided to measure the range of the Benefactor's intentions.

A chance meeting with an Arab grain merchant, following his return from Adullam after a disappointing settlement with Mansour, sowed the idea in his mind. There was a village called Gazezza in the plain, not far from Jaffa. Its landlord was none other than the Pasha of Jerusalem, and he was putting up much of the land for sale. Israel went to look at the place together with a friend who had shared his enterprise with Mansour. What they saw delighted them. The place was well-favoured by nature: the soil was rich, suitable for grain, fruit trees, and vines. Fresh springs supplied water in abundance to irrigate 500 fedans of fields. There were woods close by, for timber, and quarries where good stone could be taken to build houses.

Once Gazezza had been a prosperous village. But poor husbandry by successive administrations, coupled with unchecked raids from bandits, depopulated the village. Now only about 60 falahin lived there, and they were too heavily taxed to prosper. The ruins of many dwellings, overgrown with weeds, stood as a reminder of a better past. Those that remained were friendly—for years they had been praying that a more caring landlord would replace the present one and improve their lot. They told Israel how before the decline set in Gazezza was the pride of the region, rich in corn and full of fruit trees; how caravans of camels regularly plied the routes from Gazezza to Jaffa, bearing the produce of the village to the markets of the town.

That which had begun as a hopeful quest flowered into a dream which, in turn suggested possibilities when news reached Israel of Sir Moses's intentions: with the Benefactor's wealth and influence, more could be realized than he had ever dared to imagine. A settlement, no less. Where Jews would till the land and earn their bread by the sweat of their brow.

Clara's clear thinking focused his ideas and shaped them into plans. She had a natural inclination for practical detail. "Get all the facts right," she urged, at times impatient with him, as she sat at his side going over what he had written, "Sir Moses would be moved by feasible propositions, not mere notions, things like exactly how much land is for sale at what price, the advantages and disadvantages of the place, what would be needed to set up the settlement—tools, livestock, seeds, material, and how much all this would cost."

They worked at it unremittingly for there was little time to lose. Bit by bit the details began to fall in place. The land put up for sale was only 100 fedans, the price was negotiable; Sheik Said acted as the Pasha's bailiff in Gazezza, for which he collected a profit of 15,000 piaster annually, and 100 barrels of grain; the falahin would gladly work for Sir Moses if he could find a way to relieve them from the heavy poll tax—*numeri* they were obliged to pay the Pasha, and lift the threat of conscription which would send the men flying to the hills whenever troops were sighted in the region.

At times, when it all seemed too fantastical, Israel would despair: "Dreams. Nothing will ever come of it," he would say. And Clara would rebuke him: "If you don't believe in it yourself, don't expect anybody else to believe. Least of all Sir Moses."

When he had drawn up the balance sheet, the total sum was far in excess of anything he had known anyone to possess. Solomon retired to go over the letter in isolation. He emerged with a serious expression on his face. "Ambitious, imaginative, expensive. But not beyond achieving, I don't think," he pronounced, "I will personally take it to Sir Moses."

"After I've copied it neatly," said Clara cheerfully. She was looking into the garden, apparently deep in thought, when she turned to them and said, "A name. We must have a name."

"A name, Clara? You don't give a name to something not yet born!" Solomon cried.

"But it is born. It was born the moment we put it on paper. There!" She pointed at the letter.

"Gate of Hope," Israel said. It suddenly came to him, he didn't know from where. "If it becomes a reality, a new future would be open to us, to all the Jews here. Nothing would ever be the same again."

The evening prayers were over. The men came out of the synagogue into the stone-paved yard. They were talking animatedly, arguing about Israel Zeff's fantastic scheme which had become public knowledge piece by piece as his enquiries progressed. Only an idler, dreamer of dreams, a fool, could conceive of such a thing; the conceit of it was staggering. Or a leader of exceptional vision—no one for a moment forgot whose son Israel was.

"That Jews could go and live among the Ishmaelites to work like peasants! Why, it's unthinkable," Sheine's husband sneered.

"What are we here if not among the Ishmaelites?" someone countered.

"Cities are different. We have our synagogues. We have our ways. We know what to do. Out there, in the wilderness, why, you might as well sleep with vipers and jackals!"

" . . . Who's ever heard of Jews working like labourers! Not even the Sepharadis. . . ."

"No? Then pray tell me who built the synagogue, stone upon stone, eh?"

Voices rose and fell. Israel heard Mansour mentioned. There was laughter.

"Take no notice," Solomon said, squeezing his arm. "Just listen to what your heart tells you. Our people are fractious and faint-hearted. But they follow when the time comes. There's only Binish to worry about."

"I know. He'd oppose anything that doesn't come from him," Israel said.

"This time it isn't so simple as that."

"What do you mean?"

"Well, don't you see? Control of the haluka is what he wants more than anything. The power that goes with it. Imagine how the system would be threatened if your plan became a reality. Reb Binish realizes this. He doesn't even have to think about it, he feels it in his bones. He'll be fighting for his life, for everything he believes in. He'd stop at nothing."

"I can fight too," Israel said mutedly. Solomon looked at him long and tenderly. "Yes," he said at last, "If your faith is as strong as his."

Reb Binish, surrounded by his friends, came out into the yard. He stopped a few paces from Israel and glared contemptuously at him. Averting his eyes to look over his shoulder, he said as if speaking to a follower behind, "Young Zeff hardly had his mother's milk dried on his mouth, and already he wants to save the people of Israel. Has anyone heard his pearls of wisdom at the synagogue? Will he rebuild our Holy Temple ahead of the Messiah with the vast profits he has made from his dealings with the Ishmaelites?" Titters were heard.

"Reb Binish! You came here when times were easy. Don't presume too much on the success you've enjoyed," Solomon said in a quiet but cutting voice. For a moment the two men stared at each other. Then Binish turned his gaze on Israel. Deadly calm, he said, "Keep away from Montefiore. A great king, no mere rich Jew, once sought to carry out a census among his people. And the Lord chastened David with the plague for his conceit. Tens of thousands perished because of that abomination.

"Tomorrow I'll show you what is that so-called benefactor and what awaits those who'll listen to him. You want a gate of hope? I'll show you one. Go to the Golden Gate. That's the one, and it is bricked up until the day the Messiah will come and fling it open."

As Sir Moses and his company came out of their tents for morning prayers they were confronted by a strange spectacle. A large assembly of Ashkenazi Jews gathered at the perimeter of the camp. The men all wore prayer shawls and phylacteries. Binish was among them, easily distinguishable by his enormous hat. When they saw Montefiore, they raised a loud cry. Shaking their fists at him, they shouted denunciations. They went on rocking and chanting until, bemused and disturbed, Sir Moses retreated to his tent.

Later that day news reached him: that Reb Binish had convened a special council of rabbis which placed Sir Moses and anyone who came into contact with him under interdict, for the sacrilege he was preparing to commit.

Disappointed by the anger he had aroused, Sir Moses decamped the next day and rode to Jaffa, where a steamer was waiting to take him back to Europe. He had not forgotten Israel Zeff's letter. It had impressed him deeply. He used the sea voyage to draft a letter to the Khedive Mehemet Ali in Alexandria, outlining a plan to improve the lot of the Jews of Palestine. The plan was based on Israel's proposals. Sir Moses did not believe Mehemet Ali would approve of the plan. Nor, even if he did, it could be realized as it stood. But he knew it was a good gambit which would make possible another less ambitious project at a more propitious time.

A letter arrived at Israel's home by messenger from Reb Binish. It read: "With the Help of God. because I know you're innocent of evil thoughts, and for the sake of your revered father, I forgive your foolishness. With all my heart I pray that the Blessed Name, Creator of the World, who understands everything, may open your eyes and heart to the wisdom of your people and direct you to the path of righteousness."

Early next morning, Israel awoke to the sound of animal gurgling and flapping outside. Opening the front door, he saw a headless chicken convulsing in the dust. Its blood had been smeared all over the door and walls, and the frame of the door had been daubed with black paint. Binish had sent a supplement to his letter.

Chapter 19

At the end of summer the typhus abated. Reb Mordecai Binish conducted a public prayer of thanksgiving and solemnly invoked a period of regeneration and amnesty. He appeared full of regal pride, as if he himself had single-handedly vanquished the Angel of Death. No one dared challenge his authority. Two unfortunate men who unwittingly contradicted him were found beaten senseless, reportedly by Reb Binish's over-zealous disciples, at the behest of implacable wife, the Rebbetze Zelda Binish.

Now that Montefiore was gone, and with him the dangerous heresies that hovered about him, Reb Binish spoke kindly of him, extolling his generosity and piety, welcoming the day he would once again visit his people in the Holy Land in a humbler frame of mind. The vigour of his animosity was now turned against the Christian missionaries, for it was they who during the ravages of the plague stretched out a helping hand to those among the Jews who were desperate enough to seize it.

Sultan Mahmud II died. Rimkin explained that the deceased monarch had not been good for the Jews but neither had he been worse than Jews could expect. Better the devil you knew, he said. Prayers were recited at the synagogues of the Sepharadis for the health and prosperity of the new Sultan Abdel Majid. No sooner was he sitting firmly on his throne than rumours arrived that plans were afoot to drive Mehemet Ali out of Palestine with the help of the British navy. The British Vice–Consul William Young could neither confirm nor deny the rumours. Ashkenazi Jews came in greater numbers to register with the Consulate as persons eligible for British protection for there was no longer doubt about which was the power with the rising influence in the land.

As the Days of Awe and the New Year approached, Reb Binish himself set the tone for reconciliation. Smilingly he went about shaking hands, uttering benedictions on those he had previously interdicted. He came to Menachem Zion synagogue and read the lesson, then urged Solomon to come to the smaller synagogue across the way, where he, Binish was accustomed to officiate. "Please God, may we see the day when there'll be one united synagogue on this holy site where Rabbi Judah the Pious first built the house of worship, which thanks to you, Reb Solomon, has been reclaimed from dust," Binish declared.

"Amen," Solomon mumbled.

Before the entire congregation Binish embraced first Solomon then Israel, to show that no transgression was severe enough to divide Jews for any length of time. The Rebbetze Zelda Binish, who no one ever saw smiling, baked sweet bread for the poor. Unchastened tongues wagged that in the early hours of the morning the Rabbi's kawass went about collecting the Rebbetze's bread from the gutters lest it should be seen to have been cast away even by the hungry, and shame the Rebbetze.

Ariel prepared to sing the Kol Nidre prayer at the synagogue. It was to be a great occasion, a moment of unity when strife and differences would be laid aside, if not forgotten. A day of self-abnegation for the strong and comfort for the weak. In his mind's eye Ariel could see his father and brother standing next to Reb Binish and Rimkin and his son, listening to him sing. And he would sing his best, more beautifully than ever before. His voice would rise like a blessed spirit, and vibrate in the deep dome above the Holy Ark. The thought of a beatific peace among adversaries warmed Ariel's heart. He liked to please; nothing gave him more pleasure than seeing people happy at something that he had done. Israel used to mock him, when they were both younger, that he was too good and too beautiful for this world but would nevertheless have to endure it longer than anybody because the angels wouldn't suffer him to eclipse them in the next world. Yet now, as a youth, Ariel felt a mild displeasure with people who were too easily pleased by him. Therefore he was puzzled and strangely drawn to someone who seemed demonstratively unimpressed by him as a person or by anything he did. That someone was Reb Israel, the kinsman of the late Reb Mendle of Shklov, who came to Jerusalem after the earthquake in Safed. Ariel couldn't understand what that severe man had against him. He never spoke to him, he seemed deliberately to avoid coming near him, always looked at him with cold indifference and never smiled when somebody praised Ariel in his presence.

There was dark side to Ariel's nature. Unexplained fears assailed him at intervals from childhood. He grew up with the feeling that one day, in adulthood, his world would collapse; an invader from the uncharted hinterland of his being would vanquish him—he would be enslaved and debased. No amount of love and warmth and praise, all of which he received in abundance from Solomon, could dispel his fears. In his childhood he often woke up screaming from a nightmare. And Solomon would sit at his bedside stroking his head and telling him soothing stories until dawn. He asked about his mother. All Solomon ever told him was "She was like an angel, full of goodness and light, like you." But was it possible for such a being to die and be forgotten, and never mentioned, as though her name were a forbidden subject? The question hammered at him persistently over the years and he could get no answer, until he began dreading the answer and left the question unasked. But in his dark moods he imagined his mother the very opposite of how Solomon described her.

Praise and appreciation reassured him but doubt and fear still lurked in him. He had a natural, spontaneous compassion for suffering and injustice. But in cold moments of self-appraisal he would ask himself whether his outgoing goodness was not a deceitful device of accruing capital against the day when some unknown debt would be thrust at him. He had managed to suppress such fears the older he grew and the more successful he became. Now came this strange forbidding man, Reb Israel, and stirred them up again.

Ariel rated the Kol Nidre prayer higher than all the others in the Jewish liturgy. Not only was he profoundly moved by its beauty and mood, he also recognized the great responsibility it carried, for in it the Creator, King of Mercy, is asked in solemn supplication to forgive undertakings that have not been fulfilled and debts that have not been paid. It had always been the custom that the man who sang the Kol Nidre had to be, above all, an outstanding pillar of the community, recognized for his righteous ways and for the communal responsibility that he shouldered. To sing the Kol Nidre was an honour, borne with gravity and humility. Ariel Zeff was much too young for such an honour, but that he was outstanding in every conceivable way was not doubted by anyone.

He had a gift for opening hearts and minds. He could naturally and effortlessly simplify a complicated argument making it vivid without losing its subtlety. He could bring out the differences between good and bad, trivial and important, no matter how lost they were in the convolutions of an argument. Moreover, he could do this in a way that made people feel they themselves had followed the thread of thought sure-footedly as an ibex on a mountain path. The simple-minded loved him, for he lifted them from the fog of their incomprehension and put them on equal planes with the bright, even with himself, as though their reasons were like a precious metal that only needed polishing. Everything about Ariel, his looks, the soothing yet penetrating gaze of his blue eyes, his mellifluous voice, all were outshone by his gift of reaching out to people.

His powers had developed slowly: it was only in his penultimate year at the cheder that his teacher could say with full conviction that Ariel had a rare intelligence which, if properly nurtured, would reach such heights as were never seen in the Holy Land since the days of Reb Judah the Hassid, nearly a hundred years before. That appreciation, was now shared by almost all, including Reb Binish, and Ariel's untarnished simplicity in spite of the adulation he received, was what qualified him to sing the Kol Nidre prayer at the Menachem Zion synagogue that year. It was a happy choice, not least because it aroused neither jealousy nor rivalry, and no man felt slighted because of it.

On the eve of Yom Kippur Reb Mordecai Binish went with his disciples to the *mikve* to have a ritual bath. He put on a plain white gown and in the anteroom of the synagogue submitted himself to be lashed by the *shomas* in full view of all his followers. Not once did he wince, not once did he call "enough". Thus the high-minded Reb Binish acknowledged his sharing in common human weaknesses, and repented of his sins and omissions for all to see.

He was among the first to appear at the synagogue after the Yom Kippur meal. His flesh still tingled from the flagellation; he felt light and clean. For that awesome day at least he could demonstrate publicly how insignificant were the powers and conceit of man before the terrible immanence of the Almighty. He greeted the congregants, embraced and kissed Solomon, Israel, and Reb Rimkin and his son, then took his place of honour at the foot of the Holy Ark. Not far from him stood William Young who, combining official duties with a growing personal interest in the Jews, had come on his first visit as an honoured guest to the synagogue.

Lights flickered in the dome. The service had just begun. The men, wrapped in prayer shawls, swayed gently. Standing among them, with a *talith* round his shoulders like them, Young was moved to the depth of his soul. From his readings and conversation with Jews, he had always imagined Yom Kippur to be a mournful day, full of repentance and lamentation. What he now sensed was the majesty of pure devotion, a surge towards God's ultimate gift of imaginative understanding. Not penance but humility and full receptiveness, which entered and uplifted him in communion with the rest.

Silence fell as Ariel approached the lectern before the Ark. He looked sombre and etherial. His talith was of the purest white and sky blue, with gold threads along the hem. It was a present he had received on his Bar Mitzva from Reb Eliezer Rimkin. The congregants held their breath as Ariel raised his head and closed his eyes. William Young, in near-ecstasy, thought he had never seen such a beautiful youth, his mind turned to his Redeemer Son of God as he prayed silently.

Ariel could tell that he had done his best, even better than he had hoped. The people were so moved they wept. All but one, Reb Israel. For when Ariel had finished and looked around quickly, he caught sight of Reb Israel and his heart sank. Reb Israel's face wore the same hard indifferent expression with which he had greeted Ariel on all previous occasions.

As they were leaving the synagogue and everyone came up to press Ariel's hand and congratulate Solomon on having such a fine son, Reb Israel turned his back on Ariel and briskly walked away. No one paid much attention to this incident but the memory of the elderly man's rejection burnt in Ariel's mind. He resolved that if by the end of Yom Kippur Reb Israel had not offered explanation for his strange animosity, he would gather up his courage and approach him.

And so it happened that after the Concluding Service the following day, Ariel, coming out of the synagogue with his family, saw Reb Israel standing only a few paces away talking to one of Reb Binish's followers. He was smiling and seemed in good spirits. Most of the people were still hanging about the entrance wishing one another all the best in the New Year. Ariel swallowed, took in a deep breath, and approached Reb Israel.

Reb Israel had been conscious of Ariel all the while; it was as though he were waiting for him to approach so as to spring a trap he had set. No sooner had Ariel spoken than the older man's cheerful expression changed to one of deep repugnance. For a moment he gazed at Ariel, undecided whether to reply or turn away. Then his gaze fell on Solomon among the men near by. Measuring his words with icy precision, he said loud enough to be heard by the men around him, "What do you want of me? I said not a word to you either good or bad. All who know me will testify that I've not mentioned your name, nor ever cast aspersions on you for seventeen years. Yet you're an abomination to my eyes and a blight on my life. I look at you and I see your mother, who was a whore, a proud, deceitful whore."

His words were like a sudden squall of hail. Ariel turned ashen. His hands rose in a gesture of supplication, of defence. Reb Israel went on. This time he spoke past Ariel, to Solomon, "Didn't your father tell you that you're a bastard, begotten in lust and sin? Do you think you could hide for ever behind the name of Zeff which has brought nothing but shame and ruin to the Jewish community of Safed which had offered him a home? I did not seek this confrontation. You brought it upon yourself. Now taste the filth that brought you in to this world."

Reb Israel turned on his heels and walked away.

Ariel had run away from the place, his hands clasped to his ears. Solomon ran after him but soon lost him in the alleys and had to stop, he was so short of breath. Night fell and there was no sign of Ariel. Distraught, Solomon spent the night in vigil, walking up and down the street with a lamp in his hand. Israel could not persuade him to take a rest and let him stand watch instead. When Ariel failed to show up the next day the Jews organized a search. Israel and Abraham Karlin hired horses and with the help of a few trusted Arabs scoured the hills. They returned at night empty-handed. At that moment of crisis Reb Binish showed the magnanimous side of his leadership. He ordered a collection to be made so that searchers could be hired; he proclaimed that special prayers were to be said every morning and evening until the youth was safely home. But he did not publicly denounce Reb Israel for having caused the calamity, even when Solomon in his grief assaulted Reb Israel in the street and would have throttled him if they hadn't been pulled apart by passersby.

Disjointed and conflicting reports arrived from time to time: someone resembling Ariel was seen near Nablus; a man fitting such a description was found dead and half-devoured by hyenas an hour's ride from Jericho. Solomon, refusing to give up even against all hope, daily rode out with

Israel and Karlin in search of Ariel. A month passed and there was not a word from Ariel. The searches and investigations carried out by the Sepharadis, the Ashkenazis, the Pasha of Jerusalem's officers and informers who went into action following a formal request from Vice–Consul Young, all came to nought. Ariel disappeared as though the earth had swallowed him up.

"He's dead, I know it," Ada said in her grief. "Hush, don't say that, don't give up hope," Solomon entreated. "You should have prepared him. You should have told him the truth about his mother. Did you think you could withhold it from him for ever?" she rebuked him bitterly.

"I was going to, only I couldn't just yet . . ." was all he could answer. Then he sighed, "Nothing passes without reward or retribtuion, and now my sins are visited upon this pure-hearted innocent boy." Tears began to roll down his cheeks. "Who knows what terrible things may have happened to him or where he is. Surely we would have heard from him if he were alive and well. Not knowing, that's the worst thing. Not knowing whether to mourn or to hope and wait. A bereavement for the rest of our lives, Solomon," said Ada. Her voice sounded like stone against stone.

Early in the next year, William Young reluctantly suspended his involvement in the search for Ariel. It was not because he had given up hope, nor because he had other more pressing matters to attend to. The reason was that his movements became circumscribed by a new development, a development which he, as well as anyone in the know, had long been expecting: the British joined the forces of the Sultan Abdel Mejid in a campaign to oust Mehemet Ali from Palestine and restore the land to Ottoman rule. Young and his small staff hardly moved outside the Consulate building during the period of uncertainty. He took to keeping a loaded pistol close at hand. When the local kawasses failed to turn up for work one morning, he thought it expedient to remove the Union Jack to a less conspicuous position. At last the news reached Jerusalem that the British navy together with the Sultan's army had inflicted a crushing defeat on the forces of Mehemet Ali outside Acre. The Egyptian forces were in full retreat all along the coast.

Young set about hiring replacements for the staff who had left him, and prepared to greet the new ruler of Jerusalem.

The new Pasha wasn't long in arriving, and he made a grand entry into the city. The streets were decorated with flags. A holiday was proclaimed. The citizens of Jerusalem crowded by the Jaffa Gate, along the streets leading to the Governor's Palace, anywhere where the procession was thought to pass through, and waited to catch a glimpse of their new Pasha. Preceded by a military band, he rode in at the head of a column of troops. He was a youngish man, a high-ranking officer in the Ottoman administration. Barely forty and already two-horsetailed, His Excellency the Muztarflick waved and smiled to the people. Before the Governor's Palace, he faced the cheering crowd.

"On behalf of His Imperial Majesty Sultan Abdel Majid, I greet and embrace you," he declaimed. The cheering rose to a frenzy: no Pasha ever addressed the people on such a positive note. A new era had begun for Jerusalem, for Palestine, for the whole Ottoman Empire. And the fresh-faced young Pasha was about to give the people a foretaste of what it was about: order, advancement, new opportunities.

At last the sun shone on the British Mission out of a cloudless sky. William Young, promoted to a full Consul, was able to inform the Ashkenazi Jews that Sultan Abdel Majid had personally pledged to Her Majesty's Government to protect the Jews of Palestine, and reaffirmed the European powers' rights in protecting their citizens with full authority in judicial matters. The Jews needed no telling which European power held the most sway, and which flag beckoned them with the most assurance of security.

That year Reb Mordecai Binish was appointed Honorary Prussian Vice–Consul, and Reb Eliezer Rimkin had a similar honour conferred on him by the Austrians. A vaguer yet warmer association was offered to Solomon by the British Vice–Consul. Solomon accepted gladly. It was a time, he thought, when Europe at last looked on the Holy Land with fonder eyes.

Chapter 20

"A man has issued forth from the Wilderness of Judaea, having lived in the shadow of rocks under the brassy sky, drinking the night-chilled dew and eating locust and wild honey.

"There, in the thin dry air, this man experienced revelations. Yes, my friends, the Lord spoke to him as he had spoken to the prophets of Israel. This man learnt to understand the sorrow of the world and the evil ways of his people. In his visions he saw armies clash in the dust, crumbling cities, orphaned children and widowed women, and he wept bitterly. . . ."

The speaker was a rugged wild-looking man of indeterminable age. His face was hollow and etched with deep lines. There was something absurd yet arresting about the fierce stare of his eyes. He spoke slow and deliberate Hebrew in a voice which was too resonant and full-bodied for his stilted use of the language so that his speech sounded theatrical but unmoving. He wore a plain fustian robe and nothing on his feet. The noise he was raising together with his odd appearance made passersby stop and cluster round him at the end of the Jewish Quarter where a gentle rise afforded a sweeping view of the Temple mount and the Valley of Kidron.

"How many times did the Lord your God speak to you through his prophets and ye would not listen?" the man boomed. "How long O Israel will indifference harden your hearts against righteousness? Must you be chastised with pestilence again and again?"

The Jews of Jerusalem, no less than their Arab neighbours, were tolerant of lunatics of which Jerusalem didn't lack. But at the mention of pestilence, there was a perceptible stiffening in the crowd. Some of the boys began looking around for likely missiles. Plague and pestilence were words which evoked fearful reverberations among the Jews of Jerusalem, particularly soon after the visitation of one in which hardly a family remained that hadn't lost a dear one. The stranger seemed unconscious of the change in mood that he had wrought. He went on speaking, his voice rising like the roll of thunder: "This man I tell ye of brings you the word of the Lord. Come to him and you shall be comforted. Repent of your hard-necked ways and you shall feel the loving kindness of God. Shut not your ears to the awaited message but open up your hearts in humility and set your feet on the path to Salvation."

A low grumble rose from the crowd. Boys moved out to the shadow of a nearby wall and took up positions ready to discharge their missiles at the first sign of anger from their elders—the shaking of the fist, a verbal abuse. The man saw them from the corner of his eye and his fervour rose. "I have seen the light shining forth from the soul of this man I tell you of. I have listened to him, and my troubles were assuaged. I have brought him here from the wilderness that the children of Israel may be redeemed. Come to him for the hour is at hand . . ." The first volley of bits of wood, rock-hard bread and rotten vegetables hit him full on the front and nearly threw him off-balance. He lifted his face heavenwards and called on God to forgive his assailants. Voices rose in angry shouts. The missiles that showered on the man now were no longer vegetables but rocks. He was hit on the head and began bleeding but somehow managed to stay upright. His lips, now split, moved. He raised his arms to protect himself and looked at his tormentors with defiance.

It so happened that Solomon and Israel passed by on their way from Rimkin's home. The commotion drew them to the place and they stood a small distance from the agitation and looked on.

"A crazy man, a missionary," a passerby informed, adding "They get what they deserve. What right have they to come and preach nonsense to our people?"

Israel wanted to walk away. He hated crowds and he hated violence. The heat with which Jews responded to what he considered trivia disgusted him: they seemed to look for threat in everything. Any Christian who as much as looked sympathetically on a Jew was immediately branded a missionary.

But Solomon stood fast and hung on to Israel's sleeve. He said angrily "Shame and disgrace! Can't they see the poor man is mad? Look at him bleed! What are we turning ourselves into?"

"It's not we, Father, it's them. Stupid people behaving in a stupid way. You can't be responsible for everything Jews do in this city. Come, let's go."

"We must do something, Israel. Look he's hurt. He might be killed and then there'll be trouble," Solomon said.

The man no longer shouted. He stood there barely able to shield his head with his arms, and took the blows in silence. Something about him looked vaguely familiar. As Solomon followed by Israel advanced and made ready to intervene, the man suddenly rallied. He straightened up and in an outburst of rage and fear began to curse his tormentors in English. Solomon recognized him at once: it was none other than Mr Pike the Englishman who travelled with him to the Holy Land in search of the secret of Creation, the strange, eccentric Mr Pike.

But how he had changed! What visions, what ordeals of the spirit could have transformed that clear-eyed creature of a temperate clime into the gaunt and craggy spectre of derangement he now appeared! Israel and

Solomon stared at him in disbelief, and then at each other.

"Save him if you must but let him be, what have we to do with him?" said Israel, reading his father's thoughts.

"He saved us once, you wouldn't remember. . . ."

"I remember, and you also saved him. We want no dealings with such a man. Let's just make the people stop so that he may leave in peace."

When Solomon placed himself between the hapless Mr Pike and the Jews, the latter let go their missiles but began to reproach Solomon. One young man, a reedy fellow with a sallow complexion and a wispy blonde beard, who was renowned for the quaint way he gyrated as he prayed, raised his voice above the others. "You rush to protect a cursed corrupter of our children, Reb Solomon Zeff. If only you'd rush half so fast to support Reb Binish instead of opposing him," he bleated.

"I'll throw something at him," said Israel and bent down. Solomon held his arm tightly. "That's all we need, to fight among ourselves," he said under his breath and aloud he cried, "Shame, shame on you, ruffians. You despise the goyim for doing just what you're doing now! Leave off, you've done enough. Go back to your homes before the officers of the law arrive and things get really bad."

The crowd retreated grudgingly, like a thwarted pack of hounds, snarling, shaking their fists and cursing. No more stones were thrown. But there was vigilant attention. Only small groups hung about, watching and whispering. Solomon turned to Pike who stared at him unrecognizing and confused.

"Mr Pike, do you remember me, from the boat, and on the way to Jerusalem?" Solomon said.

The Englishman's eyes cleared and a light of recognition appeared in them.

"Why . . . yes . . . yes . . . of course," he mumbled. Then suddenly he became self-conscious and started knocking the dust and dirt from his clothes. "For the second time you've come to my help in an unpleasant situation," he said when he had finished.

"We meet in most peculiar circumstances, Mr Pike. First you seek the secrets of creation, then you disappear as though the earth had swallowed you, and now this . . ."

"I have unravelled a secret. Not of creation but one of greater importance for people. Only they will not listen. You will understand. You are a true believer, help me to help you, be my tongue and my voice," said Mr Pike and seized Solomon by the hand, his eyes became fiery again.

"Look, they know each other, they know each other, the Devil . . ." The whisper from the people grew to an angry murmur. Pike rose to his toes and cried out over Solomon's shoulder: "The Lord has hardened your hearts but like the people of Nineveh you shall repent when you hear this man I speak of."

"Blasphemy, blasphemy, woe to us for listening," the people chanted and began to close in.

"Hush, haven't you done yourself enough harm? I shan't be able to protect you from them if you go on talking like that," Solomon said, and laying his hands on Pike's shoulders, spun him round so that his back was to the people.

"This madman is an Englishman. The English Consul who's our friend, and protector, knows of him. Hold your peace," Israel shouted.

Then someone from the crowd called out: "Madman, who is this man you speak of, bring him to us that we may see him."

"Gladly, that's all I want. The rest is up to God our Lord," Pike replied triumphantly. He pushed past Solomon and stood before his accusers, arms spread out. "I stand before you with my faith and the word of the Lord as my shield," he declared, forgetting how imperfectly that shield had served him. "Tomorrow I shall return with him who brings you salvation." He pointed in the direction of the Zion Gate. "Tomorrow with sunrise we shall come. Up Mount Zion and through the Zion Gate, righteousness shall return to Zion. There you'll see him and he'll pray for you, with you." Pike's gestures and voice now became so wild that the people began to laugh. "Why not?" someone shouted, "And we'll be there, to teach you a lesson you'll never forget, English Consul or no English Consul."

After the people had gone away and Mr Pike had stalked off into some part of his wilderness, Israel exhaled loudly and said: "That's all we need, some crazy wretch to give our hotheads an excuse for creating trouble. Missionary indeed! If only the Christians tended to their own madmen and left us alone all would be well. How did you recognize him Father? I'd never have done. He's changed so much, all that mass of unkempt hair and beard."

"You don't easily forget a man like Mr Pike, no matter how much he changes. Besides, you were a young boy at the time, a mere child."

"But I remember, I remember what you did with the pirates, the Captain, everything, even what he looked like," and he shook his head.

"The disease of the mind is far worse than any plague. What are we but mere animals without reason," Solomon said, reaching for his son's shoulder.

"At least it's not contagious like the plague."

"You think not? I'm not so sure about that."

"How he stank! A billy goat rolling in its own muck is a bed of flowers by comparison."

"Back in Kedainai we used to say 'the fish begins to stink from its head'. How true it is of men too, Israel, true and sad. There was something about this man I much admired."

"He was odd. Right from the beginning, as I remember. That box he used to sit on. Mad," said Israel and added, "I wonder what poor wretch he'll drag with him tomorrow. We shouldn't go."

"On the contrary, son. We must, and take Rimkin and some of the others with us in case something untoward should happen."

There was no theatre in Jerusalem. The city's mood never tolerated levity or playfulness, at least not for the Jews. Even Purim, when traditionally children dressed up in costumes, was a sombre affair in Jerusalem. So said all those who had lived in other places. In weddings, a handful of musicians—a fiddler, a piper with an old cracked clarinet and a flute player—came together to play familiar tunes for the guests. Anyway, weddings were not too frequent, nor were other occasions for celebration like the birth of a boy and the circumcision ceremony, or Bar Mitzvas. Jerusalem was a city of funerals. Rafael Mendoza had remarked that he had never seen such a sombre collection of Jews in his life, as the Ashkenazi Jews of Jerusalem. Before he departed he charged Clara never to neglect her music-making no matter what. And she didn't, not altogether that is.

The Sepharadim were only slightly better in this respect than their Ashkenazi brethren. Their liturgy was more extravagant, their homes generally more decorated and certainly cleaner, their celebrations gayer and noisier, their food spicier; even poverty and disease appeared less debilitating in them than in the Ashkenazi Jews. But when it came to music, there was not much to speak of. And as for the other forms of entertainment they, like the Ashkenazis, had to make do with occasional visits of itinerant players with tame bears or monkeys.

The prospect of two madmen playing up to the public promised a diversion nobody wanted to miss. The word spread quickly. By late evening that day a large audience was assured. With the first light of morning the Jews hurried to the synagogue for the early service. It might have been a holiday so gay was their mood. Throughout the service young men exchanged conspiratorial glances. The elders shook their heads and winked at one another. No sooner was the service over than the young men ran to the appointed meeting place. In the alleys not far from the Zion Gate, boys were stocked up with arsenals of left-over vegetables, fruit, bread, anything which could be hurled without grievously injuring, for a warning had gone out: no bloodshed, no rocks.

A few boys stood on the wall by the gate and strained their eyes to see the pretender prophet arrive. A slow stream of morning mist flowed from the foot of the Mount of Olives into Kidron, and curled about the lower houses in Silwan. The voice of the Muezzin shot like an arrow to the sky. The colours on the hillside quickened and grains of gold seemed to flood the glinting windows of the villages. It was going to be a beautiful day.

"Here they come," shouted one of the boys who was on the lookout. Two men could be seen striding resolutely towards the walls. They had not come from close by Mount Zion, past the few houses by the Gate, but had made their way from the direction of Silwan, across Gai Ben Hinnom, and up the slope to the path which ran along the walls all the way to the Zion Gate. Thus they could be observed for a long while before they actually reached it.

Pike was walking a few steps ahead of the other man. He was wearing the same dirty fustian robe that he wore the day before, and his feet were bare. In his hand he held a shepherd's stick with a broad crook. He walked very straight, his chin stuck out, his eyes set at some point in front of him. His companion dragged his feet, his eyes downcast. He was in rags. Long dank strands of dark blond hair hung limply about his shoulders. His beard was tangled and dusty like a thorn bush in summer. He wore sandals which were fastened to his feet with bits of string and leather thongs.

By the time they reached the Zion Gate a large crowd had gathered on the other side of it waiting for them. The boys on the top of the wall started jumping up and down and pulling faces as Mr Pike and his man from the wilderness drew near. Pike came to the gate like a prince of paupers. He stood before the crowd and raised both arms in benediction but clutched his heavy shepherd's stick in his fist. The wild man stood beside him head lowered. No sooner had Pike begun to speak than missiles rained down on him and his companion. You couldn't hear a word he was saying for the shouts and jeers. Then the man from the wilderness lifted his head and looked up to the sky. He didn't say a word, nor moved as bits of rotten food splattered on his chest and face. But his face began to work and soon tears ran down his dust-caked face.

Solomon grasped Israel's arm and stifled a cry. The man's face looked tortured and hollow and intensely beautiful. In an instant everybody recognized him and gasped with horror; he was none other than the long-lost Ariel.

After a moment of stunned silence the sound of choked wailing could be heard. It was Solomon; he was crying disconsolately and beating his breast. People moved away from him. His sorrow was at once so personal and passionate that even those who knew and loved him felt helpless. They looked the other way not wanting to see him in the nakedness of his grief. Soon the street was empty. Only Israel remained hugging his father in silence, and staring at his half-brother and the Englishman.

Ariel said not a word. He just stood there loose armed, eyes downcast. And when at last Solomon came to him, threw his arms around him and pressed him to his breast, Ariel didn't move. "Light of my soul, forgive, come home, I beg of you," Solomon managed to say. Ariel's thin chest heaved but he said nothing, nor looked up to his father. "I must go," he said at last.

"I won't let you go. You are my son, Ariel. Your place is with your family, with your people," Solomon said and held on to him. But Ariel gently but firmly pushed himself away. "I must go," he repeated. "Don't try to stop me because you can't. I shouldn't have come here today. It was a mistake. Forgive me for the pain I've caused you, as I forgive you for your weakness with my mother. Yes, I know everything now. Don't think I do not love you. I must go. I've a purpose and a calling and I must obey the call."

"What are you saying? What call? There is but one call which is written in our law. . . ." Even as he spoke he realized how futile his appeal was. Ariel just looked at him and smiled sadly.

"Your son is chosen of the Lord, be blessed in him," Mr Pike said. Solomon ignored him.

"I must go," Ariel said again.

"Like that, no more words? Stay, explain, make me understand. You are so good at making people understand," Solomon cried.

"Your heart is too full of emotion now to understand. Maybe one day you will, without help." He started to move away.

Solomon stretched out his hand. Israel put his arm round him. "Come Father. There's nothing we can do. At least you see he's alive. Now that we know we can follow his whereabouts. When he comes to his senses he'll return to us." Israel said without conviction.

They watched Ariel walk down the path in the direction he had come, followed by Mr Pike. When he was no longer visible, Solomon wiped his eyes and said, "He'll never come back."

Israel felt that all the strength had suddenly left his father's body.

At the door of their home Solomon said, "Now I have only you and your family, for Ada, may God bring her peace of mind, has shut me out of her heart."

"She'll come round, give her time. I am with you, as always and everything in life that's mine, is yours, for you are everything to me."

At home, Solomon tore his clothes and sat in mourning for seven days, as was the custom. His friends and adversaries alike came to pay their condolences as though Solomon had lost a son. No one said a word about Ariel. His name was never mentioned again in front of Solomon.

Chapter 21

In Jewish myth Jerusalem is the eye of the world. Rivers and mountains are all around her and oceans put distance between her and lesser human habitations. Children are taught this at the rabbi's cheder particularly in Jerusalem where the notion helps dispel the bleakness of life. The mere breathing of Jerusalem's air puts a man in a favoured place with the Almighty which no amount of hardship can outweigh, says the myth. The goyim too knew about this, the children were taught, which was why they came here, and why they coveted the city and envied the Jews their relationship with her. Therefore, no sacrifice was too great in order to attain this supreme goal of Jewish existence.

On a hot and windless summer day, a group of Russian pilgrims clambered up the road to Jerusalem, pushing and shoving a primitive cart upon which was strapped a huge brass bell. The bell was a gift of the people of Kiev to the Russian church which was going to be built near the believed site of Calvary. Not a single stone had yet been cut for the church. But here was the bell, heavy and ornate, transported by land and sea all the way from distant Kiev, and received with great ceremony by the Russian Consul in Jaffa. A bell large and powerful enough to awaken the dead on the day of resurrection and gather to the bosom of the true church countless generations of buried pilgrims.

The Russians progressed precariously up the uneven slope. Often the cart got stuck, the bell tilted to one side threatening to come down and crush to death anyone near it. The men were unarmed. On a nearby hill stood a band of mounted Beduin who looked on, bemused. To them the spectacle appeared like ants struggling to move something large and dead and utterly useless.

Elsewhere in Jerusalem Christians of all denominations and from all parts of Europe were vying against each other to secure a place in Jerusalem and in the esteem of her government.

"Jerusalem has become a bazaar for the nations of the world," said Samuel Rimkin in a superior tone of voice. "Here they put their wares on show and scream at one another. The British, French, Austrians, you name them. All in their Consulates like stalls in the marketplace." Samuel looked very pleased with himself at having made such an observation. Married life agreed with him, made him look relaxed and grave at the same time and altogether mature beyond his years. He had filled out somewhat too.

To Israel, Samuel was already middle-aged: well-fleshed, out of breath, self-important, always right. But Samuel had always been like that; he was one of those people who are born adult. Like Israel, Samuel was contemptuous of the haluka, even though he benefited from it more than most people. Israel believed Samuel really envied the power men like Reb Binish wielded. But Samuel in fact also envied Israel's independent spirit. He was drawn to him again after their earlier animosity. He would come to see him, to enjoy vicariously Israel's defiant disregard for the established hierarchy of the Ashkenazi Jews. Israel welcomed Samuel's renewed friendship, even if Samuel too often bored and irritated him. They did after all more less grow up together. And besides, Samuel was by no means stupid or a worthless person.

"Bazaar," Samuel continued. "Vendors all selling more or less the same things."

"Like what?" Israel asked, half-yawning.

"Like what? Like protection, identity, religion. Look, the Sultan wants the Europeans' friendship so he says: 'Here's Jerusalem open for you, do what you like, get your customers, I shan't interfere." So the Europeans set up their stalls. What do they sell? Lutheran Christianity, Catholic Christianity, Calvinist Christianity, Russian Orthodox, all with their special guarantee to last for a lifetime and protect you. And who do they try to sell it to? Us of course."

"We've no currency with which to pay," said Israel.

"Don't believe it. The Arabs don't appeal to them being too unsubtle, too simple. There's no challenge for the Christian missionary to ensnare the Arab. Don't look at me so, they're arrogant and high-minded those missionaries, I tell you. Besides, what can they offer the Arabs?"

"Surely no less than they can offer us Jews." Samuel looked at him as though he were an idiot.

"The Arabs", he said slowly, pronouncing each syllable "are Ottoman subjects. They are liable to conscription and to normal taxes. The Christians can't touch them. Do you know it's an offence to try to convert a Moslem? But with us it's different. We're foreigners, *rayas*, nobodies, anybody's for the taking. But converting us will bring salvation to them, so they believe. The British, the French, the Austrians, all of them want us. With us as their citizens they have a real stake in this country, don't you see?"

"The Sepharadim are Ottomans. . . ."

"That's a different matter altogether," said Samuel impatiently. He never liked talking about the Sepharadis.

"But the Europeans can have us, most of us, as citizens to protect, why should they want to convert us as well?"

"Because, Israel, they want our souls too. They want loyalty, allegiance, not just Jews! Look how they use the poor misguided one. . . ." That was a reference to Ariel and it made Israel frown. The memory was still raw. Israel was grateful at least that Samuel didn't call Ariel the Meshumad, the damned one, as everybody else did. He said stonily, "Let's not talk of him." "I only meant to show you how he has become a part of their design. Don't you see? Through him they mean to. . . ."

"Samuel!"

The Christian missionaries in fact shied away from Ariel, regarding him not as a useful convert, which he wasn't, but as a heretic. Only Mr Pike cleaved to him, going with him preaching, rallying people to come and see and listen to him. They begged together. Kindly people gave them food. The afflicted and the destitute flocked to them. Stories spread about miraculous healings performed by Ariel. Lepers and cripples followed him wherever he went. Once, outside the Dung Gate Israel went to see Ariel ministering to the lepers. They hung on every word he said. He made them, Israel could see, forget their misery and laugh and smile, so that they were people again.

He felt no resentment towards his brother, nor alienation as all the others felt. He was relieved and pleased to see Ariel coming into his own, doing something he was naturally gifted to do well, for the good of unfortunate outcasts who had nothing to look for from the larger society. He was even proud of him, though he wouldn't have admitted it to anybody.

"My father thinks Europe is our salvation. Only he doesn't understand what this means."

"And you do? As far as I'm concerned we'd be better off with Ottoman citizenship. Then we'd be able to buy land without trouble. . . ."

Samuel made a dismissive gesture. "All you think about is land. There are more important things. Listen, I've done some thinking."

There was a town in England called Preston he told Israel. Jews lived there and worked in the weaving trade. They made famous cloth, renowned the world over. Samuel wanted to go to Preston, live there for a while and master the skill of weaving. That should not take too long he thought, he had great confidence in his abilities. When he was ready money would be raised to buy looms. Moses Montefiore's help would be sought for that enterprise.

"Come with me, Israel. Just think, Israel what we could do. And with your father-in-law in England we couldn't fail."

"They won't let you work here, I've found out that much," Israel said.

"Patience, tact, you try a little here, a little there, you persuade, cajole. . . ." Samuel said, rolling his eyes.

"And bribe Binish and his men. . . ."

"I didn't say that. God forbid!"

Israel laughed. "And all to no avail. Meanwhile your expensive looms stand idle. Don't you see? The moment Reb Binish claps eyes on your machines he'd declare them an abomination and interdict anyone who gets near them."

"I know how to deal with Reb Binish," Samuel said with quiet authority. "I want you with me in this Israel. Together we can succeed. We complement one another like Moses and Aaron."

There were a few other young men of his age that Samuel had been considering but Israel he knew the longest and best and he had proved his courage from an early age. He no longer felt any bitterness towards either Israel or his father for the past. In fact Samuel was relieved that Israel had not married Sheine. The thwarting of the union had been providential in view of Reb Binish's position in the community, not to mention the terrible blight, Ariel. No, people like the Zeffs were good friends but a liability as relations, Samuel believed. This awareness made him feel generous and protective towards his boyhood friend. Israel's reticence disappointed him.

Samuel Rimkin couldn't persuade Israel to go to England with him. The idea of weaving cloth in distant Yorkshire, away from home, did not appeal to Israel. But more than that, he was loth to leave home when Clara was pregnant once again, and his father broken over Ariel. "If I bide my time and learn the ways of the land, my chance will come, it must, I know it will. There's only one thing I want, Samuel, and I must work for it," he said.

"You'll wait and wait and wait in vain. Look around you. The young blood of the Arabs can once again buy their way out of serving in the Pasha's army. Do they work? No. They join in the age-old feud between the Yemen faction of the south, and the Kais faction of the north. Brawls, fights, pillaging, burning. You want land for such things to happen? The trouble with you, Israel, you've no imagination, no sense for new opportunities. Only courage and that's wasted on idle things," Samuel said.

"Yes, I want land," Israel said. "It is the only lasting security. It's the basis of everything. And even though my hopes with Sir Moses came to nothing. I'll always go on trying. Otherwise there is no point in living here."

Samuel left for England on his own, without saying goodbye to Israel.

Chapter 22

At times Solomon felt as though too many summers in his life had taken the moisture from his body and drained the suppleness out of his joints. He disliked summers, the more the older he grew. When his breath came in short hot gasps, he felt as though he were dying. Death didn't frighten him, not because he had seen so much of it but because he had come to think of it as a gentle person who had walked beside him unnoticed for years. Now at least he could see him. When he drew near, put his arm through his and led him to an unexpected turn of the road, that would be it.

Ada urged him to go to see the doctor from London whom Sir Moses had sent to tend to the Jews so that they wouldn't have to need the missionaries. But Solomon wouldn't. "Let him tend to those who are really sick, I'm just worn out," he said.

Forty years had passed since he first arrived on the shores of Acre. Forty years, like the sojourn of the Children of Israel in the wilderness. "I'm of the desert generation," he would say to Israel, "and I feel my time is up". And Israel would reply: "Father, you use your time doing what you like doing, and playing with your grandchildren, and let the good Lord worry about when it's up. That's His business."

He preferred to pray on his own rather than go to the synagogue, and in his solitary devotion, reflections spaced out the Liturgy. Had he reached the Promised land he set out for in his youth? Oh, he had a notion that he had passed through it. Dinah. The impermanence of it was too painful. The promise of the imagination makes any "Land" illusory. Was it old age that let in the wilderness into his soul, even among his son, daughter-in-law and grandchildren? He had looked forward to old age, to the simple joys of sitting out in the soft morning sun, and watching his family bustle all around him. To telling them about the past; yes, that more than anything, the urge for telling comes with age: it's the old man's equivalent to making children. He might have been happy if it weren't for Ariel who reminded him of his failures, who flew in his wilderness like a fire bird. And Ada.

When he looked at her he saw all the hardships and sorrows they had gone through together recorded in her face. So that he could barely remember the beauty of her first love. None of the joys. She was old. Not in a pleasant way. Her presence accused him of all the wrongdoings he had committed against her. But it no longer tore his heart to shreds; the intransigeant gaze of her eyes no longer moved him. He accepted his penance, like carrying a load. He was relieved, not merely for her sake, to see her face light up whenever the children played with her.

If age was cruel to Ada, on good days it showed gracefully in Solomon. His back was as straight as ever, his eyes clear. He could still swing the two younger children round and round until Clara would call to them, "Enough, you'll tire Grandfather." Yoel was devoted to him, never tired of listening to his stories. He had just turned thirteen and at his Bar Mitzva dazzled everybody by the brilliance of his delivery. Solomon, who had coached him, had every reason to feel proud. Yoel was a quick learner and an attentive listener. He would question anything that seemed improbable or stop Solomon when he was repeating himself. Such demands sharpened Solomon's powers of recall. Or was he reliving his past as he lay awake in the small hours of the morning, woken by the need to relieve himself out in the yard? When you piss in sprinkles too frequently and in between dreams of your past, that's when you know there's no more future.

Memories crowded his mind: his youth in Kedainai, Mad Berl on the roof, the miraculous journey to Palestine. Was it madness, like Berl's? So few of those who came with him to Jerusalem were still alive. But if he concentrated he could hear their voices. The sound of them brought tears to his eyes. Dinah. Oh, above all else Dinah. The memory of her touch could still excite him, as that of her rejection could still hurt. He never mentioned Dinah to Yoel. Nor did he ever talk of Ariel. But he was always in his thoughts, and very much alive. The Consul William Young had taken him under his wing. And Ariel grew confident, perfected his technique. His appeal widened. He became a familiar feature of Jerusalem, untouchable. At times an embarrassing liability to the British consulate, at times an asset. The latter was how Young's successor saw him, James Finn, who came to Jerusalem with his wife in the year 1846, fluent in Hebrew, full of biblical fervour and love of the Jews.

No longer did the Jews consider Ariel a pitiable lunatic. He was a false Messiah, a threat to the community's integrity, a dangerous heretic. They would have killed him if they could. Countless stories circulated in Jerusalem how he had cured this man of the palsy, restored the use of that man's limbs, gave the power of speech to a dumb child. He was king of the beggars, guardian angel of the sick who flocked to him as hungry birds fly to a field of corn. Ariel, in spite of rumours Reb Binish spread about him, remained true to his own personal faith and did not convert to Christianity, even though he had been seen on several occasions disputing points with missionaries and churchmen. It had to be said to Reb Binish's credit that not once did he impute any blame to Solomon and his family on account of Ariel. Not only that, he vigorously chastised anyone who tried to do so. Ariel, he decreed, was an eccentric affliction for which no single Jew was to blame. So it was, until an incident occurred which shook Jerusalem and brought about the intervention of the authorities.

There was a poor tailor who lived with his Sepharadi wife in a ramshackle hut on the edge of the Menachem Zion compound. Abner Teitleboim was his name. Abner was bitter because he was a pauper and felt hard done by in respect of the haluka money. His workmanship was of such poor quality that no one but the most needy came to him and they seldom had anything with which to pay him. Only on holy days did Abner and his wife have a reprieve from want when people gave them gifts of money or food. Abner accepted the gifts because he needed them. But he was a proud man. It made him hate himself and others.

Teitleboim married late in life a woman who was also past her prime. They had a son who was his light and joy, for there was no one else in the world to keep his name alive. Therefore Abner guarded the boy like a treasure. At the time of the plague, when the boy was barely three years old, Abner burnt incense, which he bought at great expense or stole, in the boy's room, to purge the air of pestilence. He let no stranger come near the boy nor allowed him to stir out of the house for the duration of the plague. For all that, just as the plague abated, the boy came down with a strange illness which left him blind and paralysed. When no cure could be found, Abner shook his fists at the sky and shouted: "What kind of a God are you! I had a lamb and you've destroyed him." His wife blamed this blasphemy for their son's deteriorating condition. Abner turned on her and beat her until he had no more strength; it was the first time in his life he had ever raised his hand in anger against anybody.

The boy lay in his bunk by the peeling wall, neither alive nor dead and so it was for years thereafter. The two grief-stricken parents fed and washed him. Abner prayed for his son's recovery. Then for his death. Rabbis and healers came and went. Nothing changed. Then Abner renounced God and turned to magic practised by pagan holy men and witches whose whereabouts were known to some in the souks. It was at this stage that the Englishman Pike brought Ariel into Abner's anguished world.

It was Good Friday. A group of Christian pilgrims made ready to process along Via Dolorosa, bearing a large wooden cross. Pike, who on that day had been praying for the salvation of all Jews and Turks, had persuaded Ariel to come and watch the procession. At the first station, near the ruined Church of St Anna, where the Turks had their main barracks, Pike and Ariel joined the crowd of pilgrims. At the Forth Station where, according to the Christian faith, the Nazarene met his sorrowful mother, a group of beggars recognized Ariel and clamoured round him stretching out their hands to touch him. Ariel stopped and talked to them. Teitleboim was in the crowd. Why he had come he couldn't tell. Later he said an Angel of the Lord had spoken to him.

But Ariel caught Abner's eye and was held by his stare, so compelling was the expression of despair on the man's face.

"Do you know this man?" Ariel asked Pike.

"I've never seen him before," Pike answered.

"Let's go and talk to him," Ariel said.

That morning Israel rose early and rode out of Jerusalem with Yoel astride the horse behind him. They were bound for the village of Ajun, a few hours' ride to the east where, through the good offices of the British Consul, Mr Finn, Israel had leased a field from a gentle Arab who lived on Mount Scopus. It was a happy day for him; the wheat, sown before the rains, now stood knee-high. He wanted his first-born son to see the place, to share his happiness.

A group of falahin and their womenfolk were working on the edge of the field. The men stood up and greeted Israel and Yoel who returned the greeting. The sunlight was softened by a broken cover of cloud. The wheat, already turning gold on the swollen sheathes, swayed in the breeze. The harvest would be good; after paying the rent of the land there would still be a profit. Israel's heart swelled with pride at the thought. He picked an ear of wheat, and broke off the still green seeds into Yoel's palm. "Feel it. Feel the goodness of the land," he said.

They sat at the edge of the field, eye-level with the heads of the corn whose ripples sent shades of green and yellow racing across the field. Israel broke the bread Clara had tied in a kerchief for them, and blessed. He handed a piece to Yoel. "Eat and remember what you're eating, the fruit of the land which the Lord our God, blessed be He, gives us to eat."

Skylarks hovered tremulously over the field filling the air with their song. A sweet drowsiness came over Israel and Yoel: they might have been drinking wine instead of talking about the nature of the soil and the various trees and wild flowers whose names Israel had learnt.

When the sun reached the highest point of its course, the falahin took a break. Yoel helped Israel saddle the horse and they mounted to ride back home. From the prominence of Mount Scopus Jerusalem spread before them like a pan of molten silver. They had not reached the city walls when the youth Clara had sent to keep a lookout for them, came running towards them in great excitement.

No one had actually seen what Ariel did when he followed Abner to his home. He looked at the paralysed boy, then asked to be left alone with him. A group of men, Arabs, Christians and a few Jews, waited outside. After an hour or so Ariel came out and motioned Abner to go in.

Abner Teitleboim came running out of the house, his eyes wild. He waved his arms like a man possessed and made straight for the home of Reb Mordecai Binish. On getting there he tried to force his way in but was barred at first by the formidable Rebbetze Zelda and then by a couple of hefty youths who arrived running at hearing the commotion Zelda had created. They grabbed hold of Abner and threw him violently out from the door. He fell in the gutter bleeding from his nose. But in his excitement he took no notice. "My boy's well, healed by the true man of God, Blessed be He. A miracle has taken place," he yelled. "I've come to tell the Rebbe and you treat me like a dog, damn you!" Someone threw a rock at him. Teitleboim stood up and launched into a loud tirade. He denounced all the rabbis in the coarsest language, then shouted, "For how long will you go on deceiving the poor while you grow fat in your corruption? Your words are empty! Your prayers are hateful to the Blessed Name! The Messiah Son of David has come to save Israel and show up your falsehood. I curse your religion. I curse your lying synagogue! May your name be wiped from the book of life, may you rot in your bed. . . ."

The crowd which was quickly drawn to Reb Binish's door by the noise, stirred and divided: there was violence in the air. Abner Teitleboim had given vent to his fury and would have turned back home when the youths who attended Reb Binish set upon him and beat him. The violence spread to the bystanders. There was a great clamour out of which, like a rising pulse, a chant emerged: "Where is that blaspheming dog who calls himself the Messiah? Let's go kill him." Just then Reb Merdecai Binish appeared on the scene.

At the Dung Gate the zealots saw Ariel and Pike making their way out of the city towards Silwan. They raised a cry and rushed at the two men, but the beggars at the gate rose from their torpor and seizing whatever lay at hand, attacked the Jewish zealots. The noise attracted a small crowd of Arabs, and they too armed themselves with rocks and sticks but as yet stood by. The zealots were too many for the beggars. They fought them off and seized Ariel. They began dragging him towards the valley of Ben Hinnom. The beggars and the Arabs followed some way behind.

When they reached Ben Hinnom, they shouted: "Let us do to him as our fathers did to desecrators even in this place of execution." And they flung Ariel against the rock face. One of them picked up a heavy piece of rock and hurled it with all his might at Ariel. The stone hit him in the chest. He staggered but kept upright. Then he lifted his eyes to the sky and prayed silently. "Look at him, how he blasphemes," the zealots cried and pelted him with rocks.

A detachment of soldiers came running on to the scene for the news of the disturbance had reached the garrison's commandant. When the beggars saw them they rallied and charged at the zealots. This time the Arabs joined in the fray, brandishing daggers.

The soldiers lined up, took aim, and discharged their muskets.

Israel and Yoel arrived home to find Solomon and Ada there with Clara and a few other friends of the family. Their home was sturdier than

Solomon's with shutters that could be tightened to better withstand an assault. Everybody was in a state of excitement. Rimkin, they learnt, had gone with Reb Binish and the Sepharadi Haham Bashi to see the governor in an attempt to quell further violence before it broke out on the streets. Nine people had died at the scene of the stoning, including two Arab youths. But Ariel had apparently got away. No one knew how, or where he was, whether or not he was hurt and if so, how badly. Solomon was beside himself with anxiety.

At sunset the Pasha's criers went through the Jewish Quarter and the nearby Arab neighbourhood, declaring a curfew; anyone found loitering in the streets after dark would be shot on sight it was announced. Clara arranged makeshift beds wherever there was space. Night fell. The men stayed up and read psalms aloud.

In the following days the British Consul, James Finn, went to and fro, from the Jews whom he felt were his charges to the Arab notables with whom he had formed excellent relations, to the Turkish Pasha who held him in high regard, and back. His efforts bore results: no incidents occurred. He sent a letter to Solomon telling him that Ariel was in his home, being taken care of, for he had broken ribs. It was expedient, Finn stressed, that Ariel should remain in safe keeping at the Consulate until he and Finn together could decide what he should do next.

One evening there was a knock on Solomon's door, and there was Mr Pike standing in the gathering dusk. He no longer wore his Man of the Wilderness rags. He was dressed in a European suit, old but clean. His hair and beard were trimmed and brushed. He was carrying a cane in one hand and his hat in the other. He looked very thin. When Ada recognized him she let out a scream and covered her face with her hands. Pike winced, then said,"I'll not come into your house. I know you hate me. You seem to think it's because of me that you son Ariel has left you and has recently nearly lost his life. But your grief has made you blind, Solomon. You have no quarrel with me. Providence has thrown us together. We're brothers. I've come to say goodbye to you, from him too. We'll leave Jerusalem, maybe Palestine too for a while, until Ariel is ready to return in glory. There's much work to be done elsewhere. Much darkness for him to light. He sends you his greetings and everlasting love."

"Tell me about him, how is he? Where will you go? What will you do?" Solomon said.

"He is well. A stone had hit him on the chest, and broke two of his ribs. But he is mending. In a day we shall be able to travel. Don't worry about him, he's in good hands. I'll never abandon him."

"In your hands! You call that good! Look what you've done all that time since we first met."

"I'm not altogether without means," Pike replied gravely.

"Won't you take me to him so that I may at least see him before you depart?"

Pike shook his head. "He specially asked me not to do that. To save you both pain, you understand. But one day he will come to you . . ."

Solomon waved his hand to make him stop. He felt tears coming to his eyes. He fought to control his voice. At last he said, "I don't hate you, Pike. I think you're one of God's misguided fools, much more so than my son Ariel. My wife curses the day we saw you. She believes you corrupted Ariel. Solomon paused. "I don't know. Perhaps he was brought into this world corrupt. Perhaps I corrupted him. Perhaps . . ." he hesitated, "he is right in his ways and we're all wrong. He was a good boy." Again emotion made him stop. "You say you'll never abandon him. Look after him then for all you're worth and for all you value. He's no longer my son, and I know I'll never see him again. Go now."

On the first Sabbath in the month of Iyar, Reb Binish led a service of thanksgiving. He commended the young men who fell in the name of the Lord, shot by the soldiers, and praised James Finn for all he had done. Then he cleared his throat and began: "I want to talk to you today about purity. Throughout the ages our people survived through purity. It is the one thing that kept the light of Israel glowing. No persecution, nor any number of disasters which overtook our people wherever they were over the centuries, managed to extinguish that light. We bring up our children in this purity of purpose and destiny, we suffer to preserve our way in the purity of our sacred law, the Torah, for without it we are as the other nations, less in fact, for without our special bond with the Almighty we lack even the basic things other nations have. . . ." When Binish sermonized he always quoted extensively from the sayings of the sages, from the Talmud, from the Torah itself. In learning there was none to equal him; his mind was like a turning sword. Now he spoke plainly, eschewing all references to scripts. His voice was firm, unyielding. "Would we have survived to this day against all adversity, when mighty powers rose and fell, were it not for the unquestioning faith of our sages and teachers? And how can we keep this precious purity except by safeguarding our people's unity at all cost? Not for nothing has it been said that through Israel's internal strife and causeless hatred was our holy Temple destroyed. Not for nothing has it been said that everyone of Israel is accountable and responsible for his brother before the eyes of the Lord.

"But man is not a dumb obedient thing. When Adam ate of the fruit of the Tree of Knowledge his mind was opened to the wisdom of creation. He understood the loving kindness of the Blessed Creator. But his heart was also seduced by the evil ways of the devil. This is man's heritage: the good, and the bad, which together make a whole. . . ."

When Binish started to talk of good and evil, a quiet hum went through the synagogue, and Solomon, whose mind had been wandering, was recalled from his reveries as if by a jab of something cold and hard.

" . . . when Israel goes whoring after idols the anger of the Lord is quick and retribution follows. So it has been in the past and so it will be to the end of time, so long as we err in our ways."

Reb Binish's voice fell, became threatening, almost a hiss. "And if someone in our midst in his conceit builds monuments to his sinful pride pretending it is for the glory of the holy community of Jerusalem and the blessed memory of the saintly Rabbi Judah the Hassid, should we be surprised if such a man neglects to bring up his offspring in the ways of our God, thereby bringing shame and abomination to his Name? When he condones most the repulsive blasphemy and consorts with vile missionaries in the stealth of darkness, is he blameless of what has happened? And will not each and every one of us have to give account for it before the Supreme seat of Judgement?"

Never before had Reb Binish denounced anybody so violently in public. His speech was so deliberate that it could only have been premeditated. It struck Solomon like a bolt, all the more because he couldn't understand why Binish chose this moment of his deepest hurt to turn on him so savagely, when he had shown leniency if not compassion over Ariel in the past. There was stunned silence in the synagogue as Binish rounded off his attack and prepared to say the prayer. A voice was heard. "Shame, Reb Binish, forbear, in the name of compassion, in such a place as this, and now. . . ."

It was Rimkin. Solomon got to his feet. He was so white, Israel had a fleeting fear that he might have a seizure. He stood for a moment glaring at Binish, unable to speak. Then he said in a clear loud voice, "May God from whom nothing is hidden, forgive you, Binish, for the terrible things you've said, and all of you who sit here in silence, in this synagogue to which I've dedicated my life and strength." Then he walked out with Israel.

The incident at the Menachem Zion rent the Ashkenazi community as a lightning cleaves an oak tree. All the old animosities between the two camps were revived so that the division engulfed every aspect of communal life. Binish's camp waged a ruthless war against the missionaries; Solomon's friends maintained that such a course would only give the missionaries more attention than they deserved; better to maintain contemptuous indifference. Newcomers from London, acting on Sir Moses Montefiore's behalf, opened a vocational school in Jerusalem. Solomon's camp welcomed it. Binish's declared it a work of the devil—worse than the missionaries—on the grounds that secular education caused idleness and moral turpitude in the young, as well as defeated the basic purpose of the Jews' existence in the Holy Land. Eliezer Rimkin and his friends were torn for a while between the two sides, until old friendship and Samuel's letters from England made Reb Eliezer join Solomon's faction.

"Reb Binish has gone too far," he told Solomon.

"Why, why did he say those things? What harm did I ever do him?"

"Reb Binish is jealous and afraid for his power. He'll move against anything and anybody that threatens it. It was that, not his hatred of you that made him say what he said. And if it hadn't been for the Rebbetze, he wouldn't have gone to such excesses. She's a wicked woman, a bad influence." And Rimkin sighed deeply. "It is written that God created woman to be man's helpmeet. I think the devil also created some women to destroy men, and Zelda Binish is an example."

The Sepharadi Jews looked on bemused; their impatience with their Ashkenazi brethren was growing. In recent years Sepharadi Jews arrived in Jerusalem to settle. They were prosperous Jews from Iraq, from Pera and Salonica, and a few from Holland. They brought with them wealth and an easy-going elegance which won the hearts of the Arab notables and the Ottoman authorities. They were merchants with worldwide connection. Among them was a banker by the name of Maurice Pinto.

The Sepharadi Jews whose charm, generosity and ability, did much for the Sepharadis' standing in the city, in as much as they took sides in the Ashkenazi dispute, favoured Solomon. They knew him the longest and respected him. Reb Binish's imperious manner and his clannishness alienated them. Seeing the Ashkenazis at one another's throats, they drew away, enhanced their own haluka system and, with the help of men like Pinto, strove to strengthen their own institution apart from the Ashkenazis.

When Reb Binish attacked Solomon in his sermon at the synagogue, he could not have foreseen what a deep and bitter rift would ensue. When he realized that instead of consolidating his power, he diminished it and, to make things worse, created a situation beyond his control, he sought ways to bring about peace. He called on Rimkin and urged him to negotiate a truce with Solomon and his friends. A truce was what he wanted—nothing more. No concessions nor retrenchments, only a period for taking stock without pressure and deciding on the next step. He was worried that the strife would spread to the administrators and clerks of the haluka abroad. Rumours had reached him that Solomon's faction was making moves to break away from the haluka administration which Reb Binish controlled in Palestine, and form their own organization to compete with his. If there was one thing Reb Binish dreaded, it was precisely that such a thing should come about, for he knew that even his most ardent supporters abroad would frown on him if an irreconcilable division among the Ashkenazis became a reality. Eliezer Rimkin didn't have to be told what the dire consequences to the entire community would be in such an event. It was this knowledge rather than Binish's appeal which convinced him that he must act.

"I'll never speak to him. I'll never set foot again where he officiates. I'll never join in any public activity with him," Solomon swore.

"A wise man, Solomon, always keeps his options open," Rimkin reasoned. "Will you undo all we've both been working for for so many years because of one man? Reb Binish has faults, we all know that. He's his own worst enemy. But he also has many good qualities. If God forgives, won't you?"

"He must apologize."

"Hasn't he done so by asking me to talk to you?"

"Explicitly, Reb Eliezer, and publicly!"

"He's not the kind of man to admit fault, but in his heart he knows and repents, believe me," Rimkin said, and added when Solomon's silence threatened to break their communication, "You ask for too much, both of you, can Jews be such bitter enemies?"

"In my heart I forgive him, Reb Eliezer. I shall not fight him if he leaves off. But I shall never have anything to do with him, and that's my last word on the subject," Solomon said. "You know Solomon, the trouble with us Jews is that no sooner is life a little better for us than we make it worse by our own hard-necked truculence," Rimkin sighed. "Must we always have disasters to bring us together, God forbid?"

Solomon and Binish avoided one another but Rimkin's mission had not been in vain, for no more harsh words were uttered by one against the other. The truce Binish had so much wanted was achieved. The two men even nodded at one another at the synagogue, and in his heart Binish prayed that Solomon would be taken soon to a better world.

At the feast of Tabernacles, Israel decorated his *succah* with wheat sheaves from his own field. The yield from the harvest had been disappointing. But he was overjoyed when Clara baked bread from the flour he had brought home. It was hard, dense bread and not very tasty. They ate it with love. He had given a loaf each to his parents, and to the Rimkins. None had the heart to say anything but that it tasted like manna from heaven. Not a word was said about the debt to the Arab landowner, to pay which Clara had sold some of her prettiest clothes and pieces of furniture. As they sat for the festive evening meal in their succah, the stars twinkled through the palm fronds of the roof. The air was filled with the fragrance of pomegranate, citrus and fig, the light danced on the few painted decorations Yoel and his two sisters had prepared.

Israel blessed and broke the bread, handing it round the table, first to Ada, then to Solomon, leaving the children and himself to the last. "One day, one day, we shall be taking this for granted, as our natural due, but it'll never taste as sweet as it does today," he said as he dipped a piece of bread in honey.

Spring came with a dazzle of colour and gusts of balmy air. "You could get intoxicated just from breathing deeply! All the beautiful flowers on the hillside. Oh how good it is to be alive here," Clara cried, and clapped her hands. Her joy and gratitude were miraculously rewarded by the sight of a small herd of gazelles which came bounding in elegant arcs into the open space beyond Kidron. It was a perfect day, a day out, a sabbath to glorify creation.

"Look," Yoel said, pointing to the sky. High up in the deep blue, a flock of storks came flying from the north.

"Reliable as ever, bringers of good tidings, like our good tidings yesterday," Israel said.

Rafael Mendoza had written to say that he had wound up his affairs in England and was returning to Jerusalem for good. God had been with him; he had been successful. Now he longed to be with his grandchildren. Clara's two brothers would remain in England and manage the business. Mendoza expected to arrive in Jaffa at the beginning of August.

Israel agreed that Yoel should come with him to meet his grandfather at the port. The lad had never seen the sea. But had read that at this time of the year the sea was brilliant blue and inviting. Besides, Mendoza was arriving on board a steam ship. Such a marvel of human ingenuity simply could not be missed.

The steamer was large and white. It stood some distance from the harbour belching smoke. A crowd of small boats swarmed around it and into them the cargo and passengers were lowered. For the last few yards to shore the passengers were carried on the backs of muscular porters who stood thigh-deep in the water waiting for the loads to come. Mendoza was dressed in a white suit and a matching broad-rimmed hat. The moment he saw Israel and Yoel he started waving his arms so wildly that the porter who was carrying him nearly lost his balance.

He had not changed at all. He looked well and happy and brimming with life. He scooped up a handful of sand and kissed it. He flung his hat in the air and embraced Israel and Yoel. "Dear blessed God, that I should see you again and hold you in my arms," Mendoza said with tears in his eyes. "There's no air as sweet as this air and nothing better than arriving to be met by you. Tell me everything. How are you? Yoel, my my, you're a man. I'd never have recognized you! and how's my beloved Clara?"

His joy could not be contained, and when Israel suggested that they should rest for the day and start for Jerusalem the following morning, Mendoza cracked his cane against his shoe and said, "Absolutely not. I won't hear of it. We'll start for Jerusalem at once if it's possible. I've already rested ten long days on a perfect sea voyage, and I cannot wait to see Jerusalem and home."

The Jewish Quarter was unusually subdued. Something oppressively silent hung about the place and Israel sensed it at once. "There's something wrong, I feel it in my bones," he said.

"The Ninth of Ab fast, and we've all forgotten," Mendoza said and slapped his forehead.

"That's in two days' time Grandfather," Yoel said. Israel broke into a run, leaving Mendoza and Yoel with the porter who carried the luggage to trail after him. He reached his home to find it locked with no one inside. Forgetting Mendoza he ran with his heart pounding to his parents' home. Here he saw a crowd of people gathered at the open door. The windows too were open, and the room was full of people. Some of them were weeping. He pushed his way in and bumped into Clara. "What's happened?" he cried. She took his face in her hands. "Your father. Go to him," she motioned with her head to the closed door of his parents' bedroom.

Solomon was lying on his back covered with a white sheet. His face was sallow, as if cast in wax. There was a bandage round his head through which a large stain of blood kept spreading. Dr Frankel, the doctor whom Montefiore had sent to Jerusalem some years before, was at his side. Ada was sitting on a chair at the corner of the room silently rocking back and forth. Solomon's eyes were closed. He was breathing heavily through opened mouth. Israel stood frozen. The doctor motioned him to approach.

"In heaven's name, what's happened?" Israel whispered. "Will he live?" Even as he said this he knew that his father was dying.

"He's very strong," the doctor said, "But he's lost a lot of blood and his head is badly hurt. It's a wonder he's still alive. We mustn't give up hope."

Israel knelt by the bed and took hold of his father's hand. It felt cold and rigid. The only sign of life was a tiny twitch as he kissed it. Solomon's mouth moved but no sound came from it.

"All we know is that he staggered home early this morning with a terrible wound at the back of his neck and head. He had been to pray at the Western Wall. A sword thrust, the doctor says. Who could've done such a thing. To him of all people," and Clara broke down and wept.

All day Israel and Clara sat at Solomon's bedside. Rafael Mendoza, having changed, also came. He and Clara did whatever chores and errands needed doing. Poor Ada remained in her chair, her face set like stone.

"He won't die," Mendoza said. "It'd take the sword of the devil himself to lay low a man like your father, and even then the devil would have to strike several times. No, I tell you, he'll live."

But by evening Dr Frankel put all his things back in his satchel and left. There was nothing more he could do, he said, and the way he said it told Israel that his father's end was at hand. He brought Yoel to look at Solomon and hold his hand. Then he sent everybody away, and putting his arm round Ada, sat at his father's deathbed holding her. A little past midnight Solomon breathed his last.

All the Jews of Jerusalem mourned him as though a dearest son, a father, their guide and leader had been taken away from them. Reb Binish wept as Israel recited the Kaddish prayer at the graveside. Then Binish eulogized in a loud tremulous voice saying, "A great man has been taken away from us the like of which we may never again see. A giant in his time, a leader who adds glory and valour to the history of our oppressed people. May his name be forever bound in the wreath of life, may the Blessed Creator who has gathered his favoured son to his merciful bosom, console his bereaved people. My brothers, I tell you, an era has come to an end this day." Only Rimkin really understood the true meaning of what Binish was saying. Solomon had been more than a friend to him: he was the measure of their achievements.

For the seven days of mourning life in the streets of the Jews virtually came to a standstill. Ada had surfaced from the depths of her desolation. Serene in her black weeds, she sat in the front room and received the never-ending stream of people who came to pay their respects and express condolences. Neither she nor Israel who was always at her side, nor his family and friends, had fully realized until that day how widely respected and admired Solomon had been. On the second day of the Shiva, the Pasha of Jerusalem himself came to pay his respects. Taking Israel aside, he told him that the assassin had been caught and confessed his crime. He was an Arab, a Beduin of no known connections, who had been hired to kill Solomon. But he wouldn't, even under torture, say who had hired him and why. The murderer was to be publicly hanged at sunrise the following morning.

After a month, the headstone on Solomon's grave which was in the Jewish cemetery on the slope of Mount of Olives, was consecrated as was the custom.

Carved in it were the words:

"Here lies buried our teacher Rabbi Solomon Zeff of blessed memory in peace and beatitude for eternity, who redeemed the Ashkenazi synagogue on the site of Judah the Hassid synagogue and laid the foundation to Menachem Zion. Gathered unto his world on the 6th of Ab in the year 5611 to the creation of the world."

Ada died a year later, defeated by the land and the experiences it gave her, and was buried at his side. For years afterwards, wicked people whispered it was Reb Binish who had been behind the murder of Solomon Zeff. Righteous folks who heard it would spit three times and say, "Cursed be the tongue which utters such evil".

Chapter 23

The people of Jerusalem had been waiting and praying for rain. Moslems flocked to the El Aksa Mosque where special prayers were held. The Christians sang masses and gave alms to the poor. The rabbis, Ashkenazi and Sepharadi, declared days of fasting and the unseasonal sound of the shofar could be heard throughout the day. A pious Hassid called Tevye Hilfgott, who in his unshakeable innocence believed he alone could move the Almighty to pity, drew a circle on the ground outside the Menachem Zion and declared that he would not stir out of it nor eat a morsel of food until the Lord relented and sent blessed rain. A group of children gathered round to watch him and see if they could provoke or tempt him out of his circle.

Not a cloud was seen in the sky: prayers and cries of lamentation rose, and fell unanswered. Tevye sat panting in his circle, ready and waiting to die. It was late December and the falahin were saying the late summer sowing would come to nought. Shopkeepers began pushing up the prices of flour, dura seeds, lentils—any storable foodstuff—in anticipation of shortages. But worst of all was the situation of the water as the cisterns and wells in the city began to dry up. The water vendors' calls became less frequent; the price of a skin of water which was normally one piaster, doubled then trebled. Within the walls there were some 950 cisterns, thirty-four of which—and the largest—inside the Temple complex and only Moslems received water from those. The water in the city never tasted as sweet as that from the springs in the hills, and in time of drought, it was slightly brackish, fit only for washing and for animals.

Now, as at any time when water was in short supply, the water vendors neglected the Jewish Quarter. The vendors of the better, dearer water stopped coming altogether and would turn their backs on Jews who pursued them to other parts of the city. The men prayed for rain and the women watched over the jars of drinking water as though they were more precious than gold.

At last a cold wind began blowing from the north. The Mufti of Jerusalem spread his prayer mat on the dusty flagstone outside El Aksa and, facing the wind, squatted there, waiting for the first drops of rain to fall. It was Sabbath. With dusk, it began to rain. The rain was thin, like needles, but it persisted through the night and in the morning the earth breathed and the houses gleamed in the cleansed air. Hilfgott, drenched to the bones and shivering, stepped out of his smudged circle convinced that it was his self-sacrifice that moved God to relent. He died of pneumonia hardly a month later and no one but the children remembered his stubborn tussle with the Almighty.

Relieved at last by the downpours Jerusalem turned her attention to the news which, like the rain, arrived very late: war had broken out between Russia and the Sultan and his allies, the English and the French. The first skirmishes had occurred in the Crimea three months before and no one in the Governor's Palace knew about it or properly understood what the war was all about. The Crimea was far away and held no interest to the Province of Syria. And the Ottoman Empire was vast: communication flowed through it like leaves on a slow river. But at last the Imperial order arrived: troops had to be mustered, new taxes levied.

The British Consul in Jerusalem briefed the Pasha on the war aims of the allies, and what was involved. Jewish merchants informed him about where the Crimea was. Ships were expected in Jaffa to ferry the troops to their destined battlefields. Here and there, Russian pilgrims or Russian subjects—including Jews who claimed Russian affiliation—were set upon, beaten, and robbed with impunity. The new war mood gathered into a festive climax when on a clear sunny morning, after the first rains, the garrison of Jerusalem paraded west of the City in an area known as the Maidan, for the ceremony to mark the first departure to that distant and meaningless war.

The area had been cleared of rubble and marked out the day before, when gangs of sulking peasants picked and scratched at the muddy soil, supervised by a whip-wielding *rais*. Now flags cracked in the breeze. Representatives of the allied consulates took their places as far away as possible from the ragtag band which, having managed some sort of co-ordination, struck up a shaky march.

The troops arrived from the direction of the Damascus Gate, followed by a large crowd. It was a beautiful morning, and the people wanted to see the soldiers off no matter where they went.

Two battalions of foot soldiers, dressed in bits of ill-matching uniforms and carrying an assortment of weapons, awkwardly formed into an open-ended square three ranks deep. Some were armed with muskets, some carried lances and swords. Those who had none of those sported *nabuts*—the heavy clubs local thugs often carried—slung musket-fashion across their shoulders. A couple of squadrons of light cavalry, the bashi bazooks, mostly recruited from the hill Beduin, fidgeted untidily behind the infantry. A team of mules dragged an antiquated artillery piece from the Napoleonic wars all the way from the Citadel to the parade grounds. It was to be fired ceremoniously as the main event of the parade.

A fanfare proclaimed the arrival of the Governor of Jerusalem. Seated on a glossy grey gelding, he trotted past the troops accompanied by the garrison's commandant and a small retinue. The commandant had brought with him a supply of chains and manacles to be used on reluctant recruits whose families could not or would not pay the ransom bribe for their release.

Even here, in mountain-locked Jerusalem—a half-forgotten outpost of the Ottoman Empire—the people had seen more exciting public spectacles than the departure parade mounted by the Pasha. Certainly, it could not match for sheer excitement and colour the appearance two years before of a roving circus, with jugglers, a bearded lady and a pack of singing, saluting dogs. The troops mustered, formed and reformed on the churned-up parade grounds, and the Pasha rode past the columns, smiling and waving his horsetail switch. The people cheered and clapped their hands; any harmless distraction was a welcome release.

Reb Binish invited a select number of leaders from the Ashkenazi and Sepharadi communities to a special meeting at his home. The people he invited were carefully chosen, some not less for their tractability as for their social standing. He showered honours on them, spoke of duty and responsibility, then revealed the purpose of the meeting. The time had come, Binish declared, for a more authoritative and responsive leadership of the two communities. Those present would constitute a special council which would decide on all matters of importance concerning the Jews of Jerusalem. The council, which he proposed to call the Council of the Sages, would be vested with full powers to represent and to adjudicate, like the Sanhedria of Talmudic times—Binish stopped short of drawing direct comparison. Thus the House of Israel would be governed, as of old, by the Spirit of the Word.

Mendoza was there. So was Israel. Neither of them wanted to come. It was Clara who had insisted that they go: "Hard times are coming," she reasoned. "We mustn't let someone like Binish take us over completely, without anyone restraining him."

Binish's wife, the Rebbetze Zelda, a large, mean woman, had prepared the most secluded room in the house for the meeting. Once the door was shut, she positioned her ear to the keyhole so as not to miss a word of what was being said inside. Reb Binish sat on a high, throne-like chair. He had a batch of notes in his lap, which he acknowledged from the start, were compiled with the help of Reb Samuel Rimkin. He launched into an analysis of the situation.

The Crimean war was in full swing. As he had predicted, communication with Europe was increasingly capricious. Already the haluka money was coming in dribs and drabs. Soon it might stop altogether. No need to dwell on the consequences, everyone present could envisage the hardship ahead.

"To think that the European powers start a war all because of the petty squabbles among the sects in that church they call the Holy Sepulchre, it's insane!" The speaker was a newcomer from Odessa out to make his mark on Jewish life in Jerusalem, and feeling somewhat vulnerable for coming from Russia.

Reb Binish peered at him coldly over the rims of his spectacles. He didn't like interruptions when he was talking, particularly irrelevant ones.

Palestine, he continued to explain, no longer had troops to speak of with which to maintain order. He had fresh news of Beduin tribes crossing the Jordan in force, and moving west. Tribes in the south of the country had decamped and were moving north. Alliances were broken and remade. Without the Ottomans to check it, the ancient feud between the Yeman faction of the south and the Kais of the north was flaring up again. Even now, agents of the Al Anazi Beduin and the Bani Sacre—he paused to examine his notes so as to get the names right—were pouring into Jerusalem to size up the situation in the city. Danger lurked round every corner.

Israel and Mendoza looked at each other and made a moue. They had to admit, Binish displayed a formidable grasp of facts. The picture he presented was coherent if grim.

"The Ishmaelites thrive on chaos," Binish said, putting down his notes and removing his glasses. "For them chaos, weakness of government, means freedom from the Ottoman yoke. No more taxes. No conscription to the army. No one to tell them what to do. Instead, the familiar rhythm of work, plunder, and fighting, interspersed with commerce and natural disasters. That's what they are used to.

"For us Jews, chaos spells disaster. Always has, in any country any time. When order breaks down, Jews are the first to suffer.

"Now all we can do at this stage is to husband our resources wisely. To keep the community together. To see that all the necessities of life are shared equitably among all. That no widow or orphan will go hungry when there's food to be had." His finger shot out. "To see that all this is done, there must be discipline, even harsh discipline if necessary. There must be an authority to enforce such a discipline and to punish transgressors when necessary."

In the silence that ensued no one was left with any doubt as to who would be the authority Reb Binish had in mind.

"Many pitfalls face our people," Binish went on. "Not least among these is the threat of the Christian missionaries. Every day I hear of more of them arriving. They have wealth. They say they want to help the poor and the sick." His voice dropped, became threatening. "Let no one be fooled as to their true intention. They are out to ensnare the souls of foolish, weak Jews. When the body is made frail with want, the mind surrenders to the blandishments of material comfort. Money, yes, they give it out freely to any Jew who would kneel before their cross. But we shall fight them with all our might and with the help of the Lord our God. This I swear to you." For a moment Reb Binish looked subdued by his own commitment.

"When you return to your homes, ponder on what I've said. Think of ways we could serve the community. Consider your responsibilities," Binish concluded on a conciliatory note.

The Council of Sages was to meet regularly to draw plans and make decisions. Instead, it convened only at Reb Binish's bidding to approve of actions he had already set in motion. When Israel and Mendoza realized this, they ceased to come to the meetings.

Reb Binish's dire predictions proved right: communication between Jerusalem and Europe virtually stopped, and as it did so did the haluka money from abroad. With no money coming in, poverty bit hard into the Jewish community. There were weeks when too many children in too many families had nothing more than a thin gruel to eat, and once a day at that. Children became sad-eyed and lethargic, and easily succumbed to illness. In the summer there was dysentry; in the winter ague racked and often killed the old and weak. The Christian missionary organizations opened hospices and infirmaries where nurses and doctors offered loving care to all the needy, particularly Jews. Here there was food and rest in comfortable beds. Yet only a handful of Jews—the poorest, who had nothing further to lose—found shelter there. A curse and banishment from all things Jewish awaited anyone who either went near the hospices or encouraged somebody else to go there. The Angel of Death himself could not wear a ghastlier mark than Reb Binish in his wrath.

Chapter 24

The British Consul in Jerusalem, Mr James Finn and his wife Elizabeth, built themselves a stone house on land they had purchased with money raised in Britain by various Christian organizations. The plot, about fifty fedans—some thirteen acres—lay not further than half an hour's ride to the south on the outskirts of Jerusalem. You reached it riding from the Jaffa Gate along the western ridge of the Kidron, through the village of Abu Tor, to a broad brow of a hill from where, on a clear day you could see the Dead Sea. There, on the hillside sloping westwards, Finn built his house. From it fields rolled down into a wide saddle, then climbed up again the slope of the hill opposite.

The house was large, even by the standards of richer landowners. Finn moved into it many of his books. He was a pious Christian, a learned man, well-read in the ways and customs of the east, and fluent in Hebrew and Arabic. The view from the windows pleased him: he loved the sweep of the land and its deep changing colours. Elizabeth made accomplished sketches in watercolour. Looking at the hills early in the morning, or at dusk, he was often filled with awe. In his mind's eye he saw sheaves of wheat and barley, bending before the sickles of biblical reapers; shepherds tending their flocks under the luminous night sky. On the first morning when the house was completed, he and his wife watched the sun rise over the hills across the Jordan River. Then overcome by sudden emotion, they knelt down and prayed.

What had he not done already? He had travelled the land from the slopes of Hermon in Syria to the heart of the desert in the south. His notes and descriptions of plants and animals of the Holy Land were published in respectable journals in Britain. No other foreign envoy enjoyed such high esteem among the local populace as he did. And he had won the trust and friendship of the Jews. This, he considered his greatest achievement, the thing his heart had longed for ever since he set foot in Jerusalem in 1846. Israel and his father Solomon, when he was alive, were regular visitors to his home. Reb Eliezer Rimkin was his friend. And the Sepharadi Jews whose quiet dignity and grace won his heart, how he loved them!

It was not for his own enrichment that James Finn built the house and purchased the land, but for the Children of Israel. He had seen them arrive from distant lands, from Europe, from the Mahgreb, from Asia, road-weary and bewildered. He had seen them die of hunger and disease—they were the first to succumb to illness, being less robust than the Arabs. His heart went out to them. At last, he felt, he could play a small but real part in the Divine purpose of reconstituting Zion and redeeming the world. The land was for the Jews, to be worked by them, as in the days of the bible. One day, he was given to believe as he looked lovingly on the rolling field before the house, they will return, and each man will sit under his fig tree, beside his vine. Centuries of dispersion had alienated them from the soil and from physical work. They were like birds which, being caged, had lost the use of their wings. They needed time and patience to rediscover their true form. Finn called the plot of land Abraham's Vineyard.

The fields were strewn with rocks that had to be cleared. But the land, he knew, was fertile. He worked out plans, made calculations: the Jews would be paid a day's wages for their work, the same as hired falahin were paid. And they would be fed. The wages would ease the poverty which now ravaged many a family since money from abroad had ceased to come. The fresh air would invigorate them and the work strengthen their sinews. Elizabeth too, had plans: while the men worked in the fields, she would teach the young women useful womanly skills and give them the rudiments of education, for she had seen how ignorant they were.

Finn bought hoes, two ploughs and two pairs of oxen. The Arabs from Abu Tor, whom he hired to clear the land of rocks, laughed at the thought of Jews working with them in the fields under the hot sun: you could no more make Jews work than you could turn a camel into a Haj, they said. Finn paid no attention to such jibes. Every morning he rode to the field on his horse. For a while he would look at the falahin working. Then, satisfied with the progress, he would canter off to begin his day's work at the consulate.

The news of the British Consul's astonishing enterprise became the talk of Jerusalem. Representatives of the other European powers, were sceptical, but also envious. For a long time they had regarded Finn as something of a curiosity: an eccentric scholar and mystic. But a most unprofessional envoy. They sent home cynical despatches knowing that the message would be conveyed to the English through diverse channels. The Arab notables of Jerusalem, who liked the British Consul, were bemused and amused: here was another sign of European naïveté, they agreed among themselves, a waste of good intentions and, more importantly, of good land.

Reb Binish had always kept his distance from the British Consul. While the activity around "Abraham's Vineyard" was in full swing, Reb Binish said not a word about it, nor made any reference to it. But secretly he had instructed his henchmen to take down the names of all those who came in contact with James Finn and his wife. At last Abraham's Vineyard was ready to receive its sowers and reapers, and James Finn made a resonant public appeal for the Jews to come. A week passed and nothing happened.

Then tentatively, the poorest and most hungry among the Jews came and hung about Finn's home. They accepted gifts of bread and flour. Then, one morning, a rabbinical student called Joseph, an orphan, stepped forward and said he would work for food and wages. Within a week ten more joined in. Before a month had passed Jews of all ages could be seen making their way to the fields every day with sun rise. They were not used to work. They tired easily. The heavy tasks were invariably left to the few Arab falahin whom Finn kept permanently employed. Sitting on his horse Finn would watch the Jews bent over the soil, and imagine their murmurs to be Hebrew incantations. In fact, they were muttering and complaining in Yiddish. He would greet them in Hebrew as Boaz greeted the reapers in his fields "Shalom Aleichem"—Peace be unto you—and they would look up and smile, and return his greeting.

On one such morning Reb Binish, surrounded by a large group of surly youths, arrived at the field. He and his followers wore prayer shawls. One of them carried the Holy Scroll. Their faces were stern. The workers stopped to look at the new arrivals. James Finn saw Binish and dismounted to greet him. Binish looked through him. His implacable eyes were fixed on the group of Jews who stood leaning on their hoes, sweating, not knowing what to make of the unexpected visit. He pointed at the Torah scroll which his followers now raised high above his head and roared "Will you throw this too to the dust and trample upon it as you have done with your self-respect? Is a bit of hunger enough to make you shame the pride of Israel and scratch the earth like hens for scraps of food? You pitiful dogs, you nothings, worse than slaves. Stop this debasing work at once. Go back to your homes or you shall be spewed out of the House of Israel and your names rubbed out of the Book of Life." His rage gathered like thunder. The men about him worked up a frenzy. A shofar was produced. At the first note Binish's men raised a great cry of lamentation, pounded their breasts and shook their fists.

Finn stood by shaken, and watched helplessly as the workers dropped their tools and scuttled away. When no one was left on the field but the Arabs, Reb Binish turned on his heels, and flicking the hem of his talith over his shoulder, left the scene without as much as a look at Finn.

That night at the synagogue Reb Binish published a strict interdict on Abraham's Vineyard and on any Jew who set a foot in it. He compared it to the work of the Devil, who made things appear pleasant only in order to ensnare the souls of the weak. But he held back from denouncing Finn.

The congregation listened in silence. Glances were exchanged. Those who had been working in the fields hung their heads. Binish's men were there, a reminder if such was needed that there was a court presided over by him, and heavy arms to enforce his judgement.

"He would be King of Israel," Israel whispered to Yoel, "and he would chastise us with scorpions, if he's given the chance, that's the kind of King he'd be."

Yoel pulled a face. "I don't think so," he said. "But the whip, yes, he'd chastise us with whips if he were king."

Israel had much comfort from his son Yoel. He thought of him almost more as a friend than a son. There was a sweet accord between them rarely to be found in fathers and sons. At fifteen Yoel was sharp-witted, a keen observer and above all, steadfast. In temperament as in body, he was sturdy, durable and economical of his energies. Yoel was not a loner like Israel, or to a lesser degree, Solomon. He liked doing things with other boys and he could persuade them to do things his way without bullying, hectoring, or cajoling. He could simply convince them quietly and rationally that his way was the best. He had patience and firmness allied with a sense of responsibility that was rare for a lad of his age. Israel knew he would never have to worry about Yoel: the boy was life's favourite son. Clara appreciated that for Yoel loyalties and contracts of friendship meant more than warmth. She was, therefore, sparing of hers with him.

The fear of Reb Binish was great. But not as strong as hunger. When the haluka money stopped, Binish had little other than words to give the people besides threats. Those who could not subsist on the pittance they received from the officers of the community ignored Binish's warning and returned to work in Abraham's Vineyard. Their ranks swelled steadily. Binish threatened and denounced but was unable to staunch the flow of men to James Finn's fields.

One morning the Jews failed to come to work on time. Finn waited for them with growing anxiety. Towards noon one man showed up. His clothes were torn, he had blood on his face and hands. He was so shaken and exhausted that he was hardly able to work but said nothing to Finn or to any of the Arabs who worked with him. The next morning he too didn't come. No one came for the next two days and Finn learnt that Reb Binish had posted a gang of strong-armed men at the Zion Gate, and these set upon the workers as they made their way to the fields in the morning, and beat them with sticks and leather belts.

Although Binish denied direct involvement in the deed he justified it on grounds that an example had to be set: an act by a few irresponsible individuals which threatened the moral standards and integrity of the entire Jewish community could not be tolerated. The people, worn out by hunger and worry, could not summon the will to oppose him.

Not content with the end of Abraham's Vineyard, Binish was determined that the threat should be removed for ever. Through the court he had set up to bolster authority, he proceeded to root out with ruthless severity any deviations from the path of righteousness as he saw it. A woman accused of adultery was stoned and her young daughter taken away from her to the orphanage run by Zelda Binish; male offenders were dragged to the lower rooms of Binish's court, and whipped. Stories were circulating about iron rings attached to the wall, to which those in for punishment were manacled. There had been the case of an old Austrian Jew who had come on a pilgrimage and stayed at the house of the Synagogue's shomas; he was found dead in his bed the next morning. The Austrian Consul who came to register the death was satisfied that the old man had died a natural death. But such was the mood among the Jews in Jerusalem that it was believed the old man was throttled to death by one of Binish's thugs, for it was a custom that if a Jew died while in Jerusalem all his possessions and money were taken over by the administration of the haluka to be distributed to the needy of the community.

Yoel had been right: Reb Binish reigned and chastised his people with whips for the entire duration of the war.

On the day when peace was proclaimed from the Congress of Paris, Clara suffered another miscarriage which nearly killed her. The doctor told her that she couldn't have children any more. When she recovered, she said to Israel, "I think it's time you put your mind to Yoel's marriage. He is of age. Go see a good matchmaker." He was astonished at how conservative she had suddenly become.

The rains had stopped. The hills blossomed with crocuses, cyclamen and anemones. The Zeff family celebrated the Passover with cautious optimism, like someone recovering from protracted illness which he cannot forget. The first ship that arrived at Jaffa after the war brought Sir Moses Montefiore on his third visit to the Holy Land. This time he came with plans and a purpose which would not be thwarted. He wanted no time wasted, for the hour of great changes was at hand, of that he had no doubt.

He also had an unpleasant task to perform in Jerusalem. A group of notable London Jews, acting on behalf of the Ashkenazi leadership of Jerusalem, had lodged a formal complaint against James Finn with the Colonial Secretary. It was charged that Finn had used his position as British Consul in Jerusalem to work with the missionaries for the conversion of Jews to Christianity, and that he had received bribes for his efforts. Sir Moses had been asked to enquire into these allegations.

Chapter 25

In the early 1830s—when Israel was a youth, shortly after Pasha Mehemet Ali established his rule in Palestine, there arrived in Jerusalem a Russian Jew called Abraham Karlin. He was poor when he came. No one had heard of the village in the Pale where he was born, and Karlin could not mention names of rabbis by way of reference. All he had on him were the clothes on his back, and a tattered pouch containing his prayer shawl, phylacteries and a small leather-bound *sidur* of daily prayers printed in Odessa. He told people that he had walked all the way from his native village, across Europe, through Turkey, down the Syrian coast, to Jerusalem. It had taken him over three years—he had lost count of the exact number of days and weeks. During that time he had lived on his wits which, unlike his clothes, were none the worse for wear, and never once prayed in a *minian* for he never had the good fortune of meeting nine Jews all at once to form the required prayer congregation of ten men.

Because he was destitute and not learned Karlin met with indifference in Jerusalem. Although these were days of relative prosperity when the haluka money flowed regularly into the community's coffers, Karlin's allotment barely enabled him to subsist. He had no skills with which to earn his living. But he was a handsome fellow and could tell a good story at a drop of a hat, particularly since he had plenty about which to tell. He hung around synagogues and the mikve where Jews came on the eve of Sabbath to bathe, and soon developed the knack of telling at a glance who he could charm with his tales for the worth of a dinner. His reputation grew as his skill developed. No longer did he have to scrounge, people began inviting him to their homes. Soon no social occasion was complete without him, Karlin the story-teller. With the food often came small gifts. He was doing well, and taking a hard-headed view of his new vocation, he learned economy: his stories were measured in length and quality to the remuneration he expected.

But if it was among his fellow Ashkenazis that he earned his daily bread and a lot more besides, it was in the warmer bosom of the Sepharadis that he found real friendship and eventually true love. One day Karlin saw the elder daughter of Shalom Elissar, a wealthy merchant from Baghdad, chaperoned on her evening walk through the Armenian Quarter. He didn't know who she was but a passing glance from her dark eyes told him that if Fate had any ruling in the lives of men that comely shy girl was destined to be his. Leah, Elissar's daughter, was somewhat past her prime and no suitor was knocking at her father's door. Old Elissar, who had three younger daughters already married, consented to the marriage. As it happened, Karlin and his father-in-law found a kindred spirit in one another. Abraham Karlin gave up story-telling and, with Elissar's wealth behind him, launched himself on a new career as merchant and go-between in land transactions. He worked with Arabs, learned their language and customs, and over the years won their respect and affection.

A chance transaction drew the attention of the entire Jewish community to him so that almost overnight he became a public figure, a man to reckon with. Even those who in the past had treated him with disdain now pretended that all along they had been friends and admirers. It came about as follows.

Five miles west of Jerusalem, there was a village called Kolonia. Its name dated back to the days of the Romans. The village was not a large nor particularly noteworthy one. But perched on top of the summit of a hill, it dominated the route from Jerusalem to Jaffa. The Mukhtar of Kolonia, a mean man, known for his avarice and deceitfulness, was a kinsman of Sheik Abu Gosh. His greed was matched only by his fear of his powerful kinsman. Over the years the Mukhtar of Kolonia, using threats and schemes, dispossessed all his villagers of their land and leased it back to them as tenants. Only one man held out against him: Muhamad Raif. Raif's land sloped gently towards the Jaffa–Jerusalem road. It was no more than two fedans in size and Raif worked on it with his half-brother for he was newly married and as yet had no children.

The Mukhtar coveted Raif's land but the more he did the more determined Raif grew not to part with it. "Rais," he said to the Mukhtar, "you have much land. All I have are these two fedans of land on which my father lived and his father for countless generations. Without it I have no name, I'm nothing. I'll die before I sell my land to anybody." But Raif's obduracy only whetted more the Mukhtar's appetite for the two fedans with their carefully terraced fields and almond trees.

As King Ahab was obsessed with Naboth's vineyard, so it came to pass that the Mukhtar of Kolonia could not put Raif's land out of his mind for a minute. It disturbed his sleep and plagued his peace of mind, Raif continued to turn down one offer after the other. In the end the Mukhtar did the meanest thing an Arab could do to another Arab: he denounced Raif to the authorities for illegally avoiding his military service.

The day after the bashi-bazooks dragged Raif away in chains, the Mukhtar forced Raif's distraught wife to sell the land at a much reduced price and soon after had her removed from the village.

But ever since that day the Mukhtar ceased to enjoy life. Sheik Abu Gosh withdrew his patronage from the village and as he did so gangs of bandits raided, frequently despoiled the fields, and made off with the livestock. The villagers rose against the Mukhtar's authority. He became a hated and despised man. Broken and isolated, he lost his health. Nothing could please him any longer and he wished himself dead.

Years went by and one day a holy man passing through was given hospitality for the night at the Mukhtar's home, as was the custom. When the Mukhtar told him his story, the holy man said the Mukhtar would surely die in misery unless he sold the land at the price he paid for it to a complete outsider, a foreigner.

This was how Abraham Karlin became the first Jew to possess land in the vicinity of Jerusalem. The fields were registered in the name of Leah, Karlin's Sepharadi wife, who was an Ottoman subject, and as Abraham took possession of it, the Mukhtar mounted his horse and accompanied by his slave set off on a pilgrimage to Mecca.

Karlin had neither experience of land nor a particular feeling for it. But he was a shrewd, practical man and he realized that not gold, not warehouses full of merchandise or barns bursting full of grain were so lasting and dependable a currency as the two fedans of gentle land he now possessed. Besides, he relished the idea of being different, and in his imagination he saw many long-term possibilities. He knocked down Raif's hovel and built in its place a house of stone with a wide veranda. He planted apricot and pomegranate trees, apples and figs. His home was in Jerusalem in the house of his wife's father. But the more Karlin visited Kolonia, the more it came to him that one day, not too far off, he would leave the city altogether and settle here where the air was pure, the water sweet and plentiful, and the only sound to be heard was the song of the birds, the distant bleating of sheep, and the rain dropping on the leaves of his fruit trees.

Karlin rode a large ambling piebald horse which he bought from a horse trader who in turn had bought it from a French pilgrim. There was no other piebald horse in Jerusalem, or indeed anywhere else in the country that anyone knew about. It wasn't much of a mount to look at but the horse was sweet-natured and reliable. Karlin could be seen from great distances as he rode to and from Kolonia and Jerusalem. The Arabs called him deferentially 'Effendi'. Or, affectionately 'Abu il-hisan Al Abqa'—Owner of the magpie horse. He was the only one who openly and fearlessly defied Reb Binish.

Karlin was always ready to try new things that no Jew had tried before. He met a German Jew who in his native land made bricks and roof tiles. Karlin took it into his head that bricks and tiles were just what Jerusalem builders needed if only they could be persuaded that sloping roofs were superior to the flat roofs and glazed domes of the Jerusalem houses. He built a kiln at the extremity of his land, and employed the German Jew to make the new product. The bricks proved useless. The tiles piled up in the yard without a buyer in sight. Sceptics jeered. His father-in-law kept a stiff and dignified silence. Karlin shrugged his critics off. "You never get anywhere unless you try new ideas," he said. It was after he abandoned the kiln that he joined Israel in their ill-fated incursion into farming with the Arab Mansour, for which he, Karlin, received the greater share of the blame. He had lost money but gained a friend, for the experience brought the two men, Abraham and Israel, together in a friendship that was to last and grow in their children.

In 1856 Sir Moses visited the land for the fifth time. He was eager to fulfil a mission. A pious Jew from New Orleans, called Judah Touro died and left in legacy a large sum of money to be spent on improving the conditions of his brethren in Jerusalem. He had nominated Sir Moses Montefiore in his will as executor for that sum of money, for Touro had seen how committed Montefiore was to his people. Montefiore remembered the letter Israel had sent him sixteen years before. But after taking counsel decided against embarking on a scheme like the one Israel had suggested. Instead he bought a tract of land west of Mount Zion, overlooking the shallow reaches of the Ben Hinnom gorge. On this land he built rows of houses, workshops for Jews to work in wood, in metal and precious stones; workshops for weavers where Samuel Rimkin could revive the half-forgotten skill he had acquired at such expense in England. And a windmill too, so that Jews could mill the grain from all the surrounding villages and prosper thereof.

All at once there was a demand for Karlin's bricks and tiles, so that he was able to point at his critics and say, "Never say a man is finished until he has breathed his last."

The houses stood, but no one came to live in them. In spite of the cramped, insalubrious conditions in the Jewish Quarter, no Jew dared leave the security of the walls to live in the new houses out on the open hillside where bandits roamed in the night, and under the curse of Reb Binish. The workshops were abandoned before their completion. The windmill broke down and no one came to repair it. It stood like a crippled giant, its arms stuck out in a gesture of despair. Reb Binish held his head high, contemptuous and impatient with his people: once again he had been vindicated, and still the people wouldn't learn! But at least for a while there would be no whoring after new-fangled ideas after Montefiore's failure, nothing to distract the people from the Torah and observing God's law, for who would dare try where even the great Montefiore had failed? Israel and his friends gave up hope. Abraham Karlin brooded in his Kolonia fastness and thought of new schemes.

Karlin had a son called David Joshua. David Joshua and Yoel grew up together and went to the same cheder. In youth they became close friends, although they were as different from one another in temperament as night is from day. Yoel was restrained and thoughtful. David Joshua was expansive and spontaneous. Yoel had a prodigious memory and a relentless line of logic. David Joshua's mind drifted like a butterfly, alighting on this or that as the fancy took him. Yoel was tenacious of purpose. David Joshua wanted only to please and be liked. Yoel's peers respected and followed him. But David Joshua they loved. In appearance too, the two youths were the opposite of one another. Yoel resembled Clara in colour, he had auburn hair, and a fair complexion. His eyes were clear hazel. His movements were strong and deliberate so that he gave the impression of premature adult solidity. David Joshua was dark, linear and quick as a colt. What they had in common, each in his own way but both to a high degree, was a spontaneous love of adventure and the unconventional.

By the time they were seventeen—for their birthdays were a month apart—they had been out together into the heart of Samaria and as far east as the Jordan River. These excursions materialized from challenges they used to set one another. They travelled on foot, armed with sticks, and slept under the stars or in shelters they found on the way. Sometimes they came into Arab villages where they were given the customary hospitality extended to all travellers and strangers. They had grown up fed on stories about the perils of the open countryside, of wild beasts and robbers who lurked in byways ready to fall upon travellers in the hours of unwatchfulness. Many times they saw bands of Beduin horsemen in the distance and prayed for their lives. But the Beduin looked on and rode away. The fact that nothing happened to them on any of their adventures did not dull Yoel's awareness of danger but taught him that it had to be accepted as an inescapable part of life which, if you recognized, was a useful sign of the presence of death, like the hiss of a snake that warned you of its coiled tension. David Joshua had complete faith in his friend's courage and judgement, to the point that he believed following Yoel was as good a guarantee as any against misadventure. This became his response to people who rebuked him for exposing himself to risks and worrying his family and friends in doing so.

David Joshua had become betrothed that year. His intended bride was the daughter of a wealthy Sepharadi who originated in Tunis but travelled halfway round the world before reaching Jerusalem in the halcyon days of Mehemet Ali's rule. At fourteen, the girl had the smoothest olive complexion ever seen, laughing dark eyes, with a look that promised a paradise of love. They were to marry after Lag Be'omer the following year. David Joshua was set for a life of comfort and pleasure. He was impatient to possess her, and he shared his hot fantasies with Yoel.

Yoel's future looked less predictable. Clara consulted Rimkin's wife, who in turn held council with a number of other active wives of social standing. The word passed from the Mikve baths to the back galleries of the synagogues to the tables of rabbis and busybodies who nodded, pulled at their beards and volunteered opinion, until at last Goldfarb the Matchmaker was approached.

Goldfarb was a widower and childless. Therefore his allowance from the haluka was small. In his native Russia he had been a dealer in rags and all sorts of discarded things. All his days he had barely been able to eke out a living and was forever bitter about the injustices of life, until one day, feeling at the end of his tether, he resolved to go to the Holy Land to die there. But in Jerusalem life unexpectedly winked at him. Starting as a go-between for anything, he progressed into negotiating marriage agreements and finally marriage fixing. Here his true gifts were finally revealed. Goldfarb became the prime marriage broker in the land, for the best and most exclusive families. As luck would have it, all the marriages he arranged turned out successful and blessed with first-born sons. At the height of his power, Goldfarb's standing was such that he could pick and choose whom to work for and whom to turn down.

He took his time choosing a bride for Yoel, he wanted it to be just right, for he had great respect for Israel and this was to be—even from his professional standpoint—a labour of love after which he planned to retire.

The girl Goldfarb finally chose was called Hannah Sarah Gotlieb. Her family, though not rich—her father was a book-binder—could boast a lineage of rabbinical distinction on both the maternal and paternal sides, going back a hundred years, and recorded in the annals of Jewish communities in Frankfurt, Antwerp, Riga and Safed. Reb Isaac Gotlieb, Hannah's father, was renowned for moderation in everything he did, for his breadth of knowledge and the quiet self-deprecating sense of humour he had. His word was as good as a bond, and what he didn't know about books was not worth the trouble of learning.

Yoel's first meeting with Hannah took place at her home, after Clara had gone to see the girl's mother and Israel had met and talked over the arrangements with Reb Isaac. When that was done Israel took his son for a walk and talked to him about the importance of marriage, the holy commandment of procreation, and the incomparable value of a good wife. The secret of a fulfilled life, he went on, was the perfect partnership between man and woman, for without a woman a man was but half himself. Because he knew that abstract moralizing was not in the nature of his father, Yoel realized the contract had been completed. And when Israel concluded by saying that beauty was a passing thing, like a mood in the beholder, Yoel understood that he was about to marry a plain girl.

The encounter was, therefore, a pleasant surprise. Hannah was a small compact girl but she was not ugly. While the two fathers and mothers exchanged compliments and extolled the virtues of their offspring, she sat quietly, her hands clasped in her lap, eyes lowered, but watchful. She wore a white sarafan embroidered with red at the hems. Her dark brown hair pulled up and gathered with a velvet ribbon on top of her head. She was sixteen years old. Yoel thought she looked older. He watched her from the corner of his eye, for it was improper to look at her direct, and waited for her to move and say something.

That night he thought of love-making, but instead of Hannah, it was David Joshua's voluptuous bride whose naked body danced and heaved and finally drowned him.

Israel too was surreptitiously looking at the girl. He remembered how Goldfarb had passed his hand over his breast and said in Yiddish, "Here she has very little, unfortunately. But in her heart and head, there's enough to pass on to many generations."

Reb Isaac was talking to Israel, "And what will the young man do to support his wife and children, may God grant many wise and healthy ones?" he asked in his musical voice. "Will he be a learned rabbi? I hear he is a clever student. Or will he go into business? There are opportunities for those who seek them. . . ."

From the corner of his eye, Yoel saw Hannah raise her head and look at him. Her eyes startled him: they were hard blue and large, with long black lashes. She looked at him steadily and all the energy of her small body seemed suddenly to concentrate in that clear, serious face of hers. "Whatever he does, he'll not disappoint, of that I'm sure as I am anything" Israel said. Reb Isaac chuckled. "Like father like son, and your own father Reb Israel. Acorns do not fall far from the oak."

The weddings of Yoel and David Joshua took place on the same day at the Menachem Zion synagogue which had been extended and decorated over the years and now served as the focal point of Askhenazi devotion as well as the only real social centre of the community. The union between the two friends and their women was symbolic of the marriage of the two communities, the Ashkenazi and the Sepharadi, the Haham Bashi declared as he blessed the newly-weds. All but Reb Mordecai Binish and Zelda his wife came to see the two friends with their brides—the one a full-bodied beauty, placid and amiable, the other self-possessed and keen as a hawk, and both radiant in their white wedding dresses—standing together beneath the canopy. When the glass tumblers cracked under the feet of the bridegrooms the guests cheered and cried Mazel Tov.

But beyond that happy festive interlude, time flowed languidly on, marked by little more than Reb Binish's ever-innovative excesses. The houses Sir Montefiore had built stood empty, invaded by thorns. Pious Jews spat and turned their heads away at the sight of them. Arab shepherds used them to shelter their flocks at nights.

If Israel still had dreams of breaking out of the city he no longer talked about them. At Kolonia, Abraham Karlin sat in his rocking-chair on the stone-paved veranda of his house and watched the sun set behind the hills to the west, where he no longer ventured. All his enterprises had come to an end and his beloved piebald horse had succumbed to old age and died. Karlin was content to be still, and healthy, to watch his trees blossom and the fruit ripen, and look forward to grandchildren whom he would tell tales of wonder and adventure which had filled his life.

On a bright spring morning Yoel and David Joshua rode out of Jerusalem to Kolonia to spend the day with Abraham Karlin and his wife in the rustic tranquillity of their home. Instead of taking the main road they branched off to a path across the hills that eventually descended into Kolonia from the height of the ridge. There, prickly shrubs grew among the rocks in profusion, along with carobs, oaks, and pines, all scarred by the ravaging of the Arabs' goats. A westerly breeze fanned the scent of flowers and wild tree blossom into the air. The rocks shone as though they had been polished and the earth was dark and musky. The horses, stimulated by the crisp air, pricked their ears and chafed at the bit. Yoel loved riding out in the country with David Joshua. Only here was he able to forget the tedious routine of life in Jerusalem which marriage and the responsibility that went with it only emphasized. He was not unhappy in his new life as a married man; it was the tunnelled progress of life in Jerusalem, from which there was no escape, that often oppressed him.

Hannah could hardly compensate for that even though she surprised and delighted him more than he had dared to hope. She was slow to unravel; they were discovering one another tentatively even in their lovemaking. But one thing he already knew: she was deeper and more understanding than all those who had praised her to him could understand, and she had a quick sure grasp of things. They were quietly and undemonstratively falling in love with one another without it affecting the contractual responsibilities of their union; as though their love and friendship had grown independently of their marriage. She always took him at his word when he said that he wanted to do this or that which nobody else had ever done, and tacitly she was throwing challenges at him. She was ambitious on his behalf without pushing him. Because her imagination was earthbound her determination was forever wedded to practicality. He might have tested the feasibility of an idea from her reaction. Yet he needed David Joshua's warmth and his expansive, leaping flight of fancy to spice the too doughy flavour of his home life in Jerusalem. Nowhere were David Joshua's qualities so potent as out in the country, on a day like this.

David Joshua prided himself on his horsemanship. Many times on festive occasions in the village of Abu Gosh he contested with the young men in horse races and always acquitted himself honourably. It was he who taught Yoel how to ride and provided him with the horse for the outing.

Yoel rode a steady grey gelding, more accustomed to carrying loads than riders. David Joshua rode a little bay colt with dancing feet, only recently broken in. He would let the colt go, gallop a short way ahead, then wait for his friend to catch up with him. When the pale dun and blue houses of Kolonia came to view, he reined in alongside Yoel. "You carry heavy thoughts from Jerusalem in your head," he said. "What's wrong? Is that what I got you a horse and took you out here for?"

"I've been thinking. . . ."

"You always do. That's the trouble with you. Learn a little from me. I take things as they come. And out here nothing bothers me. Out here I'm King.' He gave the colt a loving pat on the neck. "So be my guest. Drive all thoughts from your mind today. They're worse for your system than Shabas cholent."

"Not your mother's cholent. That's light and delicious," Yoel laughed.

David Joshua waved his hand, "Even my mother's. No cholent today, not for the stomach, not for the mind. Today it's minted tea, apples, honey, and freshly-baked bread and cheese. That's all my father will have and he says it'll keep him healthy for a hundred and twenty years, if he wanted to live that long."

"May we all live that long."

"No, only those of us who know how to enjoy God's creation, like me, and Father," said David Joshua shaking his head.

"What about me?" Yoel smiled.

"Only if you learn new ways of course."

"Oh, you'll never grow up, a boy you'll remain to the end of your days!"

"And you, Reb Yoel, you grow up too soon. You have Yom Kippur in your heart and mind the year round. I have Purim in my head and the Rejoicing of the Law in my trousers. I'll have many children," David Joshua laughed and gave Yoel's horse a gentle kick with his toe.

"Blasphemer!"

"Prophet of doom!"

"You call me prophet and I have nothing to say."

"Don't say. Feel, see, touch, try."

"Yes, I want all that, but you still need words, good words, like bricks to build with," Yoel said.

"I don't. You want to change the world."

"No. Maybe to improve it a little. Just our world, it's not a very big one."

David Joshua fell silent. As they were reaching the village he said, "You should write then. Print and publish, start a journal. No one's done that here. Well?"

Yoel looked at him open-mouthed, smiling. "God's word from the mouth of a fool, David!" he cried.

"Come now, get your lazy horse to pick up its feet." And the two friends cantered down to the village.

The day was slow to age in Kolonia. Abraham Karlin never used a watch or kept a clock here. He could tell the time from the length of the shadows and the pitch of the bul bul's song. He was proud of the country wisdom he had acquired and he was not in the least offended if at length the young men got tired of listening to his observations on nature. Dusk fell. Leah Karlin stood at the door of the house and reminded the men that supper would be ready soon. She began lighting the lamps. Abraham looked at her lovingly. Her beauty never dimmed in his eyes after all these years, but like nature itself was full of variety. In everything he did he blessed the good Lord for having given him Leah. Suffused by the warmth of that sentiment, he said, "Now I have something for you young men that'll warm your hearts."

He went into the house and presently returned with a glass cask. When Leah saw that, she screwed up her face. Karlin poured a rich red liquid out of the cask into four tumblers and raised his: "Lechaim", he said.

It tasted sweet and bitter and sharp. Karlin smacked his lips and waited. Leah took a small sip and put her tumbler down. Yoel dutifully followed his host's example and drank it all. David Joshua pulled a face and clutched his throat.

"Father what's that stuff?" he cried.

"The first cask of Karlin pomegranate brandy. A cure for every known illness of the body and the mind," Karlin said.

"Only if you believe in demons!" David Joshua said. "No demon could stand this, it's awful, Father."

"Good things are wasted on some people," Abraham said with a touch of hurt dignity.

In the middle of supper, Karlin became thoughtful. He stopped eating and said, "Germany. . . ." They looked at him questioningly.

"I was thinking of what you were saying earlier," he went on. "I know something about bricks. For making good bricks you need a good kiln. For making good printed words you need a good press. And you need to learn how to use it. You won't learn it here. Germany's where you should go, if you're serious. I like the idea. But there won't be many who will. You'll have to fight and fight, and fight."

Yoel's and Hannah's first-born son, Leib Isaac, was circumcised according to the Covenant of God with Abraham, Isaac and Jacob, a week before Passover the following year. To David Joshua and Rachel a daughter Naomi, was born. After the two families settled down again, Yoel and David Joshua set out for Germany with the blessings and money of Rafael Mendoza and David Joshua's maternal grandfather. David Joshua's decision to go was late and spontaneous: he wanted to see new horizons, different countries. And starting a printing press had after all been his idea.

Two years they spent in Königsburg where Yoel learnt the printing trade and David Joshua learnt more about life. They stayed in the homes of wealthy Jews, lovers of Zion and donators to the haluka. The Jewish Community of Königsburg was a rich and generous one. It was famous for its fine Hebrew printing. When Yoel had mastered the basic skills of printing, money was raised and a secondhand press, complete with Hebrew typefaces was bought. The two young men were seen off, showered with gifts and felicitations. All through the sea voyage to Jaffa, Yoel lovingly watched over his precious press, and thought of battles with Binish, of triumph of ideas, of opening gates for change.

In Jaffa his hopes were shattered: the primitive crane which lifted the press from the ship's hold broke. Yoel stood on dry land and saw his dream and the result of two years of hard work, plunge into the blue sea and disappear out of sight.

As the first hamsin of 1860 scorched the land, followed remorselessly by more hamsins, poison bubbled up from the dirty bowels of Jerusalem. A few days before the fast of the Ninth of Ab, cholera broke out in the Jewish Quarter. It spread through the city like fire. The Angel of Death was thorough and indiscriminating in his visitations.

Chapter 26

The sickness seized Yoel suddenly. He was at his parents' home and they had had only tea with a lump of crystal cane sugar which Clara believed was a good guard against infection. He was talking to his father when he began to feel shivery and faint. He said it was nothing. Clara said the outbreak of the disease put ideas into people's heads and made them afraid of the smallest upset and every cough. Nevertheless, she watched him anxiously. Then a terrible weakness came over him, and the vomiting began. Before he passed out there was pain, then nothing, then disconnected scenes began coursing through his mind. He thought his end had come, he just about managed to mumble "Hear O Israel, the Lord is one. . . ."

The first thing he saw when he came to, was the whitest ceiling he had ever seen, on which a pale shadow, like a wing, moved to and fro. He heard nothing but the sweet song of birds. Something cool and gentle touched his forehead. He closed his eyes and thought he must have died and was in Heaven—it never occurred to him that he deserved anything less. The thought of his grandfather Solomon came to him. He wondered whether he would meet him in this quiet clean haven. When he opened his eyes he saw his wife Hannah leaning over him, wiping his brow with a piece of damp linen. Her head was covered with a white kerchief and she was wearing a sort of white gown. Her eyes were larger, more luminous than ever. It occurred to him that she too must have died a little ahead of him, and was here in Heaven with him. He tried to rise and nearly fainted from weakness. "Lie still, don't try to move," Hannah said, and added, "Thank God you've got over the worst. I knew you would." Her voice was low but there was no mistake about it, it was that of the composed Hannah, not a spirit.

"Where am I?" he asked.

"In a good place, where there's clean water and fresh air. Rest." The shutters were closed but the light came through and formed rows of bright strips on the reed mat that covered the floor. Not far from the low bed on which he was lying, stood a large earthen jar full of water. Hannah tilted it to dampen the linen. When his senses adjusted to the room he perceived that it was freshly whitewashed, and that there was a smell of camphor in the air. He also sensed that outside it was bright and hot, though the room was cool. The weakness from the effort to rise made him nauseous. He no longer cared where he was, it was enough that Hannah was at his side, the rest didn't matter. Once again details were becoming blurred before his eyes. Only this time he knew that he was drifting to sleep not sinking into oblivion.

It was dark when he woke up. An oil lamp was burning in the corner of the room, and Hannah, seeing him stir, came over to him. He felt a little stronger, he was able to eat a little of the hot clear chicken soup she had cooked for him. She told him that they were in Kolonia, in Abraham Karlin's home, she and little Lieb. Then suddenly he felt himself sucked into a vast and terrible emptiness. He was safely with his wife and child, yet another reality in the darkness of his unconsciousness, was claiming him.

"My mother, my father, where are they?" A panic was rising in him.

Hannah held him down. "Rest," she pleaded.

"Where are they, where are they?" He almost screamed at her. Then he calmed down, "Tell me, please. I must know, I might as well know now."

"They are dead. They died within hours of each other, two days after you fell ill. There was nothing I could do. Nothing anyone could do. They died peacefully."

"My sisters . . . they too are dead?"

"Yes," she said.

He was too weak to weep. Besides, there was no moisture left in him, he felt, only a great empty and dry wilderness in which nothing was recognizable and nothing mattered. He turned his face to the wall. "Why didn't you leave me there? What's the point, when there's nothing left?"

She turned his face towards her. "There's me, and there's your son. There's still life about, and people who've lost their families. That night when you fell ill I rushed to your parents' home. By morning they too were ill. I took your sisters to our place. I kept going from one home to the other, nursing you and your parents, and your sisters in turn. There was no help to be got. People were dying by the dozens and the city was put under quarantine.

"I did all I could. While there was hope, I fought. When your parents died, and then your sisters, all I thought was of saving you and our son. Would you've preferred us all to die? If it weren't for David Joshua we would have died, I'm sure. He came and took us away. Strapped you on the back of a mule, bribed the soldiers at the gate. That's how we came here. Don't say there's nothing left to live for. We're alive, it's a miracle. We are safe here with Karlin and his family, where the air is clean and the water good."

At last he could weep. He let his despair flow freely, and she held him in her arms and rocked him until, drained of energy, he fell asleep.

As soon as he was strong enough, Yoel went back to Jerusalem to bury his parents and his two sisters. He had never seen a sadder sight than that which greeted his eyes at the Jewish Quarter: it was almost deserted. Heaps of ashes lay everywhere. The smell of burning was in the air. Only the burial teams of *Hevra Kadisha* were seen in the streets, and the only sounds were those of lamentation. He buried his parents and sisters in the cemetery on the slope of Mount Olive, next to the graves of Solomon and Ada, and returned to Kolonia to what was left of his family.

For a month they stayed there, and Yoel spent the days in contemplation and prayer. The death of his parents and sisters seemed to sever his past from him. He felt rootless, stripped of all that he had. His grief was inconsolable, his only relief the gentle distractions of Hannah and his son Leib's company. He would take them both in his arms and hold them tight.

Hundreds had perished from the cholera. Among them were Rafael Mendoza, Eliezer Rimkin, Reb Mordecai Binish and his wife Zelda. Reb Binish it was told ended his life in a blaze of courage and affirmation. Undaunted he went about helping people, visiting the afflicted and praying without the smallest regard for his own safety. Death overtook him in an act of devotion, and all the furies were drained from his body in one terrible cataract.

They went back home where together they repainted the walls and doors and windows. An emissary was immediately sent to Europe to acquaint the clerks of the haluka with the extent of the disaster. Samuel Rimkin was the emissary. Hannah's family survived. Reb Isaac Gotlieb and his wife had declined to go with Hannah to Kolonia but stayed behind to help others, and the Lord spared them. At Reb Isaac's suggestion, Yoel threw himself into public affairs, helping people and attending councils where plans were drawn to get the community back on its feet. His work distracted him from his own loss. Slowly, his appreciation of the disaster became influenced not by the extent of the damage it caused but by the extent of the community's extraordinary resilience.

Looking at the resurgence of life around him, he would see children going to school laughing and playing, and he found comfort in the thought that Death the Reaper visited wars and plagues and famine on the community which like the grass was cut only to grow again. There was no loss of continuity, no break with the past, nor did his parents' death signal finality. It came to him that he would never again fear loss; he wondered whether he would be afraid even of death.

Reb Binish was succeeded as Chief Rabbi of the Ashkenazis by a scholarly and sweet-natured man called Samuel Salant. The rigour of Binish's days melted and became a myth. But the authority he had established lived on with his successor who exercised it more gently but no less resolutely. Reb Salant was as conservative as his predecessor without being a warrior. He was not going to try to dam the flow of progress if that was how people saw the advent of new fashions. He believed that true merit ultimately wins the day. He opened his arms in welcome to the Sepharadis and invited them to join their Ashkenazi brethren and work for the common good of all the Jews in Jerusalem and in the Holy Land.

The regeneration of the Jewish community after the devastation of the plague affected Yoel profoundly: he too experienced a rebirth of a kind. Hope, like fresh vegetation, grew to cover the wasteland of his loss. As he threw himself with ever-increasing commitment into communal activities; it seemed to him that his experience, all the jarring contradictions of his vision, were gradually smoothing themselves into a sense of order in which simplicity and complexity, sadness and joy, were melded together. Finding his direction, he began to write.

That year Hannah gave birth to a baby girl. They called her Tiqva, meaning Hope.

PART THREE

Chapter 27

Yoel acquired the habit of rising at dawn. Except when baby Tiqva woke up screaming, it was the only time of day when he was assured of silence and privacy. He learnt not to force his concentration but wait patiently until it gathered and his thoughts began to flow freely into a stream of narrative. In these pregnant moments before he began working, his memory was like a well, deep and resonant, and almost invariably it was Solomon's voice which spoke to him through the spaced-out sounds of the yet unawakened day. Solomon, whose stories he had read over and over again, whose stories seemed to grow and develop in his own imagination, was his starting point. Before him there was nothing he could relate to, nothing to give his vision of the past wholeness, and Yoel could not conceive of a meaningful future without an equally meaningful past.

Today he was impatient to record his thoughts: nothing he had written before linked him so vividly to all he had heard Solomon and his own father say over so many years, than what he was about to put down on paper. He grappled with the form and decided on simplicity just when the voice of the Muezzin cut into his thoughts. David the baker's pushcart clattered along the broken alley. He took up his pen.

"The third day of the week, five thousand six hundred and twenty-seven years to the creation of the world, month of Nisan. Blessed be the Lord," he wrote.

"Yesterday morning David Joshua and I went for a walk. It was a beautiful spring day. David Joshua suggested we walked to the compound the Russians started building ten years ago, and have been adding to ever since. It's a pleasant place situated not further than two miles west of the city, on a gentle rise. Here the Russians have built rooms and chapels for their pilgrims, and on a day like this, the place and the visitors make a cheering sight. We had not gone far when we came upon Rabbi Salant showing a group of visitors round the new Great Synagogue Beit Yakov. We greeted him and went our way, but my mood had changed so that by the time we reached the Jaffa Gate, David Joshua felt compelled to rebuke me for spoiling such a perfect day with my sullenness. I said to him: 'I see Reb Salant proudly showing our great synagogue, and I feel ashamed.' He looked at me perplexed and a little annoyed. 'My grandfather Solomon Zeff came here with nothing and left this world with his dream fulfilled, he redeemed the plot of the ruined synagogue and saw the synagogue Menachem Zion built in his lifetime. And my father got land. He failed in the larger thing he tried to do, but look, even he carried on where his father had left. Didn't he help raise 35,000 pieces of gold to build this great synagogue close to Menachem Zion? Look at it, is there a more majestic building in the whole of Jerusalem? Generations of our people will be buried on the Mount of Olives and Beit Yakov will still stand as a monument to my father's and my grandfather's generation. And here am I, getting set in my ways, no achievements, nothing in sight.'

"'Achievements', David Joshua replied, are a matter of chance and timing. If an opportunity comes your way and you seize it, achievement will follow."

"We had walked about a mile when we came upon a field which had been sown with peas. The crops were fresh green, the pods were glossy and swollen. I touched the soil. It was dark and moist, it crumbled in my fingers. A group of falahin, five of them, were standing at the edge of the field taking a rest. They were happy and laughed a good deal. When they saw me bend down and touch the earth, one of them called out, 'Hey, you Jews, what are you doing there soiling your hands like peasants?' There was no malice in his voice, he was friendly. On a sudden impulse I answered him, 'We've come to see if you'd sell us your field so that we may grow peas, like you.'

"David Joshua looked at me as though I had taken leave of my senses. But the Arab called back, 'Is that so? Well, you're in luck for the field belongs to an old man who would gladly sell it at the right price. Come back tomorrow at the same time and we'll talk about it more.'

"It was only when we passed the Damascus Gate, some ten minutes later, that we both realized what had happened. We looked at one another and laughed. Then David said, 'You see? How impatient you are!' And I said, 'It can be done. It must be done, and if not now then when?'

"Today we shall meet the old man and negotiate the purchase. There are men with money who are interested in coming in and sharing in the venture. I know I can raise the money. Today is the greatest day in my life.

"Our people are still sceptical but they don't look at you as though you were mad when you talk of breaking out of the city's walls. That is something the plague has made us all realize, how unhealthy conditions are in the Jewish Quarter. People are still afraid of any innovation. That's human nature, and Jewish nature. But who survived when the cholera was killing every night by the hundreds? Those few who dared return to the neglected houses with the tiled roofs 'the turbaned goat pens' as Reb Binish called them, built outside the walls with Sir Moses's money. Those houses and their dwellers, on whom Reb Binish had laid a curse, lived! The fresh air and the open space saved them as it did me.

"Yet even now Reb Binish's spirit lives on: there's much squabbling over the haluka money, the schools, hospitals and above all, the missionaries! The generation of the Desert will not loosen its grip!

"One day, with the help of God, I will start a journal so that wisdom and progress will have a voice. God's will will be done, I believe that. But even He needs some help. Would He have created man in His own image and given him free will for no other purpose than that he should follow rules unquestioningly? To think that God needs help is not blasphemy but the essence of wisdom. Which brings me back to the question of the fields.

"When I touched the earth yesterday morning and felt its moisture in my hand, it was like touching something very private. Like Hannah. So private and delightful that I felt shy at having David Joshua standing there looking at me. And then I knew what I wanted for the future. I wanted the earth's fragrance close to me. Always. And the fresh air and the smell of things that grow.

"I see that the falahin, even in their poverty, look healthier and happier than the city dwellers. It was the same in Europe. I saw it in the countryside I passed through. The reason for this is clear to me. What was the Garden of Eden if not a place where the earth gave forth fruit and flowers in abundance, all things to please and satisfy man? But the city is man's creation; the streets and tall houses a monument to his conceit. What can be a higher form of worship than to strive to return to Eden, to God's grace. I cannot believe that my grandfather Solomon, may his soul be woven in the wreath of eternal life, came here merely to walk in the dank alleys of the Jewish Quarter! The goyim think we are weak and sickly. I've heard an English missionary quoted as saying that Ashkenazi Jews were the most unwholesome looking people he had ever seen. But out in the fields, when we till our land and make things grow, no one would be able to say that of us. I want my children to recognize the partridge, the kestrel, the finch and the turtle dove, not point at anything with wings and just say "bird". And I want them to walk among the trees and know the wild carob from the oak, the fig tree from the pomegranate, and the scent of the hill pine. I'll build my home in the fields. For Hannah for my children and their children. For posterity and for the glory of all Israel, Amen."

Seven men, including Yoel, banded together and bought the land which they divided into seven plots. They were Samuel Rimkin for his son Asher, David Joshua Karlin, son of Abraham, Jacob Fishbein, Mendle Kovarsky, Joshua Raab and Aaron Mendle Fuchs. All upright men, pillars of the community, with families. The land purchase was registered under the name of a widow called Malke Weiss. It was forbidden for *raya*, non-Ottoman Jews, to own land officially. But for legal purposes at least, Ottoman law rated women as nothing, and land could be easily transferred to the use of a new tenant so long as the official owner was "nobody".

The homesteads were completed before the rain came, in the year 1867. Bunched together on a flat slope west of the city, they stood tightly together like a congregation seeking safety in their closeness to each other. They were modest buildings, two rooms each at the most, with an outside lean-to and an improvised fence marking the boundaries of each house. The doors were solid. The windows had shutters with slits to see through. The homes of Raab and Kovarsky had red tiled roofs from Karlin's yard. They stood out against the faded hillside like torches at night.

On the first day after the New Year Holy Days the seven families moved out of the city to their new homes. It was a day of celebration for the entire Jewish community. The small convoy of mules, donkeys and a camel, marched out of the Jaffa Gate. The men and women walked alongside, carrying small loads or children who were too small to walk. They were accompanied by a crowd of young men dressed in holiday clothes and broad-rimmed hats, who danced and cheered and clapped their hands as they sang, "David King of Israel is alive and does exist". Kovarsky's nephew, a strapping young man with a sandy beard, blew the shofar.

Some distance from the city walls, the path sloped sharply, the ground dropped. Ahead stood the seven houses, small, surrounded by a vast emptiness. The city looked down on them, high, formidable, secure. The people stopped, looked back. Suddenly the open hillside looked unfamiliar and exposed. The voices died down. Those who had accompanied the settlers hung back; it was the point of farewell. Yoel raised his voice and cried out pointing to the houses ahead: "There, our homes. A mere stone's throw from the city, almost in the shadow of the walls. Do you tremble like leaves to move just a few steps?" Without a word, Hannah took hold of the reins of their mule, and pulled it forward. The mule wouldn't budge. Hannah pulled and pulled and cursed until exhausted, she broke down and began to cry. It was the first time Yoel had seen her shed tears.

The paralysis didn't last long. In a moment Rabbi Salant could be seen, walking at a brisk pace at the head of a group of followers. He had his prayer shawl draped round his shoulders. There was a big smile on his face as he drew near and stretched his arms out. He had come himself to nail the mezuzas on the doorjambs of the new homes and bless the settlers.

Night falls quickly in the east; twilight is brief and luminous. Yoel and Hannah had been so busy unpacking their belongings and arranging their new home that they became aware of the gathering darkness only when they paused to rest between chores. Then the stillness of dusk suddenly seemed to amplify their own voices and those of the children.

"Light the oil lamp, Hannah," Yoel told her.

Through the window they could see the stars getting brighter against the deepening night. A jackal howled. The dogs in some nearby village began to bay. The tall withered grass whispered in the night breeze. The wind carried every sound, now bringing it closer, now taking it further away. Hannah pulled her shawl round her shoulders.

"We should get a goat, maybe some hens too. And ducks. I've always wanted ducks," she said.

"The jackals and hyenas will come and eat the hens and the ducks. But a goat, yes. A good white milking goat," Yoel said.

"If we build a good fence the hens would be safe," Hannah insisted. Leib, tired from the day's excitement, fell asleep on the mattress by the wall, near the cot of his sister Tiqva.

"I should go back to the city, just for the childbirths," said Hannah.

When they ran out of conversation they became aware of how silent it was. Not a sound came from the neighbouring houses. Yoel looked through the window. The houses stood massy in the dark; no light came from them. He closed the shutters. Hannah was looking at him.

"They've gone," he said quietly. "Stolen away without saying a word."

"All of them?"

"So it seems."

"Call out," she said. "Maybe someone's still there."

He started for the window again then stopped and turned back.

"No, I'll not advertise our shame, particularly if there is someone who's stayed behind. I'll not shout into the darkness as though we are afraid."

She was silent. "What shall we do?" she said at length, and added weakly, "The mule's out in the yard."

He stared at her, "What are you saying?"

She lowered her eyes, "Nothing. Maybe you should bring the mule in. If she gets stolen we won't be able to afford another one."

"She won't get stolen." He came over and put his arm round her shoulder. "We've done enough for one day. Come, let's put out the light and go to bed. In the morning we'll get up and go about our business. Most probably the rest will return and we shall act as if we didn't know they had gone and when they see that all is well, they'll stay. That's all."

They lay close to one another under the blanket, the sounds of the night were close, and alive. He knew them well from on his excursions with David Joshua. Only now it was different: they seemed louder, and personal, as though they were directed at him, as though the house was calling attention to itself, challenging the indifference of the night. He was here, inside the house he had built, with his wife and two children, and the mule outside. Held down by the house, marked out by the snorting mule. He became a little afraid.

Hannah pressed closer to him. He felt her breath on his neck. She nuzzled against him and her legs moved in between his. When he was aroused, she began to undo his trousers. Her hands were deft on his penis.

When he touched her thigh he was surprised to feel that she was already naked. She wriggled herself on top of him and took him in. He lay back and let her warm assured thrusts build up to a climax. But suddenly she stopped and went stiff. In an instance she was off him. Her breath came in short frightened gasps. He heard, or thought he heard, the sounds of steps outside. Quickly he buttoned himself up; he was grateful that he hadn't taken off his boots. His mind went over the dark room as he thought of likely weapons. Then it occurred to him that the first thing thieves would do would be to steal the mule, and a swell of helpless rage came over him.

The steps receded then came back again right up against the door. Hannah stifled a cry and began to mumble a prayer as she scrambled up to where the children lay.

"Yoel, Yoel, are you there?" they heard a voice whisper.

It was David Joshua.

Both let out a cry of relief, and Yoel, jumping to his feet rushed to the door and unbolted it. Even in the near pitch darkness he could see how frightened his friend was.

"Thank God you're here," David Joshua said.

"Where else would I be?" The relief of finding the danger he had feared illusory restored his confidence and made him gruff. He was angry with himself for having been afraid but very happy at seeing his friend.

"The others have gone," Yoel said.

"I know. They were frightened to stay the night out here after someone spread the rumour that robbers were coming to attack us."

"But you didn't go," Yoel said.

David Joshua laughed. "I fell asleep and so did my wife. We were so tired we didn't notice that the others had sneaked away. When we woke up it was dark. They had taken my mule. I said to her, 'Wife, Yoel wouldn't have gone away and left us here,' and she said, 'There are seven houses here, more than enough for a thief or two. So let's lie quiet and hope that the thieves will go to the other houses and leave us alone.' She pleaded with me not to go outside. But I had to, the thought of you sitting in the dark not knowing what to do or think, I had to come and let you know we're here too."

Hannah began to laugh. She said, "Go, David Joshua, bring Rachel here and let us spend the night all of us together and cheer one another up."

They lit the lamps and Hannah made some tea on the little oil stove. Throughout the night the jackals howled but their voices did not sound sinister any longer. Towards morning a few shots were heard in the distance, perhaps in some village a score had been settled, or a celebration had begun.

Yoel said, "This night we shall remember for the rest of our lives. And we shall tell our children of it and they will in turn tell their children."

"And years from now God alone knows what the story will be. Perhaps that we were attacked and saved by a miracle."

"Perhaps. But our being here is in itself a small miracle, David Joshua. Think about it. I believe in miracles. But they don't just happen, you have to work at them."

David Joshua laughed. "I was thinking how small things like last night can turn into legends."

"Don't laugh at legends," Yoel said pointing a finger at him, "they are the spice of life. Try eating your food without spices and you'll see how important spices are."

In the morning Yoel and David got up and began to work at setting order to their plots. A few Arab peasants who came to work in the fields nearby, greeted them in friendliness. They showed no surprise at seeing the Jews there.

By noon, all the five men had returned, but without their families. Yoel did not rebuke them, in fact not a word was said about the previous night. The men set about their work as though nothing had happened, and David Joshua found his mule tethered to the post outside his door. That night no one returned to the city. In a week, the families moved in, and the seven families could look at the city walls in the golden light of the evening, and say with pride to one another, "We were the first. This is our home and here we shall stay. Let the others come to us." The small settlement was named Seven's Estate.

Chapter 28

On 14th April 1856 the two dilapidated cannons in the Citadel had fired a few discordant salvos from the battlements. The soldiers had lit the fuses then ran for cover; no one could say with certainty that the old artillery pieces would not explode. The occasion was the end of the war in Europe. That night shops were kept open by special dispensation from the Pasha, and fireworks were shot from the top of the Tower of David and the Jaffa Gate. Those who had witnessed the day never tired of telling what a great occasion it had been. But the war had come to an end a month before, on March 18th. It had taken twenty-eight days for the news to reach Jerusalem.

Kamil Pasha's chief Clerk, Mahmud Latif, remembered the day clearly. He was a junior clerk at the time and Jerusalem's belated victory day celebrations was the first major event in his career. Kamil laughed to hear his Chief Clerk talk of those bygone days. He couldn't imagine such backward primitive conditions. He was younger than Mahmud, a handsome man and one of the most promising officers in the Ottoman administration. His recent posting to Jerusalem came with a promotion; it was a challenge he was eager to meet.

That morning, when the Austrian Consul called on him to inform him that His Majesty the Kaiser Franz Josef will be making a private visit to Jerusalem after his participation in the opening of the Suez Canal ceremony, Kamil Pasha was able to smile in bland superiority and, over a cup of sweet bitter coffee, tell his guest that he was already in possession of the news, it had come a week before direct from Constantinople, by the telegraph!

Nothing so miraculous as the telegraph which had been stretched to Jerusalem some five years before, nor even the Suez Canal, could excite Kamil Pasha out of his calm suaveness; men like him took achievements and innovation for granted, like promotion and benefits that came with it. But the visit of the great European monarch was an event which Kamil Pasha recognized, would have a direct bearing on his own life and career. He felt as though Providence had chosen him to be at the very eye of history. When the faithful Mahmud remarked how fortunate it was for the Sultan that a man of Kamil Pasha's abilities should be Governor when the eyes of the world are fixed on Jerusalem, Kamil could only smile and call for the plans he had drawn for the highway from Jaffa to Jerusalem. For once there would be money from the Imperial coffers. Only time was in short supply; and Kamil had no intention of wasting any. He looked forward to the excitement of creation and to a reprieve from the tiresome affairs of the Jews which, with the ever-growing number of them arriving, had been claiming his time and attention not least with their stubborn, irrepressible desire to buy land.

For the ordinary people of Palestine—Jews, Arabs, and Christians—the Suez Canal signified the height of human achievement, an unbelievable feat which defied imagination. The news of it reached Beduin tribes even in the most remote wilderness. A stretch of desert cut like bread and two continents pulled apart to allow the passage of ships between them! Nothing so stupendous had been done since the Almighty rent *Yam Souf* to let the Children of Israel escape the chariots of Pharaoh. Was this good, or was it bad? The rabbis were for once at a loss, except to agree that few things could hereafter remain immense and mysterious if man can contrive successfully to shrink the awesome vastness of creation.

The work on the Jaffa to Jerusalem highway began at once. Kamil Pasha saw it as a point of honour that the road should be finished or at least usable before the rains came. Hordes of labourers were mustered; the prisons throughout the region were emptied and the prisoners taken in chains to work on the site. Every morning with sunrise teams of workers armed with picks and shovels came out of the Jaffa Gate and made for the points appointed for them by the engineers along the line of the road. All day until sunset the hills rang with the sound of hammers and picks against the rock. Day by day the white scar cut deeper into the hillside, progressed from Jerusalem, past Abu Gosh, and down the winding ravine of Bab el Whad. On some mornings Kamil Pasha would come to inspect personally how the work was progressing. Mounted on his black charger, he would ride a whole morning's way, then race his adjutants back to the city.

When the road was finished and Kamil Pasha opened it ceremoniously with the blessings of the Mufti, the Anglican Bishop, the Latin Bishop, the Ashkenazi Rabbi Salant and the Sepharadi Chief Rabbi the First in Zion Rabbi Gagin, a contraption meant to resemble the Imperial coach harnessed to four horses rattled out of the Jaffa Gate towards the western end of Bab el Whad to test the new road. It was never seen again. The next day the horses were brought in ridden by Kamil's soldiers.

As it happened the Kaiser's visit disappointed expectations. The Austrian Emperor wished it emphasized that his visit to Jerusalem was private and personal. The ceremony laid on for him by the Governor was hindered by surging crowds which had to be contained by gendarmes wielding club and whip.

For the Ashkenazi Jews the royal visit marked much-awaited recognition, for Kaiser Franz Josef epitomized all that was good and magnificent in temporal power. Dressed in their best clothes, they lined the streets where the imperial procession was to pass, but all they could see was the brilliant white plumage of the Kaiser's hat through sweat-covered flanks of horses in his entourage.

But the Kaiser did not forget the Jews: he had been told of the Jews in Jerusalem, many of whom were his subjects, and mindful of the Jews in his own Empire, took time to confer the title of Knight of the Empire on the leading Jewish personage in the city. The honour mistakenly fell to the retiring and bemused Sepharadi Haham Bashi who said a special prayer for the health and well-being of the Kaiser in the Sepharadi synagogue, Tree of Life.

Only the new road remained, a symbol of change and a memento of the Kaiser's visit. It wasn't much of a highway by European standards. The stones used for the roadbed soon worked loose and broke up, hurting the animals' feet and shaking the carts that now trundled regularly between Jerusalem and Jaffa. But for all that, the journey was cut by more than three hours, and was safer. The powerful clan of Abu Gosh through whose lands the highway passed, levied toll and took means to protect the traffic. Bandits may have watched from the hill tops the caravans and carts going to and from Jerusalem, but seldom swooped down on them as they used to do before. Slowly, judderingly, the world was reaching out to reticent hill-locked Jerusalem. Travellers from foreign lands no longer excited interest as they had done before, for with spring Jerusalem would be crowded with them, from as far away as America, Argentina, India, and the farthest reaches of Russia. The souks were filled with hitherto unknown or unobtainable goods and gadgets the use of which people didn't understand but bought all the same.

The small settlement beyond the walls had struck root and began to grow. Seven's Estate, no longer a cluster of a few small houses grouped together in a bare field, spread up the slope towards the city. The path from it to the Jaffa Gate had cut a crease into the hillside; it looked as permanent as any road. When the Jews of Jerusalem saw how content were those dwelling outside the walls, and heard the laughter of the children playing among the trees, they too longed to emulate the pioneers. Yoel Zeff, David Joshua Karlin and Asher Rimkin, the three main founders among the seven, became the moving force in the community for any innovative action which was not, at the same time, either eccentric or irresponsible. Their shared authority drew them together; there was nothing, no new enterprise, no act of charity, in which they were not involved.

"It is the highway," Yoel wrote in his diary, "not I, nor any of the others, that has brought this remarkable change in the attitude of our people who are ready to do now what they would have trembled to think about before. The road is like an artery that brings fresh bubbling young blood to this too still and fearful city." As he wrote, he thought of Hershle Zunshein and his cousin Nahman Fuchs, two Jews from Transylvania, ignorant and unaccomplished in anything except brawls, who had nothing to lose between them and nothing going for them. Nahman had a wife called Bella. Bella feared no one in this world or in the hereafter. She was quiet until roused to anger, then you could hear her bellow louder than a roll of thunder. It was said she could drive a thick nail into a doorpost with one clout of her fist. Bella towered over her husband and his cousin, and ungainly though she was, she brought a child into the world every year. At Bella's initiative the cousins managed to raise money as soon as the road was opened, and gain concession to run the ancient caravanserai at the mouth of Bab el Whad. Bella and Nahman ran the place and turned it into a passably good hostel, providing food, reasonably clean accommodation, and a change of horses. Hershle bought a cart and four mules and struck up a lively haulage and passenger business between Jerusalem and Jaffa. Before two years had passed, they had paid off all their debts and were making a handsome profit. Woe betide any of the cousins' detractors if he chanced to find himself on Hershle's cart or in Bella and Nahman's caravanserai.

Yoel and his friends used to joke about the fearsome trio's success, at times not without a tinge of envy and admiration. But if the prosperity of the hostel at Bab el Whad and Hershle's growing fleet of carts showed what daring and application could achieve, another enterprise of an entirely different nature reawakened in Yoel an ambition that had accompanied him from youth, an ambition which had in fact been passed down to him from his father.

There was in Paris a group of pious but forward-looking Jews who years before had formed an organization they called the Society of the Friendship of Israel. The Society, amongst whom were wealthy Jews, was particularly interested in education and had been involved in the founding of a vocational school in Jerusalem run by a man called Krieger, a colourful personality with a rare gift for languages who had learned Arabic and was so well-versed in the ways of the land that the Pasha had appointed him his personal secretary and translator. The Society's projects brought back to life all the forgotten reflexes that so dominated communal life in the days of Reb Binish. But none more so than the agricultural school which opened in the year 1870 on land purchased near Jaffa, and which was called Mikve Israel – Fountainhead of Israel.

The fact that he was drawn into a controversy which surprised him by its fierceness, did not distract Yoel from the challenge that Mikve Israel threw at the Jews of Jerusalem. Nor could he be distracted, for it was to that challenge that the guardians of the haluka responded when they condemned the school and cursed the new highway that tied it to Jerusalem.

"They have put the cart before the horse. A school for farmers but no land for Jews to farm," Yoel said to David Joshua and Asher Rimkin.

"What does Mikve Israel tell us? It says go, try again with renewed determination, get land so that the school is justified, if for nothing else."

Before the new year of the Mikve Israel's first anniversary, the first issue of a bi-weekly journal, the *Pisga*—Summit—appeared in Jerusalem. A man called Frume, who had a passion for the printed word and some experience in printing, joined Yoel and together with David Joshua as an inactive partner, they acquired a secondhand press very much like the one that Yoel had brought back from Germany and saw plunging into the sea less than ten years before.

The *Pisga* sought to extol the virtue of the land, to support Jewish self-sufficiency, and to give information about the country. It gave Yoel a voice and a flag for like-minded people round which to rally. The journal, innocent as it was, made its entry into the communal affairs just when the Mikve Israel school came under its most severe test: because it was established on some 200 hectares of land requisitioned by the Sultan from the nearby village of Yazour, the Arabs of that village began attacking it. First they drove their flocks on to the fields. When the staff and pupils failed to drive away the intruders, the Arabs became bolder and set fire to the buildings and attacked their occupants with clubs.

As the new school came under attack, Yoel wrote passionately in the *Pisga*, calling for support, exhorting the staff and patrons of Mikve Israel not to give in. Within two months of the *Pisga*'s first publication, another journal appeared in Jerusalem. Called *The Clarion*, it was owned by an experienced printer and writer called Israel Bloch, and backed by the most conservative elements in the Ashkenazi community. Whatever the *Pisga* supported, *The Clarion* attacked; whatever *The Clarion* propounded, the *Pisga* contradicted. If Yoel, returning from a journey to Jezreel and Galilee with a party of friends, wrote that they found friendly Arab villages who grew splendid citrus trees whose fruits, the highly-priced etrog used for the ritual of the Succoth holiday, could be bought and even exported, *The Clarion* followed with a story of how dangerous such adventures were, and that none of the etrogs grown by the Arabs in the villages Yoel Zeff described could pass the tests for unblemished excellence required by rabbinical law.

These were petty skirmishes. But slowly old feuds dating back to Reb Binish's war against the resurrection of the ruined synagogue, resurfaced and the two journals were used with mounting acrimony as weapons by the opposing factions. Yoel was more fortunate than his father and his grandfather Solomon had been. His standing was strong among his contemporaries and elders. Even when he was set upon and felt like a bear bated by dogs, he always preached conciliation. In private he was often near despair at the spiral of hatred spun out of nothing and seeing nothing but waste and destruction.

"Out of needless hatred the Temple was destroyed, and by needless strife and hatred we may well destroy ourselves," he wrote in the *Pisga*. He was becoming so weary of his communal commitments that on certain days he couldn't bring himself to step out of his home. Here at least he had happiness and peace of mind. Leib was a strong healthy boy with a loud voice and boundless energy, his daughter Tiqva was the apple of his eye, and that year Hannah gave birth to another baby boy whom they named Chaim. His friends were many and loyal; it was they, led by Hannah, who forever kept pushing him into more involvements and confrontations he would have given anything to avoid.

It was at their pleading that he travelled to Europe to raise money for the foundering hospital Visitation of the Sick, which had been opened soon after the end of the war with Sir Moses Montefiore's blessings and money from Europe. The money that Yoel had raised was used to re-equip and enlarge the hospital. The day it opened its gates, hordes of sick people gathered, begging to be admitted for treatment. The porter, an old Sephar-adi Jew who was blind in one eye, and a little deaf, came out holding a batch of blue chips. The chief administrator of the hospital was proud of his blue chips system, each admitted one patient to the infirmary. When the crowd surged forward, the porter threw the chips in the air and retreated behind the doors. A scuffle ensued as the sick scrambled to get hold of the chips. Those who were stronger succeeded; those in real need of care, were left out. That night fist fights broke out outside the synagogue amidst accusations and counter-accusations. Within two months the hospital was closed after the staff left complaining of poor conditions and incompetent management.

A year passed and then another group of Jews from Hungary, inspired by the example of the Seven's Estate, formed a company, purchased land north of the city outside the walls, and built a settlement which they called Mea Shearim—a hundred measures. Yoel's interest in the running of the *Pisga* waned, or was submerged by the contingencies of his public life. Frume was now in full charge of the journal, assisted by a young enthusiastic deputy. Yoel wrote essays, some of which Frume published. He was nearing forty; thoughts bred in solitary meditation about the meaning of life led him to write poetry, which Hannah read without a muscle moving on her face, and put down.

Then, just as David Joshua always believed, the chance he had been waiting for came. Or so it seemed. At the beginning of 1875 the Ottoman Government published a tender for the sale of 4,000 dunams of land not far from Jericho, a tract of land watered by springs from the mountain slopes to the west, a land described as fertile.

All Yoel's weariness and scepticism vanished like mist under the sun. At once his energy returned tenfold. He worked tirelessly and within a week gathered around him a group of fifty men committed to placing an offer to the tender. A company was formed, with Yoel, David Joshua, and Asher Rimkin as the active representatives. It was decided to divide the land into a hundred plots and, should the venture succeed, place a value of a hundred Napoleons on each plot. No sooner was the agreement drawn than the three representatives rode to the place and Yoel was able to report on how good the land looked, a report which he followed with an enthusiastic description in the *Pisga*.

But, as *The Clarion* soon disclosed, there were other bidders for the land, no less than Mussa el Huseini, one of the richest and most influential Arabs in Jerusalem, and a rich Armenian from Egypt who wanted to buy the land for the Armenian church in Jerusalem.

After consultation with Krieger who knew el Huseini, a delegation of Ashkenazi and Sepharadi dignitaries went to see el Huseini, who was persuaded to withdraw his offer in return for a free gift of one-tenth of the land, and a thousand Napoleons. That being done, the representative committee prepared to make overtures to the Armenian Patriarch who was known to be sympathetic to the Jews. There was an Ashkenazi Jew called Reb Arie Neeman who had had dealings with the Armenians, and he arranged the interview. The Patriarch received the four Jews in his office. When he had heard what they had come for, he said, "And what will you do about the curse Joshua laid on the man who rebuilt Jericho?" And Yoel answered him and said, "Joshua's curse applied only to the first, for is it not written in the Book of Kings 'In his days did Hiel the Bethelite build Jericho'?" And the Patriarch was pleased at this, and after further discussion promised to write to the Armenian in Egypt to ask him to withdraw his offer.

Three months passed, and one morning the Pasha of Jerusalem, Ali Bey, sent a messenger to Yoel Zeff. The Government in Constantinople, the message ran, wanted to know who were the prospective buyers, whether they were Ottomans or aliens. Yoel called for a meeting of all the members of the company. He urged them to present a list of names of people who were Ottoman subjects, pointing out how the Government viewed with prejudice the request of aliens to buy, particularly if they were Jews. But the men argued against him saying that if the land was bought in the names of Ottoman subjects they would all be at the mercy of the Pasha without the protection of their respective European consulates. In the end a list was drawn with the names of the members and their European nationality. A month after the list was presented to Ali Bey, the messages from Constantinople returned: The Sultan Abdel Hamid had decided to buy the land himself rather than alienate it, and had put in his own bid.

"Think of it like this, the move was made, the people rallied round you. Maybe it was for the best that the land in Jericho slipped out of our grasp, maybe the Lord has something else, and better, in store for us which wouldn't have come about if we had got the land in Jericho, think about it this way," David Joshua pleaded.

For a few days Yoel was inconsolable. "Once more the Gate of Hope appeared only to be shut firm in my face," he said to Hannah.

Another attempt to buy land, this time in a place called Duran west of Ramlah in the coastal plain, failed. *The Clarion* rejoiced. A young firebrand of a rabbi out to build himself a reputation, wrote a lengthy article attacking Yoel Zeff. He denounced him for his arrogance in presuming that his forefather's pre-eminence entitled him to mislead the people into idle adventures. Yoel replied with a rational conciliatory article in which he tried to explain why the two previous attempts had failed and why even in their failure they blazed a path to more realistic hopes for the future. But his heart had gone dead; he had no faith in his own calm exhortations.

One night, two years later, after Yoel had ridden with his friends up and down the country again and again in search of suitable land, hoping against hope that luck would be with him, David Joshua came to his home together with a new friend, an Hungarian Jew by the name of Stamper. David Joshua's face was radiant. He was smiling happily. "Leave off your brooding and forget about all the quarrels here in Jerusalem," he said. "At last I truly believe our big chance has come."

Chapter 29

The river was muddy green and still. Reeds grew in great clumps along both banks. In places they joined across the entire breadth of the river, choking it. Swarms of insects moved over the hot pools among the reeds. A smell of rotting hung over the place; there was no breeze and no escape from the bad smell or from the flies that attacked both horses and riders. The path followed the course of the river but never came too close to it: it had its own stubborn independence. When it wound off and led to a rise, you could see the flatlands pan out to the dull horizon and the pale hills in the east. The river looked as though it had no life in it. Nor could the five riders who made their way along the cracked path see any living creature among the few stunted trees that dotted that land of unrelieved desolation.

Yoel looked at his companions for signs of dismay, or regret. He saw strain, nothing more. David Joshua, catching his eye, pulled his mouth down and wiped his brow, then smiled. The Greek fell behind. His white mule glistened in the sun.

Beyond the bend in the river and the rise a distance of about a mile from it, lay 3,500 dunams of land belonging to a Greek merchant and moneylender called Kassar, who lived in Jaffa. Kassar had taken possession of the land after its previous owner, an Arab sheik, defaulted on his debts. The transaction had not been properly recorded because the land Registration Office had challenged Kassar's rightful ownership claiming that the land was *Miri*, that is, government-owned land over which another owner may secure right of tenure only after cultivating it for three years. It had taken a lot of patient negotiation and bribing of officials before the transaction was completed.

The land bordered on that of the village Amlabes to the south, and land belonging to another Jaffa Arab called Tayan, a part of which had been for generations leased to the Amlabes villagers.

Away from the river towards the rise, the soil was dark loam, suitable for growing cereal, cotton, and potatoes. On the northernmost slope of the rise, conditions were right for planting fruit trees, even vines. Yoel had hastened to look at the land. On that cool limpid morning it lived up to his impatient expectations, so that he had been blind to the bleakness, to the taste of the air, and to the sallow look on the faces of the falahin he had passed on the way. All that mattered to him was that the land was theirs for the asking, unlike government-owned land which could not be bought by Jews.

He needn't have worried about the resolve of his friends and partners in the venture: David Gutman, Joshua Stamper, Eliezer Raab, and his son Judah, Leib Katz, all stalwart Jews from Hungary, Zora Barnet from London, and his own faithful friend David Joshua. Nevertheless, he described what he had seen in rosier terms than reality could support: "The land is good and fertile and yields handsome harvest. And it's suitable for planting orchards of fruit trees and vineyards," he said. And when Gutman fixed him with the sharp stare of his pale blue eyes, he added, "Only the bad air from the swamps by the river makes the place insalubrious, and the water is brackish." He had hung his head, and waited, until he heard Gutman clear his throat and say: "Swamps can be drained. Sweet water can be drilled for." That settled it, for it was Gutman who commanded most of the money needed for the purchase of the land.

They trusted Yoel. They were carried away by his confidence. Only after the land was theirs did the others venture to go and look at it. On that day they hired the services of a Greek doctor and scientist called George Mazrikos who lived in Jaffa and was reputed to be an expert on health conditions in the Coastal Plain.

Dr Mazrikos was not in an agreeable mood. On such a day he preferred to sit in the shade of the spreading jasmine, on his verandah, where the sea breeze fanned him cool. He was not familiar with the place to which he was being taken, but he knew of cases of malaria, trachoma, and hepatitis in people who lived in the vicinity of the Uja River. He knew of Kassar and disliked him, all the more for being a Greek and therefore a disgrace to a tradition Mazrikos revered. Nor did he have much sympathy for the Jews with whom he had had to work on several occasions. He found them excitable; he didn't like wasteful agitation over trivia. And they were fractious and argumentative even on matters about which they obviously knew nothing.

Dr Mazrikos hated being irritated unreasonably. But more than anything, he hated being the bearer of bad news. Even now, as they were drawing close to their destination, his heart was sinking at the thought of what he might have to tell these strange men who had sought his advice and paid for his services. He couldn't understand the intensity of their feelings but it communicated itself to him and made him brood. He disliked their silences even more than their earlier chatter in a language he couldn't understand.

David Joshua, riding a grey light-footed mare he had recently acquired, fell a few paces behind Yoel. Nothing could better convey to him the oppressive mood of the place than the sullen listlessness of his mare. He was troubled. In his mind's eye he saw the land they had traversed turn into impassable stretches of heavy mud under the winter rains. Their settlement—would it really come to that?—shot out of orbit, engulfed in darkness and surrounded by marauding bandits. Along the river, they had come across Arab peasants from nearby villages. They looked sick. Their eyes were dull. Many were blind. The children had spindly legs and swollen bellies. Would their own children be like that too? He wondered what was in the minds of the others: the deeper they progressed into the interior, the less they spoke. Now, not even a glance passed between them. He worried about what Gutman would say when he saw their estate.

The river bent north then east again. Within its sluggish loop a group of peasant women were busy gathering bits of dead wood. Dr Mazrikos's professional interest was aroused. He looked at them long and searchingly. Yoel reined in his horse. It was somewhere here that a less well-trodden path broke away from the river and led to Kassar's land. For a moment he rode around trying to remember. Then he saw it. Spurring on his horse, he led the way. Their land stretched over a shallow rise which then dipped towards the river. In the distance, though not far, they could see the village of Amlabes whose people, they had been assured, were peace-loving and neighbourly.

The land looked dry and bare: apart from wilted tufts of grass nothing grew on it. The fetid smell of the river hung in the air even here. "There it is," Yoel said, and pointed out the boundaries of the land they had bought.

Dr Mazrikos clambered down from his mule and began poking into the earth. It felt powdery and dead. A tree stood over a fold in the ground. So dusty and misshapen it was that he couldn't tell what species it belonged to, but it afforded some shade and branches to which the animals could be tied. The five friends dismounted and unsaddled their horses.

"Before we proceed any further, let us partake of some food and bless the Lord," Gutman said. Katz rubbed his hands together; they had not eaten a crumb all day, and momentous events always made him hungry.

"This day generations to come will judge us either as fools, dreamers of dreams, or as visionaries and pioneers," Gutman said. He held the bread in his hands. "There's nothing wrong with being fools in a good cause. But. . . ." He broke the bread, gave it round, then said the blessing. The sun was like a battered shield: the sky dull. There was no movement in the air. "By the look of things being pioneers in this place would be a good deal more painful than being fools," he said with a sigh.

Yoel only half-listened. His attention was fixed on Dr Mazrikos. The Greek had left his mule under the tree and walked some hundred paces up the rise. There he stood, looking now here, now there. He removed his cork helmet and held it above his head at arm's length as if to shield him from the sky.

"What's he up to?" Katz said. "I wonder if the sun has got to him." He touched his temple, "What could he tell us anyway?"

"We shouldn't have brought him here."

"Let him be, he knows what he's doing, what do we know of science?" David Joshua said and added, "I've seen Arab peasants do this sort of thing when looking at a piece of land."

"He's trying to find the direction of the wind," Gutman suggested.

Katz shrugged his shoulders. "Wind? There's no wind."

Dr Mazrikos came towards them. There was a sad expression on his face. He had put on his cork helmet with the scarf trailing at the back; he looked ominously official. The men rose to their feet. Dr Mazrikos stopped a few paces away as though what he was about to say could not bear proximity. Katz opened his mouth to speak but Yoel took hold of his arm and squeezed it.

"Gentlemen," Dr Mazrikos began, "I've taken samples of the soil and I've made careful observations here and on the way." He paused and began shaking his head.

"Katz was right, we shouldn't have brought him here," Yoel thought. But there was no stopping the Greek now.

"This is not a healthy place," Mazrikos said. "There is disease about, you can tell from the faces of the people. All this I can see. But I thought perhaps, perhaps there was still hope. Gentlemen, you may ask why I stood there looking at the sky. Tell me, you've been sitting here now for a good few minutes under this tree. Isn't there something you miss?"

They looked at one another, then at the Greek.

"Did you hear the sound of birds singing? I didn't, and that surprised me. I went up there and looked about and up at the sky. Not a bird in sight. This, gentlemen, is the surest sign that a place is unhealthy, for no bird would live in a place where the water is unclean and where there's disease." With that, Dr Mazrikos began to walk towards his mule. Halfway he stopped and turned. He really disliked disappointing people just as he instinctively recoiled from any form of violence. But he had a duty which he couldn't avoid. For a moment he considered returning the fee he had charged. He said, "If I were you I would give up the idea of settling on this land. It is not a place fit for human habitation, for people like you."

For a long moment the men stood looking at one another in silence. Never before had they felt so isolated from the rest of the world and so close to one another. Their joint commitment suddenly bound them together with a bond stronger than blood. Yoel looked down at the dark powdery earth. Memories stirred in him: the failures at Jericho and Duran. He remembered his father's unfulfilled ambitions. He was standing on land they had bought but felt no intimacy with it. Had it all been an illusion? In his mind's eye he saw their defeated return to Jerusalem, and tasted the great emptiness that would settle on him after the recriminations and reassertion that not only were Jews unfit for farming, they weren't even capable of acquiring land suitable for farming! He thought of Sarona, the thriving German Templars' village not far from the spot they were standing on. Of course, the Germans were experienced farmers, but had God given this too unwelcoming land to them and their seed? A great weariness of spirit came over him; he felt like a withered tree rooted in a desolation starker, more irredeemable than the land on which he was standing.

Then he heard Gutman's voice cut the silence like a knife: "And still, in spite of everything, it's a great day. May God bless this land and strengthen our hands and our hearts." He spoke for them all, and Yoel felt at once relieved and ashamed for having doubted his friends. Gutman reached out to Yoel and hugged him; they were all hugging each other with tears in their eyes.

Dr Mazrikos, witnessing this display of emotion, thought the Jews were crying over the money they had lost. He began to console them saying, "What is money when human health is at stake, think only of your wives and children, the misery you'd be saving them from." But they paid no attention to him until, dismayed and baffled, he mounted his mule and started back for Jaffa.

After the Greek had gone the intimacy of possession transformed the land for them. They began to discuss where the houses should be built, when to make the move, how things would be. Joshua Stamper, who had been the most sceptical among them, now became the most enthusiastic. He regaled them with stories he had heard about settlers in far-flung American wildernesses inhabited by savages and wild animals, about the hardships of nature and battles with Indians. "And did these settlers in the vastness of America walk upon land promised to them by the Almighty who had made a covenant with their forefathers to the end of time?" he concluded, "did names of places in their new land recall their past as the names of places here have survived to remind us who we are and where we came from? And could we do less than they?" Sitting beneath the stunted tree in the still and empty landscape, they were strangely stirred by Stamper's words.

At last, tired from the excitement of the day, they fell asleep. When they woke up the sun was dipping towards the sea. A red glow suffused the fields. "We'd better make haste and return to Jaffa before it's dark," David Joshua said. Yoel said he would stay behind and bivouac for the night under the tree. No amount of persuasion would make him change his mind, nor would he agree to David Joshua staying with him. He watched his friends ride away until they faded into the hazy light and the sound of their horses' hooves was no longer heard.

As darkness fell the lights of Amlabes flickered on cluster by cluster. Soon the dark became so immense he couldn't tell where sky ended and earth began; the lights of Amlabes looked as distant as the stars. He could hear the bullfrogs croaking in the river, and a light breeze carried the smell of decay. An owl hooted. So there were some birds here after all. He lit a fire and boiled water for coffee. He made coffee the Arab way, thick and bitter. This was his night of vigil; he wanted the secretive spirit of the land to enter him. He was not afraid: "If a passing bandit should fall on me, and slay me," he thought, "so be it. Better now, when I'm alone." He thought of Hannah, of the night they made love in their new home outside the walls, and listened nervously to the noises of the night. What would she say now, about this place, stuck in the middle of nowhere, with no friends nearby? In winter the river often flooded its banks. They would be cut off from the rest of the world. What help could they hope for if, God forbid, one of them should fall sick? And will the others hold fast, not scatter with the first setback?

He remembered someone once saying to him: "Fear of the moment sharpens your mind. Fear of the future kills your sense of purpose. Fear of the inevitable is cowardice." Yet who didn't fear death, the most inevitable thing of all?

The cock crows from the village woke him. He got up, washed his face, then said his morning prayers. A herd of goats and sheep issued from Amlabes with the tinkling of bells. He heard the shouts of the shepherd boys above the bleating of the flocks. After eating of the bread and cheese left over from the day before, he saddled his horse and set out on his way back to Jaffa. But instead of following the path they came on he took another route which brought him to the fields of Amlabes. A few peasants and their womenfolk were already working, bent over rows of vegetables which he couldn't identify. As he rode past, they stood up and greeted him, "Marchaba, salam aliecum". "Salem aleichum" he replied. There were larks in the sky, their song rose and fell and filled the air. "When we've tilled our fields and sowed, these birds will sing for us too," he thought, and with that the last vestige of gloom from the night vanished. He was happy, and confident. Spurring his horse, he cantered on past the village, to Jaffa.

They named the place Petach Tiqva—Gate of Hope, as it is written in Hosea: "And I will give her her vineyards from thence and the vale of trouble for a gate of hope." And as they stood on the spot where the well would be sunk Gutman said, "May The Blessed Name grant that this vale will be our gate of hope for the redemption of the land and the resurrection of our people in body and spirit."

The *mada'fa*, where the Mukhtar of Amlabes received honoured guests, was a small room annexed to his home. The walls had been whitewashed too long ago. Here and there the plaster had fallen off to expose the mud and straw bricks. The reed mats on the uneven floor were frayed and dirty. The old Mukhtar didn't see all that for he was blind—the river had done that to him, he said, many years ago. His wall-eyes stared in the direction of Yoel and David Joshua, who had come to pay their respects on behalf of the Jews, soon to be Amlabes' neighbours. His grandson served bitter coffee and stuffed the old man's water-pipe. He was a young man, perhaps in his early twenties and already there was a look of old age resignation in his eyes.

"Once Amlabes was a great village, yes, don't think we've always been as we are now," the Mukhtar said, and sighed, and made a gesture with his hand, "Allah's will. Everything comes from Him. Listen, I'll tell you."

The Hija clan of Amlabes once owned some hundred thousand dunams of land which went beyond the valley to the south bordering on the Jaffa highway, to the west up to the foot of the Musrara hills, and to the loop of the river near its source, to the north. The springs which gathered into the source of the river watered the valley and made it fertile. But the blessing turned into a curse when the people neglected to drain the land. Marshes formed. Reeds grew in profusion, choking the river. Animals that wandered into the treacherous ground drowned and their carcases rotted in the fetid water. The air become poisonous, and death stalked both sides of the river. The people of Amlabes became listless and succumbed to illness. Shepherds who came from distant villages to water and graze their flocks by the river, drank the water and their bellies swelled. The sickness weakened Amlabes and depleted its population until the village could no longer stand up against the strong villages like Magdal and Yahudiya who rode roughshod over Amlabes stealing its crops and livestock. Amlabes was held accursed by the neighbouring villages.

A great warrior came down from the hills of Samaria. Hammad Nablusi was his name. He had left his native Nablus because of a blood feud and went west with his large family, retainers, slaves, and herds of sheep and cattle. He came to the Uja River and saw how fertile the valley was, and coveted it. He waged war on the Hija clan and prevailed against them. Then he pitched his tents on the land of the vanquished Hija, and on those who survived his sword he levied heavy taxes. For a while he prospered and grew rich. But soon the curse of the river fell on him too. Year after year members of his family and his slaves fell sick and died until there were more graves by the riverside than tents in the valley. The rumour reached Nablus that Hammad's power had waned so much that the falahin in the region no longer feared him and stopped paying his taxes. A host of his enemies came riding from the hills and butchered Hammad and his family to a man. They dipped a white kerchief in Hammad's blood, fixed it to the point of a spear, and rode back whence they came.

Years later, when Ibrahim Pasha, son of Mehemet Pasha came and conquered Palestine, many came up from Egypt with him to seek land and riches. Among them was one Hammad el Masri, like the other Hammad, a renowned warrior. He had with him forty slaves and his family. He too liked the Uja valley, and finding the village of Amlabes almost deserted, paid compensation to the few falahin there, and settled in the village. But as happened with his predecessor so it happened with him, and over the years many of his slaves and people died of fever. Hammad el Masri then left Amlabes and settled in another village not far off with what was left of his family. Year by year he saw his land shrink as trespassers took bits of it over, until he was left with less than 14,000 dunams. When Hammad el Masri saw that Amlabes was doomed and he was sinking into debts, he turned to a Jaffa merchant called Tayan, to ask for his help and a loan. Tayan cheated him and extracted from him a bill of sale for half the lands of Amlabes. When el Masri realized this, he began legal proceedings against Tayan, to meet the cost of which, he sold 2,000 dunams of the best land to another Jaffa merchant, Salim Kassar. El Masri lost the case and died soon afterwards. What was left of his land was taken over by those who worked on it.

"This is the land you have bought from Kassar," the old Mukhtar concluded. "May you have more happiness from it than those who owned it before you."

"This day, the first of the month of Elul, 1878, we pitched our tents in Petach Tiqva, praise be to God," Yoel wrote in his diary. "With the first light of dawn we set out from Jaffa where we had been living in anticipation of the move for the past week. Everything was ready and David Joshua and I loaded the two camels and five mules with all our equipment and material before the others had even got dressed.

"It has been a day of sinew-cracking labour but we have prepared the first site of our dwellings and the contractors from Jaffa have set up the rig nearby for boring the well. God willing, tomorrow they'll start drilling and by evening we may have fresh water!

"My arms and back are aching from the work, for I must have worked as hard and as long as any of the seven falahin whom we hired to help us. How poor Reb Gutman must feel, I daren't imagine. He is older than any of us yet he worked as hard as any, and wouldn't let up even when we implored him to rest.

"I'm sitting in the tent I've pitched with my own hands. The oil lamp is throwing dancing shadows on the ground and on the canvas. In the nearby tent the others are exchanging impressions and talking about tomorrow. I can hear the bullfrogs from the river and the intermittent howling of the jackals. Music. Never a sweeter sound. We shall take turns in standing watch tonight. Tomorrow with dawn it's back to work. To think that a settlement, a thriving permanent habitation where Jews live, are born, and die, will grow out of the present disorder of this place, fills me with inexpressible joy so that I grow impatient for the morning."

The men who on that morning rode out to the site of Petach Tiqva, were David Gutman, Joshua Stamper, Leib Michael Katz, Yoel Zeff, David Joshua Karlin and Zora Barnet from London. They were joined by two newcomers, Nathan Gringrot from Jerusalem, and a clean-shaven fellow, recently arrived from Hungary, who professed to considerable experience in farming in his native land. David Ragner was his name. The womenfolk were left in Jerusalem, to be called only when the houses were put up and the place was ready for proper habitation.

Except Hannah. Leaving Tiqva Chaim and their youngest son Malachi in Jerusalem, she came with Leib to Jaffa where she took a small room with a Jewish family, and waited for Yoel to allow her to join him. "We didn't marry to be separated," she told him. "Wherever you go there I'll go with you, no matter what, even in the face of mortal danger."

The well-borers came later the next morning, four of them, including the overseer. He announced, to the settlers' disappointment, that after second thoughts he didn't hold much hope for finding an aquafer at the depth of up to 18 metres on that site, even though the site was as good as any on the Jews' land.

They started to drill with little enthusiasm. Ragner couldn't bear standing by waiting for the result upon which their entire enterprise depended, so he saddled one of the mules and rode out to survey the fields. In his mind's eye he already saw straight furrows and crests of corn.

In the latter part of the afternoon the overseer sauntered over to the tent where Yoel and the others were taking a rest. "Hawaja Zeff, we've reached 18 metres and there's no sign of water," he said.

"Drill deeper," Yoel commanded. The faces of his friends reflected the panic that was rising in him as he tried to keep calm. The overseer smiled insolently. "How deep?"

"Twenty-five, up to thirty. . . ."

"It'd be a miracle if we find water even at that depth, the earth the drill has been bringing up doesn't show there's water," the man said.

"Drill all the same. Miracles have been known to happen," Yoel insisted. But the overseer shook his head. "We said 18 metres. Deeper will cost more money."

"Tell him to go ahead and drill to thirty and we'll pay," Gutman said grimly. The overseer went away saying they would return the next day and drill to thirty metres.

"Let's pray they find water tomorrow, or else . . ." said Gutman and clasped his hands together.

Early the next morning the overseer returned with a fresh team. They started work right away. Yoel and his friends took themselves some distance away from the site of the drilling. They tried to occupy themselves with various chores but the rhythmic thudding of the machine held their attention. Shortly before noon the noise suddenly stopped. The men stood up. Then the shout came from the overseer, "Water!" At twenty-eight metres they had struck the aquafer. The water was cold and sweet-tasting. They brought up jugful after jugful, drank and spilled it on one another laughing like children while the four Arab workmen and the overseer looked on, sharing the Jews' happiness and wondering at their luck.

After the workers had left with their gear, Yoel said "Now we have water. Let's waste not a day but bring the news to the people in Jerusalem that they may join us here and start building the houses, till the fields and sow for the first rains."

David Joshua jumped to his feet. "I'll ride right away. This day my fast mare will be put to the test."

"Go and God be with you but be gentle with yourself and your horse, we've waited long and another few hours wouldn't make that much difference," Gutman said.

"Tonight," said Yoel, "I shall sleep with my wife and son in Jaffa. Tomorrow I shall bring them here and together we shall start to build our home."

The horizontal wheel on top of the well was the best and most modern that was to be had. When that was fixed, they built a duct which ran from the lip of the well, to a long trough. This wheel was turned by two mules. But for household uses, there was a hand pump. It was a beautiful well, the falahin said, and the water was fresh and plentiful. "This is our source of life, and round this point we shall build the village," Gutman said, and added, nodding in the direction of the falahin who had come to watch, "Let whoever is thirsty come and drink, there'll be no restrictions."

The sacks of wheat and barley for sowing which Ragner bought in nearby Kalkiliya were stored in the square stone shed built not far from the well. It was the largest building in the settlement, and was used also for gatherings and prayers. On Gutman's instruction a motto was painted on a strip of cloth and hung on the wall. It read: "Walk in modesty; talk little, and do much."

Not far from the store-house, stood the stable where the mules, the horses, and the three pairs of oxen for ploughing were kept. From these two buildings and the well, the houses stretched out in either direction to form a line, a street, alongside which trees brought from the farming school of Mikve Israel, were planted. The falahin of Amlabes helped in the building of the houses, except for that of Zeligman's the American. He wanted his first real home, as he put it, to be more than a mere frame of baked mud bricks and wattle. He contracted a builder from Jaffa, bought stones, and built the house to last for ever.

Twenty homes lined the street of Petach Tiqva. Twenty homes of those who had taken part in the venture and now arrived from Jerusalem to make good their commitment. They were joined by a few newcomers. The Arabs who occasionally came to avail themselves of the settlers' invitation and to water their animals at the well, could not hide their admiration, and Petach Tiqva's reputation spread by word of mouth and was magnified by distance: far-lying villages spoke with awe of those new Jews who were not "Children of death" but farmers, able to work as hard as any Arab falah.

David Ragner felt proud at the responsibility that was vested in him. He wanted to succeed beyond anything that was expected of him. His passion for land and his first steps in farming in his native Hungary had ended leaving him landless and broke. Now Petach Tiqva threw at him the most formidable challenge he had ever confronted, and at the same time Providence at last seemed to smile at him as if it were ready to make up for past hardships, and offer personal redemption to boot. Ragner, unlike the others in the village, was not a homestead owner but a hired man. He hoped that success on a spectacular scale would earn him what money, which he didn't have, could have got him: a place of his own and a standing in his new society.

But when he faced Gutman and demanded a proper European plough, the old man's face became severe. He was loth to part with communal funds over which he was entrusted. "We have the oxen and we have the ploughs, haven't we already spent much more than we anticipated?" he asked.

"The Arab plough is primitive. It doesn't turn a deep furrow but merely scratches the earth," Ragner began to explain. "If you don't turn the soil it won't yield as much as when ploughed deeply. I could buy a plough cheaply from the Germans in Sarona."

Notwithstanding Yoel's support of Ragner on this matter, Gutman wouldn't budge. So Ragner designed and built his own plough, and it was an impressive machine, with four ploughshares arranged in a row. But when they hitched the oxen to it, they were not strong enough to pull it. Gutman pondered over the problem. The new contraption fired his imagination. Besides, the larger Damascene oxen Ragner now recommended as a solution, sounded like a shrewd investment.

All the men in Petach Tiqva turned out to see Ragner's invention at work. The two new oxen towered over their smaller local cousins. They were thick and tawny and docile. Even so Ragner's plough heaved and strained but hardly moved. Until Yoel and Leib Katz, a strong large man, pushed with all their strength against the shaft behind the oxen; only then was Ragner able to stir a straight deep furrow at a reasonable pace.

The first rain came early and was heavy. The fields looked dark and steamy under the sun. Ragner prepared to sow. But the falahin from the nearby villages who had been following how the Jews were progressing warned against it. When the first rain came early as this, they said, it was a sure sign that later rains would be late in coming. This rain is like a miscarriage in the sky, they said. Better wait for the real rains to come before sowing or all your labour would be lost. Ragner wouldn't listen. "We farm by modern European methods, not according to Arab superstition," he said, and went ahead with the sowing. Gutman stood at the store-house door, and counted the sacks of seeds as they went out. "They that sow in tears shall reap with joy, it is written. Let it be so with us, for we've had too much tears," he said under his breath.

"We sow in joy and we shall reap with greater joy still, have no fear," Yoel tried to reassure him.

The Zeffs' home was among the last to be built and also among the smallest. It stood at the outward reach of the colony like a sentinel. From the window Yoel could see the green swell of the young wheat they had sown, and next to it fields of barley and maize. Whenever he looked at it, which was often, he remembered with pleasure the back-breaking effort it had taken him and David Ragner, and the two Raabs, father and son, to plough and how all the men came out to sow together with a few hired hands from Amlabes.

Beyond the deep green of these fields lay stretches of dusty dun-coloured earth, around Amlabes and beyond, further than the eye could see. The Arabs were right. After that first rain no more came and the sky remained hard and opaque. If it didn't rain soon all they had sown would wilt and die. The Arabs were already talking of drought and holding special prayers for rain. The agronomist from Mikve Israel who had come to look how the new settlers were managing, had shaken his head and told them they had been too hasty in sowing: they should have listened to the falahin. It was the end of Kislev, the thick of winter. Cold winds began to blow from the sea but not a sign of coming rain showed in the sky. Ragner held his head high, dismissing all scepticism. But in private, with Yoel and his family with whom he spent a good deal of his spare time, he often gave in to doubt and despair. "It's my luck. All my life I've been followed by bad luck in everything I do," he lamented.

Then one night the sky became so dark not a star was seen. Lightning hissed through the blackness, once, twice, again and again. Then the thunder rolled in from the sea and unleashed the fury of the storm. The horses screamed and kicked against the stable walls. Yoel rushed out and was drenched before he got more than a few steps beyond the house.

It rained non-stop for days on end. Blessed rains, they called it. Until roofs began to leak and some of the houses built with mud bricks insufficiently baked, collapsed. The people gathered in the store-house, taking with them blankets and whatever food they could grab hold of in a hurry. Huddled together among the sacks of corn and potatoes, they took comfort from one another. Hannah had the presence of mind to bring the samovar and tea which she had handed to Leib before they all ran through the whipped-up mud to the store-house.

Lamps were lit; a small stove gave pleasant warmth. The children were gathered round it to dry. Hannah started preparing piping hot tea for everyone. The women took stock of the food that was there and set about distributing bread and fig jam to go with the tea. The rain grew so fierce they could see the water flashing beneath the door. Presently Yoel and David Joshua came in soaking wet. They had seen to the animals. All was well, unless the stable collapsed, which didn't seem likely. When Joshua Stamper heard that, he clapped his hands and began to sing. Soon everybody joined in. It was a familiar song in Yiddish:

> Leave off crying and joyously sing,
> Go to the land of your fathers, there
> to live as a King.

After they had sung and laughed and drunk the tea, someone remarked that Zeligman and his family were not present. Perhaps he should be fetched? "Why worry? In that fine stone house of his no harm could come to him," said Zora Barnet whose own house had suffered extensive damage, and who was wrapped in a blanket and shivering.

Zeligman's house was not far from the store-house. Leib Zeff peeped through the window. "I can't see any light there," he said.

"Probably they've all gone to bed," Gutman said, and winced as another flash of lightning lit up the sky.

Soon afterwards Zeligman came in with his wife and two young daughters. He was a large man with a jolly craggy face. Standing at the doorway in his broad hat, with his wife and children at his side, he looked like a monument of human endurance. "The roof began to leak," he said in his slow Yiddish, "I said to Minnie, it's a good time to go join the others." Then he produced from beneath his soaking cape a little bottle and held it high, grinning. "Nothing better to warm body and soul on such a night than a bit of this," he said.

Towards morning they were wakened by a noise from outside that began like a groan and grew louder to reach a climax in a mighty crash. The rain had not let up. But shapes were emerging from the nacreous light, surrounded by churning stretches of water. The shape that loomed out with violent fixity was that of Zeligman's stone house. All that remained of it was a heap of mud-washed rubble between two broken walls.

Neither Zeligman nor his wife said a word. But after a moment of silence he stepped out into the rain. Eliezer Raab tried to stop him but Yoel put his hand on his arm.

"Let him be," he said. "No harm will come to him."

"In this rain? He'll catch his death. What can he do? What can anybody do now?"

They watched Zeligman walk over to his ruined home and disappear behind the jutting broken walls. "Zeligman, Reb Zeligman, come back," Raab shouted. There was no answer.

"He'll come back soon enough," said Yoel. Hannah put her arm round Minnie Zeligman to steer her away from the door. But Minnie only smiled tightly and patted Hannah's hand. No sooner had they settled down again when gun shots were heard. The men rushed to the windows to look out. Outlined against the pale light, stood Zeligman, on top of the heap. He had found his precious repeating rifle which he had brought from America, and now discharged shot after shot into the sky.

When at last the rain stopped, the men hitched the mules to the two carts they had, and went to Jaffa to buy building material and contract builders. For weeks the only work that was done in the village was on the houses. This time Zeligman personally supervised the rebuilding of his home for he had been cheated by the first builder who, in Zeligman's absence, had substituted mud for cement. Before the next spell of rain came, all the houses that had been damaged were repaired.

It was a hard winter: rain by day and frost by night. The River Uja burst its banks. All around it were marshes and great pools of mud. If it hadn't been for Tiqva Zeff the dreadful hazards of being cut off may have not impressed themselves on the settlers and daunted their spirits. The cold and the dampness proved too much for Tiqva. She fell ill. Tiqva was by no means frail. In fact, she was more robust than anyone in the family except Leib. She was also plain, uninspiring, and undemonstrative. But Tiqva had an uncanny way of magnifying ordinary setbacks into portents of calamity. She didn't merely become ill, she was deliriously feverish, visibly waning, and it seemed that all the harshness and fury of the winter allied with her malady to make it as awful as was possible.

"If you don't get the doctor Tiqva will die," Hannah said. A dark endless ride to Jaffa unwound itself in Yoel's mind, scene following scene, beyond the limits of hope and of fatigue. He didn't believe Tiqva would live anyway but Hannah's implacable will got him to his feet. He made ready to go out to saddle the horse when Leib said, "I'll go, father. No one could get to Jaffa faster than me. I'll bring the doctor."

Two hours later Leib returned, drenched to the skin, and on foot. He had tried to ford the river. The water was deep and fast. The horse refused to go in. Leib, a masterful rider, might have known better if the urgency of the occasion hadn't shut everything but the mission from his mind. He forced the horse. Horse and rider leapt into the rushing river. The horse lost his footing and fell. Leib felt the horse swept away from under him and heard it scream. If it hadn't been for a couple of Arabs who happened to pass by and threw him a branch of a tree to seize on to, Leib would have drowned. He got out to see his mount some distance downstream on the other side of the river, kicking its last out of the murky water.

Yoel buried his head in his hands and wept.

Some said it was the Arab healer from Amlabes who saved Tiqva's life with his herbs and amulets. He came the next day when the word got round that Yoel Zeff's daughter was dying, and Hannah, keeping a watchful eye on him, allowed him near the sick girl. By the time Leib made another, this time successful, attempt to reach Jaffa the following day, and brought the doctor back the day after, Tiqva's fever had abated. But her illness left her nearly deaf, and Yoel, stroking her head as she sat weepy and dejected against his knee, prayed saying, "Blessed Lord, if it is your will that there should be a price for what you granted us, make me alone pay it, and comfort my poor girl with the heavenly sound of your goodness."

The wheat, barley and maize grew thick in the fields. No one could have dreamed of such a rich harvest, not even David Ragner as he stood there squinting against the spring sun. All this, contained by a hazy horizon, had been granted him in compensation for all his past failures, a reward for his faith and patience. The Arab rais who had brought falahin to help with the work, whistled through his teeth and said, "You Jews have done even better than the Almains of Sarona." Ragner didn't like the tone of the Arab. It sounded not congratulatory but grudging, as though the Arab believed it had all been achieved by trickery. "They think they can teach us everything," he thought, "but they are nothing but simple superstitious peasants, no wonder they are poor and downtrodden. Better for us to keep away from them."

Ragner's sentiment found no echo with the rest in Petach Tiqva as everybody prepared for the Passover, the first in the freedom of their own land. They were proud, they felt generous; all the hardship of the winter was forgotten as each family scrubbed their home clean and collected together all their leavened food to be put in communal storage until the Passover was over. Minnie Zeligman, lantern-jawed and pigeon-chested, dragged out into the yard the huge flat bowl in which she prepared the Matzo dough and took a moment's rest in the gentle sun. She shaded her flinty eyes and bellowed a greeting at Tiqva who had just come to the well to draw water. The swaying fields in the distance filled her with happiness, she looked forward to the harvest. Bit by bit, sack by sack, the village's leavened stuff—grain, whey, all food that had been preserved by smoking and salting—was taken out to a collecting point by the well, where it was to be sold symbolically to the Arabs that afternoon so that the settlement might be purged of all impurities for the Passover.

At midday the headman who deputised for the Mukhtar of Amlabes was seen approaching the village with a few of the village's elders. They were greeted with refreshment after which Yoel explained the purpose of the transaction. The headman looked at the village's bounty gathered at his feet. He smiled politely and wished the Jews happiness on their holiday. But his eyes were cold and uncomprehending. On the way to Petach Tiqva they had walked through the fields and had seen the crops. Fortune had not smiled on the fields of Amlabes that year; their granaries were almost empty. Now the Jews were emptying theirs, making him count the sacks to be his and his fellow villagers for a week. Their strange exuberance grated on his and his companions' nerves; it was like defying Providence, wantonly and arrogantly. But they were neighbours. And for all his distaste, the headman still had reverence for ritual even such as he couldn't understand.

The Seder table was set in the newly-painted and purified store-house. It was covered in clean white sheets and laid with the best plate and cutlery that Petach Tiqva had. Candelabras glowed among dishes full of food that the women had been preparing for days before. Gutman, being the oldest as well as the wealthiest of the settlers, presided at the head of the table. His face expressed the gravity and splendour of a patriarch as he broke the matzo and blessed. He began reading the Hagada. So magical was the moment that when the door was opened for Elija, as was the tradition, even the adults could believe that any moment he would come in to partake of the meal.

Then Gutman raised a glass of red wine and said: "This night we are commanded to remember the wonders and miracles which our God worked for our forefathers when He brought them out of slavery in Egypt into freedom in this land which He promised to Abraham and his seed. But we must doubly give blessing to Him which hath sustained us to this day, since we have lived to establish the first farming community in our land and thereby to blaze a path for those who will follow in our footsteps. We are like the harbingers of dawn, and the Lord lights our path. This is where the sun shall rise, and the spirit of Israel shall be revived, and the House of Jacob will rejoice and walk in the ways of the Lord as it was once, in purity and holiness."

When he had finished talking, everybody came and pressed his hands and blessed him saying, as was the custom, "Next year in Jerusalem."

Malachi Zeff, being the youngest child, asked the Four Questions in a clear loud voice, to which Yoel and Gutman took turns answering. Yoel knew he was expected to say a few things after the songs were sung. The wine made his head light. He felt happy and relaxed as he listened to Reb

Stamper speaking ecstatically about his experience in Hungary and all the hopes and hardships he had gone through, all of which were vindicated by this night. Then he felt Hannah's elbow in his ribs, and saw all eyes fixed on him. Stamper was standing arms outstretched, calling him the man who like Moses had led the Jews from Jerusalem to this place of self-redemption. Yoel covered his face with his hands and laughed. Then, as the people began to clap their hands and call his name he rose to his feet. A small gust of wind made the open door creak on its hinges. Yoel pointed at the door. "Look," he began, "all the time we've been celebrating the Seder tonight the door has been open. Has anyone here been worried that a thief, a robber, would come in and do us harm? Listen to the night. It does not make threatening noises; its sounds are the sounds we know and love. Because here in our homes we dwell in peace. On this festival of freedom and redemption, we throw our door open and welcome any passerby who might come. This is freedom from fear, freedom to be generous to the stranger who might pass by as it was in the days of our judges and kings.

"But if Passover is the festival of our redemption from slavery, here we're also redeemed from the bondage of fear, of humilation and of disease caused by overcrowded conditions, so that we may work for our living and observe the laws of God.

"Passover is also the festival of spring. What flower, what sign of spring did you see in Jerusalem? Look now at the fields we have ploughed and sown, did you ever imagine spring could look so beautiful?"

He took a pause. Was he being carried away? Hannah's face could tell him nothing. The wine made everything seem so perfectly easy. Gutman was looking at him, smiling, and Stamper, leaning with both elbows on the table, nodded vigorously.

"I could say a lot of things to you, and no doubt in time they will be said whether by me or someone else," Yoel went on. "But we've all worked hard. Let us sing and thank God for all He has given us. Let me just say this, when we've reaped our fields, let us take of the harvest, all that's beyond what we need, to Jerusalem that our brothers may see what we've done and eat of the fruit of our labour. We didn't open this gate of hope just for handful of families but for all our people to come through."

Tayan never forgave the Jews for having preferred Salim Kassar's lands to his, and when he heard of their success, he hated them with all his heart and devised ways of frustrating their endeavour. His land lay mostly along the river but part of it ran into and overlapped the land formerly owned by Kassar, which now made up a part of Petach Tiqva's fields. Tayan leased his land not to the villagers of Amlabes but to outsiders further north. The men he hired to work for him were hard men, violent and quick to pick a quarrel.

David Ragner had shallow-tilled that part of the land which was contested by Tayan's tenants, and sown it with grass for hay-making. The grass was almost ready to be cut when Judah Raab came running into the village one morning holding a bloodied handkerchief to his head. He had taken a walk to that part of the land with a girl from the village he was fond of to show her the storks which had recently arrived in great flocks and seemed to favour that particular field. They had not been there for more than a few minutes when ten Arab shepherds of Tayan arrived and drove their herd of sheep and goats on to the field. Young Raab had the presence of mind to send the girl home at once and he himself began to remonstrate with the shepherds. They threw rocks at him and chased him away saying they would kill any Jew who came to challenge them. "They will not do such things to us, and laugh at us back at their homes!" Leib said. He was white with fury. He ran into the house to fetch his pistol but Yoel called him back.

"Leib, Leib," he called. "Leave your gun where it is. Let there be no bloodshed. We'll go to meet them and we shall not yield. But let no blood be spilt."

That day the Arabs learnt something about the Jews they didn't know before, and Leib earned a reputation for being a fearless fighter. Many were hurt in the fight. Yoel headed the fifteen-strong force and received a gash on his head and a heavy blow from a club on his shoulder. But the Arabs were forced to retreat and the Jews drove their herd into Petach Tiqva and penned it by the well there to be held until the Arabs paid for the damage they had done to the field.

Michael Leib Katz had been unaware of all that had happened in the village. Early that morning he had set out to Kalkiliya to buy more grain and some fresh vegetables and eggs for the village. He hadn't noticed a gang of Arabs who had been following his progress from a distance. Slowly the Arabs closed in on him, and as he reached the shallow dip between two rises, they attacked him. Katz was a big strong man and feared no one. He lay aside the reins, grabbed hold of a club he had beside him and standing up on the cart fought like a lion until the cart was overturned on him. One of the mules escaped and came running into Petach Tiqva. A party went out in search of Katz and found him lying unconscious beside the smashed cart. He would have surely died had he not been found in time.

The village closed in on itself. Zeligman got out his repeating rifle and loaded it. He knew a thing or two about siege warfare, he announced. Leib said, "Let's mount up and go teach them a lesson they'll never forget." But Yoel prevailed. There was a time for teaching a lesson, he said, but this was not it. Now a complaint had to be made to the authorities before the matter got out of hand.

Leib Katz was driven to Jaffa for proper medical attention at the small hospital. Gutman, being an Austrian subject, made a complaint to the Austrian Consul in Jaffa who happened to be his friend and had much influence with the authorities. As a result, a platoon of gendarmes was sent to arrest Katz' attackers. They were brought to Jaffa's jail in chains and confessed to being commanded by Tayan to attack the Jews. Tayan, who had never before been bettered in a court case, was publicly humiliated and made to kiss Gutman's hand and pay compensation for the damage his men had done. After that incident the Arabs of the nearby villages greeted the Jews of Petach Tiqva with great reverence for they said, "If they could humble a Leviathan like Hawaja Tayan, all strength to them, better for us to be their allies and friends." But Yoel said to Gutman, "We've won this little battle and we shall have a little respite. But we'll never have peace until Tayan is no longer our neighbour."

Pentecost that year fell soon after harvest time. The fields yielded far above Ragner's most optimistic estimate. The weather was balmy for the heat of summer had not yet begun. Everybody who could work turned up for the reaping. The men in short sleeves and bare arms, advanced in a line across the field cutting with sickles as the falahin did. The women behind them gathered the corn and tied it into sheaves, ready to be taken to the threshing floor nearby. The warmth of the sun on the ripe golden corn gave the women's arms and cheeks a healthy glow. Yoel was working beside Leib and Chaim, father competing against sons, each urging one another on. Even Gutman came to cut a few swathes before retiring to sit a way off and watch the rest at work. Coming up behind with the women, was Toive, Yehuda Raab's sweetheart, black-eyed and full-bodied, how her large breasts swayed as she worked, making the young men cast glances in her direction, or stop to go back on whatever pretext they could think of. And at night there was talking and laughing by the threshing floor. Happy days, over-flowing with golden hours.

At Shavuoth when in biblical times the best of the fruit of the land was offered in the Temple, the men loaded a portion of the harvest on two camels and set out for Jerusalem. Ever since Yoel and his friends settled on the land they called Gate of Hope, the Jews in Jerusalem—and indeed elsewhere in the country—had been following anxiously the progress of the settlement. Now they were to see with their own eyes, and taste! Leib, on a new horse Zeligman had bought, rode at the head of the small convoy, his pistol tucked into his belt. Behind him, pulling the lead camel, was Yoel, proud of the day, proud of his son.

The Jews of Jerusalem were overwhelmed. "To see our falahin brothers healthy and sun-tanned, bringing to us the wealth of the land, the fruit of hard labour, patience and hope, was enough to infuse with faith even the greatest sceptic and to chase away all shred of doubt about the abilities of Jews to work on the land," *The Pisgah* wrote, and went on to say: "Such scenes as the caravan coming first into Mea Shearim then into The Seven's Estate before ending its journey in the Jewish Quarter, giving grain and fruit wherever it stopped, was reminiscent of Jacob returning to his father Isaac's tents with the wealth he had made during his sojourn with Laban."

But the jubilations and questions that followed them wherever the men went proved too much for Yoel. The stress of the severe winter had taken its toll, and no sooner was he back within the walls at his father-in-law's home, than he fell ill. The men returned to Petach Tiqva without him. His protracted convalescence in Jerusalem was to determine the future of Petach Tiqva: her growth, and her subsequent disintegration.

Chapter 30

Ibrahim Kalantar leant against the railing at the stern of the steamer and watched the port of Constantinople fade into the horizon. He was a terrestial creature and he hated the sea: even the smell of it made him sick. But for once he was glad to be here on the ship, drawing away from the mainland. The drone of the engine and the cry of the gulls which bobbed and weaved in the wake of the ship reminded him that he was safe.

There had been months of tension and vigilance as he led his large querulous family from Bukhara across half Russia, and into Turkey in daily fear of his life. It had taken skill and courage, not to mention lots of bribes, to reach this point, when at last he could relax. Nothing save the caprice of nature or an attack by pirates could harm him now. He had heard that the Mediterranean had been made free of pirates, and the steamer, he was assured, was of the latest and fastest built ships operating in these waters. Even a warship couldn't overtake her. Once in Jaffa with his fortune, he would start a new life. It wasn't what an old man in his position should look forward to but at least he would be free to do as he liked. He had half a million gold Napoleons concealed in bales of cloth and barrels of spices in the hold of the ship. Enough to secure comfort in his last years no matter how backward Palestine was—yes, he had heard stories about that—and even with the free-spending ways that had become second nature to him and his sons. Kalantar no longer sought power. Years of intrigue and association with sycophants at the court of the Emir of Bukhara had made him weary; he wanted peace and rest.

The ship was more or less at his command. And he had paid enough to make the journey profitable even without further cargo or passengers. So the captain and the crew were at his beck and call. Now that his keen mind no longer had to grapple with the contingencies of his flight, it crept like shadows into the events which had led him to be where he was, to his disgrace, and fall. Thinking about these things made him angry, and when he was angry he tended to be sharp with his tongue and liberal with his whip. When the furrows above his nose deepened, all who knew Ibrahim took distance from him and left him alone.

Ibrahim didn't like his family. They were all mendacious, indolent, and imperious. The last offended him most: imperiousness born of indolence was the worst of vices, the very thing which singled out weak, stupid despots. Back home, his wife Bonu by whom he had three sons and a backward daughter, had tired him with her schemings against his concubine

Zulika and her son. Often in his vexation he lashed out at them both with his cane, which he later regretted. His sons, Yussef the eldest, Yacub, and Nissim, he considered as deceitful as any in the Emir's court where they grew up. Ibrahim felt he could look to no comfort from them in his old age. They were weaklings, he despised them. His loneliness sometimes moved him to dissemble affection, mostly for Yussef, his heir. He was glad none of them knew about the money hidden below. If they did, they would be at one another's throats. He couldn't rule out their trying to poison him too, their own father! Only Aram, his devoted servant who had followed him, knew. Good faithful Aram. He too was getting old. And what would become of poor Aram in this strange land they were going to when Ibrahim was gathered to his fathers? Of all things that question alone could make Ibrahim sad.

He knew very little about Palestine, and what he did know did not appeal to him in the least. He had grown up among people with courtly manners; people who enjoyed poetry, the flight of a falcon, and thoroughbred horses. The gardens of Samarkand and domes of Bukhara were imprinted on his memory as was the moody grandeur of the landscape where he had hunted with courtiers and his master the Emir. What was there in Palestine but coarseness, bleakness and Ottoman boorishness?

The shouts of the Turkish sailors broke into his thoughts, irritating him even more. How he loathed them, a dim-witted race which only knew how to fight and destroy. And what could one look for in a backward country, populated by cunning Arabs and ruled by Turks? Yet when it came to cunning he knew a few could match himself. If it weren't for cunning and foresight would he not be at best languishing in prison, or dead, executed with a sword in Bukhara's main square, instead of sailing on this calm sea to the Promised Land?

Ibrahim had a religious imagination and temperament even if he had always been casual about ritual. Oh, he had seen the warning spelt out unmistakably. He recognized the hand of God. He might have gone to America as did a few of his countrymen, but all at once atavistic reverberations impelled him towards his Judaic roots, like a commandment he couldn't ignore: "Get thee out of thy country, and from thy kindred, and from thy father's house, into a land that I will show thee."

If only he hadn't been encumbered by his kindred! Only in spirit he was free of them.

He knew he would miss Bukhara, his old lifestyle, the rich earthiness of his mother tongue; even now he did. What would that be which would fill the emptiness in him from what he had lost, he didn't know. Except that it would be an immanence he couldn't yet comprehend. He conceived of it as a kind of calm luminescence glowing from within. He tried in anticipation, to enter into a state of gracious abdication of power, of passion, of everything that was hard and material. In Palestine he would invest in land, thus securing his children's future and discharging all parental obligations to them. For himself he would build a house with a garden, he would sit under a tree in the shade and bask in the soft light of old age. Thinking about his family shattered his self-induced tranquillity. His right calf began to ache where it had been accidentally pierced by a lance during a boar hunt many years ago. "Aram!" he shouted. The old servant emerged from behind the mast.

"Yes master?"

"Go fetch my nargil and fill it with hashish."

Aram padded away. Presently he returned with Ibrahim's ornate water-pipe of silver filigree and blue glass. Packing it deftly he put the glowing amber to the top of the leaves. Then he puffed on it until the fire caught. Only then he changed the mouthpiece to a fine amber one, and handed it to Ibrahim. Ibrahim inhaled a few times and felt better. He would have taken off his turban to let the sea breeze cool his balding head if his damask throne-like chair with the parasol above it hadn't reminded him of his position. How could he bare his head to those uncivilized sailors? A man without a turban was worse than naked, like having his name obliterated.

"Shall I rub your leg with camphor and oil, Master?" Aram asked.

"Yes, do that, Aram." He loved his servant. Even though Aram called him "Master" there was more dignity in him and more independence of mind than any number of his fawning former peers who had betrayed him. Aram could also play a good game of chess. Occasionally win too, discreetly, with consummate delicacy.

"In the Holy Land, Aram, I shall change my name to Abraham. No more Ibrahim. How does that sound to you?"

"It's the man, Master, who gives the name its sound. It will make no difference." Aram's tact never failed him. He did everything with a perfect sense of timing and aplomb, from washing Ibrahim, or helping him dress, to procuring a young girl and instructing her on how to arouse the old man.

Ibrahim puffed away on his water-pipe. "Scoundrels and traitors, all of them. May they die like dogs" he said, but no longer in passion. His memory began to uncoil with the sweet langour of the drug.

Ibrahim had not always been rich. His father, a Georgian Jew, came to Bukhara before he was born. Nobody knew why or much about the man except that he was illiterate and ruthless. When Ibrahim reached eminence, the thought of his father, whom he never knew for he died shortly after Ibrahim was born, was like a scar in his mind. The father married a local woman whose family was well-connected but poor. Ibraham's mother did not outlive her husband by very long and when she died Ibrahim was committed to the care of her family who treated him as though he were a servant's bastard, not a relative. When he ran away at the age of thirteen, never to see them again, he vowed that never again would he have to depend on anybody. He had more or less kept that promise to himself. In his nature, native intelligence, resilience, and a ruthless sense of opportunity combined to assure the best prospects for survival even in the most adverse circumstances. As a young man he travelled a good deal; first to the east as far as Persia and the borders of India, then to the west, into the heartland of Russia, where he struck up lucrative trade connections which eventually attracted the attention of the Bukharan court and catapulted Ibrahim Kalantar to prominence and success. God's most adaptable creatures—weeds, sparrows—could not be more successful in the face of change than Ibrahim proved to be. Just as hardship had not bowed him, so good fortune didn't soften him. Unfettered by tradition, he soon acquired courtly manners. Riding and hunting came as naturally to him as dissembling or plotting a rival's downfall. He learnt to lance a target and slice a pumpkin in half with a sabre at a full gallop. As he advanced up the social ladder of Bukhara, he enjoyed with a kind of malevolent perversity to see the elders of the Jewish community seeking his attention. Among practising Jews Ibrahim would have been considered an ignoramus; he barely knew how to pray. Now it gave him pleasure to be called to the ark in Samarkand's main synagogue, to read the lesson. How the most honoured Jews smiled forgivingly at his errors. His wife Bonu was the youngest daughter of a rich carpet merchant, a courteous learned and pious Jew, the main pillar of the community. Ibrahim had haggled heartlessly with him over the dowry. No sooner were they married than Ibrahim brought his courtesan into the household. Humiliated, Bonu ran away to her father's home. Ibrahim sent his servant to fetch her. For a week he locked her in her room allowing her only bread and water until she begged forgiveness. The quiet blend of submissiveness and detachment excited Ibrahim. They had a child every year, but only four survived.

When the Chief wizir to the Emir Muza'afar Khan passed away, Ibrahim was chosen to replace him. It was the greatest honour ever bestowed upon a Jew. The courtiers used to joke that Ibrahim Kalantar was born a Jew only by mischief of the devil, for in appearance as in manners he was as Moslem as any of them. Ibrahim worked hard at his new office. Under his stewardship the Emir's wealth grew twofold, threefold, the Emir himself didn't know by how much, some said it was tenfold. Ibrahim knew exactly. The responsibilities of the highest office in the land sharpened his instincts and mellowed his fiery temperament. He began to discern the difference between himself and his fellow courtiers. Then gradually out of the security of power his Jewish identity began to emerge. In the privacy of his palatial home he made sure that his sons learnt the holy script and gained an understanding of who they were. Years passed. His sons, raised in the court as princelings, grew up. Times were good for the Jews of Bukhara, thanks to Ibrahim.

Aram's hands were working on his calf, round his knees, up his thigh. Good hands, they were, patient, firm, trustworthy; hands that would never be raised against their owner's benefactor. Faithful Aram, his mind repelled the very notion of treason as oil repels vinegar.

"Good, Aram, good. Now lower down," Ibrahim said. Aram had a special understanding of legs, human legs no less than horses' with which he was masterful. "Tell me Aram, what are they up to now?" Ibrahim referred to his family as 'they'; it was easier to justify the mistrust he had for them when they were thus lumped together with anonymity.

"Quarrelling as usual, Master."

"Not poking around in the hold are they?"

"No Master. I watch them."

"Not even Yussef? He's a crafty one."

"He sits around moping or reading. Or he walks on the deck."

The confines of the ship concentrated Ibrahim's dislike of his family. They were his wife's people, like those who had betrayed him at his moment of vulnerability. The children he fathered were more hers than his, and through them she was working a slow revenge on him. He had to watch out.

His decline began when the old Emir Muza'afar Khan, his patron, died full of years and steeped in honour. He was succeeded by his son, Achat Khan whose playmate Yussef had been and who as a child Ibrahim had often bounced on his knees. The young Emir was shifty, intolerant, and impressionable. Ibrahim, better than anybody, understood the danger of such qualities in a despot. He began to make plans. Soon Achat Khan fell under the spell of Mullah who hated Bukhara's great Christian neighbour Russia and held it to be the devil's creation and a source of corruption to Bukhara's Islamic way of life. At last the opportunity came for Bonu's menfolk to avenge themselves on Ibrahim for the humiliation they had received at his hands. Stories began to circulate about Ibrahim, how he always prayed secretly for the Tzar's health. The young Emir was reminded by courtiers how Ibrahim Kalantar made his wealth through connections with Russia. The poison worked in deadly lassitude until young Achat Khan began to fear Ibrahim, and wonder how the alien Jew, despised even by his own people, could have so corrupted his father's judgement that he never realized a Russian agent had insinuated himself into his trust.

Ibrahim sensed the change. His advice was no longer heeded. Cold looks now greeted him. He was avoided by the courtiers and his free access to the Emir was restricted. His instincts told him that worse was yet to come if he didn't make a move quickly. Ibrahim had never forgotten his past, his ability to remember without self-pity or self-congratulation had made him a supreme survivor. He took vicissitudes of fortune for granted, neither fearing them nor seeing them as his due.

The move he made was as bold as it was imaginative. For two weeks he feigned illness. So convincing was his malingering that not only his wife and sons, but even Aram, was taken in by it. At the end of two weeks he obtained an audience with the young Emir. Dressed in a mendicant's garb, he told him that he had had a dream in which the Angel Gabriel appeared to him, and told him that he was about to die, but to save his soul, he must make a pilgrimage to Jerusalem and be buried there. He begged Achat Khan to give him leave to go and fulfil that last commandment. The Emir, a deeply devout Moslem, couldn't refuse. Reconciled with his ruler, and with his blessing, Ibrahim prepared his last journey. He sold his property and ostentatiously gave alms to the poor. Having sought and won his wife's forgiveness, he persuaded her to accompany him with their sons as far as Constantinople. He settled a generous sum on his concubine Zulika and sent her away. No one had a shadow of doubt that Ibrahim Kalantar was indeed about to be gathered unto his fathers, realizing which he sought grace by renouncing all his past sins.

On the pretext that he had to put the last of his affairs in order, he sent his wife and sons ahead of him to Constantinople. Then he contacted secretly a clerk of the treasury whom he had raised and who was loyal to him, and through him gained access to the treasury. The night he left Bukhara, Ibrahim took as much gold as could be loaded on four swift horses and rode out for all he was worth across the Bukharan border into Russia. By the time the theft was discovered, Ibrahim Kalantar had been received for an audience with Tzar Alexander II and given safe conduct into the Ottoman Empire.

It wasn't really theft, Ibrahim kept telling himself. He had been wronged; he had taken what was due to him after a lifetime of unremitting work for the Emirate—all the trade, the wealth the Emir had gained through his endeavours! With that thought in mind, Ibrahim was able to put the past behind him. His wife had wept and tore her hair. The sons protested. But they understood that the way their father left Bukhara, there would be nothing but shame and disgrace if not actual retribution for them in their native land.

As Ibrahim expected, Ottoman courtiers and officials were even easier to bribe than the Bukharan, and cheaper too. He left the Turkish shores an honoured Ottoman subject. No news of misdeeds had reached the Divine Port by the time he set sail for Palestine. If or when it did, they would be laughing at the Emir, Ibrahim knew.

The ship rocked. Through the seat of the chair Ibrahim felt the soothing vibrations of the ship's engine. The hashish was working on him. His mind flowed like a river. The scent of jasmine and pomegranate was in his nostrils. He closed his eyes. A pink light flooded his vision. Aram began to sing softly.

"You're a good man, Aram. God knows what I'd do without you."

"May Allah grant you many happy years, Master," said Aram.

"May He so. If only for your sake, Aram. I wouldn't like to think of you alone after I'm gone."

"I'm not worried, Ibrahim Bey."

Ibrahim sighed, "We're both old, Aram. We've been through a lot together. Now when we should see our last days in peace and honour, here we are on another journey."

"One cannot choose what happens in one's life Master," Aram said.

"True. But, God willing, we shall yet have a good time. No more horses and hunts. There'll be a garden with trees and a wall all around. We'll sit there and enjoy the soft hours playing chess. I promise you."

Even as he said it, reality began to intrude. His brow knotted. "Go fetch my son Yussef," he said.

Yussef came sauntering across the deck. He had his father's robust physique. His dark eyes had heavy lids. His carefully tended beard was like glossy rivulets of liquid ebony. On his deck strolls Yussef wore a loose white gown held at the waist by a broad glittering sash and into which was stuck an ornate dagger; still the prince with his black turban topping his head in arrogant frivolity. When Yussef saw the unfocused look in his father's eyes, his mouth curled down a little.

"You called me, Father," he said, bowing perfunctorily.

Ibrahim stretched out his hand palm down. Yussef hesitated. Ibrahim's eyes hardened. Yussef took the proffered hand, bent his head and touched it with his lips. As he did so, Ibrahim jerked him forward, reached for the dagger, pulled it out and flung it overboard. The speed of movement took Yussef aback.

"You don't wear that when you come to see me," Ibrahim hissed.

Hatred flickered in Yussef's eyes but only for an instant; the old man could still be dangerous.

"What are you doing down below?" Ibrahim demanded.

"Reading, Father."

"And your brothers?"

"They are with our mother. She's crying."

"Crying? Why is she crying?"

Yussef shrugged. "How should I know? Women cry often for no reason."

Sensing a rebuke, Ibrahim wanted to strike him for his insolence. He knew why Bonu was crying. It was for her hopelessness. Now she had no one but him to look to, no one to whom she could run away, nothing to do except obey him, and poison his sons' minds against him. Against that he had no remedy. Yet she could make him suffer pangs of conscience. How he longed for peace, even at the cost of contrition.

"Yussef, come read me some poetry," he said in a conciliatory voice. The Court poets of Bukhara could not recite poetry as beautifully as Yussef. Even his own verse which was dense and inelegant sounded good when he read it. And Yussef could never turn down an invitation to recite. He went to fetch his volume of Persian poetry.

Stirred by the lilting cadence of his son's voice, Ibrahim had visions of sadness. He saw himself old and unloved in an unfamiliar country where no one respected his ways, his money squandered by spendthrift sons and on bribes to greedy officials. Mortality in Palestine suggested squalidness not divine grace. Tears began to roll down his face.

Yussef accepted his father's show of emotion as a tribute to his gift. As he rounded off one poem and prepared for the next, his mind turned over possibilities for reward.

Ibrahim heaved a sigh. "Ah, Yussef my son, love is greater than might, dearer than gold, more precious than anything man in his conceit can devise. Love, happiness, blood bonds. These are the essence of life. Not for nothing is it written in our holy writ, 'Honour thy father and thy mother'. Think about that Yussef, think about it now and forever."

"I do Father, I cherish that commandment above all else," Yussef replied, and cleared his throat.

Gradually Ibrahim's head began to sink. His white beard fanned out like a peacock's tail on his chest. In his sleep he looked gentle. Yussef closed the book and walked over to the railing where he stood gazing into the sea. He was still numb from the events of the past weeks. Incredulously his mind tried to piece together what his father had done to bring about their flight. As he pondered over this he recalled the period when they were in eclipse, when even his own friends avoided him, let alone his childhood playmate who was now Emir. He began to suspect that the crisis was not precipitated arbitrarily but that his father had planned everything, from his gradual withdrawl to his sudden religiosity and their abrupt departure from Samarkand. Ibrahim Kalantar's judgement was infallable: he would never be caught in any situation unprepared. That much Yussef knew about his father, therefore it was unthinkable that they were out here on this Ottoman steamer without some secret advantage from the affair. Wrack his brain as he did, Yussef couldn't progress beyond that apprehension.

But this disruption to his life made him feel older than his twenty years. He turned to look at Ibrahim. He was still peacefully asleep, and Aram was sitting like a heap at his feet. "He's getting old and weak," Yussef thought. "In that foreign land we're going to it won't be the same for him as it was back home. I'm young, and he has taught me patience, to lie in wait, to endure. I'll take whatever there is to take from him when my time comes. For all that he has done to me, my brothers and my mother."

Yet the doubts about what, if anything, Ibrahim had which could be taken from him, surreptitiously gnawed at Yussef's mind, sowing fear, fear that he might have to struggle to earn his living, a task for which he was unqualified, and which terrified him. His hands tightened on the poetry book. In a spasm of anger he tossed it away and horrified, watched it bob on the waves as though it were his soul. His adam's apple began to work. He was grateful that no one saw him trembling like a maid.

"Abraham, tell them Abraham Kalantar, a wealthy Jew from Bukhara and an Ottoman subject, has come to the land of his fathers with the blessings of the Sultan," Ibrahim instructed the captain to say to the Turkish officials in Jaffa. The officials were not impressed but they were in an accommodating mood. Only the week before a French duke had departed. It had been a colourful day in their lives, and they had received handsome bonuses. Ibrahim was much reassured when told about the distinguished visitor. A land to which princes come couldn't be all bad, he told himself, and cheered beyond his expectations, he gave liberal tips to the porters and port officials. By the time the Kalantar family and their possessions had cleared Jaffa port, an army of agents and hangers-on surrounded them, offering advice and diverse services.

Money needed a safe repository. Ibrahim recognized only one safe way of keeping money, and that was translating it into property. It so happened that soon after the family moved into rented rooms in the more salubrious quarter of Jaffa, a friend Ibrahim had won on the first day of his arrival came to inform that a large house with a spreading garden was up for sale. Its owner, a Lebanese merchant, had died and his widow and sons were anxious to sell and join their relatives in Beirut. Ibrahim went to see the house and liked it immediately. It was a solid home, set apart among tall palm trees and fragrant oranges. It had a stone wall surrounding it—Ibrahim liked walls—and a strong iron gate. He bought it at once.

The news that a rich Jewish man of affairs—for so he had presented himself—had come to retire in the Holy Land and had bought the pink house on the promontory overlooking the bay, spread fast. Agents of notables came to size him up. There were delegations of Jews. Ibrahim was generous and forthcoming. With hardly an effort, he fell into the rhythm of his new country of residence. He travelled to Jerusalem, made contact and bought another house no less grand than the one he owned in Jaffa. He employed servants and bought fine Arab horses. The oblique but elaborate politeness of the Palestinian wealthy society stilled his anxieties. He entertained a good deal and never failed to show respect to the Pashas of Jaffa and Jerusalem whom he showered with gifts. He became their confidant. When he saw with what confidence and skill Yussef was making new friends, he began to think of his wealth. One by one the bales of cloth stored in the cellars of the house were unfolding. Ibrahim's stolen riches were invested in land and houses.

Faithful Adam did not take well to his exile. Like a foreign plant that would not take to a new soil, he wilted. Soon after he had seen his master settle down his tired mind returned to distant scenes of his childhood. He could no longer carry out his duties as in the old days; even the horses did not respond to his touch. One evening, as Ibrahim sat on the verandah of his house and watched the sun sink into the Mediterranean, Aram quietly passed away in his servant's quarters. Ibrahim grieved deeply. He had him buried in the garden, among the almonds and the pomegranate trees, and sitting there, would sometimes call Aram's name.

Only after Aram's death did he change his name officially to Abraham, and with that, he felt the last tie with the land and culture of his birth was broken.

Abraham preferred Jaffa to Jerusalem. He liked sea air and the orange blossom fragrance carried on the breeze in the evening. He would sit on the verandah smoking hashish and be tranquil. In Jerusalem the importuning of the beggars at the gates vexed him as did the quarrels of the Jews. Jerusalem made him think of mortality. He had never been frightened of death. Now, with Aram gone, he thought of it as a gentle fading away. With this in mind, he bought a plot in the Sepharadi cemetery on the Mount of Olives for himself and his wife, and to enlarge his last base before the eternal repose, he also purchased more houses and land in the city and around it.

But for Yussef and his brothers, Jerusalem twinkled like a bright star out of the darkness, all the brighter because their father was set on remaining in Jaffa.

Chapter 31

Petach Tiqva's main street—the only thoroughfare in the settlement which could be called a street—was named Hovevei Zion, in honour of the movement 'Lovers of Zion' which made Petach Tiqva rise from her ruins and live again. One end of the street opened on to fields. The other pointed towards Yahudia—Petach Tiqva's now reduced other half—and towards Jaffa. Roughly in the middle, between one and the other, was the old well around which a natural cluster of buildings had formed a circle. The settlers named that, significantly of the new mood of optimism, 'Hovevei Zion Square'. The old store-house was still there, opposite the well at one side of the Square but it no longer dominated the street as it had once done.

Trees grew on either side of the street; without them it would have looked no more than a wide rut in the ground, with alleys, like veins running across it and branching from it. No design dictated the course and shape of the alleys: they sprouted haphazardly from it but avoided intersecting at a right angle so as not to configurate the Cross.

In winter the street turned into an archipelago of mud islands bridged with a criss-cross of wooden planks for people to cross. The traffic of carts and horses made deep ruts. In summer clouds of powdery dust would stir up with every puff of wind and in the afternoons hot stifling breezes would rake the street from one end to the other. Hens poked around between the houses. Occasionally a stray goat would wander into the street. Dogs lay panting in the shade of the houses, and the horses, tethered outside Katz's tavern, stood shifting their feet and swinging their tails to chase the flies away.

The Street called Hovevei Zion was the heart of the settlement—or colony—as outsiders called it. In it you could see Petach Tiqva's variety, her cautious acceptance of progress, and her conformity with the past, which made her so different from the larger, more outgoing settlement, Rishon le Zion a little over half a day's ride away.

Thirty-nine families now lived in the village whose total population was about 200. The houses, no longer crowded together as if seeking protection by proximity, were concentrated around Hovevei Zion Street. They were larger than their predecessors, more private, and surrounded in many cases by eucalyptus trees, fruit trees, and small gardens. No longer were the village's livestock all kept together. Each man stabled his animals behind his house. But in the old storehouse, the common grain was still stored as well as the communal machines which now included a number of different ploughs and thrashers.

The street would wake up at dawn to a chorus of cock crows. Boroch Kraus would light the ovens in his bakery. The smell of freshly-baked bread spread through the street. One by one the men made their way to the synagogue not far from the well—a handsome unassuming building with a modest dome, like a skull cap. They were already in their work clothes, clothes which betrayed their way of life, for the men of Petach Tiqva never gave up their traditional trousers, the long coats and broad hats. To an emissary of the Lovers of Zion movement who once came to look the village over, their garb seemed so inconsonant with the times that he had reported contemptuously: "What is the point of giving aid to these people when you see them walking about dressed like yeshiva students in Jerusalem?" To which Gutman had retorted, "Look at our fields. It's the men who do the work, not the clothes!"

As the men would be making their way to the synagogue for the morning prayers, Yudit Winkler drove her brindled cow together with four others belonging to her neighbours, down the street towards a grassy meadow where they would graze for the day. She shouted at them in a mixture of Rumanian and Yiddish, just as Boroch did when he was vexed with his ovens. You could hear many different voices in the Street of Hovevei Zion in the course of a day: Rumanian, Hungarian, Russian from Bialystok.

As the men came out of the synagogue and dispersed for the day's work the children came running, skipping, chasing one another on their way to school fast by the synagogue. It was 1885, a good, trouble-free year. The hardships that brought Petach Tiqva to her knees only four years before, were all but forgotten. At least the people preferred not to talk about them, for recalling them is painful. Yoel Zeff for one—steeped in honour though he is, in Jerusalem, as in Petach Tiqva where together with Gutman he is the chief authority—Mukhtar of the Jews—cannot distance himself from the events that had led to Petach Tiqva's disintegration. Feelings of guilt and personal failure are still raw in his memory; a memory that is merciless in its judgement, vivid in its recall, meticulous in detail, for Yoel had committed himself to chronicling.

"With the help of God, Sivan year 5639 (1879)", a past entry reads. (His incursion into journalism developed his sense of history and had got him into the habit of noting down the Gregorian year alongside the Jewish one). "When the people in Jerusalem had seen the success we had with the first harvest, their appetites knew no bounds. 'Reb Yoel, are the Arabs friendly?' 'Reb Yoel, and what about the children, are they well and happy?' they asked. And then they wanted to know: was there more land to be bought, and at what price? How could I not be glad to see there was so much interest? There was this man whom I'd never met before, Azriel Litman, and he gathered a group of people round him. 'Look at the men from Petach Tiqva,' he said, 'how healthy and sun-tanned they look, and we're pale and sallow-faced. Shall we dwell in the shadow of the walls when there are open fields waiting for us?' He was good at stirring people with words, this Azriel.

"He came to me with ten men, when I was still weak from the fever and convalescing. 'We want to buy land in Petach Tiqva,' he said. And I welcomed them with open arms. I tried to assuage any fears they had, I told them their decision to join the settlement was brave and right."

Reb David Gutman had not been so forthcoming as Yoel Zeff. He saw problems, he wanted to wait so as to be sure the right people came, people who were suited for farming life and to the small closely knit society of the settlers. He wanted no idlers, no troublemakers. There had been arguments, with Yoel saying the momentum of settlement must be kept even at a risk of failure, partial failure that is. Besides, land was land: you never lost buying more of it. He reminded Gutman of the troubles they had had from Tayan's people, trouble that would be removed for ever if they bought Tayan's land. In the end Gutman agreed. Though his heart wasn't really in it, Yoel could tell from the way his nose twitched with fastidious irascibility. "My nose tells me . . ." Gutman used to begin before he ruled something out. Only this time Gutman didn't listen to his nose. Was he going to be the one to put the brake on what they had all hoped and prayed for? There was the question of money: even Gutman couldn't raise enough to buy the 8,500 dunams of Tayan's land along the river. The man who saved the situation was a former collaborator of Yoel's in the *Pisga*, Reb Yehiel Pinnes, a firm advocate of Jewish independence, and now happily involved with a special fund established in London, in honour of Sir Moses Montefiore. The land was bought hastily with funds from London and a loan underwritten by Reb David Gutman and had to be sold to settlers, plot by plot, to recover the money. Azriel Litman with his group headed the queue.

"They were too keen, like children in a garden full of pleasant surprises. We had the experience; we knew the deadly breath of the river. But they wouldn't listen to us. Children seldom heed the advice of their elders. If they did there might be less sorrow in the world. But on the other hand, how much spontaneity and discovery would be lost? This thought alone absolves us of guilt for what later happened to myself, Gutman and my dearest friend David Joshua. Yet if I had not been so weakened by the fever, and if there had been more time we might have selected the newcomers more judiciously."

Azriel and his friends, some twenty families to which more were later added, built their homes in the shallow valley that overlooked the river bank. Compared to their more prosperous co-settlers on the rise they were poor. No sooner had they moved into their homes than it became apparent that most of them could not repay the loan on their plots in anywhere near the allotted time. The fact that they owed money at all, rankled with Azriel in particular, so that every bit of advice he received from the people on the 'rise' he rejected out of hand. "The Millionaires on the hill," he called them contemptuously. The name stuck. "The River idlers", the settlers on the rise reposted. Mutual irritation mounted.

For a while all went well with the newcomers. They had zest and hope. They conjured up fantastic schemes. Several times Yoel had ridden over to see how they were faring. "Don't use the river water," he had warned. "Come and use the water from the well, as much as you like." But they paid no attention to him. They had plans: groves of fruit trees, vegetables, all watered by the plentiful water from the river. Azriel Litman talked of fishing and pleasure sailing, of groves of mulberry trees for growing silk caterpillars. "You think you have everything there on the hill, your granaries full, your homes aloud with the laughter of children," he said grandiloquently to Yoel. "Just wait and see what we shall do here."

Winter came with heavy rains, knocking down some of the houses; the river heaved itself from between its banks and flooded the surroundings. With the hardship that followed people lost much of their ardour. Then, like an evil spirit out of the river, came the fever.

The fever first struck the people of the river at the end of the summer. One morning two of the children from down by the river fainted at school. Within an hour they were delirious. The doctor arrived from Jaffa two days later. By that time seven people were already down. It was malaria, the doctor said, the whole area by the river was infested and should be evacuated. The older settlers on the rise remembered the warnings they had given the newcomers and became resentful.

The men and women from the river gathered on the path leading to the rise. They were grief-stricken, bewildered. They didn't want to stay in their homes where they feared death but had nowhere else to go. That day and the day before, they had buried four of their number: two children, and two women. What was the point of going up the rise? People were dying there too. What could the others do to help? But Azriel Litman urged them on, drove them as a shepherd drives a reluctant herd: they had stayed aloof when help was needed, those people on the rise, he said, using their less fortunate brethren because the founders were bent on buying land and settling on it no matter what. "Our lives are no better than dogs in their eyes, I tell you," Litman cried out. And so the people lumbered after him towards the centre of Petach Tiqva.

"I'm not a healer nor a prophet. I cannot make death stand at bay. Yet if I had given more of my time to those unfortunate people, for those settling by the accursed river I must accept some responsibility, the tragedy might have been averted. I keep quiet. I cannot accuse other people of indifference or negligence when I myself stand accused of these very charges," Yoel had written. "They say the river Uja has defeated us. I say this is an excuse men make when they daren't face the truth about themselves. A river is a stretch of water in a stretch of land; it has a character, it offers advantages and it imposes hazards. Man has the ingenuity to turn natural advantages to his own use, or he is nothing. Indolence, contrariness, and impatience have defeated us, not the river and the fever it exhales. But what difference does that make when you see the pain of defeat on people's faces, all their shattered hopes?"

The malaria spread and hit Petach Tiqva on the rise. When the Beduin and the Arabs of the distant villages saw how weak the Jews had become that they no longer came out to confront them when they drove their herds to their fields, they came and went to the fields of Petach Tiqva at will, and there was no one to stop them. Families began to leave. No longer one by one, the departure turned into a rout which rapidly depleted the village's community. Jerusalem, which only two years before, welcomed the jubilant villagers with their first harvest, now received them hopeless and sick.

Yoel Zeff with a few of the others, mostly the founding fathers of the village, were the last to leave Petach Tiqva, but they didn't move far. They set up homes on the 130 dunams of land bought with great difficulty and at a great expense near the village of Yahudia, with money raised by David Gutman and Michael Pines.

The feud between the river dwellers and those on the hill did not end there; it was transported to Jerusalem. Accusations were countered with accusations. It transpired that some of the would-be settlers by the river had bought the land but instead of settling themselves, sold it to others and made profits. Now landownership and debts were disputed, for the first time, among Jews! The bitterness intensified as bit by bit, like terrible shameful secrets, past machinations behind the scenes were exposed.

Only the news of the pogroms in Russia, which began to reach the Jewish community of Jerusalem in the spring of 1881, and shook it to its foundation by the next year, distracted the people from the failure of Petach Tiqva and the controversy around it. Out of that disaster was born the movement 'Lovers of Zion' which begat several new Jewish settlements in Palestine, and resurrected Petach Tiqva. That year the Ottomans banned immigration of non-Ottoman Jews to Palestine. Newly-arrived immigrants had their papers taken away from them at the Port of Jaffa, and were issued with the Red Card, good for one month's stay in the country. Mehemet Rauf, Pasha of Jerusalem, jealously enforced the regulations against illegal building, and fought in vain against the corruption of his subordinates in Jaffa who allowed Jews to get round the Red Card restriction. Corruption didn't leave the Jews unstained either: fictitious real estate companies were formed whose agents greeted new immigrants at the port, having ascertained that they were people of reasonable means, arranged for their immigration restriction to be removed by bribes, and sold them land which was not theirs to sell. Scores of young men, often with their families, were stranded in Jaffa or Jerusalem with no money and nowhere to turn to, and became a burden on the Jewish community before they found whatever employment they could get, whether in Jaffa, in Jerusalem or in the new settlement of Rishon Le Zion.

Out of sorrow, deceit, but also determination, Petach Tiqva rose from her ashes, repopulated by those who had the heart to return, as well as by newcomers.

At about that time too, Abraham Kalantar bought land in there and through that acquisition, became involved with the Jewish settlement whose moving sentiment he never understood, and whose endeavour he held in little regard. Thanks to his good relationship with the Ottoman officials in Jaffa as well as with Rauf Pasha himself, the settlers were allowed to build their homes unmolested. Then, on 6th December 1884 an event took place in a town in Poland which set Petach Tiqva on the road to prosperity, or so it seemed. The executive of Hovevei Zion Movement met in Katowice and decided to take Petach Tiqva under the Movement's wings, and allot it 10,000 francs so that the marshes might be drained, eucalyptus trees planted, and the threat of malaria removed from the village for good.

On a sultry Friday afternoon of early summer the street was empty. All the work in the fields had been finished well before noon. Hot gusts from the east stirred up dust and rattled the shutters. The hamsin had not yet begun but you could tell it was on its way because the night before the sky was milky and a wide ring encircled the moon. Hamsin made man and beast torpid; even your thoughts moved in heavy lassitude.

Mendle Wolfe, the blacksmith, was asleep in a chair on the porch of his house. His lips flapped over his toothless mouth as he breathed. Mendle was thin. You could see the bones of his chest and his ribs when he worked, for he would take off his shirt and hammer away at his anvil with only his talith bodice on. But his arms were knotted with muscles like ropes. He could take a wheel off a wagon singlehanded and toss it away as though it were a piece of wood. Mendle was hard of hearing, therefore irritable. Because of his deafness the village alarm bell had been posted next to his door. From his porch Mendle had a full view of both ends of the street. If danger approached he would rush up to the bell and hit it with a hammer for all he was worth.

Soon the village would stir from its slumber and prepare for the Sabbath. But hopefully not before the return of the young men, who early in the morning had set out for Jaffa to bring provisions and the post.

Malachi Zeff came out of the house. He sat at the edge of the porch and lowered his bare feet into the warm dust. Narrowing his eyes he made the space before him shudder and open up into depths. But even his imagination couldn't fill that space with anything: the emptiness seemed endless, stubborn. Inside, Hannah, tired from the day's chores, was asleep. So was his sister Tiqva, or she was locked in her unwelcoming silence: a dour young woman, unloving and unloved. Yoel was away in Jerusalem, staying with Chaim and Grandfather; he wouldn't be back for another week. In his absence, they were invited for the Sabbath meal to Gutman's house.

When the wind changed to a sea breeze the heat would ease, the brass would go out of the sky and a flush of lilac would spread across the horizon. Then swallows would come, cutting through the air, whistling like knives. Hannah would wake up and call him in to wash—he could hear her voice in his imagination, see the impatience in her face as she came out of the door hands on hips, squinting. She would wash him in the yard, out of a pail of water that had been standing in the shade of the lean-to, and comb his chestnut side-curls and dress him in a long white shirt and the dark trousers which he wore on the Sabbath. Then he would sit in the room—for Hannah would forbid him to go out again lest he should get soiled—and watch his sister Tiqva plait her dark hair in front of the small mirror on the wall. They would all wait for Leib.

Leib, the Lion, his eldest brother. Leib, tall and strong, fire in his dark eyes; his beard like a lacquered shield. Leib, on his grey mare; the best horseman in the village—who could shoot like lightning from his horse. Leib would come back from Jaffa covered in dust, wash and dress, put on his wide-sleeved white shirt. Standing in his high damask boots, he would look taller, more than ever the hero. He would come with them to Gutman's home, sit at the table and answer questions with easy confidence that often, as Malachi had seen, disconcerted his elders. Mouth the prayers while his mind and heart were elsewhere. A little sooner than was polite, he would be off to some other house in the village where his comrades were waiting for him, where they would talk and laugh and retell their exploits.

"Take me with you," Malachi had begged the day before.

"Little boys of ten don't get taken to Jaffa," Leib had said.

"I'm eleven."

"Makes no difference," and he slapped him a little too sharply on the head.

Malachi knew better than to whine and plead.

Once before, Leib had taken him to Jaffa. He had left him in the house of a Jew from whom the village bought things, then went off on other business with some of his friends. Malachi stood in the shed and watched the provisions being stacked up. The trader had a son, a year or so older than Malachi. "Want to go and watch the sea?" the boy offered. Sitting on a ramp of broken wall, the two boys watched the sea beyond the harbour. The shifting blue and the advancing white crests of the waves made

Malachi's head reel. He could have sat there for hours mesmerized by the vastness before him, if his host weren't anxious to entertain. "Got any money?" he asked.

Malachi shook his head.

"Never mind, come."

Weaving their way through the throngs in the bazaar, the older boy showed him how easy it was to steal in the crowd. Among the palms, away from the crowds, they sat and sucked on the sugar cane the boy had stolen. The smell of the sea was everywhere, invigorating and lulling. The French man-of-war—the boy seemed to know everything—lodged far out in the blue, looked like a toy boat surrounded by yet smaller toy boats.

"One day I'll sail away from here."

"Where to?"

"America," the boy said. "Over there," and he flung out his arm to indicate how far it was.

Malachi was thrilled. America! At that moment of magic, at the edge of the enticing sea, everything seemed possible. Soon they were on the move again.

An Arab woman leaned over the balustrade of the balcony on the second floor of a house not far from the port. Her shrill voice arrested Malachi. She had long hair. The front of her dress was open. Her breasts, resting on her forearms, swelled out like melons. She was, like the sea, reaching out to an unknown world.

"Butrus!" she shouted.

A barefooted urchin not much older than himself stopped to look up.

She waved her bangled arm at him. "Butrus, go fetch me water to wash myself." Another woman appeared at her side. They talked in loud voices and laughed. Just then the door of the house opened and Malachi saw his brother Leib come out into the street. He looked to his left, to his right, then walked briskly away. For an instant their eyes met. Or so it seemed to Malachi. He never was sure if Leib actually saw him and pretended he didn't. But on the way home he was strangely silent and broody.

Malachi loved Leib more than he loved Tiqva or his other brother Chaim. Loved him, in fact, almost as much as he loved his father whom, in his boyish mind, Leib complemented. Tiqva was difficult to love: she was intensely private, unpredictably irritable. Chaim was distant, not only geographically—he lived and studied in Jerusalem. A clever, fastidious young man of nineteen, Chaim disliked the country; he was contemptuous of Petach Tiqva. Leib was here, ever close, brusque but caring; deeply serious in spite of his frequent frivolity; a rebel yet a conformist; warm even in his terrible anger. Above all, loyal. Malachi could never understand why Leib and Tiqva were so close to each other. At times, he felt envious of them. Chaim, on the rare occasions when they met, would go out of his way to be nice to him but Malachi always felt ill at ease with him. Tiqva he couldn't reach: she would simply shut him out. There was no getting through the barrier of her privacy. But Leib, oh he knew and understood him, intuitively; knew his strengths and his weaknesses. He could hurt Leib. Therefore he loved him.

But he never wanted to be like Leib or anybody else, not even like his father whom he knew was the best, the wisest, with the strongest will among men. Somewhere in the distance of later life, a special destiny awaited him, Malachi believed; his world was out of the common run of things, full of strange creatures and hitherto unseen landscapes. Dangerous and magical. How lucky he was to be able to move in such a world. How lucky and lonely, like being stamped with some rare feature that sets you apart from the rest. Except that nobody realized this. Only his mother had some understanding of the kind of boy he was, not his father who in his frustration would sometimes take the strap to him, and certainly not Leib. One day, when he had learnt to concentrate the full power of his imagination, he would be able to make things happen just by making pictures in his mind, he told himself.

A spotted dog, outcast from Amlabes, which always hung about the store begging for scraps of food, lumbered out from the shadow across the street and stretched itself. Ugly animal, with a yellow stare and cropped ears for falahin cut the ears of their dogs down to a stump so that the rain would keep them awake at night. You could count the ribs on the dog's flanks, so thin it was. But it was a harmless dog and a good deal more alert than the few village hounds that often turned on it and chased it away.

Malachi was contemplating throwing a stone to make the dog jump, maybe bark and wake Mendle, when suddenly it stiffened and stood staring in the direction of the village's eastern approach, ear stumps pricked. Malachi could see nothing. But the dog just stood there, fixed. Then it lifted its muzzle to let out a drawn howl before retreating down the street. Mendle the blacksmith went on sleeping. Beyond the village, a few stunted carob trees quivered in the heat. The dog was barking sharply now, as when an intruder approaches. Then Malachi saw the horseman.

He appeared all of a sudden, a blurred outline buckled by the heat. He moved forward, or so it seemed, in a prancing motion, the horse's hooves hardly touching the ground. Now Malachi could see the lance's point high above the rider's turbaned head, steady as a pivot from which rider and horse might have been suspended. The man sat very straight in the saddle. His face was covered with a black veil that came down from his turban. As he drew near, he loosened it and let it fall to one side. He had the strangest face Malachi had ever seen. It reminded him of a buzzard he had once seen on a broken tree by the river, impassive expression, remote yet watchful. But oh, how magnificent was the horse! Tall, well-rounded and rippling with light. No Beduin Sheik was ever seen riding such a noble animal.

The man on his black, electric horse, might have ridden through the village and out the other side, armed as he was with a lance and sword, and still, for all the dog's frantic barking, Mendle was asleep, and nobody was coming out to see what was happening.

Malachi ran across the street to the bell. It hung a little higher than he could reach, and the hammer that lay beside it was heavy. Holding it with both hands, he swung at the bell, giving it only a glancing blow, but enough to wake up Mendle, who blinked, then rose to his feet and reached for his belt that hung over the banister. He might have set upon Malachi with his belt if the boy hadn't gestured wildly in the direction of the horseman who now was within yards of the village entrance. So Mendle stood gaping and rubbing his eyes, then looking at Malachi as though expecting instructions. Meanwhile the horseman reined in and stood perfectly still a little way from Yoel's house, amidst the shifting dust. The lance point remained high; Malachi would have wanted to see the point lowered and shot through the village's sleepy street propelled by the charge of the amazing horse. The rider hesitated, looked at the boy and the man with his impassive stare, and would not move.

"Just one of them," Mendle muttered, gripping the hammer, "and on the eve of Sabbath too."

"Maybe he's the leader, maybe a hundred more are waiting beyond the trees for him to give the sign to attack," Malachi suggested.

Mendle rubbed his nose. "You think so? Nah, he's a stranger, not from these parts I can tell. Must have lost his way. What is there here to attack? What is there here to steal? And he has no gun. . . ." Still he gripped the hammer and moved closer to the bell. "And the boys are away in Jaffa. . . ."

"Talk to him, Mendle. No, strike the bell first, then talk to him," Malachi said.

"Wake up everybody? For what? Maybe all he wants is water for himself and his horse."

Malachi grew excited. "Just water? Look at him, have you ever seen such a face, such a horse? He doesn't need water, he needs nothing! He could, he could. . . ."

The horseman passed Yoel's house at a walk and was drawing near them. He looked at them undecided whether to greet them or not. Mendle lunged towards the bell and gave it a mighty whack. The ring was flat and cracked. Nevertheless, the horse shied and reared, and for a moment the rider looked humanly vulnerable.

The people of Petach Tiqva didn't rush out to the street weapons in hand. Here a window swung open, and a head stuck out, there a sleepy man appeared at his front door, his shirt front unbuttoned. Slowly they came out and gathered at the sides of the street to look at the stranger. Until Zeligman came out and stood in the middle of the street, squinting, feet apart, cradling his frontiersman repeating rifle in the crook of his arm.

Because Zeligman looked ready to face a challenge, it was towards him that the horseman advanced. The horse cantered at a walking pace, like a rocking horse. The rider's face showed neither alarm nor aggression, in fact nothing at all. The lance remained high, steadier than ever. When he was only a few paces away from Zeligman, who hadn't budged an inch, the horseman suddenly smiled and said in a throaty Hebrew, "Shalom, peace and blessings of Abraham, Isaac and Jacob be upon you."

Chapter 32

He was Malachi's discovery, if not his creation. No one could or wanted to deny him that. From far-flung zones he had pulled in the miraculous warrior, awakened his spirit, stirred the quivering power of his horse, and bade him ride to dusty somnolent Petach Tiqva on that Friday afternoon, when not even Leib's impending arrival with the provisions from Jaffa could promise to give distinction to a dull Sabbath. And to think he was Jewish! Who had ever seen such a Jew, unless in some fantastical dreams?

But Yahya Salem Tahari—even the name conjured unknown, distant wildernesses—would not be owned, nor credit Malachi with as much as a nod of the head.

Tahari unsaddled his horse and fed it at Mendle's yard. He indicated that he would welcome a stay in the village, and Mr Zeligman, having been denied a confrontation, was eager to play the host. This, however, Tahari declined in a manner that was at once courteous and appreciative. Instead he accepted the humbler facilities of Mendle's household, so that he might be close to his beloved horse.

Everybody in the village, most of all Leib and his friends, wanted to know about the stranger. So Gutman, whose sense for the occasion never failed, improvised a feast and invited all who cared to come.

In the front room Malachi watched his brother Leib comb his beard before the broken mirror. Leib, stripped to the waist, except for his talith bodice, caught his boy brother's critical gaze in the mirror, and turned.

"Have you nothing better to do but stand there gawping?" he asked. Malachi shrugged his shoulders. He had already washed and dressed.

"Will you take your pistol along?"

Leib laughed. "On the Sabbath? What will you think of next! And what do I need the pistol for at Gutman's home, eh?"

"For show, you like to show," Malachi said.

"Cheeky! I'll *show* you something if you don't go away!" There was a note of irritation in his laughter as he reached for his belt.

"If it weren't for me he might've ridden right through the street and out at the other end and nobody'd have known. He mightn't have come at all."

"Is that so!"

"Yes."

"Well, what do you want me to do, give you a prize?"

"I don't need prizes."

"So what do you want?"

"Nothing. Only that you should know when you sit next to him, as though you brought him from Jaffa yourself, with the goods."

"Ho ho, so that's what this is all about, is it?" Leib said and reached for Malachi's head. "You make him out to be I don't know what, the Messiah, or something."

Malachi dodged. "Then why are you standing in front of the mirror all the time, trying to make your beard look bigger?"

"Very well, little brother. I'll see to it that you sit right on his knee, if he'd have you. As for me, I'm interested in his horse."

Because of the number of guests and the atmosphere he wanted to create, Gutman did away with the table. The simple fare was arranged on bits of carpet and other suitable spreads which had been borrowed from neighbours and the guests sat eastern-fashion on cushions. Positioned thus, among his guests, Gutman had a fleeting sense that he was reaching far into their common origin, while outside the swallows made their last swoops through the lavender-tinted sky.

Malachi found himself sitting among the children, nowhere near the visitor's knee, as Leib had promised. From there he was able to watch every movement on Tahari's face, but barely hear a word he spoke.

But Tahari hardly spoke a word. His language was one of gentle gestures and looks. He listened intently, observed all that was taking place around him, and when Gutman said the prayers, he shut his eyes and his lips moved, as though he were trying to remember what he had once known, a long time ago, early in his life. Malachi admired his restraint; everything he did seemed calculated with utmost economy. How coarse by comparison all the others were, most particularly Leib whose bull-like strength looked clumsy beside the refined disciplined power of the stranger. Only Mendle was unmoved by the occasion. He sat quietly stuffing food into his rubbery mouth, Tahari was just another man to him. He had done his bit, rang the bell, didn't he? There had been no calamity. Calamities were the only stuff of life that could agitate Mendle.

Everybody wanted to hear how Yahya Salem Tahari chanced into Petach Tiqva, and from where. They had seen him pray; no one doubted any longer that he was in fact a Jew. Tahari was in no hurry to tell his story. The Sabbath songs visibly moved him. He sat with his eyes half-shut, listening to the songs, rocking gently. And watching him, Malachi understood that to him the street of Petach Tiqva, the men who now sat around him, not least Gutman's home, were as exotic and mysterious as he himself was to them.

Tahari could recite prayers in Hebrew but his language was Arabic which he spoke with the thin sharp accent of the southern Beduin. Throughout the meal he had said hardly a word. But later, when pressed by his host, he prepared to tell his story. Now Leib, whose Arabic as well as warriors' jargon could be trusted, was called to his side to translate his words.

In the depths of Arabia, Tahari began, there was an ancient tribe of Hebrews. It was a proud warlike tribe which traced its lineage to King Solomon and has lived and fought with Arab tribes long before the emergence of Islam. This tribe, which had once been feared and respected, has all but vanished: its people have died, drifted away, or merged with the Arabs. Now only a few families have survived, to one of which Tahari belonged. An old Tora scroll, handed down from generation to generation and jealously guarded, was the only thing that kept their Jewish identity alive. So submerged was their Judaism in the customs and idiom of the people amongst whom they lived, that the Arabs took them to be members of some eccentric deviant of Islam. They were left in peace, in so far as peace could be found in that turbulent part of the world. "A man may lose his strength with age, and his senses fail him. But his name survives and gives him respect among the people. So it was with us," Tahari explained. "We were few, we no longer had wealth or power, our herds were small, our horses few. But people remembered what we once were. Bards at festivals would recite our deeds, and so the respect we had outlived our prowess.

"My mare", Tahari continued, "is a rare, beautiful creature of the noblest blood. She is the eye of my life, my heart and soul. Her dam, herself a peerless mare, died at her birth. 'Ya Salem Ibn Masud,' people said to me, 'this poor orphan will surely not live another week!' But I fed the foal on camel's milk until she could eat by herself. Such a beautiful foal was not to be seen anywhere. I hunted gazelles and put them with her in a large enclosure so that she might learn speed and agility from them. I called her Ahwa, Wind, for she was as fast and as light as the morning wind from the west. And when I rode her people looked and said: 'There goes Yahya Salem Bin Masud Tahari on his mare which is fit for kings.'"

Malachi looked at Tahari's hands; they were small, delicate and dark; hands for gesturing where words failed. He couldn't imagine them wielding a sword or a lance.

Tahari's heavy-lidded eyes became doleful, then fierce. "But people are greedy and jealous of others' good fortunes," he went on. "When it was seen that Ahwa could outstrip any horse ever raced against her, and after I'd turned away all the men, agents of Sheiks from distant parts, who sought to buy her, threats were made. 'Sell the horse, Yahya,' my old father told me, 'for it will bring you nothing but sorrow.' How could I answer, except to say that to sell Ahwa was worse than to sell my soul?

"One night, I remember it so well, it was a dark night and the wind was high, the kind of night when raids are made and thieves do their work, I heard the dogs bark louder than usual, and some shouts. The men were shouting that thieves were rustling the goats. Like the others, I grabbed my sword and rushed out into the night. We heard the thieves retreat and gave them chase. When we returned to the camp I realized what had happened and how I had been fooled. Ahwa my mare, who had been tethered to a post by my tent, was gone.

"For a year I wandered in search of her. I swore before the elders and the entire *hamula* that I would avenge my dishonour. But they only shook their heads and said they knew all the time this would come about, for such a horse would put his owner's life in constant danger.

"Banishment from one's home and family needn't come from an act of others but from your own heart," Tahari said with a sigh."And so it was with me, the loss of the one thing I loved, and the hope, which seemed at times no more than a dream that one day I shall find it. When I left my people it occurred to me that I may never see them again."

Of all the things Tahari had said, nothing moved Malachi so much as his leavetaking from his people; the terrible finality of it—trajecting himself as it were, into the unknown, never to see his family and friends again. "It's like dying," Malachi thought, because he couldn't conceive of death as a total void. It occurred to him all of a sudden that Tahari might be a ghost, someone from the past accidentally strayed into Petach Tiqva to remind them all of something and that he, Malachi was the only one to realize this.

"In the desert there are no boundaries. Time is meaningless," Tahari went on, sounding spectral to Malachi's ears. "You drift like sand. Each night at a different camp fire, when you look at the sky the stars tell you new things about yourself. The night chill distances you from the heat of the day. You shrink one day, you swell the next. Days, weeks, months pass, you lose count, and what you'd set out to find becomes a vague idea. The quest becomes an end in itself, like a ghostly hunt with never a quarry in sight.

"There were nights of splendour. Sitting in the tents of Sheiks I'd hear stories of heroism, listen to the bards sing of past, fantastic deeds which you could believe only for the night, under those cold blazing stars, while the horses stood motionless in the dark, and the hawks, hooded, brooded on their perches. On such nights I would try to find a meaning in my people's past and weave into it the heroism, love and hate and fear and revenge I was hearing about in the stories of the bards. Not the Jews, *dhimmies* and Children of Death the Arabs always talked about, but warriors, like King David, Joshua, all those stories the elders of my tribe used to tell us children. How vividly I recalled them during those nights in the desert, among the Beduin whose language I spoke, who received me as a brother yet who one of them I was not." He paused to take a sip from his coffee tumbler and the magic by which it seemed to Malachi he was communicating directly and solely with him, was momentarily broken as he became aware of his brother Leib, rounding off the last translated sentence.

"One day I heard that preparations were being made for a great *fantasia*, to celebrate the wedding of a wealthy Sheik's son. Horsemen from all over the country were coming to the feast, to pit their skill against one another, and test the speed of their horses. A certain horseman, a renowned warrior who had fought in battles all over Arabia, and had made a pilgrimage to Mecca, was said to be going there. Men talked of his horse, a mare of surpassing beauty and speed. My heart leapt as I heard the mare's description, and at the same time I was filled with foreboding. I knew, as if a prophecy was about to come true, that my wandering was at its end, that at last I was about to be reunited with my mare, Ahwa.

"We rode there, a company of guests and kinsmen who invited me to come along, a day's ride from the camp where I was staying. My mount was a humble one, I knew I could not participate with pride in the races, and I racked my mind for a plan of how I should retrieve my Ahwa if indeed it was she whom the warrior rode. Who would believe me if I said she was my horse which had been stolen from me?

"The wedding feast was splendid. Many lambs were slaughtered. Black tents spread out among the palm trees of the oasis. There were many horses, camels, flocks of goats, so much colour. . . ." Tahari's eyes shone. "And all the while I was praying in my heart 'let me see Ahwa, but not too soon, not before I'd surfeited of the splendour, not before I'd heard the stories and believed them'.

"Many fine men came, young men, strong, eager to prove themselves. And the elders, the wisest as ever got together under the desert sky. But I did not see the famed warrior with the legendary horse. Then, on the night before the great fantasia, after the guests had presented their gifts and praised the bride and bridegroom, after I had given a five-jewelled dagger to the bridegroom, I went for a stroll before retiring for the night. It was a moonless night but the stars were so bright that the sand around the oasis gleamed white. I had reached the boundary of the camp and was about to turn back when I saw the horse, and my heart nearly stopped. Tethered to a lanyard of a tent alongside another fine bay colt, I recognized my Ahwa. Her unlawful owner must have arrived late that day unnoticed by me. As I drew near, Ahwa pricked her ears and neighed softly. That noble sound was like music to my ears, I would have recognized it among a thousand horses. And she too recognized me, for she neighed and pulled at her tether. I went up to her and stroked her neck and head, and she pushed her muzzle into me as if to say, 'Where have you been so long, how did you let me be taken away from you?'

"Should I have taken her there and then and ridden off? All the best of the desert tribes were gathered there, the Tarabins, the Sarahin, Bani

Sukre from up north across the Jordan River, and the Wahabis from the south. A horse of blood has honour and pride, like a prince. A horse like Ahwa cannot be sneaked away in the middle of the night. I didn't have the heart to deprive her of glory in the races that were to take place the next day. Thoughts like this passed through my mind as I stood there holding her. But I knew that if I didn't take her that night I'd lose her for ever. May God forgive me, I resolved, after much painful deliberation, to take what was mine like a coward, in the hour of the night, when all were asleep, for the thought of parting with my horse again was unbearable.

"At the darkest hour of night, when nothing could be heard but the snoring of the men in their tents, when even the dogs relaxed their vigil, I took my belongings and stole out of the tent. Ahwa might have been expecting me, for she was alert. I saddled her quickly, untethered her and was about to mount. She agitated and neighed. Then, to my horror I heard stirring within the tent. Before I could mount the man who had stolen her from me, that renowned warrior, came out, sword in hand and set upon me in great fury. We fought. I slew him."

Silence fell as Leib translated the last of Tahari's words. A man who confessed to having killed another man was sitting at the Sabbath table; the very idea was stunning, all the more so to Malachi who could imagine it all so vividly. Leib often boasted he could, and would kill if he were forced to. Malachi almost believed him. But Leib was talk, and a pistol was not nearly as deathlike as a sword: the Angel of Death used a sword not a gun.

"After that," Tahari broke the silence, "I knew my life wasn't worth a grain of sand among the Beduin tribes. I rode north. I'd heard stories about Jews in this land, I've heard about Jews who lived like farmers, here. I looked for you. I found you."

When they went back home that night, Leib didn't speak a word. When Malachi tried to ask him about Tahari, Leib put his hand on his head affectionately, but wouldn't be drawn out. Malachi had never seen him so wrapped in thought.

It became plain that Yahya Salem Tahari would gladly stay in Petach Tiqva if he were allowed to. That he would engage in none of the village's daily chores was equally clear. He was like a rare exhibit. He hung about Mendle's house with his lance and sword on display. People, the boys in particular, came to look at him and the magnificent horse. The women brought him food. Tahari sat there receiving the gifts and attention with nothing more than a nod of the head and a smile. Sometimes, as if to break the monotony, he would mount his mare and canter up and down the street under the admiring eyes of the folks. The street was his domain; he wouldn't stray from it. There was no question of his going out even to look at the fields where the men were working.

The men of Petach Tiqva took council among themselves. Mendle was happy to give the stranger room under his roof and to share his food with him for he was lonely. But his means were humble, it wouldn't be for long that he could afford to keep Tahari even though he ate little and was generally undemanding. The mare, unlike her master, ate a great deal.

No one had the heart to tell Tahari to leave. For the older men his charm, pitched so high by his exotic appearance in the village, had begun to wane. He had no money. His customs were alien. He seemed disdainful of work—to what use could he be put? But for all that, he was a Jew, a fugitive from Gentile vengeance. That alone demanded that shelter must be given him. But what if the violence he had fled should catch up with him and embroil Petach Tiqva in a feud they had no part in nor wished to have? It was difficult enough being in a semi-wilderness surrounded by unpredictable Arabs, with the Ottomans' grudging eye on the village, without having a stranger importing his troubles. Such were the sentiments of the men who sat down to discuss what was to be done with Tahari. Meanwhile, the young firebrands of the village—Leib and his friends—gathered round Tahari, trying to gauge his warlike skills, which made it all the harder for the elders to reach a decision. There was no denying, Petach Tiqva needed a trusty watchman to guard the livestock and the crops, and Tahari seemed, if nothing else, eminently suited for the job. Except that Zeligman had his doubts: he alone was unimpressed by the stranger, and once he expressed his doubts, he was joined by others, Ragner among them. "There's something about the man I don't like," Zeligman said, "I don't know what it is. Besides, even a bad gun is worth a dozen swords."

Because opinion was so divided, no decision was made; those who looked favourably on Tahari—Gutman, Stamper and David Joshua foremost among them—hoped he would take on the guard duties to earn his keep. The most the opposers could do was hope that Tahari would get bored and leave of his own accord.

When Yoel Zeff returned to Petach Tiqva, a strange spectacle greeted him. It was early evening when he crossed the river with Zora Barnet, heading for the village. The muffled tinkling of bells was carried on the breeze. Amlabes' flocks of sheep were homeward bound. It was a welcome sound to Yoel's ears reassuring him that all was well. His stay in Jerusalem had made him doubly appreciative of the familiar sounds of Petach Tiqva and her surroundings. He looked at Barnet to see if he too were enjoying the return as much as he did. The two friends winked at one another. Barnet said: "Thank the Lord we're back, not a day too soon." He had hardly said this when they heard the sound of pounding hooves and shouts coming from beyond the bluff where there was a field recently levelled. Barnet looked at Yoel, eyebrows raised, then they both spurred their mounts and cantered towards the commotion.

A line of posts had been stuck into the ground at intervals of thirty paces or so along the entire length of the field. From each pole hung a melon in a string cradle. The young men of Petach Tiqva, riding at a full gallop, were tilting at the melons with improvised lances. So engrossed they were in their game that they didn't see Yoel and Barnet rein in above them on the edge of the bluff. But Tahari, astride his mare, lance in hand, did, and pulled short just as he was steadying his mount for the charge.

"You'd think melons grow just like that, for the asking, the way these boys are splitting them," Barnet said gruffly, because he was so astonished he couldn't think of anything else to say. At that moment Tahari decided to charge, and levelling his lance, let his mare cannon forward. Through the dust Yoel saw Leib's face, glowing like raw meat. And all of a sudden he was shouting at the top of his voice, "What's all this? Have you gone mad?"

Tahari heard Yoel's angry shout in the middle of his tilt. He swung the point of his lance from the approaching melon and veered away, Leib's eyes were like burning coals as he glared at his father.

It was a sombre evening at the Zeff home. Leib didn't come home that night. He was angry. When he was angry like that he didn't think of what he was saying. He didn't want a row with his father which he knew they would both later regret. So he stayed overnight with a friend, Benjamin Daskal who had already established for himself a reputation as a fearless fighter although he was nearly five years younger than Leib.

Yoel washed and straightaway went over to Gutman's home. A group of men were there, talking heatedly. He was told about Tahari, the controversy he had aroused in the village. The men now waited for his judgement. He said, "We can't allow this man to set an example to our young men. We've come here and fought against nature not in order to become Beduin warriors. We're God-fearing farmers. I worry about my son Leib. What I saw this evening as I rode in fills me with foreboding." He paused. "On the other hand, we cannot turn this man out. No, this we mustn't do."

"What then, Reb Yoel? Explain to him? He doesn't understand our ways. Behind the Jewish front he's an Arab, a Beduin," Raab said.

"Beneath the Arab exterior he's a Jew, my dear Raab," Gutman said softly.

"He can be made to understand," Yoel said, "and when he understands and accepts he will be employed as watchman. He'll be given lodging and a wage. That's what I suggest."

"Employed for a wage, like an Arab?" Raab said.

"David Ragner too was employed," Gutman put in.

Zeligman raised his hand. He was the only one in Petach Tiqva to do that rather than push into the conversation. "If we dismiss our Arab watchman and give the work instead to this Tahari, the Arab will become vengeful. He has friends. There'll be much robbery."

"Then we'll see how good Tahari really is," Raab laughed.

"No, we'll have to keep the Arab watchman. Zeligman is right. But one watchman's not enough. Tahari will be the second one," Yoel said.

The news that the Jews had a warrior soon got round. The shabab—young bloods from the surrounding Arab villages—came riding, skirting Petach Tiqva to look at Tahari, to assess him. He, for his part, ignored them. He would ride some distance from them deliberately slow, watchful yet apparently indifferent. Not a stick was stolen from Petach Tiqva since he had made it his business to guard the property.

A party of ten men, all dignitaries from the proud village of Yahudia, was making its way to Petach Tiqva. The men were led by the village Mukhtar, Sheik Nazim Hadad Abu Latif. Sheik Nazim had misgivings about the visit. Affairs between Arabs should be settled among Arabs, he believed. He didn't want to be beholden to Jews. Moreover, he had made it a ruling principle in life never to ask for something he wasn't certain would be granted; there was no telling how the Jews would respond to appeals. To be indebted to Jews was bad enough; to be refused by them was an indignity Nazim Abu Latif couldn't face. But the situation called for unprecedented measures, and Sheik Nazim yielded—against his better judgement—to the opinions of the others, including that of his eldest son Latif. He had not forgotten past clashes with the Jews of Petach Tiqva, and how they had surprised him by their raw courage. Perhaps he was wrong, perhaps he was too firmly locked into the past, in convention, and getting old. He rode at the head of the party, silently brooding.

The fields were empty. Weeds and thistles grew from the cracks in the earth among the stubble where the corn had been harvested. Only the spread-out beds of melons, where the ripening fruit lay belly to the sun, provided a smear of quenching green to the parched land. High in the sultry sky, kites were riding the thermal drifts. A watchman kept an eye on the approaching party from aloft a raised platform of stakes and reed mats erected among the melon beds. The men were not armed, except with the customary dagger that was a part of every Arab male's dress. They wanted to emphasize their peaceful intent. They were carrying gifts, two lambs and two kids bound and bleating, across the saddle pommels. Abu Latif had insisted on utmost discretion: the parley was to be short and to the point. No ceremony beyond that which was necessary for politeness. And secrecy was to be observed.

In Petach Tiqva they knew about the coming visit, for earlier Abu Latif had sent a messenger to fix the time and day. Only the purpose was not revealed. In Gutman's home the leaders of Petach Tiqva gathered to meet their visitors, their neighbours and one-time adversaries. No expenses had been spared on the hospitality: nobody wanted the Arabs to come away saying the Jews were anything but generous in their hospitality, particularly if whatever it was the Arabs wanted could not be given.

New mats, recently purchased in Jaffa, were spread on the floor, decorated with bits of carpet and colourful cushions. In the kitchen, the formal repast was laid out ready to be served: *labna*, the sweet-sour clotted cheese favoured by the Arabs and now by the Jews of Petach Tiqva, freshly-baked pitta spiced with basil and sesame, sweetmeats, and the coffee, ready to be boiled with cardamom. The women departed; they were not to be seen during the conference. Presently Mendle the blacksmith came running to announce that the Arabs were in the village. "I don't know what they want. Whatever it is, they've not come here just to be nice to us. So sit and listen. We show nothing of what we feel or think, no matter what they say," Yoel instructed.

"We commit ourselves to nothing beyond what's reasonably expected of neighbours."

"Reasonably," Gutman emphasized for good measure.

"Leib, son, you sit next to me and see you keep your tongue in check. This is time for prudence and discretion." Leib scowled but said nothing.

The visitors' mounts were tethered outside Gutman's home, in the shade of a reed awning. A crowd gathered and watched in silence as the Arabs were greeted at the door by Gutman and Yoel. Inside, after the handshaking and exchange of greetings, Jews and Arabs faced each other across the mat, and began to eat. When they had finished there was expectant silence until Nazim Abu Latif began to speak.

"It's been a good year, Abu Assad," said the Sheik. He called Yoel Father of the Lion, which was what the name Leib meant.

"We can't complain, blessed be the Lord," Yoel replied smiling courteously. "And I trust things have been good for you too."

The Sheik gave a thin smile, "Allah has been merciful. There has been no sickness, the harvest was good and the flocks multiplied."

"I thank you for the lambs and the kids, fine specimens they are. May you have many like them and may we be blessed in your friendship."

"May there be peace and brotherhood among us for ever, Abu Assad," Nazim said, and touched his breast. He was a handsome, dignified man, darker and taller than his fellow villagers and kinsmen, for he boasted Beduin blood of distinguished lineage. Yoel couldn't help admiring him hardly less than did Leib who didn't take his eyes off him for a moment. A good neighbour, said the Sheik, was a true blessing, like rain at the right time, like a good healthy son. He burped discreetly. When one had good neighbours, there was no need for a recourse to the law, differences could be settled amicably and in mutual respect. Yoel responded cautiously and they both disparaged the Ottomans with polite indirectness. At last the Sheik came to the point of his visit.

"Abu Assad," he said, "when first you came to settle on this land, we thought you wouldn't last a winter. But Allah is with you, you've done well, there's no denying that. We've had our differences. Most neighbours do. But we've also helped you on more than one occasion. We've learnt to understand each other. We have common interests, and common worries." He paused.

Leib felt his pulse quickening.

"Therefore there comes a time when neighbours should stand together to protect their common interests."

Yoel said gravely, "What's on your mind, Sheik?"

"You know we belong to the tribe of El Kashek," the Sheik began, "and our enemies from time immemorial have been the tribe of Amir Al Harati whose land lies to the north by the Hawarat Valley. They're like this to us," Nazim Abu Latif grabbed his own throat in a savage gesture. "Have you ever seen locusts descend on a field? The Al Harati are like that. They leave nothing but waste behind.

"For years they have plundered our fields, stolen our sheep, humiliated our young men. We have fought them, our men acquitted themselves bravely. But the Al Harati are many and warlike, they have more warriors than we have, too many for us to fight alone." Nazim's gaze swept across, alighting on his hosts, one after another.

"Is it necessary to fight?" Gutman half-stated, half-asked.

The Sheik guessed the question which was said in Yiddish and not translated.

"Not more than a week ago there was a fight over pasture. The young men lost their heads. Shots were fired. Sheik Amir Al Harati's son was killed." He paused. When he next spoke, his words were directed at Yoel. "The time of reckoning between them and us has come, Abu Assad. We don't want an all-out war, believe me. But there's no avoiding it any longer. There's no question of a *sulcha* this time. They'll not agree to a reconciliation. Blood will avenge blood."

Yoel took his time answering, aware of the grave consequences of anything he might say. "And you've come to ask for our help, Sheik Abu Latif. What help do you think we can give your people?"

Abu Latif's mouth twitched ever so slightly. "I've heard stories about your young men exercising on their horses out in the fields. They ride and shoot well, you must be proud of them. We've also seen the Beduin warrior who lives with you. I've heard stories about him. The Al Harati have a few Beduin tribesmen from south of the Jordan riding with them."

"Our young men are not experienced in war, they're hardly more than boys, Sheik. And the man you mentioned is a Jew. He has a sword and a lance, just that. We know next to nothing about him." Again he paused. "We cannot give you an answer right away, Sheik. This is a most important matter. We have to talk about it among ourselves, this is our way. But tomorrow before evening I shall come to your home and tell you what Petach Tiqva will do to help Yahudia."

"I shall be waiting," said Nazim Abu Latif in a weary voice, and rose to his feet.

Leib kept silent all evening. When at last he was alone with his father he could contain himself no longer. The crack as he slapped his thigh made Yoel turn and stare.

"What is it with you?" he said sharply. "Hardly more than boys! I never thought I'd live to see the day when I'd feel ashamed of you," Leib shouted.

"Don't raise your voice at me, Leib!"

"You made us look like cowards!"

Yoel crossed the room and seized Leib by the wrist.

"You think you know what's courage Leib? Look at your hand."

Yoel tightened his grasp on Leib's wrist and shook it.

"Do you know what that is? A hand, a miracle of creation, capable of the subtlest of work, a hand Leib, to create, to write down thoughts. What do you do with it?" His voice rose, he was white with anger. "You use it like a hammer, to thump and hit. An ape can do that! Is that what you call courage? I'll tell you what is courage. Courage is steadfastness. Courage is patience and endurance. Courage is faith. Yes, Leib, think of your great grandfather Solomon and your grandfather Israel when you think of courage, courage is knowing when to withhold."

"That's old men's excuses, not courage," Leib roared and wrenched his hand free. "Shame, shame on us all!" The violence of his movement threw Yoel against the wall. For a moment he stared at his son in disbelief. Then he whipped out his belt. "You rude, blaspheming whelp," he said, and swung at Leib.

Awoken by the noise, Malachi scampered out of bed to peep through the crack in the door. Leib just stood there, not even raising his arms to shield his face against the lashing blows. Tears of rage were flowing down his cheeks. He kept repeating after each blow "shame". Malachi trembled. So petrified he was that he didn't feel Tiqva's hands on his shoulders trying to pull him away from the door. Then Hannah came flying out of the bedroom, her hair down. She threw herself between Leib and the lashing belt. Malachi heard her scream, "Is this what we've come to? Father against son? Better pack our things and go back to Jerusalem. What's becoming of you! animals, peasants!"

At last it was quiet. Except for Tiqva's sobbing from her bed across the room. It wasn't that which kept Malachi awake. Leib's shouting still rang in his ears. How it had stunned him. By the time he had recovered sufficiently to run to the door, his father was talking to Leib, words Malachi didn't fully understand but recognized intuitively as wise and right. The image of his father's hurt face as Leib pushed his against the wall burnt like fire in his head. Such a look of sadness he had never seen in his father's eyes before. Yes, sadness, even as he was thrashing Leib. His father, wise and strong, more dependable than anything in the whole world, had all at once become victim to Leib's toughness.

"Abba, Abba, Father," Malachi whispered to himself again and again, loving him more fiercely than ever, hoping in vain that saying the word would assuage his anguish now as it had done so many times in the past. Then like persistent thrusts, like Tiqva's sobs, it came to him that Leib's defiance of their father's authority signalled a new order of things: nothing he trusted and had always taken for granted—forebearance, the wisdom of courage not mere raw bravery, quiet decency—was certain any longer. He felt abandoned; he became frightened. He began to cry like Tiqva, and for once he felt close to her.

In the morning Leib rose earlier than usual and left for the fields without a word. Yoel washed, ate a light breakfast of bread and cheese, then left for the morning prayers at the synagogue. After the prayers, he met the community leaders at Gutman's home. He had made up his mind about what Petach Tiqva's answer to Sheik Nazim Abu Latif should be. And if the others approved, he proposed to ride over to Yahudia with Stamper and David Joshua to tell the Sheik. The message was plain: the people of Petach Tiqva supported the people of Yahudia in their moment of trial but would not fight alongside them. Fighting was alien to Jews and abhorrent to them except in the most extreme case of self-defence. It was in the nature of Jews, and their custom, to turn to the law for protection, however imperfect that law was, for which reason, Petach Tiqva would never ask Yahudia to fight for them. But because there was friendship with Yahudia, Petach Tiqva was ready to take and look after all of Yahudia's livestock and other movable property until the men of Yahudia returned, with God's help, victorious from the battle. And if the women and children needed anything, this too, Petach Tiqva would give of anything they had to give.

The men thought the message good, only it had to be worded carefully, diplomatically, so as not to offend in any way. Towards noon, they reached an agreement on the wording and after rehearsing it, Yoel and his two companions set out.

When they returned late in the afternoon, they found the village in a turmoil. Men and women were milling around the well in Hovevei Zion Square. There was shouting as people kept going in and out of the school where a meeting seemed in progress. A little way from the commotion sat Salem Tahari, smoking quietly. A few of his pupils from among the young men were with him, but not Leib. The three had hardly dismounted when they were summoned to the meeting.

The uproar, it turned out, was not over the message delivered to Sheik Nazim Abu Latif. That, having been inaccurately propagated in the course of the day, now had as many versions as people anxious to argue it. What sent the folks of Petach Tiqva rushing vociferously to the meeting hall was the fact that so important a decision had been taken without a public debate. And to make matters worse the official representative of the Lovers of Zion Movement, who ran the village's accounts, had not even been told. Zalman Aharonowitz knew about money matters and also a little about agronomy. Apart from that he understood nothing except the importance of his position. He sat at the platform table, sombre and indignant, now shaking his head, now nodding. Gutman and the others who had, with Yoel Zeff, met Abu Latif and decided on Petach Tiqva's response to his appeal, sat together to the right of the table; they did not look like men at the dock but like leaders, assured of their authority but conceding to the displeasure of their people.

Yoel rose to speak. The tremors of the audience reached him. He was instinctively aware that the agitation carried little dissent. It was anxiety and—among the young men—excitement at the possibility that Petach Tiqva could get involved in Arab tribal warfare, that stirred the people. These he could allay. Standing in front of the men and women whose lives were a part of his own, he knew he had support, that the trust between them had never been reduced. He saw Hannah and Tiqva among the women, Malachi with them. Then, as his gaze swept the crowded room, it fell on Leib, tight-mouthed and dark among his peers who clustered round him.

Yoel apologized. He explained that Gutman, Stamper, David Joshua, himself and the others had acted in good faith. It had not been their intention to by-pass the assembly. The need for a speedy response had dictated their action. As for the matter itself, it was a straightforward decision, in line with the common thinking on such matters. The group had merely anticipated what the assembly was bound to decide.

He had spoken in a reasoned measured tone. In the audience heads were nodding. Zalman Aharonowitz too began to nod because he wasn't sure what was expected of him. But a voice from the end of the room cried out, "He calls a war a simple thing, as though we had one every day!" Now the shouts and the heckling began. Yoel shouted above the din, asking for silence. Then he went on to give a factual account of the message, of the last meeting with Abu Latif, and his response. When he had finished it was clear that the majority approved of what had been done and were prepared to let the matter rest with a mild show of disapproval at the proceedings of the action. But Leib suddenly raised his arm and stepped forward.

He avoided his father's eyes but looked long and hard at the assembly and finally at his friends who now pushed to the foreground. His voice was quiet: "What do you do when your neighbour's house is on fire? Do you say to him 'Let me look after your valuables' or do you rush to his aid? Who do you call a friend? A neighbour who sits by while your house is being robbed? A coward, not a friend. That's what I'd call him. That's what the people of Yahudia will call us. Could you blame them?

"If the people of Yahudia are defeated, they'll hate us for ever. If they win, they'll be contemptuous of us." Leib paused only to let his anger rise. He spoke again, in a louder voice, "We're supposed to listen to our elders and abide by their decisions. I say nothing against them. Their honour rests intact. They made Petach Tiqva what it is. But there is the future. One thing must be clear to everyone who wants to live here. The place has its reality and it imposes its own conditions. You cannot live here among Arab villages and behave as though you were still within the walls of Jerusalem, in the Jewish Quarter. I say to you," and he turned fiercely to face Gutman and his friends, "you call on us, the young, to go and fight the Arabs when they come to our fields to steal. Hear us now and there'll be less stealing in the future. Shake off your timid past and see things for what they are."

At that Leib's friends began to chant and cheer. But their voices were drowned by shouts of "shame, shame, such brazen talk!" A scuffle broke out between two of Leib's friends and the men who stood near them. Then Gutman rose, and addressing Leib, spoke with dignity which couldn't be outfaced, "You see what the majority think about all this. The message your father conveyed to Sheik Nazim Abu Latif stands. We shall do what we've offered and no more. There'll be no help in the fighting. You Leib, and your friends shall be ruled by this. Perhaps you're too young and hot-headed to understand. So let me tell you, as no doubt your father will tell you if he hadn't done so already. With great difficulty we built Petach Tiqva as a gate of hope for future generations. We haven't come here to emulate the Arabs. We don't want to be like them. Not because of what they are but because of what we are. We are Jews! We have our values. We have our kind of courage. Obviously you don't understand it yet. But this is our way. Anyone who finds it not to his taste has no future here."

Leib came home after supper that night. Before Hannah, who had kept his food warm for him, could say anything, he said "I'd like to speak to Father alone." When they were alone in the room, he said, "I know I hurt you today. But I can't be quiet about what I believe. I'm sorry. If you want me to, I'll leave your house and stay elsewhere."

"I'm saddened by what happened today and the day before, Leib, not hurt. But you're my son and this is your home. I've always been proud to know that you were true to your beliefs. So I cannot rebuke you now for proving this again, even when I know how wrong you are. But I am sad, very sad, that you understand so little as to dismiss my judgement and think me a coward. Stay if you can. Your mother's heart will break if you leave like that, in anger." And Yoel turned away and went to his room shutting the door behind him.

A day went by and then another. No word came from Yahudia, and no movement of any significance was detected in the village by the Petach Tiqva men who went out to the adjoining fields pretending to work but in reality in order to watch. On the third day after the work was finished, the alarm bell rang and Mendle went running up and down the street, shouting that the shepherds were bringing in all of Yahudia's livestock. Large pens had been prepared in the open space beyond the street not far from the well, and the animals were driven there: sheep with the goats, camels with the donkeys. All the shepherds said was that Abu Latif and his men were making ready to ride out of Yahudia to fight the Al Harati people.

The sound of movement next door woke Malachi. Tiqva slept on, breathing steadily with a quiet rasp. He got up and tiptoed into the next room. By the light of an oil lamp he saw Leib. Leib was dressed for action —dark shirt and an Arab *keffiya*, a thick belt and boots. He was pushing bullets into the chamber of his pistol. A bundle of his gear lay on the table. When he saw Malachi he stopped and gave him a look but said nothing. Presently he pushed in the last bullet and spun the chamber. Satisfied, he put the pistol on the table beside his gear.

"Well, what are you standing there for? Go back to bed," he said.

Seeing him like that, it occurred to Malachi that he might never return; he was already half in another world. Tears came to his eyes. Leib saw this. He came over and put his arms round him and pressed his cheek to his. "I have to go, you understand, you must," he said.

"I knew you would. I know you mustn't," Malachi said. "Father's right, Leib. If you only thought about it carefully you'd see he's right."

Leib walked over to the window. It was a moonless night. Fireflies traced broken lines of cold light through the darkness. Moths from the river thumped damply against the windowpane. "There's right and wrong of the mind and right and wrong of the heart," said Leib. "Father is always right here," he tapped his head. "This time I'm right in the heart. Don't say anything more. And, Malachi, say nothing about this, just keep out of it altogether, all right?" Malachi nodded. Suddenly he said, "You'll get killed, Leib." Leib's mouth dropped for an instant. Then he threw his head back and laughed voicelessly. "Me? Get killed? Now who in this world could do this to me?"

"Any coward weaker than you. Don't laugh, Leib."

But Leib had become carefree, "I've strength to protect me from the front, and luck to shield my back. Don't worry little brother. I'll be back sooner than you think."

"Take me with you, Leib."

Leib laughed again, "What do you think this is, a game?"

"Take me," Malachi pleaded, until Leib's mouth turned serious. "Father would never forgive me. Nor Mother, if anything were to happen . . ."

"Nothing would happen if I came. That's why I must," Malachi said. And Leib who couldn't hold his gaze, looked down.

Four horsemen and Tahari were already waiting at the appointed place by the river when Leib, with Malachi sitting behind him, rode in. Benjamin Daskal, the youngest and the calmest, on his father's sorrel colt, was one of them. He saw Malachi first and a pained expression came over his face, "Have you gone mad, Leib? What did you bring him for?"

"Be quiet Ben. He's my responsibility not yours or anybody's," Leib snapped at him. Yehuda Raab was there, Ezra Stein and Avrom Shapiro —all brave young men proud of their warlike skills. Now that Leib had arrived they were impatient to move. They strained their ears for any noise of the others approaching but the only sound was that of the wind in the rushes and the rhythmic croaking of the bull-frogs. The horses began to fidget and paw the ground.

"They're not coming. I knew it," Benjamin said after a while. He spat on the ground. The others look questioningly at Leib. He saw their hesitation and said: "If any of you is afraid to go on, let him turn back now. I'll ride on if I have to go alone."

Malachi might have prayed for some power to make his brother change his mind if he hadn't realized that nothing in the world could at this stage weaken Leib's resolve. Leib turned his horse's head towards Yahudia and heeled its flanks. The others followed without a word.

How many times had they passed through that territory before? Yet never did it seem so alien. Shadows interlocked with shadows and rolled past them as they rode. It might have been a dream landscape invoked from depths of inexpressible fears, a journey shot out of time and place, with no beginning and no end. Out of the hollow gloom the horses' hooves pounded the ground like muffled drums. Malachi clung tightly to Leib's back; he felt its warm strength and remembered his responsibility.

At the outskirts of Yahudia they were suddenly surrounded by men armed with spears and clubs. They barred their path and tried to lay hands on the horses' heads. Leib called out, identifying themselves and saying why they had come. When the Arabs heard, they welcomed them and led them away a little distance from the village where Sheik Nazim Abu Latif had assembled with his men. Here there was fire and food and coffee. The Sheik himself was nowhere to be seen. Leib and his friends were told that he was conferring with the leaders on the course of the battle. The Jews were welcomed to sit by the fire and partake of the food.

"Soon the Sheik will send for us," Leib whispered to his companions. The hours dragged on. The Arabs came to chat with their Jewish guests. They circled Tahari's mare, whistling softly through their teeth. They sat by Tahari, trying to draw him into conversation. Not a word came from the Sheik.

With the first light of dawn the Arabs broke camp and prepared to move north to meet the Al Harati. Now Sheik Nazim, mounted on a large black mare, came riding past, waving to his men, shouting encouragements. Among his retinue was a gaunt fellow dressed in a black cloak. He had a wild-looking face, all pock-marked, and a great shock of frizzy hair. His beard sprouted from his cheeks in all directions, and one of his eyes was missing. He half-ran, and half-skipped behind the Sheik's mare. When Abu Latif saw Leib and his friends, he reined in his mare and greeted them. There was no warmth in his courtesy. His eyes passed assessingly over Tahari who was already mounted, standing still as a statue, then fell on Malachi. For a moment he was lost for words. Then he gave a little laugh and said, "You Jews are indeed brave fighters that you send your young boys to learn war so early in life. Welcome little warrior. Welcome all of you." And he spurred his mare to a canter.

Sheik Abu Latif's force numbered no more than seventy men at the most. Only a dozen or so, not counting the Jews, were mounted. They were armed with swords, spears, and a few antiquated muskets loaded with bird shot called sarat, which, fired at a man, would inflict a painful wound but seldom kill. The rest were a rag-tag lot noisily on foot, armed with a variety of handy weapons—clubs, swords, pikes and slings.

After an untidy march of a little over an hour, the enemy camp came into sight against a hazy backdrop of the hills. Like Abu Latif's camp this was a makeshift affair, a few black tents spread out. Dew sparkled on their flanks. Smoke was curling lazily from extinguished fires among the tents but there was no sign of the men. Fearing lest he should be outflanked, Abu Latif sent out small detachments to the wings of his line. Then he called in the leaders of his force for a conference. This time the Petach Tiqva men were invited to join. The Arabs spread out and took their positions, ready to advance. "Stay here with the horses and don't move until we come back," Leib said to Malachi.

The sun began to warm him. Nothing stirred in the wide stretch of flat land except the smoke from among the tents in the distance. So peaceful was the scene that Malachi began to think the conflict was no more than a swell of emotion in the Sheik's head, and they would soon all ride back as peacefully as they had come. A falah armed with a long spear who was crouching by a rock not far from Malachi began to sing. Then there was movement from the place where Abu Latif was holding his conference. Malachi saw Leib and the others running in his direction, and all of a sudden, as if by an agreed sign, the enemy host appeared from behind the tents, a broad line of men on horse and foot, and above them a tangle of spears.

Abu Latif leaped on to his mare. Now the wild fellow ran forward until he stood facing the Al Harati advance, a few paces in front of the Sheik. Here he began to perform a strange dance, spinning about swinging his arms, and uttering incantation in a high-pitched voice. The Al Harati had advanced to a hundred yards away from the El Kishek host before the magician had finished his curse and collapsed exhausted on the ground.

"Stay right here by this rock and don't move until I come back," Leib shouted, giving Malachi a push down towards the jutting rock. He was on his horse in an instant with his nabut in his free hand, the heavy club with the lead lumps at its head, which Leib could wield so well.

Evidently the Petach Tiqva men had been instructed by Sheik Nazim to attack on the right wing while he himself led the centre. Malachi watched his brother and his friends gallop down the gentle slope towards the advancing Al Harati. It seemed to him that the six, now led by Tahari, were putting too much distance between them and the main body of men with the Sheik, while the latter seemed to slow down as if to see the outcome of the clash between the Jews and the oncoming enemy. Suddenly Malachi realized with horror that it was there, where Leib had ridden, that the main force of the enemy was concentrated, for out of nowhere there appeared Beduin horsemen who quickly began to encircle and close in on Leib and his friends. It was at this point that Tahari suddenly let his lance drop to the ground and attempted to break through the ring of horsemen. Malachi screamed to Leib and the others to turn back but his voice was drowned in the rising din.

The Beduin closed in on the Jews. There were shouts and the sound of blows. Malachi didn't see his brother come down, only Leib's horse on its back, thrashing the air with its hooves. Meanwhile the Sheik's main force had engaged the Al Harati amidst much shouting and musket fire. "I must save Leib, I must save him," the thought flashed though his mind. He got out from behind the rock and began to run towards the thick of the fray.

He had a notion that he was running but getting nowhere. Blood red spots refracted the light and blurred his vision. His head was burning, thudding like a hundred hammers. When the hammering died down he thought he caught sight of a large body of horsemen galloping soundlessly and overtaking him; he thought he saw his father at their head. He felt his legs give way from under him, and managed to whisper: "Shema Israel. . . . The Lord is One. . . ."

He woke up to see mother's face close to his, heard her voice saying, "Thank God", and realized he was home.

*

If Leib hadn't been so strong and healthy he would have surely died. He had received a blow on the head which concussed him, and a sword cut that bit deep into his right shoulder close to the neck. It happened all too quickly, before he was able to recover from the fall and draw his pistol. The others all received cuts and blows none of which were serious. If luck hadn't been with Malachi, he too would have died, for he was hit a glancing blow on the side of the head by a flying rock which would have brained him had it hit him directly. If it weren't for the fact that Malachi too was missing that morning when Hannah went into his room to wake him up, Yoel might not have sent a rider post-haste to alert the authorities and himself ridden with twenty men from Petach Tiqva to the scene of the battle. They arrived just in time to break through the ring of the Beduin horsemen and rescue Leib and the others. Leib was unconscious and bleeding heavily. They put him and Malachi in the cart which Zeligman had the presence of mind to drive at break-neck speed behind the riders, and straight away made back for home where Dr Goldshalk had already prepared his infirmary for emergency.

Sheik Nazim Abu Latif and the men of Yahudia claimed a qualified victory: had it not been for the Jews who brought the Ottomans charging on to the scene, firing in all directions, they would have defeated the Al Haratis, would have taught them a lesson they'd never have forgotten. Sheik Amir Al Harati, for his part, claimed that had it not been for the arrival of the gendarmes, not a single man from Yahudia with the heart to stand his ground and fight, would have got away alive. For all that, both sides allowed the Ottomans to negotiate a reconciliation. At the *sulcha* feast the two sheiks agreed on new boundaries between their pasture lands. Thus the dispute was grudgingly settled.

Two days later, four dignitaries from Yahudia came to Petach Tiqva with shepherds to collect their livestock. The senior among them came to Yoel's home to pay respects on behalf of the Sheik, for Leib's courage in battle. Truly he deserved the name "Lion" after the way he had fought, and no less was due to the boy Malachi. The visit was brief, too formal. The men went back to Yahudia with their flocks and left behind Yahya Salem Tahari, bound hand and foot, his hair and beard shorn off. "Your warrior, a present from the Beduin," they told Yoel. "If it weren't for respect to your brave son, they would've killed the wretch."

Leib took a long time to recover. The sight in his right eye was badly impaired as a result of the blow he received on the head. His right arm was weak, would never recover its former strength, Dr Goldshalk pronounced. During Leib's convalescence Yoel spent much time with him, talking comfort to him, waiting as one waits for the rains, for Leib to open his heart that they may be fully reconciled.

"I'm only half a man now, and for what? For nothing," Leib said and laughed bitterly.

"No, Leib. There's a lot more to a man than strong arms." Leib fell into a brooding silence. After a while, he said: "You know what they did to us, Father? They let us ride on purpose into a trap, then held back. They wanted us killed. Like David did to Uriah the Hittite. Why? We came to help them, and they betrayed us!"

"We don't count for much in their scheme of things, Leib. That was partly why I wanted no part in their fighting."

"But as men . . ."

Yoel passed his hand over his son's head. "You see what men are when strong arms is all their strength?"

Leib lowered his eyes. He leaned closer to his father.

"You tried to tell me that," he said forlornly.

"I tried, Son, and I failed. Because I was selfish and impatient. Because I didn't look hard enough to see the greatness in you. Nothing's ever wasted, Leib. If you learn from experience your strength increases not lessens. That's what being a man is about, Leib. Not an animal, not an unthinking savage, but a learning being. Think about it Leib. Think of me with all my faults and become better than me, better in your own way, son."

In his silence Leib accepted his father's offering. Yoel, perceiving this, pressed Leib's head to his chest and was grateful.

Yoel began to talk about future plans to quell their emotion, things they would do on the farm when Leib recovered. Hannah wanted a cow. The crescent-shaped field behind the house could be sown with millet before the rains. There was a good price for millet in Jaffa. Zeligman was interested in fruit trees. The settlers in Rishon Le Zion under the guidance of Baron de Rothschild's officers, were experimenting with vine-growing. Perhaps they should ride over to have a look. Leib listened, nodding his head. His mind was only half-taking in what his father was saying. At last he said, "To think he could deceive me like that, the impostor!"

"Let him be, Leib, the poor miserable creature. Don't think about him."

But Leib wouldn't let go, "A horse thief. And he made us believe he was something noble, a Jewish warrior! Now all the Arabs for miles around will laugh at us, make jokes."

"They'll remember how the five of you fought, Leib. They can't make jokes about that."

Yahya Tahari had been taking shelter in Mendle's home. Without his horse and weapons he looked reduced, almost unrecognizable. His manner too had changed: he no longer carried himself with superior reserve but was docile, ready to do any chore Mendle assigned to him. His only way to escape the ruins of his world was by seeking a new identity. So changed he was that even the children of Petach Tiqva would pass him by without paying any attention. One morning Yoel showed up at Mendle's forge. He said to Tahari, "You cannot stay here any longer. Don't be afraid, we shan't cast you out. There's a place for you, a new home where you'll have food and shelter and earn your living."

Tahari was taken into Abraham Kalantar's household in Jaffa as a groom in Kalantar's growing stable.

The battle near Yahudia grew into a legend. Wherever young Jews in the settlements, from Rishon Le Zion to Zichron Yaakov in the Carmel sat down by the fire to sing and tell tales, the story was told. Leib Zeff, Benjamin Daskal, Yehuda Raab, Ezra Stein, Avrom Shapiro and Malachi, became heroes whom everyone wanted to meet and listen to. Of the five, only Leib steadfastly declined to talk of the experience. When people cajoled him he would fall silent, then change the subject. That year, on Rosh Hashana, he became betrothed to Tzila Daskal, Benjamin's sister, and his mind turned to what kind of work he could best do with his disability. He wanted a home, he wanted children. His searching roots drew courage from his father's love.

Chapter 33

The sun setting into the Mediterranean lulled Abraham Kalantar into drowsiness. Lustrous red grains twinkled on the water of the harbour, appeared and disappeared among the ripples, then deepened and spread until the whole sea was the colour of wine. The sea breeze carried the fragrance of jasmine and honeysuckle from the garden. Abraham inhaled. The garden pleased him. It was not a large garden. It was mellow, overgrown, and evocative. On such a night it brought back to him the smells and sounds of another garden set in a landscape which he was already beginning to forget. On such a night, how easily his imagination roamed, what distances it covered. Old age's sole luxury: the langorous ease of far-sailing imagination. He liked the thought. Another time he would have asked his servant to write it down so that he'd remember. But now he was past such conceits. Besides, his servants were local barbarians, not scribes.

The house glowed in the sea-tinted light. He had made a good buy. By the standards of the land this was as palatial a home as any he could own. Big enough to contain his noisy quarrelsome family and still afford him the peace he sought so much. Even now they were curtained from his awareness by the constant hum of the sea. He learnt to be grateful for such moments.

If motion now wearied him, soothing sound was his salve; he hankered after music as never before. But there were no musicians after his taste to be had: only the bul buls, warbling their evening song in his garden, his sanctuary. Abraham forbade his family from setting a foot in the garden in the evenings when he was there.

The sea breeze murmured in the lemon trees, softly, like the voice of a Persian courtesan he once had. He no longer wanted women nor fine horses to ride. The change of life and country had made him heavy with lassitude. He liked to think of himself as maturing, like dark wine, rather than growing old. His eyes, having seen so extravagantly, were dimming. A gentle twilight, dulcet sounds, that was all he asked of life. For which reason he resented his wife's constant clamour and his sons' greed for sensations; they alienated him and heightened his isolation. And if such intrusions were not bad enough, he had to endure another tribulation that came upon him like a bolt out of the sky.

A month before, his former concubine Zulika suddenly arrived on his doorstep with their son Bezalel. The servant, taking her for a beggar, saw her off but Zulika raised such a wail that Abraham was stirred to investigate what the row was about. He couldn't believe Fate could be so vindictive to him. The once sweet and pleasing Zulika had walked all the way from Bakhara through Turkey and Syria, to find him. Why? Had he not settled his affairs with her handsomely? Could she believe in her foolishness that here their son whose begetting he had so enjoyed would have a better future? None of this could make sense to him, only that God was enjoying a coarse joke at his expense.

Hardship had changed her. What had once been ingenuity in the art of pleasing had turned into implacable harping, and a resourcefulness surprising in its variety, and threatening. Yet he couldn't turn her away, she and the torpid weak-eyed youth, his bastard son. He put them close to the servants' quarters but forbade her to see him unless called for on pain of flogging and eviction to the street. His wife accepted the addition to the family as a part of the host of indignities she had to endure in this inhospitable and unendearing country. So the days went by. Abraham withdrew more into himself, his sons grew imperious in their self-assertion and waited for him to die.

He became aware of someone standing a few paces behind him in the shadow of the almond tree. It was his servant Ali.

"Come forward Ali, don't stand there like a shadow. What is it? I don't want a smoke nor sherbet. Bring me minted tea, but later." Abraham liked his servants, like his family, to show deference, but timidity irritated him. He also disliked people standing half-hidden from him. "Hawaja," said Ali, "The Pasha El Husseini is here to see you, he waits in the front room."

Abraham sighed. He motioned Ali to come near, clasped his hands round his neck. Ali strained to raise his master to his feet. He knew that his employer was perfectly capable of getting up on his own but accepted the old man's eccentricities as a token of trust. In the evening, both of the day and of his life, intrusions on his solitude, the tiresome necessity of social contact, made Abraham feel too inert: if Ali brought the news, let Ali labour on its account, he reasoned.

Pasha El Husseini was small and thin with an austere face and a mobile mouth, the constant movement of which was accentuated by a sparse moustache. He always wore a red fez; The amber worry beads never left his deft elegant hands. Levantine urbanity was stamped on every aspect of him.

"On such a splendid evening, Abu Yussef," El Husseini intoned as he embraced Abraham, "one is reminded of the bliss that is yet to come in the hereafter."

"Long may we live to be reminded of this," Abraham replied, for even now he was by no means ready for the hereafter. The Pasha drew up a chair and sat opposite his host. He inhaled the fragrant air and closed his eyes. Abraham clicked his fingers and told Ali to serve minted tea.

"When I retire, Ibrahim, perhaps I shall move to Beirut, build a house overlooking the sea and spend my last days gazing at the sunset, just as you're doing here," El Husseini said, and sighed wistfully. "And I'll remember my days in Jaffa with affection."

"Vanity of vanities; all is vanity," Abraham quoted, to forestall requests.

The two men exchanged platitudes until the sky turned deep purple, the waves heaved darkly against Jaffa's promontory, and Ali lit two lanterns above the table. Abraham pulled a rug of Bukharan kashmir over his legs and allowed his wattled chin to sink on to his chest. The sea hummed. Jackals howled in the orange groves vying with the sea for the audience of the night. When cosmic infinity became too much to endure, Abraham was moved to ask, "Well, El Husseini, to what do I owe the pleasure of your visit?"

"What else but our friendship, Ibrahim? What is life without the pleasant company of friends?" El Husseini slurped his tea.

"Shall I tell Ali to bring the *shesh besh*?" Abraham suggested.

"When you play such a fine game of chess, with those beautiful ivory pieces you possess?" The Pasha laughed a tight laugh. "I'm weary of chess, Ahmed. Too much thinking, too much like life."

The Pasha tossed the dice, moved his pieces across the backgammon board, and made his gambit.

"Allah has showered blessings on you, Ibrahim. You're a wealthy man, a big landowner," he said, staring portentously at the board.

Abraham grunted and began to rattle the dice.

"I've always looked favourably on your transactions, Ibrahim, even when there was, how shall we say . . ." he grinned slyly and turned his palm this way and that. Abraham was unmoved.

"I've always tried to spread my blessings among my friends and the less fortunate," he reminded the Pasha, and shot the dice.

"You're a good and generous man, no one will deny that."

There was silence as Ahmed El Husseini contemplated his move.

"What we do, Ibrahim is one thing, between friends, within the family. . . ." he said with significant emphasis. "But irresponsible land-buying, grabbing at every dunam on offer, that's bad. Bad for the falahin, bad for the effendis, bad for the country."

"You keep saying, Ahmed."

"Not you, Abu Yussef, don't misunderstand. You know who I mean. But," he added, "you help them. All those newcomers, Jews, they buy anything, pay too high prices. The falahin are troubled. What is now no more than disquiet will grow into bad trouble, mark my word. And then," he passed the edge of his hand over his throat. "I don't like them. They are not Ottomans like you and me. When they need something, when there's trouble, do they come to Pasha El Husseini? No Ibrahim. They run to the Franji, their European consuls. You and I, Ibrahim, we've always understood one another, in friendship and in business." He brought the dice to his lips and blew on them. "Now I begin to wonder." The dice struck the board peevishly.

Abraham watched him impassively. He too disliked the newly arrived Jews. Sometimes he could see them from the high windows of his house, disembark at the port. On a number of occasions delegations were sent to him, asking for money, help in securing permits for this and that. He was conscious of their strange fervour, their determination, impoverished though they were. But more than the immigrants he disliked the agents who teemed about the port like pimps.

The land he had bought at Petach Tiqva—he neither knew nor cared how much, or why—was the least successful of his investments. He suspected his eldest son Yussef had been behind the purchase. If it had been worth selling, or if it weren't for his atavistic reluctance to part with land once bought, he'd have got rid of it. All it brought him was bad news: Jews fighting one another, raids by Arabs, disease—he had been told of babies being born looking old and dying within weeks of their birth. He never visited the place, even the name struck him as false and pretentious. He had little idea of what his agent or Yussef were doing with it. But small, insignificant though it was for him, it was a constant source of trouble, the only piece of land he possessed which ruffled his smooth relationship with the authorities. Petach Tiqva, a mere few thousand dunams of second-rate land, and so much fuss! But those Jews were given to excesses, that much he had learnt about them.

He began to wonder if it weren't something to do with Petach Tiqva that brought El Husseini to his home in a deviously censorious mood. Pasha El Husseini knew very well that it wasn't easy for him, Abraham Kalantar, to hold aloof from the Jews now that his past was catching up with him. Jews from Bukhara had begun to arrive in numbers. People who had known him, or heard of him, relatives of his wife too. He could not turn his back on them. And they made demands on him; they looked to him for help, for leadership. They had been persecuted back home, they said. Well, hadn't he told them? For which they heaped abuse on him, betrayed him like Joseph's brethren.

Jews were Jews, Sepharadi, Bukharan, Ashkenazi, it didn't matter. His own ethnic reflexes wouldn't die; he had a nightmare vision of his own odious family expanding to fill a world. Time for Yussef to take over, he prayed in his heart. But Yussef was weak, arrogant too. No telling what he would do left on his own, in Jerusalem of all places, where new ideas like gaudy baubles seduced susceptible minds.

Ahmed El Husseini began collecting the pieces he had won. "Shesh besh, Ibrahim, is a funny game. Like life itself. Luck and skill go together.

Neither will do on its own," he mused. As he made a near-clean sweep of the board he added in a tone of light rebuke, "you're not playing a good game, Ibrahim my friend. It's a bad, costly habit not to play well, disrespectful of your friends, too."

Abraham frowned. The hint was not lost on him. He was well aware of his son Yussef's dealings which he, no less than El Husseini, found distasteful. El Husseini was not above accepting a present. But open bribes offended him, particularly when they were offered with presumption by someone he didn't consider his equal. Yussef Kalantar had tried to bribe El Husseini openly, indelicately, without making an effort to win his friendship. When he failed he turned his attentions to the Governor's more susceptible deputy. That was not all. During his frequent stays in Jerusalem Yussef had got to know the Governor of Jerusalem and the entire region, Mehemet Rauf Pasha. The two became friends of sorts—Yussef knew how to please a friend he needed.

There was little love lost between Mehemet Rauf and Ahmed El Husseini: the first was a Turk, a high-ranking—three horsetails—official; the other, a scion of a distinguished Palestinian Arab family, a subordinate *Mustarflick*, governor of a town within Rauf Pasha's province. Both resented the influx of European Jews. But it was Rauf Pasha who had introduced the Red Card regulation and insisted on its enforcement. Yet when El Husseini ruled that six Jews who had recently settled in Petach Tiqva in violation of their entry permit should be arrested and deported, his order was overruled by Rauf Pasha. It was an entirely arbitrary reversal of policy, as well as an outrageous interference. El Husseini felt insulted, humiliated, all the more because the whole thing was done through his deputy, in his absence. He had no difficulty knowing who was behind this.

Abraham understood at last the purpose of El Husseini's visit. He realized at once that unless he did something to curb his son, this gentle Arab, who was beating him at backgammon, could turn into a dangerous foe.

As Ahmed El Husseini picked up the dices and offered them on an open palm, Abraham made a decision. Yussef will have the independence he wanted so much, but with restrictions. Let him set up house in Jerusalem. His allowance will be supervised; no more mischief, no more wild spending. His visits to Jaffa would thereafter be strictly family visits. Yakub, his middle son, was a fool. He'd set him to work doing something useful. As for Nissim, timid harmless Nissim, let him stay in the house to please his mother. In pursuit of domestic tranquillity Abraham could be inexorable as a god. "Effendi El Husseini, I'm an old man. My sons have ideas I don't share. Yussef likes Jerusalem. So be it, let him stay there and bother us no more. I'll see to that." He turned the dice cubes langorously in his fingers.

El Husseini smiled, "A wise move, my friend Ibrahim," he said.

Yussef's departure from his home for Jerusalem was precipitated as a result of an unfortunate incident involving his brother Yakub. Yakub was the very opposite of Yussef: ponderous of mind, trusting, guileless. Misfortune seemed to hang over everything he did. Yet he hated no one nor feared anyone. He was, in fact, a thoroughly agreeable but dull fellow, with an innocent suntanned look and a stocky, powerful body. In Yussef's urbanity, Yakub saw all his own imperfections magnified. He worshipped his brother, obeyed him slavishly. Abraham distrusted Yussef at times to the point of hatred. But he had a grudging respect for him. On Yakub he vented all his anger and frustration. Even as a child, Abraham used to thrash poor Yakub at the slightest provocation. Now, in the prime of his youth as in his defenceless boyhood, Yakub never rebelled. He would take his punishment with a look of uncomprehending hurt on his face as though he had disappointed his father through some fault he was unaware of. Which only added fuel to Abraham's fury, and at the same time wounded him.

The house in Jaffa boasted one edifice of which Abraham was particularly proud. It was a throne of a lavatory with a veined marble base like a pedestal, and a rosewood seat, broad and polished. Abraham had it made to his own specification from the best materials money could buy. It was set on a reinforced platform, over a specially dug pit, in a room hung with damask draperies and decorated with wrought lamps which shed a soft unobtrusive light. Here Abraham would sit and contemplate while waiting for his bowels to move. At times the expectation and the fulfilment of release so gratified him that he allowed members of his family or early petitioners to communicate with him through the shut door. If any such solicitor peeped through the keyhole he could see a stretch of pink-scrubbed flagstones at the end of which was Abraham, seated on his lavatory, his robes flowing on either side, his slippered feet resting on a cushioned stool —for he was a short man—his face so awesome in concentration that even a fart sounded oracular.

One cold blustery night, Yakub was awakened by the urgent need to relieve himself. He had been feverish for some days, and his bladder was swollen. As if tempted by the devil, he made his way half-asleep to the hallowed lavatory. He couldn't see a thing, it was pitch dark. Nor did he hear any sound. He walked in, positioned himself where he calculated the lavatory's orifice was, and pissed. The roar his action raised hit him in the face like a clout. He turned and ran, pursued by his father's curses.

Lights were turned on, servants came rushing. Yussef emerged from his room stick in hand. Had robbers broken in, he asked? Attracted by the commotion two passing gendarmes were knocking at the gate. In his terror Yakub hid among jars in the cellar, from where he heard the thunder of his father's fury. Abraham was shouting that he would kill Yakub. He heard his mother wail, then shriek as the old man lashed out at her. When the turmoil subsided, he stole back to his room, grabbed whatever clothes he could find in the dark, then climbed over the wall and ran away.

He was gone for a week no one knew where, until an agent of Yussef's reported that poor Yakub was languishing in the most unsavoury part of Jaffa, hungry, dirty and frightened. Because the story got round how Yakub pissed on the old man in the dark—the joke became a set piece of entertainment in the highest social circles of Jaffa—Abraham would not agree to Yakub's reinstatement in his household. He wanted him far away and forgotten—Australia came to his mind as a possibility, where Yakub might redeem himself by learning some useful trade. Yussef had other ideas. He said: "Father, what will people say if you banish your own flesh and blood to a far-away corner of the world for something he did by mistake, out of stupidity? Let him go to Petach Tiqva. Let him have that piece of land to make of what he can."

Abraham agreed. Thus Yussef moved to Jerusalem, with a bigger sum of money than he had expected, and a small retinue of servants including the hapless Tahari, while Yakub was banished to the place which neither Abraham nor Yussef knew or cared about.

Kalantar's Jerusalem home was one of the finest houses in town. Surrounded by a tall stone wall, time-mellowed and brindle, it stood some way off the main road from the Jaffa Gate to the coast. A handsome stone archway opened on to a cobbled drive which led to the front of the house. From the archway the pale-honey-coloured façade came into view, sequestered among tall dark cypresses. There were painted shutters over the wide windows. Wrought-iron railings braced elegant balconies. The front door was massive and always open. Visitors dismounted, if they were on horseback, by the round ornamental garden well, and allowed Tahari to take their horses to the stables at the back of the house, where Yussef's team of greys and his gentle mare were kept. Yussef, dressed in flowing robes and smiling would come out to greet them, if they were important enough, which they usually were. On a fine day, they would sit in the shade of the trees in the garden, drinking sherbet or minted tea, and making light conversation full of import and allusions, until the real purpose of the visit emerged. Or he would entertain his guests in the large front room with the vaulted ceiling and marble floor on which the best, richest carpets in the land were spread. There were silk-cushioned divans, attentive servants. A large silver samovar hummed forever on the table, and from above the hearth, a huge portrait of old Ibrahim Kalantar in his Bukharan robes of office, looked down in majestic benevolence which he never possessed in real life.

Yussef perfected a way of making powerful friends, and dangerous enemies. His hospitality became legendary, his garden was like the mythical well into which people whispered their most hidden secrets, and heard others' secrets wafted back at them.

Yes, Yussef enjoyed life, and the hazards of being the repository of so many secrets, intrigues and indiscretions added excitement and a sense of power to what otherwise would have been no more than luxurious idleness.

Ahmed El Husseini said in a cautionary tone, "They say Ibrahim, that nothing of any importance happens from Alexandria to Beirut that your son Yussef doesn't know about. They say he's overreached himself dangerously, for Rauf Pasha is like a leopard. One moment he'll let you stroke him, the next moment you're halfway down his throat." El Husseini raised a finger. "Your son doesn't understand what he's getting into. He's young, inexperienced. What may happen to him would touch you deeper than perhaps you realize. He's your son, Ibrahim."

Husseini, Abraham knew, was not in the habit of giving idle warnings. What he said troubled Abraham's sleep for weeks. Until, unable to dispel his anxiety, he decided to go up to Jerusalem to see for himself how his son was faring.

Yussef's servants' patronizing indulgence gave Abraham the feeling of being a guest in a place where he should be master. Servants mirrored their employer's attitudes, that much he knew. The smooth opulent running of the household surprised him too. He hadn't thought he had allotted Yussef so much money, and Ahmed El Husseini's understated warning suddenly alarmed him. He was too weary to fight Yussef who had learnt the subtleties of the land, he realized, better than himself. Jerusalem looked alien and dangerous to him. A view of the garden through his window made him homesick for Jaffa. He longed for the wide uncluttered horizon beyond the sea-blown promontory.

"I wish I had daughters instead of sons," he said to himself. "A man needs daughters to comfort him in his old age, to marry well, men he likes and can trust."

All of a sudden the thought of death came to him, not with fear but like resignation. "Let me not die here," he prayed, "but in Jaffa, and be buried in my garden, next to my poor old Aram." He didn't even want Yussef to say Kadish over him.

In the morning it was time for telling and for listening. Abraham did most of the listening. What he heard unnerved him but he began to have a new if uncomfortable respect for his son. For his part, Yussef listened with barely concealed boredom. Until Abraham took up a twig and held it in his gnarled but still powerful hands. "Look," he said, and snapped the twig in two.

"What is that supposed to mean, Father?"

Abraham collected a bundle of them and lined them up in his hands. "See? Not so easy now."

"Well?" Yussef smiled.

"If you stand alone, one day, when you've outlived your usefulness, as you're bound to, the Ottoman will break you like a twig. But if you've got people behind you, you have power, you have security. Understand? Don't neglect your people, Yussef. Be good and generous and loyal to them and they'll stand by you when you need them. Serve them now and they'll serve you in your hour of need. Not only our people from Bukhara. The old community. The Ashkenazi too, all of them. Invest in them, Yussef."

Yussef nodded his head.

"I've given you freedom to do as you like," Abraham went on, "your life is your own. You may lose or you may gain as God pleases. But there's one thing I won't let you do with as you like." Yussef looked up, remembering that the old man could exert authority. "My name, Yussef. If you debase that, I'll cut you dry. I'll strip you of everything you have here."

To show him he wasn't quite the profligate he appeared to be, Yussef took his father on a sightseeing tour of the city. Yussef pointed to a row of shops by the citadel, the owners of which waved and bowed as the open carriage, pulled by Yussef's greys and driven by Tahari, rolled past. "Ours," he said smiling obliquely. Gendarmes by the Pasha's residence doffed their hats when they saw Yussef. Further north, close by a new quarter which Yussef explained had been built by Jews from Hungary, Arab labourers were busy on a building site. "I bought the land," Yussef said. "There'll be rows of houses. For our people, Jews from Bukhara. Those who can pay will pay. The poor will have it for nothing, just a small rent. The name of Kalantar will be in their prayers day and night."

Abraham couldn't help being impressed. Which didn't escape Yussef's vigilance. "I want you to be proud of me, Father," he said, sounding sincere.

Abraham nodded and patted Yussef's knee. Jerusalem made him tired. He liked her now even less than when he first saw her. The Arabs had a sharp look in their eyes. The Jews were either wretchedly filthy or too energetic. He sensed intrigue in the air everywhere. He wanted to get away, back home to Jaffa.

Sensing surrender, Yussef allowed himself to be magnanimous. "Father," he said, "I've tired you, let us go to a place where we can relax and wash the dust of the streets from our bodies."

They were handsome baths, Abraham had to admit, clean, well fitted, unlike other Turkish hammams he had visited in his time. He didn't much care for public ablution—the closeness of bodies and the steam invited the assassin's knife, oh he had seen things. But this was different. Yussef had bought it. He had his own private rooms, and a Circassian bodyguard of enormous stature.

The hammam was staffed by Sudanese, like those who guarded the Temple compound. For an extra fee they would rub you down with olive oil and camphor. Or, as it seemed to Abraham, slit the throat of your enemy. Yussef had added a special section for a mikve, for Jewish men and women to bathe on the eve of Sabbath.

The private chambers were opulent but functional: a few divans and round damascene tables of wood inlaid with mother-of-pearl. A glass bead curtain separated the rest room from the private baths.

After the steam and the massage father and son relaxed on the divans. It had been a long time since Abraham had enjoyed smoking hashish, and such good hashish at that. So he wasn't certain whether snatches of conversation he heard, laughter, the occasional grunt, were real voices or his fantasy. Until Yussef shifted a small curtain on the wall and slid shut a cover over a cluster of perforations. "It was there before I bought the place," he explained almost apologetically, "still it doesn't harm to hear what the people are saying. If you look through the holes you can see too." He gave a chuckle, "I know my friends and my enemies. Their wives and mistresses too."

"Find yourself a good woman. Marry, have children," Abraham said with a sigh. "Maybe God'll look favourably on you. I can't pretend to understand your ways."

"You've told me one thing which is my guiding rule," Yussef said bowing his head.

"What's that?"

"Always to be open to all opportunities, never to concentrate all you have on one thing."

Abraham turned his mouth down. "Did I say that? I can't remember. I don't give advice any more. Take me home now, I'm tired and would like to sleep." Half-slumbering in the carriage, he said, "You've said nothing of your brother Yakub. Be good to him, now and after I'm gone. He's one of life's wretches." His eyes were getting heavy.

Abraham Kalantar died peacefully in bed a month after his visit to Jerusalem. His will made no provisions for the distribution of his wealth among his sons. The one provision concerned the house in Jerusalem: relying on Ottoman law, Abraham willed that the house should never be sold but passed on from generation to generation to the eldest son. Yussef had his father's body brought to Jerusalem and buried with full ceremony in the Jewish cemetery on the slope of the Mount of Olives. Only Ahmed El Husseini knew that his old friend had wanted to be buried in his garden in Jaffa, next to the grave of his faithful Aram. But nobody wanted to talk to El Husseini, least of all Yussef, who already at his father's funeral asserted himself as the sole undisputed heir.

Chapter 34

Yakub Kalantar came to Petach Tiqva on foot, with a pack containing his belongings slung over his back and a heavy staff in his hand. The only thing of value he had with him were the papers authenticating his ownership over three dunams of land in the village and a share in a further five hundred. There was a house too, the agent in Jaffa had told him, or at least the frame of a house had been built some time ago, the agent couldn't remember when.

It had been a long walk and his feet ached. The red sky, the dust caked on his sandals like dried blood, the brooding trees, and the houses unwelcoming in their silence, gave Yakub a feeling of banishment. From where? He had come from nowhere to nowhere which was to be his home, if there was anything left in the world he could think of as home. Experience had numbed him; he no longer felt sorry for himself. He was like Cain, except that he had committed no crime, nor ever did anyone any harm.

As he walked into Petach Tiqva's main street he was able to reflect that at last he was accountable to no one but God, free to do as he pleased. And since his life was at such a low ebb, it could only improve henceforth. Oh yes, that was what his father would've said. Some of the wily old man's unpitying practicality had rubbed off on unsuccessful Yakub. The thought didn't cheer him, only stilled his anxieties.

If the people in the street looked alien at least they weren't unfriendly. Which turned his mind on how he might locate his new home. The tavern, through the open door of which he could see men sitting at tables, seemed a good starting point. He went in. The men turned to look and were reassured when they saw the skull cap he was wearing. He ordered tea—the samovar was something he could recognize. The questions he was asked confused him: he could barely make out what they were saying to him and no one seemed to have heard the name Kalantar, until Katz, wiping his hands on his apron, sent Yossle who was weak in the head but fit for such errands, to call David Joshua or Yehushua Stamper.

Kalantar's domestic plot as it turned out, lay between Yoel Zeff's and Leib's new homestead. It was a patch of desolation. At one end, close to the road, a house had once been built but never finished. All there was to it were the four walls and the roof. The roof had been done in a hurry to prevent the building from being pulled down by the Ottomans, for the law said that once a roof had been completed the house couldn't be pulled down. That, too, had holes in it in places, almost as large as the half-finished windows. The men who directed Yakub to his father's vacant plot told him the place was not fit for human habitation. They suggested he put up for the night at Katz's tavern and find lodgings until he could get the house in order. Yakub thanked them, but declined. He wanted to go to the place at once. They wouldn't understand, he reasoned, there was no point in trying to explain.

He could see that notwithstanding the dilapidated state of his new home, it did provide shelter of sorts. Moreover, there were signs that others, possibly even less fortunate than himself had availed themselves of it—ashes from a fire, a tin pot, a threadbare mat. The sky was deepening. Lights began to come on in some of the houses. The breeze carried the smell of the river and the eucalyptus trees. Yakub came out, walked a distance away from the house, and stood in the middle of the land he had inherited. The earth was cracked and dusty, overgrown with weeds. He knew nothing of farming, he had no useful skills and little money. He knelt down and dug his hands into the dust until it hurt. He imagined this was what it must have been like for Adam after being expelled from Eden. But he would survive, he would survive because he needed so little to survive.

Tiqva Zeff watched him from the window of her room. She watched him stand, powerful and desolate like a ravaged tree in that neglected stretch of land, and her heart stirred. She watched him walk back to the gaping house, his eyes downcast, and she wanted to touch him.

Yakub was awakened from his reveries to see Tiqva standing at the doorway against the gathering dark. She had brought him blankets, an oil lamp, and food. She had honest eyes, he thought, eyes which for the first time he could remember gave him a feeling of kinship. Her mouth was sad, like his own. After she had left he remembered her calm gaze and her silence—she had hardly spoken a word to him and yet, he felt, had said so much. He fell asleep at last with a hopeful heart. Yes, there was hope: he was as certain of that as he had ever been certain of anything.

"With God's help, 3rd August 1885. My dearest Mother and Father. I wish there was some quicker way of conveying to you the news which I know will gladden your hearts. Alas, the post takes such a long time that I sometimes think we live in a different world, which indeed we are, far apart though near they are.

"The good news is that my marriage to my dear Miriam will be brought forward to after the Holy Days. It was Reb Samuel's idea. An angel of the Lord must have whispered our own thoughts, mine and Miriam's, in his ears. And why wait, when our hearts are in agreement and all the arrangements have been made? It's all too exciting. I hope you'll both come here sooner than you planned, to be with us and help in the preparations. My love to Leib, to Tiqva, and to Malachi. Your loving son Chaim."

Yoel smiled. He recognized his son's infatuation with the modern fashion of Hebrew which a certain Eliezer Ben Yehuda, who came to Jerusalem three years before, had started. Chaim—always receptive to innovation—not only tried to emulate a matter of fact conversational style, he also entered into a kind of breezy spirit which he imagined went with the new trend. So thoroughly it had affected him that he eschewed the Hebrew calendar and preferred the Gregorian instead. Samuel Rimkin was bound to frown on such apostasy. His own letter was attached:

"With the help of God, Jerusalem Month of Ab, 5645. My dear Yoel, Do not blame your sweet son for any inconvenience that might be caused to you and Hannah from this change of plans. Rather put it to the impatience of an old man to see a dream come true before his days run out.

"I've always believed, as did my father before me, that Heaven decreed that our two families should be one. For what other purpose did the Good Lord guide your forebear, the brave and saintly Reb Solomon Zeff from the ruins of Safed, and my father Reb Eliezer Rimkin, may their souls be woven in the wreath of eternal life, to found anew the holy Ashkenazi community of Jerusaelm, if it was not that their seed should be joined and multiply?

"I'm old and my health is not too good. I feel as though I'm standing on a pisgah—like Moses in his time. Behind me is a long wilderness. Hardship. Heroism. Sacrifice. Before me I can see pleasant fields of green. Peace. And God-fearing men and women. Children singing as they go to the rabbi's cheder. Just having this far away vision is bliss, a recompense for all the hard beginnings our forebears had to endure. And it is granted me by the marriage of our two great families.

"Come to Jerusalem as soon as you can with your good wife Hannah, that we may be together in the preparations for the happy day. I embrace you both as grandson and granddaughter. Samuel Rimkin."

There was another note from Asher, Miriam's father, adding his hopes to those of his father's that the Zeff family would make haste to Jerusalem as soon as possible.

"Reb Samuel, bless him, could never miss a chance of sermonizing," Hannah commented with an ironic smile as she held the letter at arm's length while adjusting her glasses. For all that, she liked the old man. That part of her which instinctively equated respectability with convention, that her nomadic life with Yoel had starved but never killed, hankered for the ordered urban life of Jerusalem. And the Rimkins touched that part of her with an ever-assured hand. They personified order and respectability to a man and woman: a large influential family. They had done well for themselves too, Asher in particular. Life in Petach Tiqva, which once filled Hannah with a sense of mission—the danger, the hardship all of which she had been ready to face—now seemed drab and laborious. She longed for the crowded streets, for new faces, for the variety of smells and sounds.

"Miriam's a fine girl. The lad's right. Reb Samuel is right too. Why wait?" Yoel broke into her thoughts.

He sensed Hannah's restiveness whenever Jerusalem was mentioned. At times he too longed to be there. It was as though his life were governed by two invisible clocks: one ticking to the rhythm of the village life, the going to and from the fields, the change from winter to summer, from rain and cold to searing heat; the other ticking to the heartbeat of the city. Leib, stalwart Leib, was a farmer in body and soul. So deep had his roots sunk in the soil of Petach Tiqva that he would never wander further than Jaffa, and just for the day, to buy supplies. Chaim had soft white hands, fingers for pointing out, for gesturing. He would never touch the soil except in his departure from this world. What was the polarized differences between his two sons, if not symbolic of his own divided condition? Yet the division was not so deep as it might have been. It was not through the Gate of Hope that the surge of Jewish rural settlement rushed; for Petach Tiqva ignored the rush of innovations in the newer villages, now under the administration of the Benefactor the Baron de Rothschild. Instead she vibrated to the tremors of Jerusalem, as though the city had reached out and planted by the stinking river a chip from her stony orthodox heart.

Yoel put his arm round Hannah's shoulder and drew her to him. "God willing, and without making a vow, we'll go to Jerusalem next week and stay there for as long as you like. What with Leib and his wife, and Tiqva, we have nothing to worry about Malachi."

Yussef Kalantar didn't entirely forget his brother Yakub. He sent him money. Not much. Just enough to subsist and buy the bare essentials with which to build his home. Yakub bought everything he needed in the village; he never went beyond its boundaries. The people got to know him and liked him. He might have seemed one of life's recognizable unfortunates, but there was a look of dignified independence in his eyes which warded off pity, which invited companionship. Besides, he did own a good piece of land. That alone placed him among peers who had the awareness—however dim—of common responsibility.

Tiqva Zeff watched him as he set about repairing his home. Instinct alone guided his labour. He worked on his own. It was like reconstructing his own beginning from so many unfitting shards. Once, when frustrated by impossibilities, he threw his tools down and slumped on the ground close to tears, Tiqva, who saw, came over. She stood discreetly by until he regained his self-possession. Then she said, "My brother Leib could show you how to do this. I'll talk to him."

Leib showed him. Leib also took him on as a paid hand. Yakub couldn't have wished for a better teacher. He was learning about farming and animal husbandry. He worked hard, harder than any Arab falah Leib had ever employed. Leib was pleased with him. Until Yakub began to look on Tiqva as the agent of his salvation.

It wasn't falling in love. Yakub didn't woo Tiqva. He trusted her completely. He depended on her support, he sought approval in her calm gaze. He seized upon her rare smiles as an outcast seizes on a friendly gesture. Then one day, in the heat of the afternoon, he returned from the fields with a gash in his forehead from a chip of stone sent flying by the hoof of his mule. Tiqva made him sit down in her kitchen and washed his face. Her touch was cool and gentle. Looking at her as she bent over him, he suddenly saw how beautiful she was.

Leib was angry when Tiqva told him she wanted Yakub Kalantar for a husband. She could see the storm gathering in his face. He raised his voice but only for her to hear him better. He said sullenly, "The impudence of the man! To sneak like that behind my back. I'd like to whip him out of the village."

Tiqva's icy response caught him off-balance. "What has *your* back to do with this?" she said.

So he snarled at her, "What is he? A primitive nobody. Does the name Zeff mean nothing to you? Have you no sense of pride in all Father has done, and Grandfather and his father, Reb Solomon?"

Tiqva stood her ground. Her quiet ferocity more than matched his anger. "You have a wife, Leib. Soon you'll have children. Have you ever thought of anybody but yourself? I'm nineteen. Did you ever see a suitor come to our door? What shall I do with the name Zeff when I alone of all our family am left to do the chores in our parents' home? I'll tell you what he is. He is a man like you, with a body and a heart. A gentle honest heart, Leib. He doesn't care what my name is. It makes no difference to him that I'm plain and nearly deaf."

"Tomorrow I'll see him off my land. Let him do what he can on his bit of ground and his hovel," Leib said darkly.

"And I shall go to him and help him, if you do that," Tiqva said, which made him stare at her open-mouthed.

"If he were half the man you claim he is he'd have done the right thing. He'd have talked to me, he'd have waited till Father was back and asked properly for your hand."

Tiqva's mouth turned severe. She was quiet for a moment, then she said, "He has said not a word of this to me. I speak for him. When the time comes he'll do what you call the right thing and we shall be man and wife whether you like it or not. But if you do anything to him Leib, I shall never forgive you. Never."

"A name", Leib said adamantly, "is like land. You don't sell it cheaply."

He didn't turn Yakub out. But he was cold and withdrawn with him. It wasn't Yakub's origin that he resented as much as the suspicion that Yakub had taken advantage of him and presumed on their easy relationship before having really proved his worth. He hated pretence, nothing alienated him more than seeing a man reach out to take something he had not earned. When Yakub saw that his employer's change of attitude was more than a passing mood, he said to Leib, "I don't want to work for someone who despises me. I thank you for all you've done for me but from now on I'll go my own way and you go yours."

Bathsheba Zeligman kept her meetings with Baruch Schwartz underneath the spreading walnut tree that stood some three hundred paces from the communal threshing floor, and marked the boundary of the land whose ownership the Jews of Petach Tiqva claimed and the Arabs of Yehudia contested. Here, one hot evening, Baruch killed a large viper and nailed its carcase to the tree trunk. After that he looked on the place as his own field of conquest, where he could meet Bathsheba on equal terms, for she was a proud, high-spirited girl.

Beyond the walnut tree, away from the village threshing floor, the land swept upwards on to a bluff on the other side of which spread the fields of Yehudia. Wind-blown seeds from the threshing floor struck root in that stretch of land forming patches of rippling gold among the wild grass and the thistles. Waiting for Bathsheba to come, Baruch would feast his eyes on that piece of land and dream of what he would do with it if it were his. He had no land of his own. His father, a widower, was the settlement's *shochet*. Baruch was an only son. When he wasn't working in somebody else's fields, Baruch helped his father rounding up the chickens in the yard, trussing them up ready for the knife. After his father had cut their throats, Baruch would stack them on wooden shelves with a piece of paper tucked under their wings on which the name of the owner was written. There they stayed until, before the Sabbath set in, the people came to collect them. His life was divided between earth and blood. On the eve of Yom Kippur Baruch would deliver freshly-slaughtered white cocks and watch them swung over the heads of children while the Rabbi intoned prayers for the sins of those young innocents to be taken away by the dead bird. The absurdity of such an idea, coupled with the Rabbi's solemnity, made Baruch want to laugh out loud. It was with such a look in his eyes that Bathsheba first noticed him, and fell for him.

Long before Bathsheba Zeligman ever set eyes on Baruch Schwartz and decided she would have him—if he lived up to her expectations—she had achieved certain notoriety in Petach Tiqva. Like her mother, she was a steadfast, determined girl. Like her mother she had an open, honest face, not pretty but nevertheless not a face a man could easily ignore, with a firm mouth and an unflinching gaze. But unlike any other woman of her time and place, she rebelled against convention which seemed stupid to her. She was not without a sense of her own worth as a woman: Deborah the Prophetess inspired the sons of Israel to greatness; Bruria the Tana'ite, whose husband was among the compilers of the Talmud, had shown as much wisdom as any learned rabbi of her time. By what right did rabbinical convention condemn women to silent partnership? The unfair presumptuousness of this infuriated Bathsheba.

It was she who organized a group of girls to meet the young men of their age and discuss topics of the day under the guidance of Dr Godshalk. There, in his library, they talked about the ideas of the Lovers of Zion and read aloud passages of literature from Dr Goldshalk's books.

Her enterprises did not please the conservative spirit of Petach Tiqva. However, so long as these were restricted to meetings at Goldshalk's home, or singing together by the camp fire on warm summer nights, the elders of the village did nothing more than shake their heads, which didn't in the least intimidate Bathsheba. It was when she tried to introduce mixed dancing after the fashion of Rishon Le Zion, that the village council came out against her in full strength: under no circumstances would they allow in Petach Tiqva the frivolities and abominations which the new secularism brought to the Baron's settlements. Tears followed arguments. Some of the girls joined Bathsheba in refusing food for nearly a week, until one of them was taken ill. In the end Bathsheba had to accept defeat: she had under-estimated both the opposition her actions would arouse as well as the tenacity of the older people when it came to matters of tradition. Nevertheless, as a concession the Council agreed that three young men of musical talent, should be allowed to learn to play the fiddle, clarinet and trumpet in Rishon so that Petach Tiqva like the other settlements, might have its own band for special celebrations.

Throughout this, Zeligman stood aloof. He recognized in his daughter the defiant streak of his family and realized that opposing her would only make matters worse. Nor did he take any action when rumours reached him about her meetings with Baruch Schwartz. She could tell from the way he looked at her that he was set against him. So as she settled down to a kind of routine with the young man of her choice, she and her father moved round each other like two antagonists sizing one another up before the inevitable clash. It wasn't that Zeligman thought ill of Baruch; he didn't think anything of him at all, and certainly not that the poor lad, even at his very best, could measure up to his daughter.

Under the tree, in the soft hours of a pale evening, sat Baruch and waited for his Bathsheba to come. Presently he saw her hurrying through the grass, holding up her skirts as she ran. He stood up. She came to him panting, and pressed her face against his chest—Bathsheba didn't like kissing.

"I thought you wouldn't come," he lied, because that evening he felt good enough to force her to submission.

"What made you think that? I always come. Sometimes I'm late, that's all," she said, and rubbed her cheek against his.

A flock of crows flapped cawing across the sky. Snatches of laughter drifted from the threshing floor where a group of young men and women had gathered. The sound caught Baruch's attention. He became pensive.

"We shall both grow old before you make up your mind to marry me," he said mournfully, seeing the strategies he had envisaged fall apart.

"We're enjoying ourselves, aren't we, aren't you?" said Bathsheba and passed her hand over his groin.

"Will your father ever accept me?" he said, almost peevishly.

"When I'm done with him he will. So will everybody. When I want it," she replied with a laugh.

"You play games, Bathsheba. With me, with your father. People are no more than puppets to you. I wonder why I don't stay clear of you."

"Jacob worked twelve years to win Rachel. Couldn't you wait just a little for me?" she said caressing him.

"Because Laban was a cheat . . ."

"Look at the fields. Rich with corn. We've never had such a good year. After the harvest, you can have me."

"You promise?"

"I swear. Father or no Father." Her hand caressing his groin suddenly stopped.

"What's the matter?" he asked. She didn't answer, so he turned to see what she was looking at. Six donkeys and a dozen or so sheep had suddenly emerged from the meadow and were making straight for the field beyond the threshing floor, which was full of nearly ripe sorghum.

"They're doing it again!" Bathsheba cried.

He strained his eyes but could see no Arabs at the bluff.

"Oh they're there, hiding, you can be sure. Waiting to see how much damage their animals would do to our fields before we do anything. But we do nothing," she said bitterly, and added, "In Rishon they teach them a lesson. No, they wouldn't dare do that to Rishon. Here they'd do anything, they know they've nothing to be afraid of."

"The animals could've strayed. I don't see anybody," Baruch said.

"Nothing strays here. Everything is by design," she cut into him. "Only the men think otherwise, so that they have an excuse not to take any action!"

Baruch stood up. The animals had gone into the field and were trampling the crops as they grazed. Baruch felt his anger rise, and in his excitement his pulse quickened.

He heard Bathsheba say, "That's right, Baruch, go round them up and drive them back to Petach Tiqva. I'll help you."

That evening before nightfall, a group of sullen Arabs from Yehudia came to Petach Tiqva to claim their animals which, they said, had strayed on to the Jews' fields. They were greeted by a band of hard-faced young men who told them the animals had been driven there by intent as on all previous occasions, and would be returned only after their owners paid the village suitable compensation for the damage they had done. The Arabs returned to Yehudia empty-handed.

It was Friday morning. The sky was still heavy from the overnight rain—the last outburst of the *malkosh*, which ends the rainy season. That day a big purchase of supplies including some new farming equipment was to be made in Jaffa. The men hitched up the carts, saddled their horses, and rode out of Petach Tiqva immediately after the morning prayers. Only a few of the younger men remained. Baruch Schwartz was one. Yakub Kalantar was another.

Malachi came out into the street and made his way to the school. Today was no ordinary school-day for him. He was all but finished with that. This morning he was to play the teacher and tell the younger boys about the founding of Petach Tiqva, stories he had heard from his father, things he himself remembered or thought he did. He felt grown up, composed. The anticipation of giving a lesson gave him a heady sense of authority. He allowed himself to be a little late so that all the boys would be there, waiting for him as he entered the room. He was about to go in when he heard then saw Mendle Wolfe the blacksmith come running up the street waving his arms in the air and shouting, "They're coming, they're coming, hundreds of them!"

The Arabs had come on foot. They didn't charge up the street immediately, but gathered at the edge of Petach Tiqva where they began working themselves into a frenzy. There was no talk of merely retrieving the animals the Jews had taken; this was a day for settling scores. They were armed with clubs and knives. Some had guns. These were discharged into the air as the assailants shouted "*aliehum*—let's get the Jews!" The clamour reached into the heart of the village and alerted the people more terribly than a dozen Mendles with their alarm bells could have done.

Then Malachi saw Tiqva coming towards him. The swell of noise followed her like a tidal wave, she might have been propelled by it. There was blood on her dress and face. "Call out the children. Go to the store-house and bolt the door," she shouted. He near froze at the sight of her.

"What are you waiting for?" Tiqva screamed, "they've killed Yossle. Who'd have thought he had so much blood in him," and she stared broken-faced at her gory hands.

The Arabs set light to Yoel Zeff's house and the one next to it. So frantic was the conflagration that they stopped to marvel at the destruction they had begun. Which gave pause for the children, the women and the old to rush to the store-house and barricade themselves inside. Those who couldn't reach the store-house sought refuge in two nearby stone houses.

Inside the store-house, Bathsheba took command. Sacks of grain—anything heavy—were moved close to the door, ready to be piled up against it as soon as Baruch and Yakub, who were fighting to hold the assailants back, arrived. Missiles were collected in heaps by the two windows, each window manned by a team. The children and the old were told to sit at one corner behind a barrier of sacks and bits of old furniture which, in dire extremity, was to be the last stand. Standing with a pitchfork in her hand, Bathsheba contemplated the shape of the assault. The children began to cry. Reb Amram, the teacher, stood among them praying. He was trembling all over. Mendle, whose part deafness almost saved him from the pity or horror of sound, looked about critically. Suddenly he got up and began heaving the heavy sacks away from the door.

"For God's sake, what are you doing?" Bathsheba cried.

"What if they should set fire to the building? We won't be able to get out; we'd burn like mice," he shouted back.

"Better use this old shaft as a beam across the door. I'll show you."

At the mention of fire terrible scenes began coursing through Malachi's mind: visions of flames licking round Reb Amram's martyred face, the synagogue at ancient York where an excited mob burned the Jews, recurring rapes of Jerusalem, the pogroms at Kishinev—everything he had been told by his elders, by Reb Amram. Fire: wedded for ever to the Jewish experience. He thought of Yossle and wondered if he understood anything before he was killed, the poor dribbling idiot.

"God full of mercy," Reb Amram intoned in a tremulous voice. Malachi began to shake slightly. He sought Tiqva and went and sat close to her. The blood had clotted on her dress. It smelt rancid.

"Don't be afraid. No harm will come to us here. I shan't let anyone touch you," she said as she put her arm round him. For once he could believe her.

Suddenly there was banging on the door. The people inside, thinking it was the attack, leapt to their feet, seizing whatever weapons they could lay hands on. But it was Gutman, "Open up," he was shouting. "Let us in in the name of God."

Mendle removed the beam and cautiously opened the door. Reb Gutman staggered in supported by Yakub who was bleeding from a gun wound in the thigh. Gutman was shaken but unhurt. Soon he recovered his breath and calm. He began to reassure the people that once the Arabs had spent their fury burning a few houses and looting, they would go away: They had no stomach for killing, Gutman said.

In the lull that followed, Bathsheba suddenly became aware that Baruch was not there. "He's gone to Jaffa to get the men back," Yakub said, "He ran, said he would run all the way. It was the best thing to do."

And certainly if anyone was to do that Baruch was best qualified: he was fit and as fast on his feet as a colt.

The noise of the Arabs in the heat of plunder rolled down Hovevei Zion street and crashed against the barricaded door of the store-house. The attackers, in a second sally, at last found their main target. They began to ram the door, shouting rhythmically, "Yala, yala, yala." With each blow the walls shook. Bits of stone began falling from around the door frame. The besieged piled the sacks against the door adding their own weights to push against it. No one paid attention to Reb Amram who collapsed and lay motionless among the children.

The door miraculously held. Then there was a lull. They could hear the Arabs arguing what to do next. It occurred to Reb Gutman that he should try reasoning with the attackers. "I'll go out to them. Let them have me and leave the children and women in peace. Let's see if they are so godless as to strike down a defenceless old man," he said. So confused he was that instead of the door, he went to the window. No sooner had he opened it and stuck his head out than a hand grabbed at his beard. He would have been yanked clean out if Yakub hadn't brought the shaft of a pick he used as a club with all his might on the offender's arm.

The ramming was renewed. The door began to crumble. Yakub, his eyes blazing, gripped the pick shaft with both hands and stepped towards the door. He wanted to go out, engage the attackers and draw them from the door which would be shut behind him. Before he could do that, or be restrained, the door groaned then split down the middle. The Arabs stood red-faced at the gate. Yakub roared and charged swinging his club. Both sides raised a terrible din. Malachi saw the women move forward and form a barrier in front of the children. There was Bathsheba, defiant, the pitchfork in her hands poised for defence. He too moved forward, adding his voice to the clamour.

How he managed to stay on his feet in the mêlée seemed a miracle to him. No smaller miracle was the sudden withdrawal of the Arabs. They disengaged and moved across the street where they stood shouting and hurling stones. Then for no apparent reason, they began walking away. It was quiet. Until familiar shouts were heard from the other end of the village: the men had returned from Jaffa and with them a squadron of gendarmes.

At no time in his wretched existence did Yossle the idiot receive so much guilt-ridden praise as at his funeral. Reb Amram the teacher was the other fatal casualty of the attack. He died of a heart attack and was buried alongside Yossle's grave in Petach Tiqva's cemetery. After Kadish was said for them both, Baruch Schwartz confronted Zeligman.

"Reb Zeligman," he said, "I know you've never thought highly of me and wouldn't hear of my marrying Bathsheba, even though we love each other. I'm now asking you once again, before everybody, for Bathsheba's hand." Zeligman stared at him stony-faced. "Because", Baruch continued, "whether you agree to it or not, we shall marry."

Zeligman raised his hand, held it for a moment above Baruch's head, then slowly lowered it and touched Baruch's shoulder.

After the seven days' mourning for the two dead, the betrothal of Baruch Schwartz to Bathsheba Zeligman was announced, and so was that of Tiqva Zeff and Yakub Kalantar.

No sooner was Yakub married than, as often in his past, sorrow came to attend his happiness. A letter arrived from Jaffa informing him that his brother Yussef had been murdered. He was found one morning with his throat cut in the private quarters of his hamam. All his property had been impounded by the Governor of Jerusalem to cover the debts Yussef had left. For all the danger it involved, Yakub nevertheless saddled his horse and rode to Jerusalem to say Kadish over his brother's grave. He was the only one at the funeral. Their younger brother, who had inherited old Abraham's property, hadn't bothered to come.

The damage to the village was not so extensive as it seemed at first glance. Two houses had been gutted. Three more had been broken into and looted. Zeff's house was a total wreck. Nothing remained of it but charred wood and heaps of ashes. The villagers rallied to the family's aid. They rebuilt the home and refitted it with bits of furniture that people donated. The humiliation of the attackers was complete: they were marched in chains to Jaffa where, after a quick trial, presided over by a reluctant Ahmed El Husseini, they were imprisoned at the notorious Kishle pending a settlement with the Jews. The overwhelming legal victory of the Jews was made possible only because the charges were pressed by the Austrian Consul on behalf of a number of Austrian subjects headed by Reb Gutman.

Nevertheless the attack sent shock waves far and wide, stronger and louder the further they reached from their source. All at once Petach Tiqva was the heart of Jewish life—a living reminder of how precariously Jews existed in the Holy Land. Tales of heroism and horror, of death and destruction, circulated with ever growing exaggeration. They reached out to Europe and returned to their source like mountain streams swelled by melting snow, until even those who had gone through the experience forgot what it had really been like and believed what they were hearing. The Lovers of Zion Movement which had taken the settlement under its patronage, revived the call for more aid to the village. Newly arrived immigrants came to Petach Tiqva to settle there. They were mostly young people of no means, ready to work, eager for sacrifice.

Chapter 35

"Don't tell me where the boundaries lie, I can see for myself. There, the green, the fruit of love and work. Life! Yes, life. Man's ingenuity conquering his surroundings. Man, recreating Eden out of bleak wilderness. That's ours. And there, beyond: that dun-coloured waste, that stretch of stony nothingness, that's theirs, the Amalekites."

The speaker was a tall, broad-shouldered young man in his twenties. His hair, glinting bronze, massed about his strong sun-tanned face like a lion's mane. His eyes, whose depth was emphasized by the high ridge of his nose, were intense blue, fierce yet innocent. He had a resolute mouth with dazzling teeth.

"Amalekites," he repeated with theatrical sonority which nevertheless carried neither drama nor hatred.

"You shouldn't call them that. They are people. Neighbours. They have their way of doing things as we have ours," Malachi protested. His eyes swept over the rows of vines bent like bows in the morning light. Beyond them were the citrus groves dark green and glistening, boxed in by a wall of young poplars to protect them from the wind. The sight, on which so many people in Petach Tiqva prided themselves, didn't please him. It looked unintegrated, like an awkward hat worn by an otherwise sombre woman.

The young man laughed. He spread out his arms as if to embrace the scenery but settled for Malachi around whose shoulders he now placed his powerful arm. "My dear cousin, I mean them no disrespect. They are as different from us as their land is from ours, and they're here to put us to the test, for us to measure ourselves against them and excel." His Hebrew sounded rehearsed and he delivered his speech with contrived formality.

"When you get to know them you'll see how wrong your attitude is, Alexander," Malachi said.

The young man tossed his head, "Maybe. But I don't want to know them, and I shan't," he said and seeing the disapproving look on Malachi's face, Alexander squeezed his cousin's shoulder and said coaxingly, "Why must we argue when there's so much to tell and to hear, so many wonderful things to do? Come, let's away from here. You've shown me and I've seen."

Malachi allowed Alexander to lead him back to the village. His thoughts spiralled around Abigail Mitavsky and her friends whose admiration Alexander so easily commanded. He envied his cousin for the attention Abigail lavished on him, which he, Alexander accepted as nothing more than some charming triviality. He was also angry with himself for letting Alexander use this as an advantage over him, weakening his will, undermining his independence of thought. Yet he had to acknowledge that his cousin possessed an almost irresistible charm. He had seen how it worked on others, men as well as women. And he felt how susceptible he was to it himself.

When Alexander Zeff arrived in Palestine that spring he knew at once that here his destiny was to work itself out. It made no difference that what he saw largely contradicted the visions of his imagination. Paramount in his mind was the understanding that he had come back, like a long uprooted sapling, to strike root in his native soil, to grow, to spread, to bear fruit. The vagrancy of his past life, his miraculous and uncertain childhood, the years of wandering across America keeping company with strange and at times dangerous men, all these things which steeled his sinews and widened his inner geography, were meaningless if they weren't to serve the ultimate purpose which directed him to the land of his grandfather's birth.

Alexander had never known his grandfather Ariel, for he had died when Alexander was a baby, so his father had said. He came to life for him from stories his father told him. He knew that Ariel Mendle Zeff was taken away by Mr Pike to England, where Mr Pike abandoned him. He had a vision of Ariel as of a brilliance which had burnt itself out all the more rapidly after he had emigrated to New York and settled to an ordinary married life. That part of his grandfather's life Alexander preferred to forget. New York, where he came with so many hopes, defeated him and sapped what little energy there was left in him. Saul, who was born in New York, was, as people said, a *nebich*, a failure. For all that Myra Kessler, a liberated girl of independent spirit, reconfirmed her perversity in the eyes of her friends when she seduced and then married him. Saul found a job as a waiter in a popular Jewish eating place frequented by east European immigrants. While he served lemon tea in glasses with fresh bagels, he would see his wife Myra sitting at a table arguing current issues with liberated spirits like herself, young artists, thinkers, dreamers, chess players, who were not inhibited from slipping a hand up her skirts. Alexander's birth—Myra wanted the boy to have a heroic name—hardly changed her way of life. She brought the baby to the café and breast-fed him there while her friends formed a screen round her.

Because Saul couldn't compete with Myra in her world, which was constantly invading his, he built for his growing son a world of myth and legend ruled by the demi-god figures of Ariel and his father Solomon. There was some victory, he felt, in that Myra abandoned them both when Alexander was six, and disappeared with an anarchist fiddler never to be seen or heard from again.

The café on Rivington Street, East Side, was Alexander's school. Here he learnt Hebrew, listened to stories about the history of the Jews, and listened to the ideas of the Lovers of Zion vehemently debated. A landscape full of colour and wild vistas was unfolding before his inner eye. That which had been left unsketched about his grandfather, he filled in himself.

At sixteen Alexander set off to discover his depth: he was big and strong enough for the world. The café in Rivington Street could no longer satisfy his impatient curiosity. His father was powerless to stop him. For two years Alexander drifted about America living on his wits, doing a job here and a job there. He learnt to wrestle; he toured with a circus. Working with wild beasts taught him to read the nature of people from looking at their mouths rather than their eyes. It occurred to him, even in the company of visionaries he had met, that no animal had a mouth so greedy and so unpredictable as man, and that women's mouths tended to be more dangerous than men's. The fact that he survived danger time and time again gave him a superstitious belief that he was indestructible, an agent of some higher design which inexorably pointed him in the direction of his grandfather Ariel's origin.

Back in New York he fell in with idealists of the Lovers of Zion Movement. He grew to despise them for talking so much about Zion in Rivington Street instead of going there to live out their ideals. For the first time in his life he began to study seriously. A group of young men and women gathered round him. Slowly, without his thinking about it, the momentum of commitment moved him towards the day when he was ready to go; there was no turning back. His father accepted that he should probably never see Alexander again just as he had accepted his own misfortunes as a matter of course. He gave Alexander all the money he could lay his hands on, then took a day off to get drunk in the company of the widow Bluma Heskis who used to press his trousers and occasionally stimulate that which was inside them, and with whom he began to see possibilities of a happy life.

Of all the young men and women who lionized Alexander in New York, only two stuck with him when it came to leaving for Palestine. They were Asa Mitavsky and his twin sister Abigail. The three of them stood on the deck among the crowd and watched Manhattan recede into the mist. "Just as well. We are the pathfinders, the agents of history. We are now a family," Asa said as he linked his arms through his sister's and Alexander's. Alexander smiled but said nothing. His thoughts were already far away across the sea.

Malachi alone among his family was uncertain about his future. Leib, his eldest brother, was a farmer as confident of his vocation and proud of his success as any tiller of the soil could be. Tiqva had found her place in the world which had been so inclement to her, and was settling down to build a home with the man she believed Providence had sent her. Chaim, who had made his mark among the clever and promising men of Jerusalem, had set his sights on a career of public service and publishing—where Yoel had left off, he began, with steady application and his own idiosyncratic enthusiasm. His home resounded to the shrieks and laughter of children: he held his world in the palm of his hand. Yoel Zeff, steeped in honour, could look on his children with a sense of fulfilment—did they not, each in his own way, reflect what he had always hoped to achieve?

It was a time of thrusting forward, of a headlong rush into modernity. The future looked to Yoel more assured yet less predictable than it seemed when he was young. It was exciting, it was demanding, it made him feel awkward, it made him worry for his family. Malachi was young, though at his age Yoel recalled, his own life was already set on a course. At times he was impatient with Malachi's searching, he wished he could find his orientation. The closer Yoel grew to Leib and Chaim, the more protective Hannah became of Malachi, her Benjamin, her favourite, and plain, sombre Tiqva with her quiet merciless understanding.

Alexander's sudden arrival in Petach Tiqva might have filled them all with wonder and bemusement had life not taught them already to accept the impossible: only three years before, the railway line between Jaffa and Jerusalem had been completed; swarms of locusts invaded the country from the east and consumed everything except the crops of Petach Tiqva; three calves were born, each with two heads; and Mendle the blacksmith, deaf as a post and without a tooth in his head, married a woman half his age. With such things happening, Yoel said, you could expect anything!

He didn't question Alexander's authenticity. He knew almost nothing about Alexander's grandfather, Ariel, for neither his father nor his grandfather Solomon had ever talked about him, except in reference to some other matter, and then the mention of the name was invariably followed by a pained silence. Old Samuel Rimkin was the only one alive and close to the Zeff family who had personal recollections of Ariel. One look at Alexander convinced him that however unlikely it was, in view of Ariel's disappearance from the world, here was his living progeny. He wanted no part of him.

But Alexander Zeff was not easy to dislike and impossible to ignore. His presence was arresting, his manner compelling, arousing either strong affection or intense dislike. Jerusalem, with her memories and natural reticence, held him at arm's length, but Jaffa, with her burgeoning life and rushed expectations, embraced him, cossetted him, was ready to swallow him. He became the focus of attention, the vessel of new ideas. Young people, new immigrants with little to lose and too much hope, found inspiration in his carefree courage. They rallied round him like soldiers round a banner.

He came to Petach Tiqva on foot, but like a prince ready to claim his inheritance. How could Yoel Zeff not accept him with open arms, his long lost relative!

The green acres of Petach Tiqva which so moved Alexander as he stood looking at them with Malachi concealed an unpleasant reality: near bondage to the officers of the 'Benefactor' Baron de Rothschild on the one hand; obduracy and resentment on the other. The first engendered servile turpitude, the second poverty.

The Baron's intervention in the fortunes of the settlement lifted Petach Tiqva from stagnation in the early Nineties. All at once the land became priceless; certainty attended every aspect of village life. Among the six hundred souls who now lived in Petach Tiqva, you could find craftsmen, artisans, farmers, and loafers. Everybody was in the Baron's employ for a wage of nine piasters per day. Even Dr Mazze who had come to replace Dr Godshalk was in the Baron's pay.

Everybody, except eight families, who refused to give up their independence, and were in turn spurned by the Baron's chief Agent, Yehuda Farb. Leib Zeff was one of these, the most determined and outspoken in the group.

As in all the other colonies run by the Baron's administration, so in Petach Tiqva under Farb's administration all the available land was planted with vines—the Indian vine which the Baron's experts considered particularly suitable for local conditions—or with orange groves, or even with new mulberry trees for the silk industry which was one of Farb's obsessions. Leib defiantly continued to till his land and sow cereal. The dark-brown colour of the turned earth would cheer the spirit of his rebellion just as the tawny gold of the ripe corn filled him with a sense of victory. He grew to hate the glossy green of the orange trees and the regimented uniformity of the vines.

Often at the end of the day the men used to meet at Katz's tavern. Here more than anywhere, the social divisions were strictly observed: the Baron's men sat grouped together, the tillers of the soil had their own corner; the newcomers, the landless labourers sat apart and listened to the two other groups contradicting each other. One such evening, Leib, lifting his eyes from his glass, met the gaze of a man who had once been a friend and now worked in Rothschild's vineyards. Leib's face clouded. After a while he slapped the table with the flat of his hand and shouted: "Don't stare at me like that. You're a slave, all of you. My grandfather in the days of the haluka in Jerusalem was freer than you. You live on charity, just like the old ones in Jerusalem."

"It's you who's a slave, Leib," the man replied, "slave to your stubborn pride. You're so blind that you don't see how things have changed. What will you do with your miserable grain that nobody wants? Why do you go on scratching the soil like a falah when you could enjoy an easier life and see your children grow up in comfort? You don't even have to bend your knee, only accept that you're wrong."

Leib sneered at him. He grabbed a piece of bread, tore it and held it in his fists. "That's wheat. Where does it come from? Mostly from the Arab falahin. All those vines that have been planted, who'll use the grapes? Is there a shortage of grapes in France, in Italy, in Germany? I've not heard any of the Baron's officers say so. What will you all do when Rothschild stops supporting the colonies with his money? Get drunk on your wine?" He bit into the bread and chewed angrily. When his mouth was clear, he continued, "You have no memory. You're destroying everything for which Petach Tiqva was built."

Such points of view were not new in the colonies. They were also being voiced by critics of the Baron's enterprise, mostly young intellectuals, followers of the thinker and writer Ehad Ha'am. They had been heard already at the first rebellion against the authority of the Baron's administration in Rishon Le Zion in 1887 and in Zichron Yaakov the following year, both of which received wide publicity and ended in the humiliation of the settlers. They attended the feverish land purchases of Yehoshua Hankin, a Russian Jew who applied himself with missionary zeal and little discretion to buying land on behalf of various Jewish settlement organizations wherever land was up for sale. They were, above all, the mark of identity, the Shibboleth of idealists like Asa Mitavsky and his sister Abigail who nevertheless reluctantly took up employment in Petach Tiqva with the hard-faced Yehuda Farb.

Leib's own sentiments owed nothing to the idealists. He despised them. He was hanging on with atavistic ferocity to the world he knew, lashing out at anybody and anything which he felt threatened it. He mistrusted the newcomers with their dreams, their presumptions, above all, their ignorant assertions. At times they gave him a sense of kinship with the Arab falahin whom he knew and whom he had fought. But more than any of them he disliked Alexander Zeff. Alexander was handsome and strong. He might have put his heaven-sent gifts to good use. Instead he idled his time, appeared frivolous and effete. The young idealists flocked round him, celebrated him as though he were a deity, but Alexander only laughed and played with them. Leib's farmer's soul abhorred waste. But his resentment of Alexander went deeper than that: Alexander had won the heart of Malachi. For this, and for bearing his name, Leib hated him.

Farb held Alexander and his friends in contempt. They couldn't really work, he kept saying, they merely pretended to. Any Arab falah could do two days' work in the time it took those idlers to do half a day. Farb was an enemy but at least he was a man, a serious and committed farmer, like Leib himself. Leib could fight a man like Farb without really hating him. He had respect for him, which was more than he had for the young men of the village whose elder brothers had ridden with him, his brothers in spirit, who were now turning their backs on the past and whoring after Farb and his inexhaustible resources. Yes, they wanted horses, and guns, wanted to dress like Beduin warriors and ride through the fields keeping watch on the property, in place of the Arab watchmen Farb hired.

These young men, nourished from boyhood on stories in which Leib had been the hero, now lowered their eyes and shuffled their feet on the floor as Leib shot accusing gazes at them in Katz's tavern. They were a good bunch—Sander Hadad, with his smooth hair and high cheekbones (the Tartar, they called him), peerless breaker-in of horses, master wielder of the leaded whip, no fighter braver than he; young Ethan Daskal, Leib's own brother-in-law, hardly more than a boy but what steely nerves! Abraham Margolis who had a girl's smile and dark curly hair. He could shoot straighter and faster than any man from Jaffa to the Carmel hills. All the others. Leib fumed against them impotently. Yet in his heart he knew that no better young men could be found anywhere in the country. If the settlement were attacked they would defend it with their lives. It was the system, and Farb, subtle, wily enemies which corrupted from within, which bred cruelty out of indolence, which took the fire and purpose out of heroism. These thoughts tormented Leib whenever he saw a Jewish horseman riding by.

Yehuda Farb was in the habit of going over the accounts in the quiet hours of the morning. Balancing credits against the debits gave him a sense of reality by reminding him that an inevitable gap existed between what he sought to achieve and what in fact could be done. He blamed the gap on the fractiousness of his fellow Jews, their disputatious nature, and lack of discipline when action was needed. They reminded him of unruly children, each one thinking he knew everything better than the next. He had no patience for them.

Farb was a dedicated man. Trained as an agronomist in Germany, he lived for his work. Foolish mistakes, imperfections arising out of slovenliness would send him into a rage. He never doubted his own judgement. The only faults he acknowledged were impatience and irritability, a release from which he always prayed for.

As he stared at the scribbled columns of figures in the accounts book anger welled in him: notwithstanding his constant admonitions, the exhortations, he saw waste—of time and of material. It wouldn't be so if the colonists had to fend for themselves, he thought. But they didn't care—it was, after all the Baron's money. "The Baron will pay" was their saying.

If Farb had his way he would run the whole colony on Arab labour. Then he'd show them what could be done! At least the falahin worked, did what they were told and no arguments. They didn't fall sick every other day, they didn't make demands or hold meetings. And they were cheaper. It wasn't that Farb didn't believe in Jewish redemption through work. He did, as passionately as anybody. If only the effort wasn't so one-sided. Every day his striving for perfection was bruised, his sense of symmetry thrown into disarray. And for all his dedicated work, how untrusting, how ungrateful the colonists remained. Instead of treating him as their saviour, which he was—he had no doubt of that—they saw him as the oppressor, the devil who stood between them and the Baron's gentle munificent heart. Well, if that's the way it was, he would teach them a lesson, he would not compromise his standards to win their affection.

In his isolation his thoughts always turned to the Zeffs: stubborn people, truculent Leib and his father Yoel, that self-righteous old man so honoured by time and past achievement that to say anything against him was almost blashphemy. But whatever they were, they were no idlers. Dangerous. They could be neither bought nor intimidated. He would break them, yes. There was no other way. And when he did there would be no more dissent in Petach Tiqva against his rule. The rest would submit like sheep. The newcomers would have to toe the line, or leave.

Laying aside the accounts ledgers, he began to jot down notes for his annual report to the chief Baron's bailiff. Bookbinder's milk cart came into view, the horse's thin neck projecting into the window frame. Farb stopped writing for a moment. He could hear the horse coughing. It was an old horse but Bookbinder wouldn't hear of retiring it, because he himself was old and frail and the horse was a clever animal, it would walk on up to the next delivery while Bookbinder was collecting the fee for the last one, and wait until Bookbinder limped along to the next stop.

Farb smiled: four coughs at the most, and the old horse would move on. Until one day, maybe tomorrow, it would collapse between the shafts before it reached the end of Hovevei Zion Street. That would finish Bookbinder, even if Farb would provide him with another animal.

It was time Mendle Pushinsky arrived. He normally came through the door before Bookbinder's cart trundled to the end of the street. Farb would give Mendle a look, mutter "Good morning" and let his young assistant settle down to his work. But sometimes, just because he felt like it, he would scold Mendle until the poor man's lips began to tremble. Pushinsky seldom pleased Farb: his account-keeping, for which he was chiefly employed, was sloppy. Worse still, Pushinsky adored Abigail Mitavsky and for the sake of impressing her he did all sorts of foolish things, like learning to ride on the most difficult horse in the village, falling off in the process and taking days off recovering. How Sander Hadad, young Margolis, and

Shapira used to make fun of poor Mendle Pushinsky, put him on Sander's impossible colt and set him galloping madly down Petach Tiqva's thoroughfare clinging to the horse's mane in fear of his life. All for the love of that imperious girl who wouldn't even grace him with a look! Farb couldn't help being attracted to her himself. He would see her bending over the vines as she worked among the rows, her hair sneaking out of her kerchief, wisps of it sticking to her pale long neck. Whenever she saw him she would avert her eyes. He was angry at himself for wanting her, even angrier with Mendle Pushinsky for adoring her so abjectly and allowing himself to be humiliated by Petach Tiqva's young bloods for her sake.

The coughing of Bookbinder's horse could barely be heard now. Other noises began to obtrude. The people were leaving their houses for the day's work. And still there was no sign of Mendle Pushinsky. Farb got so angry he couldn't concentrate on what he was doing. "I've been too lenient with the wretch," he said to himself. "But this time he'll be sorry, really sorry." The morning wore on. Still there was no sign of Pushinsky. Farb made a note to dock Mendle's pay by one day, and left the office on his rounds, his mind seething with images of what he would do to Pushinsky.

Poor Mendle Pushinsky was not the only one who was hopelessly in love with Abigail. She aroused passions in several young men in Petach Tiqva. She also had admirers in Rishon Le Zion where she often went with her brother and with Alexander for meetings. In the new country she bloomed like the Lily of Sharon. What had been not out of the ordinary good looks turned into gentle comeliness which stole on you surreptitiously so that recognizing her beauty became an act of self-discovery, intoxicating as it was surprising. Here at last she was free of convention. A sense of freedom attended everything she did. She gave her admirers a glimpse into what they suddenly realized they had always desired in a woman but could never possess, unless they rose to heights of unreachable excellence. And they tried, vying with one another not so much in jealousy as in competitive camaraderie. She was the peer of every young man of quality, without in the least losing her femininity.

Abigail wrote poetry. She wrote of the fields, of the smell of the soil after the first rains, of the star-filled dark sky, of yearnings for lost simplicity, of heroes returning to redeem their ancient homeland, and of their women —the reapers' wives, the warriors' lovers. Her poems had the forcefulness of innocence. And when she read them out aloud round the glowing fire, in her voice which was as rich and dark as full-bodied wine, even the eyes of Sander Hadad filled with tears.

Abigail's poems, her voice, her face, everything about her haunted Malachi to distraction. He had recently become the second teacher in the village school, a responsibility he seized eagerly. Yet even as he faced the class his thoughts wandered to Abigail. What was taught at school was strictly orthodox. But in his own time he would read Abigail's poems to a group of the older more intelligent pupils. He was shocked when one of them pointed out to him that Abigail's heroes all resembled Alexander Zeff: it hadn't occurred to him that it was so obvious. How could he admit to himself that he loved her in the ordinary sense of the word when everything about her was extraordinary, when she seemed more unattainable than ever when she was close to him, laughing, exchanging views in her intense yet open way?

If she singled him out for more show of affection than the others it was on account of his kinship to Alexander. For all that, Malachi couldn't detect love—not physical love—in Abigail's relationship with his cousin. She was the same with Alexander as she was with the others, with himself, with Asa, only more so. As for Alexander, he seemed to accept her affection as his due. He would put his arm round her shoulders, pat her, kiss her on the cheek as he did even with the men. If he was her prince, she was to him but a beloved courtier. Only Mendle Pushinsky suffered openly while the others made sport of his agony as if to distance themselves from what they felt, which he devalued in his weakness.

Rehovot was a thriving settlement built in some 10,000 dunams of land purchased by Yehoshua Hankin and his associates from the village Duraan in 1890, a year before immigration restrictions came into force, and at a time when the regulations previously promulgated by the Sultan Abdel Hamid II concerning the participation of Jews in local authorities promised a more or less secure future for the Jews of Palestine. The founders named the settlement after the biblical Rehoboth mentioned in Genesis. Their belief that this was the site of the ancient settlement where Isaac dug a well and "called the name of it Rehoboth; and he said for now the Lord hath made room for us, and we shall be fruitful in the land", was stengthened by the sense of vast open spaces the place gave them, and the immediate gush of fresh water which the first drilling produced. The Baron's administration never came to Rehovot. The village was conceived and planned on the ideals of Ehad Ha'am: independence, mixed farming, and economic stability. Affairs of the village were conducted with shrewd caution: nothing spent that couldn't be earned. The soil favoured vine-growing and citrus. So the settlers grew vines to supply the Baron's wine presses in Rishon Le Zion, and planted orange trees. There was hardly any trouble between the Jews of Rehovot and the Arabs of Duraan. They had respect for each other, and kept their distance. The young men of Rehovot quickly established a reputation as fierce fighters. When local Beduin saw the young men of Rehovot race through the settlement's main street in chariots hitched to camels, they told each other that a new breed of Jews had come to live in their midst.

Landowners, by common agreement, preferred Jewish labourers to Arab —not just Yemanite Jews whom overseers like Farb were prepared to accept, but all Jews. Any Jew who came to Rehovot could find an open door and welcoming arms.

A special bond existed between Petach Tiqva and Rehovot, as though the older settlement looked fondly on the younger one, happy at its success, proud of its independence, and at the same time a little shame-faced about its own failure. Here in Rehovot Yoel and Leib Zeff felt at home. To here also came Alexander soon to win fresh followers. If Yehuda Farb's heavy hand suppressed expectations and dampened enthusiasm, Rehovot offered a respite where freedom, like the nearby sea and the orange-blossom scented evening breeze, restored spent energy and assuaged hurts.

One brilliant summer morning at the early hour when larks were rising over the steaming fields, Alexander and his friends stole out of Petach Tiqva leading a pair of mules belonging to Yoel Zeff. Malachi was there too. So was Abigail Mitavsky as well as two other girls and also Mendle Pushinsky. Hidden in the orange groves was the cart, brought there the previous night.

It was Friday, and the day when many of the men, including Farb, would be going to Jaffa on business and to buy things. The young men and women who joined Alexander had been working hard all week—it was the height of the grape-picking season. Now, seizing on the chance of a day off and the availability of the mules, they had decided to spend the day on the beach near Rehovot with friends from that village. It was Asa Mitavsky who organized the expedition. He could organize anything, from a day's outing to a labour confederation for which he had gained recognition throughout the Jewish settlement. He calculated that they should be back around the time when the men returned from Jaffa, certainly before the fall of the Sabbath.

They reached Rehovot well before noon, then joined by their friends, half a dozen young men and women, they drove to the beach. The sea was calm, dazzling blue. Not a trace of human visitation on the beach apart from them. They spread a mat on the sand. The girls unpacked the food they had brought: white cheese, olives, bread baked in Petach Tiqva that morning, and a large supply of grapes and fruit from Rehovot. One of the Rehovot lads also produced three bottles of wine, a present from the Baron, he declared, then explained to his laughing companions how he had stolen them.

Alexander reeked of garlic because every morning he would eat cloves by the handful, together with bread and olive oil. So deep was his faith in himself that he didn't seem to mind in the least the discomfort his malodorous breath imposed on his companions. Indeed, so powerful was his charm that it seemed to lull the senses of his friends to the offensive smell. He believed in the therapeutic and invigorating qualities of garlic; it cleansed the blood of all impurities, it gave you a strong, healthy heart, he would explain: "We're told, Malachi, that the Roman Empire fell through moral turpitude. That too. But the real reason was that the armies lost their fighting vigour because they ran out of garlic to eat. Teach that to your pupils, cousin," he said. Malachi knew nothing about the Romans except that they had desecrated the Temple of the Lord and killed and enslaved Jews. He was never quite sure how he should respond to Alexander's unsolicited bits of strange information. On that occasion he said fuzzily, "The Romans are not an example Jews want to learn from." To which Alexander replied with a laugh, "If you don't learnt from your enemies it's your fate to be defeated."

After they had eaten and rested, Alexander stripped to the waist and waded into the sea. Shortly he returned, shaking the water from his hair and beard and snorting like a bull. The brine glistened on his naked chest and arms, highlighting the contours of his muscles. He picked up a stick and drew a wide circle in the sand. Then flexing his arms and assuming a springy crouch, he challenged anyone to come and wrestle with him. He looked magnificent and invincible. Sander Hadad was the first to take up the challenge, he could never refuse one. Their arms interlocked, their bodies strained against one another, then Sander was sent flying head over heels out of the circle. So were three more men who chanced their luck against Alexander. He wiped his brow with his forearm. "Did any of you know," he said with jovial earnestness, "that one of our great rabbis Simeon Ben Lakish was a gladiator in the Roman amphitheatre in Caesarea? We Jews have been like weak creatures hibernating in darkness for generations upon generations. But here there's light and we are free. Here we must re-discover the art of living."

He came over to Malachi, put his arm around his neck and drew him towards him. "Come, Malachi, wrestle with me." It was as though he had invited him to dance. There was no point resisting, he was so strong. He didn't throw Malachi, but passing one arm round his thigh while the other gripped him by the shoulder, he lifted him high and spun around with him before he put him down on his feet.

They were standing on the wet sand inside the circle, Malachi dizzy as if he had had too much wine, Alexander his chest heaving from the effort, one arm still round his cousin's shoulders. Then, in a triumphant gesture, he took Malachi's hand in his and raised it like two champions saluting the crowd of spectators. The others cheered and clapped their hands. Abigail's face was flushed, she was cheering louder than the others and Malachi felt as though she was seeing him for the first time.

From that moment he, like the others, lost sense of the passing hours. They were singing, discoursing, playing, until drowsiness overtook them.

The afternoon wore on, shadows lengthened on the beach, a cool breeze ruffled the surface of the water. The friends broke up into little groups, some went for a walk or searched for sea shells. Alexander lay sprawled on the sand, asleep beside his companions. Malachi rolled up his trousers and walked along the beach, letting the advancing wash lick at his ankles. A little way on he came upon Abigail. She was sitting at the edge of the water facing the sinking sun, her arms hugging her knees, her rich hair let loose. So deep was she in her thoughts that she neither saw nor heard him approach. But when he was but a few steps from her she looked up, smiled, and patted the sand beside her inviting him to sit down.

"It's been such a perfect day, I'll never forget it as long as I live," she said.

Malachi said nothing, and she took his silence to mean that he shared her feelings. They sat close to one another staring out to sea. She began to try out a combination of words to describe the way the light touched the water. He tried to help. Suddenly she broke off and said, "He's truly great. He makes things clear in one's mind without having to explain. I understood this today for the first time, I mean really understood."

"You mean Alexander?"

"Who else?"

Malachi picked up a chip of a shell and started tracing figures in the sand. "You're in love with him, aren't you?" he said at last, his heart pounding.

"What's that you said?" Abigail asked. He shook his head. "Never mind."

It took her an instant to work it out. Then she threw her head back and laughed. "In love with Alexander? Whatever gave you that idea?"

"The way you talk about him, and look at him," he replied, puzzled yet relieved.

"I love him and I love you and I love all the others, and the sea, every inch of this country most of which I don't yet know. Yes, Malachi, what are we all here for if not to love?"

"But Alexander more than anyone else," he ventured to say, at which she shook her head. "When you write a poem sometimes a word, one single word which in itself is unremarkable, turns the poem from a mere observation into a powerful insight, in fact makes the poem. Alexander's like that. In love with him?" Again she laughed. "No, Alexander's not for loving, he's for making you understand, see possibilities, as he did today, wrestling on the beach."

Malachi looked at her questioningly. "What did he show you, wrestling on the beach, except that he was stronger than any of us?" he asked, doubting her for once. But she met his gaze with such affirmation that he almost despised himself for failing to understand.

"Not stronger than any of us, Malachi", Abigail replied with earnest serenity. "Don't you see that being what he is makes any one of us like him?"

"I don't know what he is, except that he's strong, though probably not so strong as my brother Leib once was. Maybe you don't know what he is either, you're confusing him with some idea you have in your imagination," Malachi said, digging his feet into the sand.

"The imagination", Abigail insisted, "is the ultimate truth. Who can tell what will be here when we are gone. Cities? Many settlements? Will the Kingdom of Juda or Israel rise again? Or maybe it'll all come to nothing, end in defeat and emptiness, swamps and empty hillsides again, inhabited only by Arabs. It is important Malachi, for us to build settlements, to plough fields, to leave our mark on this land. But the way we do it is even more important, that is what'll be remembered. The spirit in which we create, the heroism of it. That's what Alexander Zeff means, like your father, his father, and Reb Solomon Zeff."

"You make them out to be legends, but they were just men, people like you and me. Did you ever think what fear and pettiness, and squalor went with so much of their lives?" Malachi said with a laugh. But she just shook her head. "You miss the point," she said. "What they all were as individuals might be the concern of their descendants—even they will shape them to suit their own dreams. For the rest of us, for all the Jews here in Eretz Israel, they'll be legends. Yes, Malachi. We need myths and legends to bridge our renewed existence here with our past."

"You newcomers need symbols and myths because you dream. You want redemption through work. Farb despises you because you talk more than you work. You think you'll change everything. People like my brother Leib don't need symbols or myths. Everything he does arises from the needs of everyday life. He has tradition, he remembers what he did, and what others did, you see. So who is right?"

"There is no right or wrong," Abigail said. "There are two worlds, two realities. One day they'll meet and be one. That's what I believe, that's what Asa's working for. But you, Malachi, where do you stand?"

He shrugged his shoulders, then picked up a pebble and threw it to the sea. "I wish I knew. What you're saying makes me think a lot. But I understand the old ways, I know their strengths. When I was a boy I used to think I was very special, that I could make things happen by imagining them. Now my imagination, it seems, is left behind events."

The sea was turning dark. Flocks of gulls came winging seaward.

"You *are* special. Just for living in these exciting times, you're special," Abigail said, and getting to her feet, she stretched out her hand to him.

Alexander woke up, yawned loudly, and stretched. Then he took in the near-frantic expression on the faces of his friends. "What is it?" he asked.

"One of the mules has gone," Mendle Pushinsky said in near panic.

"Even if we found it we'll never make it back to Petach Tiqva before Sabbath sets in." He was thinking of Farb, and his despondency was all the gloomier for having seen Abigail sitting on the beach with Malachi in what seemed to him close intimacy. Mendle loved suffering.

Alexander got up, shook his head like a rising lion. "Well, the Almighty will forgive us, of that I've no doubt. What do the others matter? They'll be a little angry and then they'll forget it. Let's find the mule."

The first three stars appeared in the heaven by the time the company, having found the wayward mule, cleared the precincts of Rehovot and were on their way to Petach Tiqva. They were doing the most forbidden thing, travelling on the Sabbath. Another time Malachi might have thought that any moment a bolt would shoot out from the sky to strike them dead. But Alexander raised his voice in a song, "We've come to our land and built it and be rebuilt in it." His voice defied fears, defied tradition, and outfaced the gathering night. The rest joined him. The cart trundled on, with Sander Hadad driving, urging on the mules with a deft flick of his whip.

Was it the rocking motion of the cart which made Abigail lean against him? Or was it that she wished to press closer to Alexander who was sitting on the other side, his heavy arm laid along the rail of the cart, across Malachi's shoulders so that his hand might have been touching her? The alternatives he conjured tormented Malachi, and thrilled him. The chirping of the cicadas throbbed in the night, he could smell the river sweetened by the scent of honeysuckle. On an impulse, when he noticed that Alexander's attention was momentarily claimed elsewhere, he turned to Abigail and said, "You, Abigail, more than anyone, being what you are, make me understand what you meant when we were talking on the beach. You, more than Alexander. You inspire with your words just as Deborah inspired Abinoam." He spoke so softly because he was afraid somebody would overhear and laugh at him. But she was close to him, her shoulder pressed against his chest. So he dared go on: "I keep thinking about you, wondering what kind of man you'll marry, what hero will win your heart."

She laughed softly and said, "Probably I'll never marry. There are too many exciting and important things to do. But if I did I don't think I'd want a hero for a husband."

"Not someone like Alexander?"

"No, never. Maybe someone gentle and understanding. Someone like you, perhaps," she said.

Chapter 36

The cart rolled into Petach Tiqva as dark was descending on the village. Useless for Pushinsky who now drove to slow down; the grinding of the wheels, the squeaking of the cart, the sound of the animals' hooves and their snorts, all seemed to scream obscenely against the sanctity of the Sabbath. The people in the cart held their breath. Malachi's heart was pounding so hard it alone might have shaken the people of Petach Tiqva, out of their eve of Sabbath thanksgiving, and bring them out to the street to witness the desecration.

A window opened, then a door, and another. People came out to stare in outraged disbelief. It was too late to jump the cart and run home, run anywhere, away from the accusation.

"Shame! *Shobbes*! Desecrators!" The cries swelled to a tide of angry cacophony. All the pent-up feelings the villagers had against the newcomers now erupted. "Away from here! This is a Jewish village. We don't want *shkotzim*. Out of here, corrupters, lewd bastards!" Then, like the first drop of a cloudburst, a rock hit the side of the cart. Alexander grabbed the reins from Pushinsky, stood up and let out a yell, whipping the mules as he did so. The cart shot forward and careened at full tilt down the street. At least they were safe from injury though only Malachi and Pushinsky could appreciate what was yet to come.

The whole family was gathered round the table: Yoel and Hannah, Leib and his wife Tzila and their baby son, Yoab, Tiqva and Yakub Kalantar. Malachi's place, at his mother's side was empty. They were in sombre mood. Malachi took in the scene looking through the window from the outside. He opened the door and walked in. Leib's face hardened. He half-rose from his seat. "Sit down, Leib and hold your tongue," Yoel said. "Let us not add to the shameful desecration of the Sabbath."

Without looking at Malachi, he said, "I've nothing to say to you now. Go to your room. You will not sit at the table with us tonight." It was useless, he realized at once, to say anything. When his father's face was set in that expression of stony gravity, nothing could move him. As for his brother Leib, if he provoked him not Yoel, not Hannah, no restraining force in the world would stop him from thrashing him.

In the darkness of his room he heard his family's tense silence, occasionally broken by Leib's soft grumble and his father's sharp rebuke.

He was tired and hungry. One by one the scenes of the day revisited him, again and again, tormenting him beyond endurance. He heard his father rise and clear his throat, then the others departing to their homes. At last there was silence, heavy with the hurt he had inflicted which not even Abigail's magic could assuage.

Throughout the day the heat warred against life, beating all but Leib's furious determination to finish cutting the hay before the afternoon was out. The horses hitched to the mowing machine plodded on wearily, or else stood dazed at the end of the field before the turn. Clouds of gnats buzzed about their heads, persistent and relentless as the heat. The sky was pewter-colour. The fetid smell of the river lay across the fields. "Hi, hi," Leib urged the horses; he felt the weight in their feet, like lead. As if to mock his effort, the faint redolence of the distant orange groves wafted across to him.

At the far end of the field Yoel squatted in the sparse shade of a bent fig tree. He had walked over from the village to be with his son, even though his head throbbed and his chest felt like a brass furnace, just to be with Leib so that he may not be alone when he was so angry.

From here he watched Leib straining with the machine, his shirt dusty and sticking to his back, his hair and beard caked against his face. A moon-shaped strip of sun-blasted grass still remained to be cut. Yoel called out, "Leave off Leib, enough, or you'll kill the horses." But Leib paid no attention, holding the reins in his teeth, he wrestled with the shafts as he turned the machine round. Yoel sighed. There was no point trying to tell Leib what to do when he was in such a mood, he would sooner drive himself and the horses to death than give up.

The heat rose from the earth and entered Yoel's body. He felt his weight dissolve and spill out of him on to the cracked soil. His heart beat in heavy tired thuds. "My body is old and tired," he thought. "It has been through too much and now it'll no longer endure hardships." He wanted to be home in the cool, with Hannah pressing a damp flannel to his brow. What good was it sitting impotently under the tree watching his son vent his anger on the field?

"I mustn't give in to anger," he told himself, touching his pounding chest. "Anger is a wasteful passion which makes us do things we later regret, which ruins our health and does no one any good. We're Jews, even the misguided ones with their strange ideas. We must never turn against one another. Never have such scenes again, an ugly stain on the village will not wash away soon. Rather that Petach Tiqva should lie in ruin than that should happen." A heavy sadness came over him as he thought almost in disbelief, of what had happened. His mind reeled back to so many beginnings in search of signs and portents. Strife out of needless hatred, out of intolerance, was like a canker which poisoned health. It was the climate that turned man against his brother, he told himself in his despair, the heat that made the land devour its inhabitants.

So absorbed he became in his gloom that he didn't notice Leib who had finished the last run along the field and now stood drenched in sweat before him. "Come, Father," Leib said as he bent over him to help him up, "Let's go home, it's all finished here."

For days the village was in a turmoil. Work came to a standstill, the young rebelled against their elders. In the street of the Lovers of Zion Sander Hadad and his companions loitered sullenly or else rode around, their faces covered in keffiyas, armed and defiant. Only Alexander was calm, "If they want us to leave, why, we'll leave, the loss will be theirs," he said with a laugh, and added, "The real, important things will not take place in the sleepy fields of such settlements as Petach Tiqva. Maybe this is a sign for us to move on."

But apart from Reb Lemel, a half-demented widower given to excess of emotion, who often wept loudly in public over what seemed to everybody else trivialities, no one seriously moved to expel the newcomers, let alone Alexander Zeff who had established a right of tenure there by dint of blood kinship with Yoel Zeff.

One day, while bitterness still festered in the village, a neighbour borrowed Yoel's mules for a special haulage of furniture and provisions he had bought in Jaffa. On the way back the cart broke down not far from the river. The man, a new and inexperienced settler, unhitched the mules and tried to prop up in the cart. Startled by some noise, the mules bolted. The man came back to the village on foot. Helpers went out to repair the cart and pushed it back to the village. But there was no sign of the mules. Late in the afternoon, Yakub Kalantar, returning from the fields, reported that he had seen in the distance what might have been the mules grazing near a clump of trees. One or two of the young men might have ridden out to bring them back if Mendle Pushinsky hadn't become obsessed with the mission and begged with tears in his eyes to be allowed to do it alone. It was a peaceful time, there had been no incidents with the Arabs for nearly a year, so Sander Hadad laughed and agreed. At dusk, the young men gathered in Katz's tavern to watch Mendle, armed with a heavy club and a rope, set out to bring back the mules. Someone joked that he might have been Saul going in search of his father's asses, except that even at his very best it took a good deal of fantasy to think of Mendle as the moody king of Israel.

Mendle didn't return that night. Next morning he staggered into Petach Tiqva battered and bruised, his clothes torn. Between sobs he was able to tell how he found the mules and was bringing them back, when he was set upon by a gang of Arab youths who beat him to near death and took the mules from him. He couldn't tell who they were or where they had come from.

The young men armed themselves and rode out, headed by Sander and Leib who, because the mules were his father's, waived his self-imposed renunciation of violence for the occasion. Within hours the party returned with the stolen mules. There had been a fight with the shabab of Yehudia, and Sander had sustained a wound in the arm. But the matter was settled; there was no appeal to the law from either side.

Next day the young men, presided over by Sander, gathered at Katz's tavern to judge Pushinsky. When he had finished speaking, Sander said in a deadly quiet voice, "All this time you pleaded to be one of us yet when your moment came, you failed. There's nothing more to say."

"I didn't run away. I stood up and fought. What could I do against so many of them?" Mendle protested.

Not a muscle moved on Sander's face. His voice was as cold as a blade. "The mules were taken from you. How come you're still alive?" he said. Tears came to Mendle's eyes. He looked around at the other men, not one of them met his gaze. Only Alexander could have prevailed with Sander but he was not there. Mendle walked away downcast, swearing to himself that he would never again mix with Sanders and his friends nor ever look at Abigail.

That was not the end of Pushinsky's humiliation. Two days later Farb, sitting in his office in the early hours of the morning, caught up with several omissions and wrong entries in the account ledgers, which Mendle had made during his high anxiety. Farb was beside himself with rage. No sooner had Mendle come in than Farb began upbraiding him in the foulest language. Mendle stood before his employer like a stunned animal. "Who do you think you are?" he shouted at last. "You don't own this place, you don't even do any hard work. You give orders and throw yourself about as though you were God's agent!"

"I'll show you who I am, you useless good-for-nothing mutt," Farb roared and got up from his seat. But Mendle's fury now matched his own. Snatching the account book from under Farb's nose, Mendle cracked it with all his might across his tormentor's face. Farb would've shot him dead if he'd had a pistol at hand. Blood trickled from his nose as he stood there, white as a sheet, his eyes murderous. "You've just destroyed yourself," he said, and seizing Pushinsky by the arm he dragged him out of the room into the street.

A group of labourers were standing about, waiting for Farb to come out and tell them what to do. A few of them were Arabs. They turned and stared as Farb came charging out of his office dragging and pushing Pushinsky along. In the middle of the street he flung him down and gave Mendle a kick which caught him in the stomach. Then Farb ran to a nearby cart, yanked out the long horsewhip that was stuck there by the driver's seat and rushed back. Mendle half-turned to watch Farb stand over him;

he was too dazed from the blow to move or say anything. Farb took up position, raised his arm, then hesitated. Turning to one of the Jewish workers, he said, "This man's a cheat, a good-for-nothing time-waster. Here, take this whip and give him ten lashes." The man looked at his friends then back at Farb. He shook his head and made not a move.

"Do as I tell you," Farb screamed at him.

The man said, "What? Beat one of our own people? Who ever heard of such a thing. The heat's got to you, Farb, you've gone mad."

Farb turned to one of the Arabs, a thin, gentle-looking man. He thrust the whip into his hand, and taking him by the shoulder propelled him towards the supine Pushinsky.

"Whip him!" he commanded. The Arab began to protest. Farb became threatening. So the Arab lifted his eyes to heaven, murmured something then began to whip Mendle who was now struggling to his knees. "Harder, harder, damn you," Farb shouted.

The workers, now joined by passers-by began stirring up a commotion, but none dared step forward and intervene. Yoel Zeff came out of his house on his way to the synagogue. The noise drew his attention. He changed course and approached the spot where the people were gathering. The noise of the whip cutting through the air and the dull thwack it made on impact sickened him. He felt a sense of panic rising in him as he pushed through the crowd. When he saw what was going on he gaped in horror and disbelief: he rushed between the Arab and Mendle Pushinsky. At that the Arab immediately dropped the whip and retreated. Yoel felt faint, his heart was beating so hard he had to hold his chest. But his voice came out loud and firm. "What is this abomination?" he cried. The people fell silent. They lowered their eyes as though they had been caught dancing before a craven image. Only Farb stood defiant, eyes smouldering, his face red and perspiring. Yoel turned on him, "This ground you stand on was bought at great expense so that Jews should live and work here in dignity and in fear of the Lord," he bellowed. "It has soaked up a good deal of Jewish tears and blood but not that such a terrible impious deed should take place on it. Shame on you, Yehuda Farb, shame on all of you who stand by and witness this revolting spectacle. Go now, you've no place here among us when you do such things."

Farb stooped to pick up the whip, but Yoel put his foot on it. Farb straightened to his full height. "Foolish old man," he bawled. "With your idle prattle and silly ways, all of you, you'd have starved to death if it weren't for the Baron's money and the work I put in here on his behalf. You Zeff, and your friends, you only block progress. I'll show you, I'll cut you dry of all aid until you scuttle back to Jerusalem. Yes, I'll do that if I have to!" Farb began choking on his words. The veins on his neck stood out like ropes. "You don't know what useful work is, you don't understand dedication and discipline. Now get out of my way. I'll see this useless dog out of here if it's the last thing I do." And he gave Yoel a shove that sent him stumbling backwards so that he lost his balance and fell.

Suddenly Leib was towering over him. He raised his good hand and brought it down on Farb's head. The Baron's official collapsed in a heap. Leib said, "No one in this village has ever done the vile thing you've done today. For laying a hand on my father I should tear your arms out. But I swear by my children if you're still in Petach Tiqva by sundown I'll break every bone in your body."

Farb barricaded himself in his room and didn't come out for the rest of the day. At dawn the next morning he rode out of Petach Tiqva and was seen no more. From his retreat in the Agricultural School of Mikve Yisrael, Farb wrote and published long letters denouncing the conservative nature of Petach Tiqva, justifying his deeds, and describing how his attempts to put the village on a viable footing were constantly frustrated by stubborn hostility and ignorance of some of the old settlers like the Zeff family, and by the lackadaisical indolence of the newcomers. In an open letter to the Baron, he urged him to remove his patronage from Petach Tiqva.

The controversy aroused by the Farb incident and the publicity it generated spread throughout the Jewish settlement. In Jerusalem rabbis and intellectuals vehemently debated the nature and merit of Jewish work on the land and the Baron's efforts in Palestine to stir the Jews towards self-sufficiency. In other settlements, the rebellion against the Baron's administration which had erupted some years before threatened to break out again. Farb as a person was all but forgotten, he had become a symbol, a pointer on the crossroads of the Jewish community in the land. There were rumours that the Baron himself was disenchanted and was thinking of disengaging himself from the struggles of his brethren in the Holy Land. Then what was generally called "the crisis of the vines", erupted: it became apparent that the vast quantity of vines planted in all the Baron's settlements were of no use since, there was no hope of selling the wine produced in Rishon Le Zion and Zichron Ya'akov either in Palestine or in Europe. For the first time the self-sufficiency scheme of de Rothschild's enterprise was revealed in the starkest terms to be no more than an illusion. Delegations of prominent Jews and representatives of the movement of the Lovers of Zion were sent to Paris to meet Baron de Rothschild and persuade him not to lose heart, not to abandon the Jews of Palestine. Much to their relief they discovered that the Baron was made of tougher fibre than despondency in the settlements led them to believe; he was disappointed but his resolve and commitment were not weakened.

A new overseer was sent to Petach Tiqva, a milder man who understood more about people and what moved them than about agricultural and village management. His main concern was to reassure the colonists and the critics of the settlements that the ugly incident of Farb would never be repeated. A delicate tissue gradually grew over the wounds that had torn the village apart, and as if by a healing magic, each faction emerged stronger than before: the old settlers who had resisted the Baron's administration saw their ways, the stubbornness with which they had stuck to mixed farming, vindicated not least by the vines crisis; those who depended on the Baron were chastened by the crisis and by the Farb incident. As for the newcomers, they were enthralled by a new swell of ideology which came from Europe like a great wind. It was Zionism; its prophet was a Viennese journalist of imposing aspect and rare powers of persuasion. His name was Theodor Herzl. Zionism, a potent creed, entered the mind and soul of Asa Mitavsky, pushing out all else. All his being thrived on it. We was inspired and he inspired others. Holding meetings whenever there was a possibility, writing and speaking about it, Mitavsky grew in stature and attracted attention far and wide. It seemed to his friends and enemies that all his life he had been waiting for such an ideology to blow open the floodgates of his mind and release an awesome pent-up energy. No one hated and feared him in Petach Tiqva more than Leib Zeff.

Malachi tried to explain Zionism to Leib. Leib put up his hands like a shield: "First you build your home, you raise a family, you plan your fields and reap your harvest. You measure your own strength. You gain respect of your neighbours and you learn to live with them and understand their ways. You become a man among men. When you've done all that the rest comes of its own accord. When there are Jews who are honourable, who earn their living through their own work, who have respect for their own tradition and the tradition of others, then there are roots, then there is a basis for the new kingdom of Israel. Then there are officers and judges and order. Then you have a Jewish state just as it was in the days of our forefathers," Leib thundered.

"Zionism doesn't deny tradition, Leib. On the contrary, it affirms it, it reaches down to the very roots of tradition, it is the living fruit of the past," Malachi argued, hearing Asa's voice speaking through him.

Leib became angrier: "Your friends stand things on their heads, like trying to build a house roof first. All words, nothing but empty words which confuse simple minds and hide reality," he said heatedly.

So Malachi gave up. "Once you were open-minded, Leib, now you shut your mind against anything that's new. Where there's beauty you see ugliness, where there's purity you see corruption."

Leib gave his brother one of those hard looks he reserved for irreconcilable adversaries. "Purity, beauty? You've been enchanted by that girl and her brother, you see nothing any more, you understand nothing. What more can I say to you even though you are my brother, my own flesh and blood?"

Leib made his point one windy Saturday evening barely an hour after the demise of the Sabbath. There had been neglect. Mitavsky and his friends had fallen down on their work as a result of which two calves had died at birth, so Leib said, though no one could actually connect the calves' deaths with negligence on the part of Mitavsky or any of his friends. But in the assembly Leib attacked relentlessly: those young men and women were a liability to the settlement. Not only did they waste good working time talking and preaching, not only did they show lack of regard of the religious ways of the village even to the point of desecrating the Sabbath; worst of all, they corrupted the young and they were causing loss. Because secretly most of the settlers preferred the Arab workers, Leib's words received a warm reception, though not from Yoel and not from Gutman nor from David Joshua Karlin, all of whom were divided on the issue of Jewish labour. The meeting broke up without reaching a decision. On the way home, Leib encountered Malachi walking up the street. There was a forlorn expression on Malachi's face. Leib said, "I didn't see you at the synagogue this morning, Malachi."

"I wasn't feeling well," Malachi replied.

Leib raised his eyebrows. "Oh? I know what ails you and I know the cure," he said and walked on.

Later, in the evening, Leib sought out his brother. He found Malachi reading a book in his room. "Come, Malachi, I want to show you something," he said.

"What is it?"

"Don't ask. Just come with me and you'll see something you'll never forget."

He led the way to Shapira's barn which stood at the far end of the street. It was dark inside. The barn was full of bales of hay up to the rafters, except for an empty space in the middle. The hens roosting among the bales and on the rafters made soft clucking noises as Leib slid open the door and led Malachi in. He put his finger over his lips and said not a word. A shaft of pale moonlight illuminated a patch in the middle of the barn. Once their eyes got used to the darkness they could make out the humps of straw and the wooden palisade that fenced the empty space in the middle of the barn.

"What is it, why did you bring me here?" Malachi whispered.

Leib clapped a hand over his mouth. "Don't make a noise. Just listen and see."

Like shadows out of the darkness, the voices crept across the space of the barn, snatches of laughter, words of endearment, then moans of the kind Malachi had never heard before. He stood frozen. His heart went dead. He recognized Abigail's voice. Or was it her? There was no way of telling, it sounded so strange, unlike anything he could imagine coming out of her mouth. His knees began to shake. Leib putting his arm under him, held him up.

"Look", he said, pointing to the palisade. Draped over the wooden beam was Sander Hadad's unmistakable whip, and on the ground immediately below, his boots.

"Here's your beauty and purity," Leib hissed and walked out.

"Once your brother Malachi saved your life, Leib, and now you've nearly destroyed him," Yoel said ruefully as he sat facing his son. Leib moved about the room sullenly. For two days Malachi had disappeared. He was found sitting dazed by the river. Not a morsel of food had passed his lips. "I hope he finds it in his heart to forgive you," Yoel went on. "If God forbid anything had happened to him, I know I wouldn't have been able to forgive or forget."

"Malachi's man enough to face the truth and man enough to forgive and even be thankful," Leib murmured.

When Hannah was reassured that Malachi suffered no greater bodily harm than exhaustion from two days and nights without food and drink, she let him shut himself up in his room and allowed no one to disturb his peace. Meanwhile, it had been decided that Mitavsky, his sister and all their friends who came to Petach Tiqva with them be asked to leave. "Your way of life is not suited to ours," they were told. "Go to Rishon or Rehovot where you'll be more among people like yourselves."

"We leave you with a heavy heart but this is not a parting for even here in Petach Tiqva, the mother of settlements, where the first pioneers struck roots into the soil, even here where rigidness and narrow-mindedness rule, progress will not be held back for long, and destiny shall come knocking at your gate. We shall be back, we shall sweep you forward with us to the future," Asa Mitavsky declaimed to the people who gathered by the well to see them off.

That day Alexander came to see Malachi. Hannah barred his way and wouldn't let him in, until Malachi hearing their exchange, called out for Alexander. Alexander sat on the bed beside him, put his arm round him and kissed his cheek. "I too am going, Cousin," he said.

"Don't let's lose one another. You are like a brother to me, more than that. Whenever you look for me, you'll find me, and I shall always love you dearly."

Malachi let his head fall against Alexander's shoulder. He still felt weak, confused and hurt. He started to say something, then stopped. Alexander, reading his thoughts, said gently, "We are all only people, Malachi. There's strength in us and weakness, ideas and animal urges, beauty side by side

with ugliness. None of us in an angel. But it's people not angels who build for posterity. Don't let your admiration for any living man or woman make you forget that they eat and shit and fuck, and that all that doesn't reduce them in the least. I'm so sorry the lesson had to be so painful. Don't think ill of Abigail, don't let the small things narrow your view of life, like your brother Leib. We live in a great time, Cousin, be aware of it and rejoice."
And with that Alexander got up and left.

Chapter 37

Of all the eighteen Jewish settlements which existed up and down the country by 1898, none was as independent and self-sufficient as Rehovot. A few years before, the philosopher Ehad Ha'am criticized the Baron's grand scheme of settlement on grounds that rather than redeeming the Jews, it was killing their initiative and thus perpetuating their dependency on handouts and charity. Rehovot was the living vindication of Ehad Ha'am's ideas, a vibrant creative society where mixed farming was practised, where quality and its appreciation was placed above quantity and where nevertheless over a thousand Jewish labourers had been employed since the settlement was founded.

Here Asa Mitavsky found fertile pastures for his political and social ideas. Taking the thinking of his idol Ehad Ha'am as his starting point, he wrote and preached and gained prominence as a thinker, a socialist humanist, a visionary of a brave future, in short the New Jew at his best and most impressive. His words stirred hearts among the intellectuals in Jerusalem and reverberated in Zionist circles in Europe and America. Here Abigail's poetry flourished, celebrating nature, giving melody to new sensibilities. In moonlit evenings round the fire, young people linked arms and sang wistfully songs which new composers wrote for her verse.

On a breezy autumn day, the earth smelt of the first rains. Crocuses just out of the reddish soil, gleamed and scented the air. Oranges hung heavy on the trees ready to be picked and be sent to Europe, Alexander turned his eagle face to the seaward breeze and enthused to his admirers that this was no ordinary New Year but the rebirth of Israel's past heroic age whose trailing clouds of glory were about to be swelled even as those which gathered that time of the year on the Mediterranean horizon. And as if to back his assertion, a circus had struck camp in the garden estate of Count Ustinov in Jaffa, and Alexander declared that on the day following the New Year he would enter the lion's cage unarmed to beard the king of the beasts.

The lion lay in the corner of his caged carriage, next to a pole to which a muzzled flea-bitten Syrian bear was chained. In the other cages on wheels there were a few nervous monkeys, an emaciated leopard, and two hyenas which huddled together in a heap and took no notice of the visitors. Notices in Arabic hung on all the cages saying: "These animals are dangerous, do not come near and do not feed." There was no such notice on the lion's cage, presumably because the circus's Albanian proprietor, himself an arthritic juggler, probably considered such a notification stupidly obvious and therefore an insult to his sole lion. It was an old lion with a scarred face and a mangy mane. Lying in its cramped cage on a patch of soiled straw, with the remains of its last meal strewn about, it looked anything but regal.

Surrounded by his friends, Alexander approached the cage. He stood in front of it, raised his hand like a gladiator and with a laugh saluted the beast, which yawned, displaying imperfect yellow teeth. When the Albanian circus master saw that Alexander was determined to enter the lion's cage and was willing to pay for it, he shrugged his shoulders, turned to the gathering crowd as if to say this was none of his responsibility, the Jew was clearly mad, and then started collecting money for the spectacle.

Alexander began to strip. He stood in only knee-length pants and heavy leather belt. His body was smooth as a statue. He looked invulnerable. Still, his friends took hold of his arms and tried to dissuade him from going in. "We know you're brave, none braver than you, Alexander," they pleaded. "Let's go now, don't go in there, a man is a man and a lion is a lion." Alexander just laughed and pushed them gently away.

The Albanian, seeing that Alexander was ready, unlocked the cage door. The lion pricked his ears, snarled, but didn't move. A loud sigh rose from the crowd as the people drew back in case the lion should stir from its lethargy and spring through the half-open door. Without further ado, Alexander slid into the cage and stood there, facing the king of the beasts, half-crouched, his back to the door. The lion didn't budge. It snarled once more, then blinked wearily and turned its face away. There was deathly silence; you could hear the faint whisper of the breeze moving the leaves. Then Alexander slowly opened the cage door and slid out. Immediately the people roared and cheered, "Alexander King of Israel, Alexander King of the Jews", his friends shouted as they carried him shoulder high round and round the cage, cheering and clapping their hands. The Arab spectators also cheered shouting "Sha'atr, ya sha'atr, O hero!"

On the evening which followed Alexander's apotheosis a serene majesty descended on Rehovot. It was midweek of the first week of the New Year. The Zionists organized a public meeting to which adherents from all the neighbouring settlements as well as from Jaffa, from the agricultural school of Mikve Israel and as far away as Hadera and Jerusalem, were invited. Among the guest speakers were leaders of the Zionist Movement who had attended the historic first Zionist Congress in Basle the year before, people who knew and worked with Theodor Herzl, men who brought a message of great hope, including the intelligence that Herzl himself was about to make his first visit to the land which inspired his vision, a visit to coincide with the forthcoming visit of His Imperial Majesty Kaiser William II of Germany.

The streets of Rehovot were decorated with flags and colourful buntings. The horses were groomed so that their flanks glistened against their polished trappings. The carts were hung with flowers, pomegranates and fronds of palm. In a clearing not far from the centre of the settlement a wooden stage had been erected from which the speakers were to deliver their speeches. Already hours before the meeting was to begin, men, women and children came out into the streets and gathered at the site. Everybody wore their best holiday clothes. Young men swaggered about sporting embroidered *rubashkas*—the white Russian peasant shirt which was fast becoming the fashion, their high boots dusted and polished. The women put on pretty frocks and walked about arm in arm laughing and exchanging banters with the men. All waited impatiently for the great event, all the more so since the word got round that to crown the evening four musicians, recent immigrants from St Petersburg, will play a Beethoven string quartet.

Malachi Zeff arrived from Jerusalem, where he was now teaching in the new Hebrew Teachers' Seminar, just in time to rise on the crest of the enthusiasm which preceded the meeting. He went straight to Alexander's room where he washed and changed into fresh clothes. Alexander, dressed in voluminous rubashka, his hair washed and anointed, came towards him with open arms. "Dearest Cousin," he said as he embraced him. For all the washing and soaping, he still smelt of garlic. "So you've become the conqueror of lions," Malachi said. Alexander waved his hand dismissively and laughed, "If you believe strongly enough, anything is possible," he said and taking Malachi by the arm led him out into the streets.

People thronged around the stage on which a group of sombre-looking men dressed in suits and wearing European hats sat in a row. It was Asa Mitavsky's great moment. How he roused the people with his passionate eloquence as he introduced each of the speakers. The sun was setting. Rivers of red stretched up into the sky. When the speeches were over Abigail mounted the stage to recite some of her latest poems, some of them written for the occasion. "How lovelier than ever she looks," Malachi thought with a reawakened ache in his heart which was bearable only because of the distance between them and the awareness that she was not, on this occasion—perhaps never except in his mind—a private person but the High Priestess of a new movement.

At last the moment for the concert arrived. The people settled down, some in chairs, some on cushions on the ground, and fell silent. Slowly and deliberately, the four musicians climbed on to the stage. The three men were short and self-effacing. The woman was angular and intense. They sat down, tuned their instruments, then began to play. The quartet they were playing was the second Rasumovsky Quartet.

Malachi had never heard such music before. He could find no words to describe it except that it reminded him of water flowing under light and shade. Its beauty moved him to his depth and brought tears to his eyes. To his untutored ears the themes changed and overlapped, evoking scenes, and a rush of sensations too exquisite to bear. He wanted it to go on for ever, he wanted to be submerged in the sound. Alexander's warm shoulder lolled against him and he remembered what Abigail had said to him that day on the beach, which at last, with the music, he was truly understanding. He felt his heart swell with love, for her, for Alexander, for all the people who like him listened to the beautiful sound coming from the four intense people on the stage. He prayed, "Please God, let us always be seeking without attaining. Let us move in such beauty on a long journey without ever arriving, because I cannot imagine that the fulfilment of all the promises and dreams of tonight could be so sweet and so noble as the distant vision of them." Then opening his eyes and looking at Alexander he saw that his cousin was sound asleep, his chin slumped against his chest. He was snoring faintly.

An early bul bul began its morning song. The warble climbed, deepened, reached the height of its development and was suddenly joined by others to swell into a chorus of bird song. Yoel Zeff got out of bed. Hannah moved; the rhythm of her breathing broke with a sigh. She moaned and turned on her side. Yoel kissed her head, then tiptoed out of the room. The Muezzin in the El Aksa Mosque began to call the Moslems to their morning prayers. Yoel had grown to like the voice of the Muezzin: in a different way it started him on his day too, like a lean, uncompromising command. He wondered if Theodore Herzl, in his hotel by the Jaffa Gate, had heard it too, and what it said to him.

That morning, Yoel was woken by his thoughts well before the birds began to sing. He felt fresh, full of purpose, calmer than he might have expected to feel before going to meet Herzl. Facing the Synagogue whose dome he could see through the living-room window, he recited his morning prayers. Today, more than ever, he felt proud of his grandfather Solomon Zeff. Today, of all mornings, the synagogue he had resurrected was his own credential.

In the next room slept his son Chaim with his wife and children. Their near presence to him lifted Yoel's spirits, gave him extra confidence for the day. He felt at peace with life and with the world. His time had come to slow down: the heart was weak, he had, diabetes. "You mustn't exert yourself. Relax, watch your family grow, enjoy life, and you'll live to be a hundred and twenty," the doctor had told him.

His thoughts turned again to Herzl. The great man wanted to meet leaders of the Jewish community; he had come to learn everything about the country, at first hand. The urgency of his mission wouldn't let him rest for a moment. But the religious ones, who rejected him, whom nevertheless he included in his larger scheme of things, wouldn't meet him. Except Yoel Zeff. Herzl had been told about the Zeffs, how they had arrived in the country, how they came to Jerusalem, about the founding of Petach Tiqva—the Rimkins and the Gutmans and all the others. Stories which inspired him and strengthened his faith in the national destiny of the Jews he had dreamed of. Herzl himself had asked to meet Yoel Zeff. His schedule was tight: he had come to Jerusalem for an audience with His Majesty the Kaiser. But he had arranged to meet Yoel early in the morning in his hotel because his advisers had told him Zeff was an open-minded man, free of prejudices, who wouldn't abide by the jealous restrictions of the rabbis. He, more than anyone, could tell him how best to move the hearts of Jerusalem's orthodox Jews.

Yoel made himself tea and broke a piece of bread which he topped with cheese Hannah had bought at the market the day before. Thinking of what he would say to Herzl made him reflect on his own life. "My cup is full," he thought. "Our granaries are overflowing with grain. Our homes are alive with the laughter of children. What more can I ask for that the Lord has not granted? There have been hardships and sorrows but also a great deal of joy. Happiness and sorrow don't leave you until the day you die. Only age teaches you to distance yourself somewhat from both. That's the beauty and grace of growing old."

"Our family's like an ever-widening stream, branched with tributaries. Leib has fulfilled himself, and my father's dream. Chaim, a scholar, an upright pillar of the community. Solomon would've been proud of him. Tiqva, a purer soul has never lived, has found happiness at last, thanks be to God. The children are growing. Fine healthy, loving children. Pride to their parents and to the whole House of Israel. Comfort to my old age. And Malachi, who takes after his mother. The deepest of them all. Who knows what course his life will take, standing as he does on the crossroads of our old way of life, and the new? In him I see the growing contradictions of our people reconciled in a calm, rational compromise. It's more than I could ever do. I know he'll embrace the new way of life. But I know he'll not turn his back on the old."

Yoel rested his chin in his hand. He was increasingly proud of his youngest son, Malachi, whom he least understood. He was also relieved that Malachi had recently become betrothed to a splendid girl, from a cultured and energetic Sepharadi family of considerable wealth. That kind of thrust into life he understood and appreciated all the more as he grew old.

In his mind's eye he saw Herzl's face: a noble semitic visage of a prophet. He wondered if Herzl ever prayed; he didn't know how to relate to people who didn't pray. But as he gazed into Herzl's face in his imagination, he could hear his own voice saying to him: "You wanted to learn from me about us orthodox Jews. I'll tell you more than that. The story of my family is the story of the Jews' return to the Promised Land in our time. It's been a small return, taken in small steps. No mighty signs and wonders. No crushing tragedies and no transforming joy. Just life. Like a tree that sinks roots and grows. Or a river that gushes from its source and winds away to discover its course. Only the faith and the hope have been as large and enduring as your own.

"You come as on a swell of a great tide, bringing new ideas. I feel in my heart that you cannot be turned back. I'm not sure I'd want to do that even if I could. But we are a hard-necked people. We cleave to our tradition. We walk in the ways of the Lord our God. Not you, not anyone or anything could change that. If we are swept into your current, we shall move along clinging to our baggage.

"You fire people's imagination with your vision of a Jewish state, governed by Jews, soldiered by Jews. I say, what is the meaning of a Jewish state which merely imitates others? What is the meaning of the Return, if the divine purpose is obscured by the conceit of man? How can Jews revive their bond with this too unwelcoming land, if they are not moved by the spirit of the Lord who gave it to Abraham and his seed?

"My grandfather Solomon did not come here dreaming of a Jewish state or kingdom. Gutman, Stamper, David Joshua, all my dear friends, we did not found Petach Tiqva for a Jewish state. We wanted to live in freedom and dignity, according to our ways, to earn our bread from our own work, to live among the Arabs as equals. Who would say now that we haven't succeeded?

"I'm not against your ideas, Dr Herzl. I feel in my heart that they will be realized one day, and there will be a Jewish state. I only hope it won't come too soon, when people are not ready for it. Let such a state—for it has been prophesied before you—arise out of a natural growth, not be thrust upon confused and heated people. Let it draw its life from the land and our tradition which began here, not from imported ideas taken from the *goyim.* Above all, let it be a Jewish commonwealth governed by compassion and understanding, or it's not worth the having. There's no man-devised schedule for such a thing, Dr Herzl. . . ."

Hannah came in rubbing her eyes. He loved her now heavy movement, he loved the greyness of her hair. She bent over him and kissed his head. "You got up very early, have you eaten?" she said.

He nodded and said, "I'll make you some tea."

She waved her hand. "Not yet. Later I'll make some myself. When must you go to meet that man?"

"Soon," he told her.

"Walk slowly, don't hurry, he can wait. Don't exert yourself," Hannah said. He got up. Chaim, his wife and the children came in and fussed over him. He put on his coat, his best hat. He looked his best, dignified, restful, a serious man, a Jew who looks at the world with the confidence of experience.

The streets were cleaner than usual because the Governor Ibrahim Haki Pasha had given orders that the city should be scrubbed clean in honour of the Kaiser's visit. Along the battlements on the wall, the German Flags fluttered side by side with the Ottoman; it was a fine day, just right for state occasions, and into the Jaffa Gate came trotting the grey horses which once belonged to Yussef Kalantar, just back from their morning exercise. On the way Yoel went over what he wanted to say to Herzl, adding here, omitting there. By the time he reached the hotel, he had simplified his message. Less about the past, more about the present and the future which suddenly glimmered for him with renewed hope. Yes, he would avail Herzl of his experience. Once again he would put himself out to rally support for Herzl's ideas. He felt confident that Herzl would listen to him, that he would understand. All his life had been invested in the land. He couldn't bear the thought of letting go now, with so much at stake, old and tired though he was.

There was little movement in the lobby of the hotel. It seemed that the guests were either still in their rooms or had already left, though it was early. The porter asked Yoel what he wanted. He motioned him to take a seat, then went away. After a while he returned. "Mr Herzl", he said, "has already left. He left no messages."